STYLE AND IDEA

STYLE AND IDEA

SELECTED WRITINGS OF

ARNOLD SCHOENBERG

EDITED BY LEONARD STEIN

with translations by
Leo Black

ST MARTINS PRESS
NEW YORK

CONTENTS

7

CONTENTS

CONTENTS

EDITOR'S PREFACE

The first collection of essays by Arnold Schoenberg in English appeared in 1950, a year before the author's death, under the title, *Style and Idea* (New York: Philosophical Library), with Dika Newlin as editor and translator of some of the articles. The present edition represents a considerable expansion of that volume since it includes many additional items culled from essays, lectures, fragments and sketches—for the most part gathered at the Schoenberg Estate in Los Angeles, as well as published articles in German, here translated for the first time, and reprints of articles in English.[1] In most cases, published articles and lectures have been used as the basic material—in Schoenberg's own English wherever possible, supplemented by manuscripts, in various stages of completion, which often serve to illuminate certain points which do not exist elsewhere. In all fairness it must be pointed out that Schoenberg prepared his published essays and lectures with great care, usually in several drafts, so that the rough, unfinished statements which appear frequently throughout this book are to be considered as first attempts which the author would certainly have polished up for publication.

Although the present volume contains most of Schoenberg's longer articles in both German and English, no more than a small portion of his other writings appear herein. Schoenberg was an inveterate and often compulsive writer who constantly jotted down sketches for articles on a number of subjects, inside and outside the realm of music, so that there exist numerous bits of paper in all stages of development. Most of his writings, dated and signed, whether complete or incomplete, were filed away under various classifications, often in duplicate. Schoenberg compiled several lists of his writings under such headings as *Musik, Denkmäler, Vermischtes, Vorträge, Artikel und Essays, Aesthetik, Meine*

1 A listing of nearly all of this material will be found in *The Works of Arnold Schoenberg* by Josef Rufer (English translation, 1962, Faber and Faber). The texts of some of these additional English articles were corrected by Dika Newlin in 1950 for a second, unrealized, volume of essays (see *Sources and Notes* p. 513).

Theorien, Sprachliches, Moral, Polemik, etc.[2] He may have intended one day to publish them under these headings, but, unfortunately, they do not seem to have been collected in any perceptible order, either chronologically or by subject matter. Occasional gaps and duplications in these listings make it impossible, in any case, to follow them as guides for publication, so that it has been necessary in this present edition to find other ways of classification.

The writings by which Schoenberg is best known and which have had the greatest influence on twentieth-century musical thought and practice are, of course, his books on musical theory, beginning with the *Harmonielehre* (*Theory of Harmony*) in 1911. Besides the subsequent texts on harmony, counterpoint and composition (all originally in English),[3] he conceived large-scale projects on orchestration, form and performance which were, unfortunately, not to be completed.[4] Many of the essays in this book on theoretical matters (see Parts VI and VII) are related to the foregoing published texts and unfinished projects.

The complete collection of Schoenberg's writings—books, essays, lectures, libretti, as well as numerous letters (most of them still unpublished)[5]—would fill many volumes. Though it is hoped that some day such a project will be realized, at present only the publication of his 'programme notes'—analyses of his own compositions, omitted in the present volume—is being planned.

Schoenberg's first writings that have been preserved date, according to his manuscripts, from 1909, when he was already thirty-five years of age and had established a solid reputation as the leader of new music.[6] They are essentially

---

2 See Rufer, *op. cit.*, for various listings (English edition, pp. 155ff).

3 *Models for Beginners in Composition* (G. Schirmer, 1942); *Structural Functions of Harmony* (W. W. Norton, 1954); *Preliminary Exercises in Counterpoint* (Faber and Faber, 1963); and *Fundamentals of Musical Composition* (Faber and Faber, 1967).

4 See Rufer, *op. cit.*, for a description of these unfinished projects (English edition, pp. 135ff).

5 For the first publication of his partial correspondence see *Arnold Schoenberg Letters*, edited by Erwin Stein (English edition, Faber and Faber, 1964).

6 See 'A Legal Question', p. 185. Schoenberg mentions in his listings 'Seven Fragments' (*c.* 1900), 'The Future of the Organ' (1906 or 1907; incomplete), and several other small items prior to 1909, but they were dated by him many years later. Willi Reich, in his book on Schoenberg (Vienna: Verlag Fritz Molden, 1968; English translation, 1971, Longman Group Ltd., London), mentions a pamphlet that appeared under his name in 1904.

polemical replies to hostile criticism of his music, polemics which, from this time on, colour a good deal of his writing, since he was often exposed to virulent attacks from the press—often reflected in public scandals at the performances of his music—which he answered in kind with withering sarcasm of his own. His first published article, 'Problems in Teaching Art', appeared in 1911, the same year as the *Harmonielehre*, the book which firmly established his reputation as a writer. Thenceforth followed a steady stream of articles.[7]

After the First World War, Schoenberg's articles appeared regularly in the new music publications of the day, particularly in *Anbruch* and *Pult und Takt-stock* (both issued by his publisher, Universal Edition in Vienna), which served as forums for the dissemination of new ideas in music. A high point of literary activity was reached in 1923, a critical moment in his career when the ground-work for twelve-tone composition was laid.[8] These writings are primarily con-cerned with: (1) attempts to define the principles of twelve-tone composition; (2) critical judgements of the new musical currents of the time (see Part II); and (3) descriptions of the theoretical and notational problems brought about by the new music (see Parts VI and VII).

The first article of Schoenberg published in English was 'Tonality and Form' in 1925 (Christian Science Monitor; see p. 255). This article, though originally written in German, appeared only in its translated form.[9] In 1934 'Problems of Harmony', translated by Schoenberg's first American pupil, Adolph Weiss, was published in the American periodical, *Modern Music*. During this same year Schoenberg, having just come to the United States, delivered his first speeches—among others, on Jewish problems (see p. 501)—in English.

It was in 1934, also, that Schoenberg prepared his own translation of a lecture on Twelve-Tone Composition (not the definitive one written in 1941), which was given at Princeton University. His first main lecture conceived entirely in English, 'How One Becomes Lonely' (see p. 30), was presented in 1937. From that time on he wrote nearly all of his articles in English, in his own original, vivid and forceful style. He was aided in English by several of his students,

7   For a chronological listing of the articles in this volume see Appendix A.
8   See, particularly, the articles in Part V ('Twelve-Tone Composition') and 'On My Fiftieth Birthday in Part I.
9   Quotations in translation appear in the English edition of Egon Wellesz' biography of Schoen-berg in 1925 (J. M. Dent and Sons).

at first, Gerald Strang, then Leonard Stein, Dika Newlin, and finally Richard Hoffmann.

Schoenberg's literary style reflects, in many respects, the remarkable originality of his musical mind. At the same time he proved to be as exacting with his choice of words as he was in formulating his musical ideas. In German, he liked to cite Karl Kraus as his model (see Translator's Preface). In English, despite the advice of some of his American pupils, the present writer included, he doggedly pursued his own path, even if it took days to find the right terminology. He had little use for a grammatically correct, so-called polished style of writing that would not clearly present his ideas. But, despite an occasional rough turn of phrase, an elliptical statement, or omitting of connectives, which, after all, paralleled his musical predilection for concision, economy of expression, juxtaposition of opposing ideas, preference for strong contrasts over smooth transitions, the force of his personality and creative imagination comes through boldly and without equivocation.

It is the purpose of the new edition of *Style and Idea* to bring into focus the many facets of Schoenberg's thought, perhaps revealing, at the same time, the broad lines of an autobiography of his creative life. The editor, confronted by an incredible abundance and diversity of material, has elected to arrange Schoenberg's articles into various categories, which, though not entirely exclusive of one another, strive to examine each of his main interests and fields of activities. Thus, there appear, in order, evaluation of his own career; his reaction to modern music, and one of its main offshoots, nationalism; his lively response to critics and criticism; the evolution of his most important contribution to musical theory and practice, i.e. twelve-tone composition; discussion on problems of theory and composition, performance and notation; his active involvement as a teacher; his attitude toward composers, past and present; and, finally, his response to the social and political climate of his time. This new grouping of the essays, it is hoped, will bring into sharper perspective the many and ever-broadening directions explored by an intensely curious and passionately involved mind of genius.

This volume owes much to the work and suggestions of various people: first of all, Leo Black, whose rare understanding of Schoenberg as writer and composer, stemming from his own excellent background in both literature and music, has succeeded in capturing in the most sympathetic way the tone and style of Schoenberg in translation. Then, Richard Hoffman, who checked the translations and gave valuable advice on many matters; and Miss Selma Rosenfeld, who undertook to transcribe the difficult early Gothic handwriting of Schoenberg. Many thanks are due also to Donald Mitchell who provided the first encouragement for this book. But, above all, this book should be dedicated to the indomitable spirit of Gertrud Schoenberg; her unflagging interest in preserving the materials of her husband for proper presentation, her indefatigable zeal for this project lasted until the onset of her fatal illness. She participated directly in deciphering many of the manuscripts, read typescripts of the translations, approved choices of the essays, all with the greatest enthusiasm and understanding.

Leonard Stein, Los Angeles, California, 1971

TRANSLATOR'S PREFACE

In January 1909, provoked beyond endurance by the critics' reactions during and after the première of his Second String Quartet, Schoenberg furiously wrote an article, which he then rather diffidently sent to Karl Kraus for possible publication in *Der Fackel*. His accompanying comment was 'This is the first thing I have written' (*cf*. Willi Reich, *Schoenberg*, Ch. 3). The article, A Legal Question, translated on pp. 185–9 of the present volume, is a high-spirited but crude *argumentum ad hominem* with few musical points to make. For Schoenberg this was a time filled with composing, teaching, letter-writing and many other activities, including painting (he had suddenly begun to paint not long before)— and yet little more than a year later his command of literary German had developed to the point where he could write the 135,000-word *Harmonielehre*, which is not only one of the most revealing books about music but also one of the most strikingly written. As he said in 'Problems in Teaching Art', the genius 'acquires even the things he was not born with'.

Schoenberg's stylistic idol was Karl Kraus, a supreme master of the elegantly involved but clear and meaningful German typical of the pre-1914 generation among German writers. Much of the material translated in this volume is written in a style which does not shun complexity, and whereas Schoenberg's later and typical comment on his own acquired English was 'I do not want to parade adorned with stylistic merits of another person', the problem in translating his German written between 1910 and the 1930s is the converse one: how to reproduce his own inimitable stylistic merits, including his immense liveliness and the frequent sense of direct speech, without distorting his train of thought. It would be impossible and pointless to make his earlier German articles read like his later English ones. Some degree of stylistic discrepancy is unavoidable here, but, as Schoenberg said, it is not the style that matters, but the ideas.

The articles present fascinating problems of terminology, often springing from the depths of Schoenberg's thinking and character. A few examples: for him, as these articles often insist, intellect and feelings, brain and heart, were so little different as almost to be identical. *Geist* can therefore mean 'spirit', or 'intellect', or preferably both; it can mean 'wit', and in the article 'Sleepwalker' it also means 'ghost', forming the basis for an extended pun. When a word means so much to a great man, there may well be no standard way to translate it in all contexts. Perhaps the central among all his ideas is that of *Darstellung der Gedanken*. 'Ideas' for *Gedanken* is easy enough, but what is *Darstellung*? That depends what an 'idea' is. It may be something one puts forward, expounds, 'presents' (*darstellt*), like a plan or a proposition in philosophy; or something like a stage character, whom (in sound) one acts, depicts, 'represents' (*darstellt*). Obviously it is both, but in translation it must be one or the other according to the context. An idea is in fact a complex entity, inexpressible in words (hence the need for music), and arrived at by *Erkenntnis*—another crucial and problematic concept, which for Schoenberg had little to do with the word's scientific meaning, 'cognition'. It represents something akin to intuition or insight (only there are perfectly good German words for those already), or 'realisation', and at different points this important word has had to be translated in each of the three ways mentioned. It even appears in the *Harmonielehre* bearing its Biblical meaning 'knowledge' (the tree of), and with its religious overtones it relates to the idea of *Anschauung* (vision? contemplation?) prominent in the important 1912 article on Liszt.

In translation there have been times when freedom was indispensable if the result was not to be stilted. A German crow 'does not peck out another crow's eye', whereas an English dog 'does not eat dog' (an early example, from 'A Legal Question'); but Schoenberg sometimes chooses to deliver a Beethoven-like battery of puns with some such expression as its basis. The simple transposition of metaphor then turns into a desperate search for something that will at least be amusing, even if the resemblance is hardly discernible. Schoenberg's scrupulous apportioning of subtle degrees of relative importance, the kind conveyable by tone of voice, often made him generous with what German calls the 'short words': *but, yet, indeed, admittedly, after all, anyway.* A few of these subtleties have been reluctantly sacrificed in order to make the English version flow and to prevent its seeming fussy. The provisional nature of some of these first drafts and fragments (*cf.* Editor's Preface) was bound to make them a little incoherent at times; such passages have been left as they were if this served to underline the urgency of Schoenberg's feelings, but if the result would merely have been obscure they have been tidied up a little. Naturally a choice has had to be made between certain English and American terms, and Schoenberg, as translated, refers to 'half-notes' and 'parallels', rather than 'minims' and 'consecutives'. I am indebted to Leonard Stein for advice on many of the above points, and for other useful comments which helped me more than a little in the final revision of those articles translated by myself.

Leo Black

PART I

PERSONAL EVALUATION AND RETROSPECT

1

ON MY FIFTIETH BIRTHDAY: SEPTEMBER 13, 1924

Someone has confided in me, strictly between ourselves and everyone else, that there is a secret plan afoot to surprise me on my fiftieth birthday with an issue of *Anbruch* devoted to my work. More than that, I have been invited to help surprise myself by contributing an article.

However, I am only inclined to send myself best wishes if I can give a satisfactory answer to this question: are other people the only ones obliged to consign me to the rubbish heap, or must I join in? That is to say, has my productiveness begun to slacken off or am I still capable of posing (or even solving) riddles? Are any other symptoms of old age present? In a word, am I already 'finished'?

There are various things I am not finished with; that is why I have published less than I have written, and written less than I have thought. So I need not feel that the number of works I have published points to any conclusion. However, the ideas that have lately filled my mind: perhaps they might point the way? The musical side is not very informative: certainly I shall soon write the small section of *Die Jakobsleiter* which is necessary before the first part of it can be published;[1]* then a second, shorter choral work, whose text is already completed.[2] In these, as in certain still smaller works (chamber music) I shall be concerned with developing the technique of 'twelve-tone composition', whose first steps I tried out in certain movements of the *Serenade* and the *Five Piano Pieces*, and particularly in the *Piano Suite* and the *Wind Quintet*.[3] Much the same applies to my intentions in the theoretical field. After all, I had decided a good fifteen years ago to write treatises on counterpoint, form and instrumentation (the arts of laying out and setting parts),[4] and many of my drafts (often revised) date from then or the years between. More recently, I have made some discoveries which compelled me to revise the small work entitled *The Theory of Musical Cohesion*

* See Sources and Notes, p. 513ff.

into the more ambitious *The Laws of Musical Composition*, and similarly to compile not a simple counterpoint text-book but a *Theory of Polyphonic (Contrapuntal) Composition*; and finally, to plan an article, 'Laws of Composition With Twelve Tones'.[5]

But, despite a relatively large amount of preliminary labour and considerable progress, all these works in their present state, and far as they are from being finished, need completion if I am to prove my productive energies undiminished; that will probably be the only way of restoring faith, at least for those who recognise a creator not by what he conceives but only by what he carries out. 'Let there be light!'—one may believe that, and leave it at that.

So even if it seems like blowing my own trumpet, I cannot muster the self-denial needed to keep quiet about minor matters; there are, understandably, many such—and if I pick out such trivia as 'A Genuine Twelve-Tone Notation', 'A New Explanation of Ornaments, Complex Ornaments, Appoggiaturas, etc.', 'Discussion, Representation and Correct Description of All Tempo- and Performing Indications',[6] I am all the more glad to do so since it is the best way of proving my genuine desire to see myself objectively—with an objectivity that will leave my best enemy nothing more to do.

If all this has still not convinced my incorrigible friends of something which less well-disposed people assume at the outset: that I have reached my limit, that, as a true pace-maker, I have been overtaken (for everything gets overtaken, one's co-runners and followers are so robust); that, in a word, I have arrived at the place where many people would, in the interests of their plans for the further development of musical history, be glad to see me—then I am obliged to mention one clear symptom of age which is present in my case: I can no longer hate as once I could. Sometimes, and this is worse still, I can even understand without feeling contempt.

That speaks for itself! It seems I have to wish myself all the best—so that, once here, it may give me cause to say that I am not yet ready for the rubbish heap.

Mödling. August 20, 1924

CIRCULAR TO MY FRIENDS ON MY SIXTIETH BIRTHDAY: SEPTEMBER 13, 1934

I must, above all, explain why I have been so long in saying 'thank you' for the many messages of congratulation on my sixtieth birthday. But before even that, let me say I was able to enjoy it all extraordinarily, and was fully content, even though we passed the day without any kind of ceremony and with not a single guest. The first to greet me were Trude and Nuria, then came the many telegrams, the letters, and the fabulous *Festschrift*;[1] this all gave me far more pleasure than the public could ever provide. Although I shall not forget the comfort I once derived from being fêted by the city of Vienna, and from the speech made by Mayor Karl Seitz, a man who is today so unfortunate; I should have been glad, this day, to send him a token of my gratitude, for he is a man to respect far above any party allegiance.

On September 13th our luggage for the journey was already partly packed. Some time previously we had become convinced that the best thing for me would be to go to Hollywood, or at least to California, and in the last weeks of August we decided definitely. I will now give a short survey of my first year in America, which ended on October 31st.

I have to say that for disappointments, annoyance and illness it was worse than quite a lot I have been through so far. The first disappointment came while we were still in Paris, for there was absolutely no reaction to the news that I had to leave Berlin, and we faced the worrying prospect of a very uncomfortable winter in France. I had, indeed, long since lost my earlier ideas of what an American engagement would have to offer—by now, the streets were clearly not going to be paved with gold. But then the Malkin Conservatory offered me rather less than a quarter of what I had regarded as compensation for my Berlin salary, that is to say as a minimum; by now I had been sufficiently softened up to accept this solitary offer, after a few hours' reflection. The next big disappointment, to mention only the more important things, was discovering that I had carelessly agreed to teach, for the same salary, not only in Boston but also in New York—a demand, made at a late stage, whose insidious nature I failed to detect. These journeys, every week, were the main cause of my illness. Then: on the way from Washington to Boston I asked Malkin what the conservatory orchestra was like, and on my arrival in Boston I found a little school of music with perhaps five to six classrooms. The school set its hopes on me, but it had been announced to the public much too late; moreover, it demanded fees more than double anything that could be managed during the depression, and was caught in a cross-fire of intrigues stemming from poverty and philistinism, so that in Boston and New York I had a total of 12 to 14 pupils, some of them complete beginners. There was also a bright side. The League of Composers arranged a concert (only chamber music, though!), and a very big reception —2,000 people were said to have been there; I had to shake hands certainly with 500 of them, and the Committee of Honour was said to include everyone in New York interested (in any way) in art. Soon after, there was another reception, also a very noisy affair, but I cannot recall who gave it.

The actual teaching I enjoyed. Even the more mature pupils had covered the ground-work very inadequately, but all the same I had two really talented ones and a few with some talent. Apart from this, so much new material had been accumulating in me during the previous months that I was able to tell my pupils really a great deal which was quite unknown to them, and surprised them very much. In Boston I had a concert with the resident symphony orchestra, which is extraordinarily good. There, too, I met Pollatschek.[2] The permanent conductor is Serge Koussevitzky, once a travelling double-bass virtuoso, who in the ten years he has been there has never played a *single* note of mine. In my firm opinion he is so uneducated that he cannot even read a score—at any rate, even orchestral musicians told me that he has engaged two pianists, who play him each new piece as a piano duet, as many times as are needed for him to get to know it. Even then he does not take all the rehearsals himself, but first lets the concert-master rehearse, and sits in what he thinks is a dark corner, following and conducting. As everywhere throughout the world, there are many charlatans here too. I conducted a kind of final rehearsal of the concert in Cambridge (a small town linked to Boston), but at half past two on the afternoon of the day I was due to conduct it for the first time in Boston (Friday, January 12th), I had an attack of coughing in the lift of our house; I tore something, and this gave me such violent pains in the back and chest that I could not move, even though I was bandaged. I had already been ill since the early days of December (as soon as the bad weather set in), but was able to keep going, more or less, and carry

26

out my duties to some extent, thanks to medicaments which obviously did me harm. The climate there is bad, you see, and was particularly so that winter. Within 12 or 24 hours the temperature will go down by 60 or more degrees Fahrenheit, i.e. 34 Centigrade. In March this sort of sudden change of temperature started again, and I had a horrible attack of asthma, made worse on this occasion by irritation of the heart (the doctor gave me iodine for the cough, although I had told him not to: as they call it 'iodine' and I knew it as 'Jod', we did not realise what it was. It checks, but does not heal, the illness, which therefore soon breaks out again. In addition, it did such harm to my stomach that for at least two months I could eat absolutely nothing but weak tea, ham and toast. And this affected the heart). I then had to take great care of myself in April, May and June, but during the summer spent in Chautauqua[3] I recovered very quickly, though not enough to be able to risk another winter anywhere near New York. My engagement at Malkin had expired at the end of May, and although there was interest in me everywhere (except among the conducting gentlemen), and people were anxious to secure my services as teacher (so far I have had to refuse five such offers), there was nothing that offered security, except in New York or Chicago, where I could not live. On the other hand, I was amazed, if only at the start, by the attitude of the conductors, with the exception of Stock in Chicago. Over here, butter is easier to come by than judgement about art, so that one rarely finds many people interested, and even when they are, they tend to get things all wrong. The artistic luminaries, especially the conductors, seem to get the largest ration, for they are in charge—that is what attracted them, and it is hard to think of anything else they would be good for. They have performed, at most, *Verklärte Nacht* or one of my Bach-arrangements, but, for the most part, not a single note. On the other hand, Stravinsky, Ravel, Respighi and many others are widely played. It is very much as in Europe; here too, I have a really great number of—well, what am I to call them?—one can't properly say 'adherents', because it is rarely more than a matter of their coming round at some time in the future, but they are people who will do so when the right occasion offers. All the same, I can say that interest in me is only just awakening. The younger people are all very much on my side, and the general opinion is that I am 'on the way in'. But not for people like Walter and Klemperer. It goes without saying that over here Klemperer plays Stravinsky and Hindemith, but not a note of mine, except Bach-arrangements.[4] And Walter, indeed, was always (for safety's sake I must pressingly beg you to regard what I say as entirely confidential, and to prevent its reaching the public, let alone the press. To fight these forces on that basis would at the moment be too much for me, but I shall certainly carry the fight through to the end, on a different basis!) —so, Walter is a magnificent conductor (in private, however, he has always been a nasty creature; I feel sick whenever I think of him, and avoid doing so as far as possible).

Los Angeles (Hollywood is a sort of Floridsdorf or Mödling[5] of Los Angeles, only with the difference that here they produce those splendid films, whose highly unusual plots and wonderful sound give me so much pleasure, as you know) is a completely blank page, so far as my music is concerned. From time to time someone (Goossens, Rodzinsky, Slonimsky) has tried out a piece of mine, but has succeeded only in confirming the public still more in its distaste for new music. The blame lies, as ever, with the conductors. For example, in San Francisco the Philharmonic orchestra has not played a single note of mine in 25 years; take careful note of the name Alfred Hertz! All these gentlemen, from sergeant downwards (there is no upwards), call themselves conservatives, an expression whose meaning I have worked out as follows: they have nothing else to guard, to conserve, but their own lack of ability, ignorance, and cowardice; these they guard so that nobody shall get to know about them. For that reason I have also refused to conduct concerts here and in San Francisco, for I should like to see the punishment fall on those who are guilty. This has made me many enemies, but I do not think I need fear them, for on the other hand I have many friends. As a teacher, I mean. Unfortunately I cannot demand decent fees, and receive only one-third to two-fifths of my New York price, but already I have a course with 10 pupils, and one or two in private, so I am sure that, once people know I teach, those who can pay more will also come, and I shall be able to exist here quite well. In the summer, for six weeks, I shall give two lessons every day (except on Saturdays and Sundays) at the local University of Southern California. Here again payment isn't princely, but at least the three summer months are covered. Moreover, I am now in demand in New York. We had been here scarcely more than a week when I received an offer from the Juilliard School of Music, the largest and richest American music college; unfortunately I had to refuse, because we could not risk a New York winter. But the director, Ernest Hutcheson, a very good pianist and musician, and a delightful man, whom I got to know in Chautauqua, now wants me to go next year, and I can only hope I shall be well enough to accept. That would be a very good position, in every way, since over here all the other good and important things are inseparably linked to such posts. But I should also be well content to stay here. Today, the 25th of November, I am sitting by the open window, writing, and my room is full of sunshine! Having written so much about myself, I should now like to say a little more about my wife and Nuria; this place suits them very well, too. We have a very charming little house, not too large, furnished, with many amenities customary here but hardly known at all in Europe. Once we can have our furniture—it is still in Paris, because the German government has so far refused to pay the balance of my salary for 22 months—we shall probably rent an unfurnished house. This will be still cheaper, and we shall also look for one rather more into the hills, where there is still less damp and more sun.[6] I have not yet resumed work on my opera,[7] but am writing a Suite for String Orchestra, *tonal*, a piece for student orchestras. I am writing it at the suggestion of a musician who teaches at New York University,[8] conducts a student orchestra there, and has told me very many heartening things about this American student orchestra —there are hundreds like it. It has convinced me that the fight against this awful conservatism has to start here. This piece will become a veritable teaching example of the progress that can be made within tonality, if one is really a musician and knows one's craft: a real preparation, in matters not only of harmony but of melody, counterpoint and technique. A stout blow I am sure, in the fight against the cowardly and unproductive.

Warmest greetings to all my friends
Arnold Schoenberg, 5860 Canyon Cove, Hollywood, California
November, 1934

3

HONORARY CITIZENSHIP OF VIENNA
1949

Seven cities are recorded as claiming to be Homer's birthplace.

Up to a short time ago the contrary seemed to be the case with me. Though not seven cities were involved, I still remember a man saying with authority about me:

'And if he were Mozart himself, he must get out!'

But now, after having acquired the honour of American citizenship, another honour has come to me: the Mayor, His Excellency, General Dr. Theodor Körner and the Senate *der Stadt Wien* have conferred upon me the *Ehrenbürgerrecht der Stadt Wien*. It is perhaps superfluous to state that this honour makes me extremely happy and that I am proud that it is this city for whose love and recognition I would make my greatest sacrifice.

That I have reached this goal now is abundant and generous reward as well as an unexpected one. While I vow herewith artistic allegiance to the place from which my music originated, and all my knowledge, I have to confess that, in order to do this, I had to forget that I had planned it differently.

And now, your Excellency, let me thank you and the Mayor of Vienna and its Senate again for the great honour and joy your generous action has given me.

October 23, 1949

4

HOW ONE BECOMES LONELY
1937

My *Verklärte Nacht*, written before the beginning of this century—hence a work of my first period, has made me a kind of reputation. From it I can enjoy (even among opponents) some appreciation which the works of my later periods would not have procured for me so soon. This work has been heard, especially in its version for orchestra, a great many times. But certainly nobody has heard it as often as I have heard this complaint: 'If only he had continued to compose in this style!'

The answer I gave is perhaps surprising. I said: 'I have not discontinued composing in the same style and in the same way as at the very beginning. The difference is only that I do it better now than before; it is more concentrated, more mature.'

Ex. 1 *Verklärte Nacht*, 105–10

Ex. 2 Third String Quartet, Second Movement, 11–20

Of course, if one who knows only *Verklärte Nacht* is confronted suddenly and without any preparation with music of my present style, he may well be perplexed. This shock may also be felt in comparing a few measures of *Verklärte Nacht* with some of my Third String Quartet (see Exs. 1 and 2).

The difference might not be so sharp if one compared soft melodies, although it seems obvious that the melody of *Verklärte Nacht* is easier to understand than that of the string quartet. But justice asks that we compare part of a more violent expression, and for this purpose I choose a part from *Verklärte Nacht* which, at the time of the first performance of this work (1901),[1] sounded so rough that people said: 'It sounds as if an orchestra playing Wagner's Tristan and Isolde had become confused and mixed up.'

Note here the use of the *pizzicati*.

33

Ex. 3 *Verklärte Nacht*, 135–40

This should be compared with a part of my Fourth String Quartet which uses almost similar means.

Ex. 4 Fourth String Quartet, Second Movement, 556–65

The expression and the mood is different, but I am sure that, in 1903, instead of distinguishing between the expression of these examples, the audience would have found only a similarity and would have called both of them 'very, very rough'.

As long as an audience is not inclined to like a piece of music, it does not matter whether there happen to be, besides some more or less rough parts, also smooth or even sweet ones. And so the first performance of my *Verklärte Nacht* ended in a riot and in actual fights. And not only did some persons in the audience utter their opinions with their fists, but critics also used their fists instead of their pens. So one wrote: 'This sextet seemed to me like a calf with six feet, such as one sees often at a fair.' Six feet, he said, because there were six players. But he forgot that six players possess twelve feet. And he also forgot that in this piece there also appeared parts of which everyone, even at this time, could have approved—as, for example; Ex. 5 *Verklärte Nacht*, 231–39.

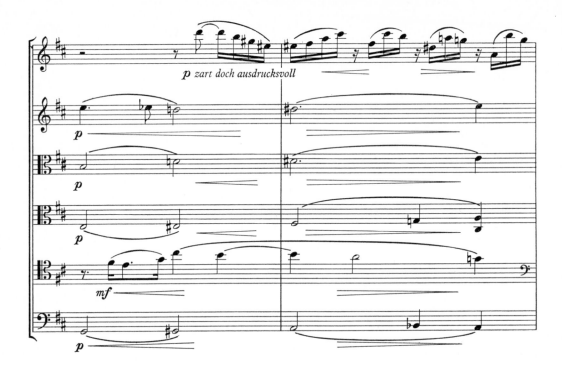

And one might be astonished that even the very end of this piece impressed neither these critics nor the audience.

It may be easily understood that a composer who knows what he has written and feels that he has been treated very badly becomes a little bit suspicious of this kind of criticism. 'Why,' one might ask himself, 'why did they mention only what they did not like and forget what pleased them? Could they not even have admitted that the eyes of this calf with six feet were nice looking? Or that its hide showed a lovely colour? Why did they speak exclusively about the six feet?' Six feet on a calf might be an outstanding feature. But in a sextet it is not surprising that there should be six or even twelve feet.

But see: an artist treated in this way becomes not only suspicious, but even rebellious. Seeing that even parts of undoubted beauty could not protect him, knowing that those parts which were found ugly could not be wrong because he would not have written them if he himself had not liked them, and remembering the judgement of some very understanding friends and experts in musical knowledge who have paid tribute to his work, he becomes aware that he himself is not to blame.

But then this happens: after having composed an extensive work, he visits a dear friend, his closest one and one whose judgement and musical knowledge seem to him perfectly indisputable. The friend looks over the whole score and his judgement is: 'This work shows a complete lack of inspiration; there is no melody, no expression; it seems to me dry, and the way you write for the voices is mere declamation, but no kind of song.'

He was speaking of my *Gurrelieder*, from which I now cite two characteristic parts : Ex. 6 *Gurrelieder*, 'Nun sag ich dir'

Ex. 7 *Gurrelieder*, 'Du sendest mir einen Liebesblick'

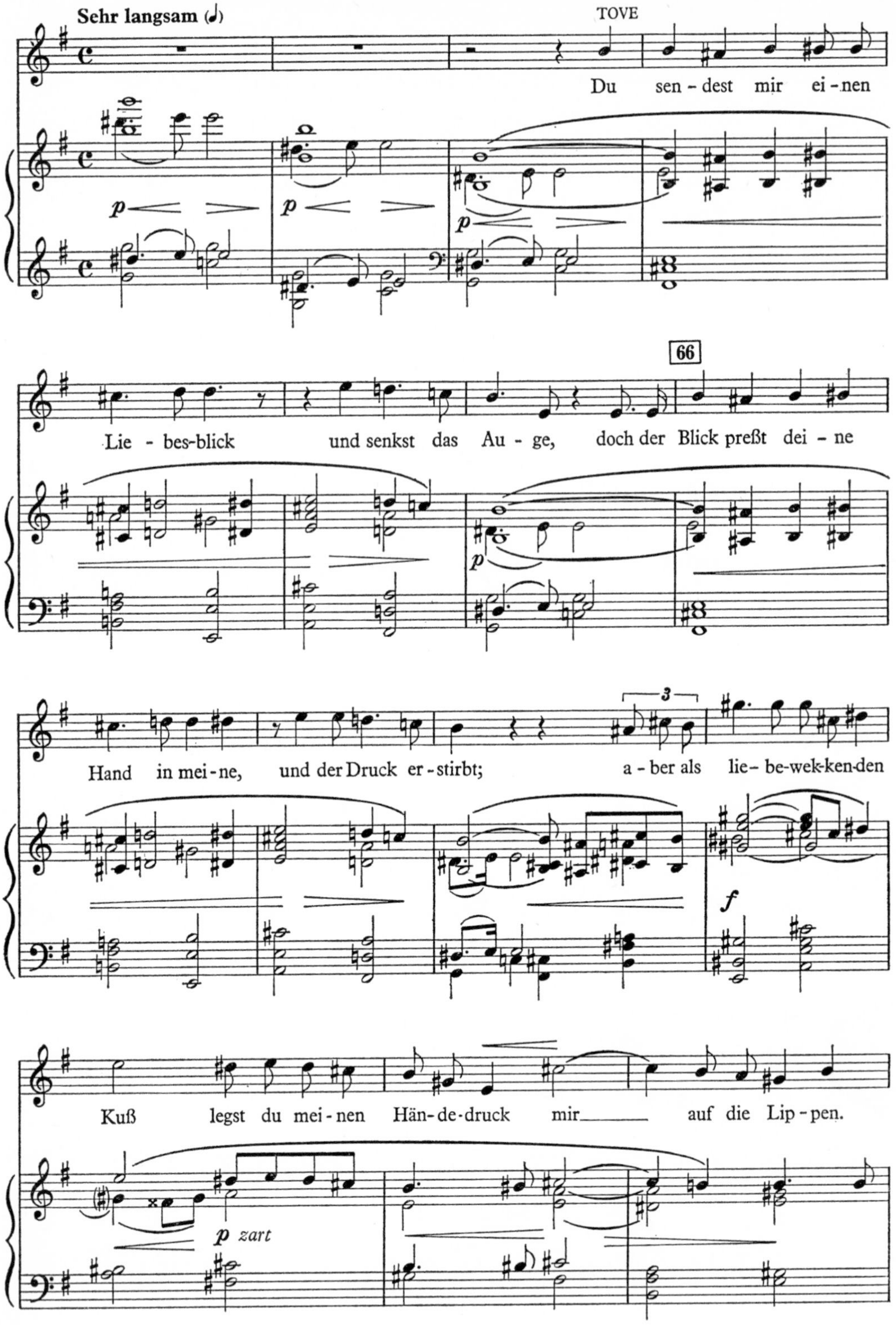

Today it seems perhaps unbelievable that my friend did not recognize the melodies in songs like these two. Of course, the designation *melody* does not involve an aesthetic value. There are good melodies and poor ones; one is original, the other commonplace; one is appealing, the other indifferent. And it may happen that a good recitative will show more emotional power, and sometimes even more inventive capacity, than many a melody. But knowing I had written melodies and feeling that they were not poor, I had the choice either of being discouraged or of doubting my friend's authority.

I decided not to be discouraged. But I had to wait for more than thirteen years before, in 1913, at the first performance of *Gurrelieder* in Vienna, the audience affirmed my stubbornness by applauding at the end of the performance for about half an hour.

As usual, after this tremendous success I was asked whether I was happy. But I was not. I was rather indifferent, if not even a little angry. I foresaw that this success would have no influence on the fate of my later works. I had, during these thirteen years, developed my style in such a manner that, to the ordinary concert-goer, it seemed to bear no relation to all preceding music. I had had to fight for every new work; I had been offended in the most outrageous manner by criticism; I had lost friends and I had completely lost any belief in the judgement of friends. And I stood alone against a world of enemies.

Alone, with one exception: that small group of faithful friends, my pupils, among them my dear friend Anton von Webern, the spiritual leader of the group, a very Hotspur in his principles, a real fighter, a friend whose faithfulness can never be surpassed, a real genius as a composer. He is today recognized the world over among musicians, although his works at the present time have not yet become as familiar to the great audience as his genius deserves. Among them also was Alban Berg, one of the dearest to me, whose death we deplored in 1935. He gained worldwide fame through his opera, *Wozzeck*, which was played in every important musical centre; he, too, was a most faithful friend to me. There were and still are many others of reputation among them. It was a fact which has always made me proud, and for many years beyond these thirteen they were my only moral support in the struggle for my work.

While today one inclines perhaps to count in my favour the fact that I was surrounded by pupils of talent and genius, in 1910 I was merely blamed for that. I was called a 'seducer of young people', and when a critic once compared me with Socrates I was not sure whether he intended to honour me or to suggest that I should be condemned like Socrates and given the cup of poison. The mildest form of rebuke for the devotion of my pupils to my music was ridicule. When, for example, my First String Quartet was played at a festival of music in Dresden in 1906, the performance provoked the same tremendous scandal that it had at its first performance a few months before in Vienna. Ten of my pupils had made the trip to Dresden to attend the performance. But as two friends of mine were generally with us besides my ten pupils, a malicious musician found a way to ridicule us by calling us 'Schoenberg and his twelve apostles'.

This First String Quartet played an important role in the history of my life. On the one hand, the scandals provoked by it were so widely reported the world over that I was known at once to a considerable part of the public. Of course, I was primarily regarded as the Satan of modernistic music; but, on the other hand, many of the progressive musicians became interested in my music and wanted to know more about it. And in this way a slogan was produced which by mistake was attributed to me. It became a custom in similar cases to say: 'He has made a *succès de scandale*—a success out of failure.'

One would not believe today that the best musicians and even friends of mine, who had some esteem for my musicianship, misjudged my music very badly. But I must admit that in 1905[2] the music sounded confusing to the ears of my contemporaries and that the score also offered enigmas. So when I showed the First String Quartet to Gustav Mahler, the great Austrian composer and conductor, at that time head of the Imperial Opera in Vienna, he said: 'I have conducted the most difficult scores of Wagner; I have written complicated music myself in scores of up to thirty staves and more; yet here is a score of not more than four staves, and I am unable to read them.' It is true the score looked, if possible, even more complicated to the eyes than it sounded to the ears, especially passages such as the following:

Ex. 8 First String Quartet, 57–77 after B

What made it so difficult to understand in 1905 was its complicated contrapuntal style. And the most embarrassing circumstance was that the harmonies produced by those independently moving parts changed so fast and were so advanced that the ear could not follow their meaning.

Again, as with *Verklärte Nacht*, parts of understandable smoothness could not calm down the public or reassure them. Two examples of such parts follow. The first one is a section of the Adagio part of this quartet in one movement [see Ex. 7 in 'Heart and Brain in Music', p. 70. Ed.]. The other example occurs at the very end of the work:

Ex. 9 First String Quartet, Ending

45

The excitement of the audiences at first performances of new compositions of mine was growing greater from work to work. Every now and then, when I believed it could not be surpassed, I discovered that it could. But, in my memory, one of the worst occasions was in connection with my Second String Quartet. The public listened to the first movement without any reaction, either pro or con. But as soon as the second movement, the Scherzo, began, a part of the audience started to laugh at some figures which seemed curious to them and they continued with bursts of laughter at many places during this movement.

A scherzo is the kind of music which should provoke gaiety. And so I could have understood a kind of smile when, as in the next example, I combined my

Ex. 10 Second String Quartet, Second Movement, 165–89

themes in a tragicomic manner with a popular Viennese song, the words of which may be translated as follows: 'Alas, poor boy, everything is lost',—the song, *Ach du lieber Augustin*. But this provoked an eruption of laughter, instead of an understanding smile (see Ex. 10).

From now on the public reaction became worse and worse. I am sure that if, at this point, the Rosé Quartet had played a string quartet of Haydn, the public would not have noticed the difference and would have continued their nonsensical laughter.

Years later I was informed that this reaction of the audience was due partly to an intrigue instigated by a powerful enemy of mine as an act of revenge for an attack which friends of mine, without my co-operation, had previously directed against him on account of his artistic misdemeanours. But I am convinced that this intrigue was not the only cause for the tumultuous rejection of my work. I came to understand that such rejection was based on my musical ideas and the way I expressed them. Something happened during the rehearsals of this work by the Rosé Quartet which was as strange as it was significant. To explain the phrasing of a certain section, I said: 'Please, would you not try to play this melody so and so?' A dear friend of mine, who had attended all the rehearsals and was therefore supposed to know the work thoroughly and who, I hoped, understood it, asked, with an air of sincerity and astonishment: 'I hear you talking about a melody; where is there a melody at all?' The section in question was the following [see Ex. 2 in 'Heart and Brain in Music', p. 57. Ed.].

If a friend, after hearing it so often, did not conceive this as a melody, why should the audience be able to understand it after only one hearing? So I should have foreseen that also my next work, the *Kammersymphonie*,[3] would not have the success which I had expected. But I had enjoyed so much pleasure during the composing, everything had gone so easily and seemed to be so convincing, that I was sure the audience would react spontaneously to the melodies and to the moods and would find this music to be as beautiful as I felt it to be. And besides, I expected much from the sound of the extraordinary combination of 15 solo instruments—that is, five strings, eight woodwinds and two horns.

After having finished the composition of the *Kammersymphonie* it was not only the expectation of success which filled me with joy. It was another and a more important matter. I believed I had now found my own personal style of composing and that all problems which had previously troubled a young composer had been solved and that a way had been shown out of the perplexities in which we young composers had been involved through the harmonic, formal, orchestral and emotional innovations of Richard Wagner. I believed I had found ways of building and carrying out understandable, characteristic, original and expressive themes and melodies, in spite of the enriched harmony which we had inherited from Wagner. It was as lovely a dream as it was a disappointing illusion. I had started a second *Kammersymphonie*. But after having composed almost two movements, that is, about half of the whole work,[4] I was inspired by poems of Stefan George, the German poet, to compose music to some of his poems and, surprisingly, without any expectation on my part, these songs showed a style quite different from everything I had written before. And this was only the first step on a new path, but one beset with thorns. It was the first step towards a style which has since been called the style of 'atonality'. Among progressive musicians it

49

aroused great enthusiasm. New sounds were produced, a new kind of melody appeared, a new approach to expression of moods and characters was discovered. In fact, it called into existence a change of such an extent that many people, instead of realizing its evolutionary element, called it a revolution. Although the word revolution had not, at this time (about 1907),[5] exclusively the ominous political flavour which is attributed to it today, I always insisted that the new music was merely a logical development of musical resources. But of what use can theoretical explanations be, in comparison with the effect the subject itself makes on the listener? What good can it do to *tell* a listener, 'This music is beautiful', if he does not *feel* it? How could I win friends with this kind of music?

In fact, I could not, and I did not expect to win friends. And I may tell you frankly that much as I liked the compositions I wrote at this time, I was equally afraid to have them submitted to the public. And I even hesitated to show them to people other than my closest friends.

But then two of my new works caused a complete change in the situation: my *Harmonielehre* (Theory of Harmony), published in 1911, and *Pierrot Lunaire*, a cycle of poems declaimed with the accompaniment of chamber orchestra.[6] Until then, I had been considered only a destroyer, and even my craftsmanship had been doubted, in spite of the many works of my first period. The *Harmonielehre* endowed me with the respect of many former adversaries who hitherto had considered me a wild man, a savage, an illegitimate intruder into musical culture. These same people were forced now to realize that they were wrong. They had to acknowledge that none of the slurs they had cast on me could be justified. Far from having no background, or a poor one, I had, on the contrary, been brought up in the Brahmsian culture; far from ignoring the works of the classic masters, I paid them profound respect and knew and understood the masterworks at least as well as my enemies; far from knowing little about the technical requirements of composing, I could explain them in a new and very instructive manner. And perhaps the greatest surprise may have been the fact that my *Harmonielehre* did not speak very much about 'atonality' and other prohibited subjects but almost exclusively about the technique and harmony of our predecessors, wherein I happened to appear even stricter and more conservative than other contemporary theorists. But just because I was so true to our predecessors, I was able to show that modern harmony was not developed by an irresponsible fool, but that it was the very logical development of the harmony and technique of the masters.

It was as embarrassing to my opponents as it was encouraging to my pupils and followers, whose number had already increased astonishingly. And so I approached rather rapidly the first climax when *Pierrot Lunaire* gave me a great success by the novelty which it offered in so many respects. I must apologize for writing without modesty of my successes. But as I have written as sincerely about my failures, I may perhaps be forgiven on the assumption that I am trying to act on my own behalf as an historian.

As soon as these two successes were followed by the aforementioned performance of my *Gurrelieder* in 1913, the public had to realize that my music was not without emotional power. Because of this change, a different type of judgement now came into use when my works were reviewed. Almost every review at this time began: 'One may think whatever one likes about Schoenberg . . .', and usually continued: 'But one must admit his sincerity.' To receive appreciation for my sincerity was of much value to a man in my position, but it is somewhat inadequate for a composer who believes in his work, and who aims for more than this moral support. And so I became annoyed as often as I read this, and said: 'They think about me what *they* like, but I want them to think what *I* like.'

Success comes in waves; and thus, after this climax, I sank into the depression between waves. It was the war which made people think differently about modern music. But as soon as the war was over, there came another wave which procured for me a popularity unsurpassed since. My works were played everywhere and acclaimed in such a manner that I started to doubt the value of my music. This may seem like a joke, but, of course, there is some truth in it. If previously my music had been difficult to understand on account of the peculiarities of my ideas and the way in which I expressed them, how could it happen that now, all of a sudden, everybody could follow my ideas and like them? Either the music or the audience was worthless.

While the music proved to be lasting, these audiences were unstable. As suddenly as they had turned their favour to me and had procured me a popularity which was not consistent with my style, and which always seemed to me unsound, the same audiences made another turn and became hostile towards my music. This was the time when everybody made believe he understood Einstein's theories and Schoenberg's music. And the *reaction* was more justified than the action. Through this turn in the mind of the public, I became for the first time in my life really lonely. This happened in 1924. I had just started to lend my new works an improved kind of structural continuity in introducing what I called the 'method of composing with twelve tones', when suddenly public opinion began to forget the emotional power of everything I had written before. *Pierrot Lunaire*, the First and Second String Quartets, *Gurrelieder*, and even *Verklärte Nacht* were forgotten, and I was called by some critics a mere constructor. By this term they wished to imply that I did not write instinctively, and that my music was dry and without emotional expression. By others, in contrast, I was accused of exactly the opposite crime: I was called an old-fashioned romanticist and my style of expression was blamed for expressing personal feelings. Still others called me a decadent bourgeois, while one group called me Bolshevist. So I seemed to unite within myself every possible contrast: I was too dry and too sweet; I was a constructor and a romanticist; I was an innovator and I was old-fashioned; I was a bourgeois and a Bolshevik.

Though the reasons my opponents gave for their opposition to my music were ridiculous, though their arguments were as confused as possible, since I could not be at one time myself and my own opposite, and though I could laugh about such nonsense, nevertheless, on the other hand, the unanimity of the rebuke was frightening. It was frightening to such an extent that even among some of my pupils an uncertainty appeared and some of them turned to the new fashions of composing which were promoted by the different composers of the so-called New Music. It was the first time in my career that I lost, for a short time, my influence on youth.[7] This took place between 1922 and 1930, and during this time almost every year a new kind of music was created and that of the preceding year collapsed. It started with the European musicians imitating American jazz. Then followed 'Machine Music' and 'New Objectivity' (*Neue Sachlichkeit*) and 'Music for Every Day Use' (*Gebrauchsmusik*) and 'Play Music' or 'Game Music' (*Spielmusik*) and finally 'Neo-classicism'. While all this happened and so many styles developed and passed away, I did not enjoy my splendid isolation very cheerfully. Although I soon realized the confusion among my opponents and although I saw with regret that many a great talent would perish through a corrupt attitude towards the arts, which aimed only for a sensational but futile success, instead of fulfilling the real task of every artist; although I knew I was right and that they were wrong, I felt lonely during this period in which I was restricted to the faithfulness of the above-mentioned small number of pupils, among whom I should not forget to include my four friends in the Kolisch Quartet. One of the accusations directed at me maintained that I composed only for my private satisfaction. And this was to become true, but in a different manner from that which was meant. While composing for me had been a pleasure, now it became a duty. I knew I had to fulfil a task: I had to express what was necessary to be expressed and I knew I had the duty of developing my ideas for the sake of progress in music, whether I liked it or not; but I also had to realize that the great majority of the public did not like it. However I remembered that all my music had been found to be ugly at first; and yet ... there might be a sunrise such as is depicted in the final chorus of my *Gurrelieder*. There might come the promise of a new day of sunlight in music such as I would like to offer to the world.[8]

October 11, 1937

5

HEART AND BRAIN IN MUSIC
1946

Balzac in his philosophical story *Seraphita* describes one of his characters as follows: 'Wilfred was a man thirty years of age. Though strongly built, his proportions did not lack harmony. He was of medium height as is the case with almost all men who tower above the rest. His chest and his shoulders were broad and his neck was short, like that of men whose heart must be within the domain of the head.'

No doubt all those who supposedly create cerebrally—philosophers, scientists, mathematicians, constructors, inventors, theorists, architects—keep their emotions under control and preserve the coolness of their heads even though imagination will often inspire them. But it is not generally agreed that poets,

53

artists, musicians, actors, and singers should admit the influence of a brain upon their emotions.

Only a few decades ago it was the standard opinion that a poet, and especially a lyric poet, was distinguished not only by long hair and a dirty collar but also by his habit of assuming an interesting pose. In place of a sober and direct word, he was expected to use one which only circumscribed an idea or a fact, if possible, obscured both a little, befogged their meaning and appearance. Thus they appeared as something out of a dream, suggesting that the reader—no, not that he fall asleep, but only that he dream without sleeping.

Though such viewpoints no longer prevail, similar outmoded misconceptions are still in circulation. One such misconception is the general belief that the constituent qualities of music belong to two categories as regards their origin: to the heart or to the brain, with the exception of some products in which both might have a word to say.

Those qualities in which a listener likes to recognize his own heart are those which he deems to have originated in the emotions of a composer: the beautiful melody or phrase, the beautiful—or, at least, sweet—sound, the beautiful harmony.

Those qualities of a less heart-warming nature, such as dynamic contrasts, changes of tempo, accentuation, features of rhythm and accompaniment, and, most of all, the finesses of organization—these seem to be ascribed to the co-operation of heart and brain and might be classified rather as 'interesting', arousing the interest of a listener without considerable appeal to his feelings.

The third group arouses neither so much feeling nor interest, but, if it should accelerate the heart-beat, it is because of the admiration, the awe, in which it is held. Counterpoint, contrapuntal style, is definitely attributed to the brain. It is honoured by the highest appreciation but tolerated only if it does not destroy the warmth of the dreams into which the charm of the beautiful has led the listener.

I believe that a real composer writes music for no other reason than that it pleases him. Those who compose because they want to please others, and have audiences in mind, are not real artists. They are not the kind of men who are driven to say something whether or not there exists one person who likes it, even if they themselves dislike it. They are not creators who must open the valves in order to relieve the interior pressure of a creation ready to be born. They are merely more or less skilful entertainers who would renounce composing if they could not find listeners.

Real music by a real composer might produce every kind of impression without aiming to. Simple and beautiful melodies, salty rhythms, interesting harmony, sophisticated form, complicated counterpoint—the real composer writes them with the ease with which one writes a letter. 'As if he were writing a letter'—this is what my comrades in the Austrian army said admiringly when, in the barracks, I wrote some music for a party given by the company. That this was not a remarkably beautiful piece but only one of average craftsmanship does not make any difference, because it often takes as much time to compose a letter as to write music. I personally belong to those who generally write very fast, whether it is 'cerebral' counterpoint or 'spontaneous' melody.

Most of the friends of my youth were also fast writers. For instance, Alexander von Zemlinsky, composer of many successful operas, while still studying composition at the Vienna Conservatory, prepared at the same time for a competition in piano which he later won. He had a peculiar method of using his time rationally, since he was forced to give many piano lessons in order to earn a living. He would alternately compose and practise the piano. Writing in ink one page of music, he had to wait for the page to dry. This interval of time only could he spare for practice. A busy life!

A week was generally considered just sufficient time to start and finish a sonata movement. But once I wrote all four movements of a string quartet within this length of time. A song for voice and piano might have required one to three hours—three hours, if you were unfortunately caught with a long poem.

I composed three-fourths of both the second and the fourth movements of my Second String Quartet in one-and-a-half days each. I completed the half-hour music of my opera *Erwartung* in 14 days. Several times I wrote two or three pieces of *Pierrot Lunaire* and the song-cycle *Hängende Gärten* in a day. I could mention many more such examples.

Thus it will be as astonishing to you as it was to all my friends when I came with the score of *Verklärte Nacht* and showed them one particular measure on which I had worked a full hour, though I had written the entire score of 415 measures in three weeks. This measure is indeed a little complicated since, according to the artistic conviction of this period (the post-Wagnerian), I wanted to express the idea *behind* the poem, and the most adequate means to that end seemed a complicated contrapuntal combination: a leitmotiv and its inversion played simultaneously (Ex. 1).

Ex. 1 *Verklärte Nacht*

This combination was not the product of a spontaneous inspiration but of an extra-musical intention, of a cerebral reflection. The technical labour which required so much time was in adding such subordinate voices as would soften the harsh frictions of this combination.

Of course there is always the possibility that in the midst of a composition there might suddenly emerge new reasons for persuading a composer to engage in such a venture. One of the most frequent of such reasons is artistic ambition, the artist's sense of honour. Indeed, the aim of an artist to elaborate profoundly upon his ideas, especially if it makes the task more difficult for his listeners—this aim should not be condemned even if the cerebral procedure causes loss of the surface beauty. Besides, an artist need not necessarily fail if he has started something to which inspiration has not forced him. Often enough inspiration intervenes spontaneously and gives its blessing undemanded.

It often happens to a composer that he writes down a melody in one uninterrupted draft and with a perfection that requires no change and offers no possibility of improvement. It has occurred often enough to me. For instance, in this melody from my Second String Quartet, I certainly did not make the slightest change: (Ex 2)

I was certainly no less directed by inspiration when I started my *Kammersymphonie*. I had a perfect vision of the whole work—of course, not in all its details but in its main features. But, while I wrote many of the subordinate themes later in *one* draft, I had to work very hard to shape the beginning. I have copied here some of the phases and metamorphoses through which the first two main ideas had to pass before I was satisfied (Ex. 3).

Ex. 3 A–D *Kammersymphonie*, Principal Theme 3

A—Shows the one rhythmic and melodic configuration, which reappears in all sketches.

Aa—Shows an attempt at a continuation, which is quite unbalanced but contains one rhythm (Aa) which does not disappear any more.

B—Already brings the ascending whole tones, though in a broader rhythmization, and the triplets (*) which also appear in the following sketch C and in the final form.

Ex. 3 E–J *Kammersymphonie*, Principal Theme 5

E—This first sketch already contains four features which are used in all following sketches and also in the final form J. The melodic form marked *a* consists here only of four notes. But already the next sketch, F, adds the fifth note (a^1). There is also under *b* the syncopated rhythm (⋀), under *c* the characteristic leap of a ninth, c to d, and the harmonic progression based on fourth chords (marked *).

G to I—Preserve the first 4½ measures and try to continue in various ways. The final form is then given in J.

In all these cases there was no problem which one would call complicated. There was no combination of voices whose contrapuntal relation required adaptation, as in the example from *Verklärte Nacht*. In these first notations, there were even no harmonic progressions which demanded control. There was at hand from the start a sufficient amount of motival forms and their derivatives, rather too much than too little. The task, therefore, was to retard the progress of development in order to enable the average good listener to keep in mind what preceded so as to understand the consequences. To keep within bounds and to balance a theme whose character, tempo, expression, harmonic progression, and motival contents displayed a centrifugal tendency: this was here the task. If one compares the difficult labour required in this case with the great ease with which most of the other themes were conceived, one might conclude that inspiration at times makes a gift to a composer in a perfect form, which at other times is denied him. In both cases it was not complexity which stood in the way of perfection, nor was it the heart which erred nor the brain which corrected.

In order to give an idea how such themes look when conceived spontaneously and written without correction, I refer the reader to the subordinate theme of the *Kammersymphonie* (No. 21, pp. 22–3 in the score). Or Ex. 4, from the same work, will also illustrate this point (see p. 62).

There are other cases which might even increase the confusion and make the determination of the share of heart or brain, of inspiration or labour, more difficult.

Some forty years ago I was composing my First String Quartet, Op. 7. Usually taking morning walks, I composed in my mind 40 to 80 measures complete in almost every detail. I needed only two or three hours to copy down these large sections from memory. From such a section of about 80 measures (which even a fast writer could not copy in less time than it took me to compose them) I want to give some illustrations and explain some of the intricate complexities involved.

Ex. 4 *Kammersymphonie*, Adagio Theme

The first violin plays a passage in measures 100–3 (p. 46 in the score):

This is repeated in 107–10 (p. 46):

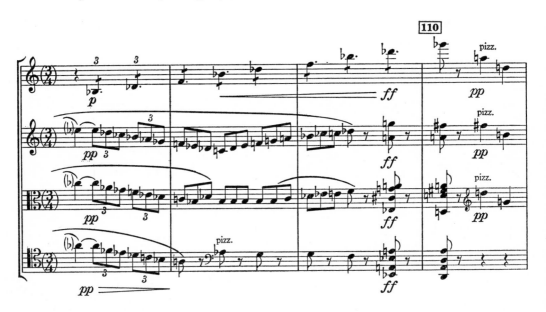

And again in 40–43 (p. 48):

These three statements differ in their accompaniment and harmonization and lead to different endings: the first to D-minor, the second to D-major, the third to D♭-major chords.

The pizzicato in 103–4 (p. 46) is part of the Scherzo theme, and is used in many transformations. In measures 1–11, after H (pp. 46–47), it accompanies a transformation of the main theme:

And in 43–46 (p. 48) a variant of it is used similarly:

65

Sehr zurückhaltend. Etwas langsamer

Note also the independent voice leading in 19–26 (p. 47):

And a similar example will be found in 63–70 (pp. 49–50). Besides the examples given here, there are numerous other contrapuntal combinations; and doubtless the entire section is of a texture one must call complicated.

One who assumes that counterpoint is cerebral while melody is spontaneous would be forced, in the face of these two examples, to conclude that cerebral products can be written faster than those of spontaneous feeling. But nothing could be more erroneous; the one as well as the other may require much or little work. Whether much or little labour is necessary depends on circumstances about which we have no control. Only one thing is certain, at least to me: without inspiration *neither* could be accomplished.

There are times when I am unable to write a single example of simple counterpoint in two voices, such as I ask sophomores to do in my classes. And, in order to write a *good* example of this sort, I must receive the co-operation of inspiration. I am in this respect much weaker than some of my pupils who write good or poor counterpoint without any kind of inspiration.

However, having been educated in the sphere of Brahms' influence (I was only a little over twenty-two when Brahms died), like many others I followed his example. 'When I do not feel like composing, I write some counterpoint.' Unfortunately, Brahms destroyed everything he did not consider worthy of publication before he died. This is regrettable, for to be allowed to look into the workshop of such a conscientious man would be extremely instructive. One would see how often he had worked hard to prepare his basic ideas for those conclusions he foresaw. 'A good theme is a gift of God,' he said; and he concluded with a word of Goethe: 'Deserve it in order to possess it.'

One thing seems certain: Brahms' mental gymnastics were certainly not of an easygoing sort. We know that it was his habit on his Sunday excursions in the Wienerwald to prepare 'enigmatic canons' whose solutions occupied his companions for several hours. Subsequently I was stimulated to try also the difficult types of canons. There were some which required much work, as, for instance, the following example. Perhaps this mirror canon required such a painful effort because my heart refused to co-operate (Ex. 5).

Ex. 5 Mirror Canon

Even though the purpose of such things is not music but only gymnastics, I must have been inspired, or at least in a good mood, when I wrote the Mirror Canon for String Quartet in about an hour (Ex. 6).

Ex. 6 Mirror Canon for String Quartet

But what assisted me in writing these canons could never have been inspiration of the same kind which produced melodies like that of the Adagio section of my First String Quartet (Ex. 7).

It is perhaps necessary to show also some melodies of my later period, especially of the composition with twelve tones, which has earned me the title of constructionist, engineer, mathematician, etc., meaning that these compositions are produced exclusively by the brain without the slightest participation of

Ex. 7 First String Quartet, Adagio Theme

something like a human heart. As an example from my later period, I quote here the beginning of my Piano Concerto, Op. 42 (Ex. 8).

Ex. 8 Concerto for Piano and Orchestra, Op. 42

71

Arnold Schoenberg, Op. 42. Reduction of Orchestra for a Second Piano by Eduard Steuermann.

An unprejudiced musician will easily find many more such melodies in my latest work. See, for instance, the Intermezzo from my Third String Quartet, Op. 30, and the Andante Grazioso of the Violin Concerto, Op. 36 (Exs. 9 and 10).

73

Ex. 9 Third String Quartet, Intermezzo Theme

Assuming that a composer is at least entitled to like his themes (even though it may not be his duty to publish only what he himself likes), I dare say that I have shown here only melodies, themes, and sections from my works which I deemed to be good if not beautiful. Some of them were produced with ease; others required hard labour. Some are relatively simple; others are complicated. But one cannot pretend that the complicated ones required hard work or that the simple ones were always easily produced. Also, one cannot pretend that it makes any difference whether the examples derive from a spontaneous emotion or from a cerebral effort.

Unfortunately, there is no record that classic masters made much ado about the greater or lesser efforts needed for different tasks. Perhaps they wrote everything with the same ease, or, as one might suspect in the case of Beethoven, with the same great effort, as Beethoven's sketch books prove.

Ex. 10 Concerto for Violin and Orchestra, Andante Theme

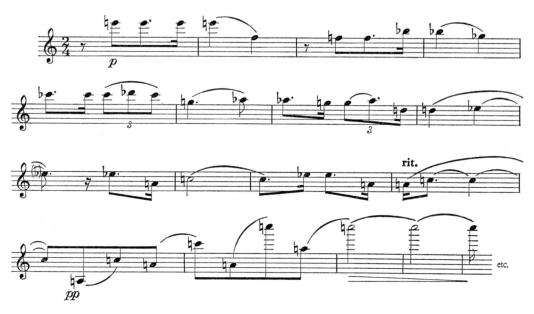

But one thing seems to be clear: whether its final aspect is that of simplicity or of complexity, whether it was composed swiftly and easily or required hard work and much time, the finished work gives no indication of whether the emotional or the cerebral constituents have been determinant.

It is necessary to remember that frequently the elaboration of unaccompanied themes and melodies in the examples I have shown required from three to seven sketches, while some of the contrapuntal sections were composed in a very short time.

It seems to me that I anticipated the solution to this problem in the very beginning of this essay with the quotation from Balzac: 'The heart must be within the domain of the head.'

It is not the heart alone which creates all that is beautiful, emotional, pathetic, affectionate, and charming; nor is it the brain alone which is able to produce the well-constructed, the soundly organized, the logical, and the complicated. First, everything of supreme value in art must show heart as well as brain. Second, the real creative genius has no difficulty in controlling his feelings mentally; nor must the brain produce only the dry and unappealing while concentrating on correctness and logic.

But one might become suspicious of the sincerity of works which incessantly exhibit their heart; which demand our pity; which invite us to dream with them of a vague and undefined beauty and of unfounded, baseless emotions; which exaggerate because of the absence of reliable yardsticks; whose simplicity is want, meagreness, and dryness; whose sweetness is artificial and whose appeal attains only to the surface of the superficial. Such works only demonstrate the complete absence of a brain and show that this sentimentality has its origin in a very poor heart.

6

A SELF-ANALYSIS
1948

If people speak of me, they at once connect me with horror, with atonality, and with composition with twelve tones. Generally it is always forgotten that before I developed these new techniques, there were two or three periods in which I had to acquire the technical armament that enabled me to stand distinctly on my own feet, in a manner that forbade comparison with other composers, either predecessors or contemporaries.

It is seldom realized that a hand that dares to renounce so much of the achievements of our forefathers has to be exercised thoroughly in the techniques that are to be replaced by new methods. It is seldom realized that there is a link between the technique of forerunners and that of an innovator and that no new technique in the arts is created that has not had its roots in the past. And it is seldom realized that these works in which an innovator prepares—consciously or subconsciously—for the action that will distinguish him from his surroundings furnish ready information about the justification of an author's turn toward new regions.

In formulating this justification it seems as if this might be the task of a musicologist. But this is untrue, because it is just the audience to whom such recognition is important. And it is the musicologist's duty to guide the audience in order to procure a fair evaluation of one who had the courage to risk his life for an idea.

Musicologists have failed to act in favour of the truth. This is the reason why my situation with the audience is often as follows: those of my works that might interest them (that is, those they consider atonal and dissonant) they refuse to listen to, and those works that are not called atonal but are less dissonant are not interesting enough—to people who do not know them at all.

Atonality or dissonance are no yardsticks for evaluation. Superficiality might base its judgements on such qualities. True love and understanding of music will wonder: What has been said? How was it expressed? Was there a new message delivered in music? Has a new personality been discovered? Was the technical presentation adequate?

Of course, to identify the style is easier and procures for one the glory of a connoisseur. But the love of the friend of art does not derive so indirectly—if it is appreciation that it aims for.

I am sure that the works of my last style would find at least the respect they deserve if the audience were given a chance to do justice to the works of my earlier periods. It was a healthier situation when Richard Wagner's works had to struggle for recognition. Then, even the most conservative friends of music recognized the value and the beauties of Wagner's first and second periods— *Rienzi*, *The Flying Dutchman*, *Tannhäuser*, and *Lohengrin*. This recognition paved the way for the appreciation of *Tristan*, *Die Meistersinger*, *The Ring*, and *Parsifal*.

I personally do not find that atonality and dissonance are the outstanding features of my works. They certainly offer obstacles to the understanding of what is really my musical subject. But why then did even the works of my first period always meet resistance at the first few performances, only later to become appreciated?

It seems that the true cause must be found in my tendency to endow every work with an extravagant abundance of musical themes. In the works of my first period this caused extension to a length that soon began to annoy me. It was, of course, the tendency of the Wagnerian and post-Wagnerian epoch. Recall the extension of symphonies by Bruckner and Mahler and other forms by Strauss, Reger, Debussy, Tchaikovsky and many others. Much of this length, except in Mahler and Reger, was due to the technique of using numerous little-varied or even unvaried repetitions of short phrases. I became aware of the aesthetic inferiority of this technique when I composed the final section of the symphonic poem, *Pelleas and Melisande*. In the greater part of that work, sequences made up a considerable contribution toward achieving the necessary expanse of the presentation, such as is required for easier understanding.

At the very start I knew that restriction could be achieved by two methods, condensation and juxtaposition. The first attempts that I made prior to this recognition—to use variation, often with far-reaching changes—did not satisfy me perfectly, though in 'developing variation' lies a far greater aesthetic merit than in an unvaried sequence. But even by that method the length of a piece was scarcely reduced. Thus even my First String Quartet, Op. 7, which I dislike as little as any of my earlier works, is of an unusual length—a great obstacle to the recognition of whatever beauty may be found therein.

Before I could master technically the difficulties of condensation and juxta-position, I was forced by my destiny upon another road. By abandoning the one-movement form and returning, in my Second String Quartet, to the organization of four movements, I became the first composer in this period to write shorter compositions. Soon thereafter I wrote in the extreme short forms. Although I did not dwell very long in this style, it taught me two things: first, to formulate ideas in an aphoristic manner, which did not require continuations out of formal reasons; secondly, to link ideas together without the use of formal connectives, merely by juxtaposition.

I admit that this style of writing does not promote easy understanding. It is the style of music since about 1920, and it requires intense attention to grasp and a good memory to keep in mind what is going on. I am sure that a full under-standing is difficult to acquire if one has not gradually become acquainted with my ideas in general and their special presentation.

Already my early works show some traits of my mature style, but seldom are all the so-called difficulties crowded into one single place. If, for instance, heterogeneous units of a work are juxtaposed, the unit itself might not be too condensed or its harmonic background might be rather comprehensible; in other cases, a slightly varied repetition might support the memory; in still other cases, subsequent elements might function as belated connectives. Thus, not all such procedures as are obstacles to the uninitiated listener will work in a sense-interrupting manner. And once the gate to understanding is open an emotional impression will not fail to appear.

May I venture to say that, in my belief, even works of my third period as, for example, the *Three Piano Pieces*, Op. 11, or the *Five Orchestral Pieces*, Op. 16, and especially *Pierrot Lunaire*, Op. 21, are relatively easy to understand today. And if I speak at present dispassionately about these works, one must not forget that they were written forty or more years ago. I can look upon them as if somebody else might be their composer, and I can explain their technique and their mental contents quite objectively. I see therein things that at the time of composing were still unknown to me.

May I venture to say that if in spite of my personal feeling about them I still like them, the idea that they are worth it seems somehow justified.

7

MY EVOLUTION
1949

Of the seventy-five years of my life I have devoted almost ninety per cent to music. I began studying violin at the age of eight and almost immediately started composing. One might accordingly assume that I had acquired very early a great skill in composing. My uncle Fritz, who was a poet, the father of Hans Nachod, had taught me French very early; there was not, as has happened in many child-prodigy-producing families, any music-enthusiast in mine. All my compositions up to about my seventeenth year were no more than imitations of such music as I had been able to become acquainted with — violin duets and duet-arrangements of operas and the repertory of military bands that played in public parks. One must not forget that at this time printed music was extremely expensive, that there were not yet records or radios, and that Vienna had only one opera theatre and one yearly cycle of eight Philharmonic concerts.

Only after I had met three young men of about my own age and had won their friendship did my musical and literary education start. The first was Oscar Adler, whose talent as a musician was as great as his capabilities in science.

Through him I learned of the existence of a theory of music, and he directed my first steps therein. He also stimulated my interest in poetry and philosophy and all my acquaintance with classical music derived from playing quartets with him, for even then he was already an excellent first violinist.

My second friend at that time was David Bach. A linguist, a philosopher, a connoisseur of literature, and a mathematician, he was also a good musician. He greatly influenced the development of my character by furnishing it with the ethical and moral power needed to withstand vulgarity and commonplace popularity.

The third friend is the one to whom I owe most of my knowledge of the technique and the problems of composing: Alexander von Zemlinsky. I have always thought and still believe that he was a great composer. Maybe his time will come earlier than we think. One thing is beyond doubt, in my opinion: I do not know one composer after Wagner who could satisfy the demands of the theatre with better musical substance than he. His ideas, his forms, his sonorities, and every turn of the music sprang directly from the action, from the scenery, and from the singer's voices with a naturalness and distinction of supreme quality.

I had been a 'Brahmsian' when I met Zemlinsky. His love embraced both Brahms and Wagner and soon thereafter I became an equally confirmed addict. No wonder that the music I composed at that time mirrored the influence of both these masters, to which a flavour of Liszt, Bruckner, and perhaps also Hugo Wolf was added. This is why in my *Verklärte Nacht* the thematic construction is based on Wagnerian 'model and sequence' above a roving harmony on the one hand, and on Brahms' technique of developing variation—as I call it—on the other. Also to Brahms must be ascribed the imparity of measures, as, for instance, in measures 50–54, comprising five measures, or measures 320–327, comprising two and one-half measures.

Ex. 1

Ex. 2

But the treatment of the instruments, the manner of composition, and much of the sonority were strictly Wagnerian. I think there were also some Schoenbergian elements to be found in the length of some of the melodies,

Ex. 3

in the sonority, in contrapuntal and motival combinations, and in the semi-contrapuntal movement of the harmony and its basses against the melody.

Ex. 4

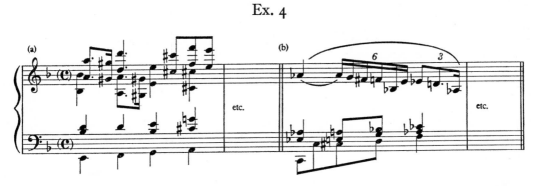

Finally, there were already some passages of unfixed tonality which may be considered premonitions of the future.

Ex. 5

True, at this time I had already become an admirer of Richard Strauss, but not yet of Gustav Mahler, whom I began to understand only much later, at a time when his symphonic style could no longer exert its influence on me. But it is still possible that his strongly tonal structure and his more sustained harmony influenced me. There were not many unusual melodic progressions demanding clarification through the harmony in my work. Qualities of this kind may be found in my First String Quartet, Op. 7, and in the Six Songs with Orchestra, Op. 8, while the earlier symphonic poem *Pelleas and Melisande* suggests a more rapid advance in the direction of extended tonality. Here are many features that have contributed towards building up the style of my maturity, and many of the melodies contain extratonal intervals that demand extravagant movement of the harmony. Examples 6, 7, and 8, from *Pelleas and Melisande*, will serve as illustration:

Ex. 6

This example also exhibits counter-movement of the harmony:

Ex. 7

This example is based on a broadly extended tonality:

Ex. 8

Here the intervals of the melody demand a rich movement of the accompanying voices.

The rhythmical texture is interwoven with syncopations and a tendency to avoid accentuation of strong beats seems to be prominent in Ex. 9:

Ex. 9

But most significant are sections of undetermined tonality, of which the following may be quoted:

Ex. 10

The climax of my first period is definitely reached in the *Kammersymphonie*, Op. 9. Here is established a very intimate reciprocation between melody and harmony, in that both connect remote relations of the tonality into a perfect unity, draw logical consequences from the problems they attempt to solve, and simultaneously make great progress in the direction of the emancipation of the dissonance. This progress is brought about here by the postponement of the resolution of 'passing' dissonances to a remote point where, finally, the preceding harshness becomes justified.

This is also the place to speak of the miraculous contributions of the sub-conscious. I am convinced that in the works of the great masters many miracles can be discovered, the extreme profundity and prophetic foresight of which seem superhuman. In all modesty, I will quote here one example from the *Kammer-symphonie*. I have discussed it thoroughly in my lecture 'Composition with Twelve Tones', solely in order to illustrate the power behind the human mind, which produces miracles for which we do not deserve credit.

Ex. 11

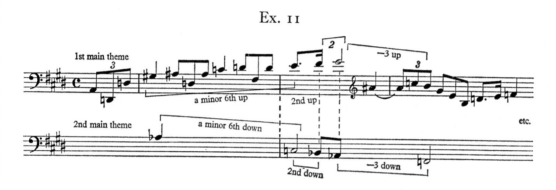

In this example is unveiled the hidden relationship between two main themes. It is based on the appearance of steps of the melody, which, in the second theme, move miraculously in the opposite direction.

Ex. 12

Example 12 unveils the relationship of the subordinate theme to the essential intervals in the first main theme.

If there are composers capable of inventing themes on the basis of such a remote relationship, I am not one of them. However, a mind thoroughly trained in musical logic may function logically under any circumstances. Externally, co-herence manifests itself through an intelligible application of the relationship and similarity inherent in musical configurations. What I believe, in fact, is that if one has done his duty with the utmost sincerity and has worked out everything as near to perfection as he is capable of doing, then the Almighty presents him with a gift, with additional features of beauty such as he never could have produced by his talents alone.

My Two Ballads, Op. 12, were the immediate predecessors of the Second String Quartet, Op. 10, which marks the transition to my second period. In this period I renounced a tonal centre—a procedure incorrectly called 'atonality'. In the first and second movements there are many sections in which the individual parts proceed regardless of whether or not their meeting results in codified harmonies. Still, here, and also in the third and fourth movements, the key is presented distinctly at all the main dividing-points of the formal organization. Yet the overwhelming multitude of dissonances cannot be counterbalanced any longer by occasional returns to such tonal triads as represent a key. It seemed in-adequate to force a movement into the Procrustean bed of a tonality without supporting it by harmonic progressions that pertain to it. This dilemma was my concern, and it should have occupied the minds of all my contemporaries also. That I was the first to venture the decisive step will not be considered uni-versally a merit—a fact I regret but have to ignore.

This first step occurred in the Two Songs, Op. 14, and thereafter in the *Fifteen Songs of the Hanging Gardens* and in the Three Piano Pieces, Op. 11. Most critics of this new style failed to investigate how far the ancient 'eternal' laws of musical aesthetics were observed, spurned, or merely adjusted to changed circumstances. Such superficiality brought about accusations of anarchy and revolution, whereas, on the contrary, this music was distinctly a product of evolution, and no more revolutionary than any other development in the history of music.

In my *Harmonielehre* (1911), I maintained that the future would certainly prove that a centralizing power comparable to the gravitation exerted by the root is still operative in these pieces. In view of the fact that, for example, the laws of Bach's or Beethoven's structural procedures or of Wagner's harmony have not yet been established in a truly scientific manner, it is not surprising that no such attempt has been made with respect to 'atonality'.

What a composer can contribute to the solution of this problem, even if his mind is capable of research, is not of much consequence; he is too much prejudiced by the intoxicating recollection of the inspiration that enforced production. Nevertheless, just such psychological details might open an avenue of approach towards an explanation.

I have mentioned before that the accompanying harmony came to my mind in a quasi-melodic manner, like broken chords. A melodic line, a voice part, or even a melody derives from horizontal projections of tonal relations. A chord results similarly from projections in the vertical direction. Dissonant tones in the melody, that is, tones of a more remote relationship to the occasional centre, cause difficulties of comprehension. Such remotely related tones are likewise an obstacle to intelligibility.

The main difference between harmony and melodic line is that harmony requires faster analysis, because the tones appear simultaneously, while in a melodic line more time is granted to synthesis, because the tones appear successively, thus becoming more readily graspable by the intellect.

In other words, melody, consisting of slowly unfolded progressions of tones, offers more time for comprehension of the relationships and logic than harmony, where analysis has to function many times as fast.

This may be at least a psychological explanation of the fact that an author who is not supported by traditional theory and, on the contrary, knows how distasteful his work will be to contemporaries, can feel an aesthetic satisfaction in writing this kind of music. One must not forget that—theory or no theory—a composer's only yardstick is his sense of balance and his belief in the infallibility of the logic of his musical thinking.

Nevertheless, since I had been educated in the spirit of the classical schools, which provided one with the power of control over every step, in spite of my loosening of the shackles of obsolete aesthetics I did not cease to ask myself for the theoretical foundation of the freedom of my style.

Coherence in classic compositions is based—broadly speaking—on the unifying qualities of such structural factors as rhythms, motifs, phrases, and the constant reference of all melodic and harmonic features to the centre of gravitation—the tonic. Renouncement of the unifying power of the tonic still leaves all the other factors in operation.

Usually when changes of style occur in the arts, a tendency can be observed to overemphasize the difference between the new and the old. Advice to followers is given in the form of exaggerated rules, originating from a distinct trend 'épater le bourgeois', that is, 'to amaze mediocrity'. Fifty years later, the finest ears of the best musicians have difficulty in hearing those characteristics that the eyes of the average musicologist see so easily.

Though I would not pretend that my piano piece Opus 11, No. 3, looks like a string quartet of Haydn, I have heard many a good musician, when listening to Beethoven's *Great Fugue*, cry out: 'This sounds like atonal music.'

I now find that some of the statements in my *Harmonielehre* are too strict, while others are superfluous. Intoxicated by the enthusiasm of having freed music from the shackles of tonality, I had thought to find further liberty of expression. In fact, I myself and my pupils Anton von Webern and Alban Berg, and even Alois Hába believed that now music could renounce motivic features and remain coherent and comprehensible nevertheless.

True, new ways of building phrases and other structural elements had been discovered, and their mutual relationship, connection, and combination could be balanced by hitherto unknown means. New characters had emerged, new moods and more rapid changes of expression had been created, and new types of beginning, continuing, contrasting, repeating, and ending had come into use. Forty years have since proved that the psychological basis of all these changes was correct. Music without a constant reference to a tonic was comprehensible, could produce characters and moods, could provoke emotions, and was not devoid of gaiety or humour.

Time for a change had arrived. In 1915 I had sketched a symphony, the theme of the Scherzo of which accidentally consisted of twelve tones. Only two years later a further step in this direction was taken. I had planned to build all the main themes of my unfinished oratorio, *Die Jakobsleiter*, out of the six tones of this row.

Ex. 13

Ex. 14

When I took the next step in this transition towards composition with twelve tones, I called it 'working with tones'. This became more distinct in some of the piano pieces of Op. 23.

Ex. 15

The first three measures consist of thirteen tones. Both D and E♭ appear twice, while C♯ is missing.

Examples 15a, b, c display how unity is produced by manifold uses of the mutual relations of these tones.

They still do not constitute a real basic set. I had at this time not yet discovered all the technical tools that furnish such abundance of variety as is necessary for expansive forms.

The closest approach happened in the Serenade, Op. 24, which, besides, already contains one really twelve-tone piece, the *Sonett Nr. 217 von Petrarca*, the fourth movement.

The tones of the first measure of the *Tanzscene* appear—in a different order—as accompaniment in the *Valse* part. The clarinet adds the remaining six tones.

Ex. 16

Still closer to twelve-tone composition is the variation movement. Its theme consists of 14 notes, because of the omission of one note, B, and the repetition of other notes.

Ex. 17

Here, for the first time, the 'consequent' consists of a retrograde repetition of the 'antecedent'. The following variations use inversions and retrograde inversions, diminutions and augmentations, canons of various kinds, and rhythmic shifts to different beats—in other words, all the technical tools of the method are here, except the limitation to only twelve different tones.

The method of composing with twelve tones substitutes for the order produced by permanent reference to tonal centres an order according to which, every unit of a piece being a derivative of the tonal relations in a basic set of twelve tones, the 'Grundgestalt' is coherent because of this permanent reference to the basic set.

Reference to this set offers also the justification of dissonant sounds. Contemporary music has taken advantage of my adventurous use of dissonances. Let us not forget that I came to this gradually, as a result of a convincing development which enabled me to establish the law of the emancipation of the dissonance, according to which the comprehensibility of the dissonance is considered as important as the comprehensibility of the consonance. Thus dissonances need not be a spicy addition to dull sounds. They are natural and logical outgrowths of an organism. And this organism lives as vitally in its phrases, rhythms, motifs and melodies as ever before.

In the last few years I have been questioned as to whether certain of my compositions are 'pure' twelve-tone, or twelve-tone at all. The fact is that I do not know. I am still more a composer than a theorist. When I compose, I try to forget all theories and I continue composing only after having freed my mind of them. It seems to me urgent to warn my friends against orthodoxy. Composing with twelve tones is not nearly as forbidding and exclusive a method as is popularly believed. It is primarily a method demanding logical order and organization, of which comprehensibility should be the main result.

Whether certain of my compositions fail to be 'pure' because of the surprising appearance of some consonant harmonies—surprising even to me—I cannot, as I have said, decide. But I am sure that a mind trained in musical logic will not fail even if it is not conscious of everything it does. Thus I hope that again an act of grace may come to my rescue, just as it did in the case of the *Kammersymphonie*, and unveil the coherence in this apparent discrepancy.

8

THE YOUNG AND I
1923

Earlier than I had foreseen, an energetic younger generation with new tendencies and a new way of feeling forces me to examine the up-to-dateness and up-to-futureness of their and my creations. Remarkably enough, I too believed that the development of music must now go the way I had pointed out, although I know that never once in the whole history of music has this in fact been the case— although I see that youth has always regarded the paths struck by its predecessors as exhausted, has found other side-paths to left or right, or even turned back to the point of departure, in order to strike out in an entirely different direction—and although in fact I myself developed in just that way in the end, for all that I did so unconsciously and believing the very opposite about myself.

But now, indeed, I must say why it was that all the evidence to the contrary could not prevent my believing what I believed. For ten years nothing new of mine has appeared. Anyone who knows me up to the last work of mine to appear is liable to assume he knows me entirely, to assume that from now on I shall simply continue in that direction, simply broaden this style, and that it is now the task of younger men to continue where I left off. The outsider considered this cessation as a fact, instead of considering symptoms which lead in another direction. I knew that I myself was hard at work enlarging this continuation of the path I had been treading, but (and this is the decisive thing) I personally had not only declined to classify myself, not merely omitted to confirm some sole particular direction for myself: quite the opposite, I was searching for something entirely new. And I found it, and believed it to be the kind of thing that points out, for all who come after, a straight way it has opened up. I forgot that the will of nature is perhaps also fulfilled via diversions. So I have not stopped, and perhaps there will still be new side-shoots at various points in my own development. Perhaps certain people feel this and therefore call me—according to the degree to which they have made themselves independent of musical understanding of my scores—their stimulus or forerunner. Perhaps some of those who strive with me will some day have to characterize me as one who ran away—that is to say, if both sides fail to stand the pace—they, of following me, I, of being followed by them. But even as a stimulus I am greatly overrated. My pupils can confirm that I tend rather to discourage. And, in fact, of all the very many who learned from me, as is now known even elsewhere, only three have become composers. All the others understand just enough to make it impossible to compose as badly as one must in order to be a modern master. Now, it is very sweet of this kind of master to admit to having been stimulated. It is good tactics, too, since they thus make quite sure nobody notices the wholly personal passages in their works where they lacked any stimulus. And they owe their effectiveness to the fact that these un-stimulated qualities are liable to be missed by the listener, since without these qualities, and the listener's way of missing them, they would be harder to grasp than those who would storm heaven can afford. But I believe that even in this respect I am overrated. A later age will have to get straight how much of their own, arisen with no stimulus, these masters have given, and that their most important things have nothing more in common with mine than, say, Don Quixote had with reality. My quixotries can never have caused anyone to get involved in a battle with windmills, but they have indeed made people aware of the danger of going near such things. So those who go near them count, rightly, as brave; they are the heroes of this age. Nor do I think one should overlook that many of the forms which I was supposedly the first to use in our time will surely be found to have been used by others long before me (even if only in unpublished works, or works perhaps merely planned)—if they did not indeed occur in earlier centuries. For example, in my *Pierrot Lunaire*, the dance-forms (waltz and polka) and contrapuntal studies (passacaglia, double-fugue with canon and retrograde of the canon, etc.), the pieces for solo instruments (*Der kranke Mond*) and for singing and reciting voice, with accompaniment for various instruments, for which I was cautious enough not to invent the title 'chamber-music songs'. In the same way, there are chamber orchestras and chamber symphonies even before the time of Bach. How pitiful and insignificant this all is, and how little true stimulus it offers! But who could overlook the fact that just these stimuli are of a purely external nature? For nobody had any closer knowledge of them than could be taken from newspaper reports, and than the very title-pages conveyed. And just this fact—that so far from my scores' being able to stimulate my successors' interest, it was merely my titles'—to nothing more than that should one ascribe the speed at which insight was attained, so that my nuisance value was reduced to that of a stimulus, and nothing more.

And since I am no longer a nuisance to the younger generation, I am more certain of their thanks than any master ever was. They render unto me what is due unto Caesar (in a republic), salute me (leaving me where I lie)[1] as they march past, feel themselves highly stimulated and will soon have forgotten that it was by me.[2]

And rightly! For whatever else they have not studied, they have studied musical history. And so they know that a new art is due to come now (Spengler foretold it long ago), and each of them already knows his role and knows what is the one and only role this leaves for me. Whatever inspiration I may still have, it can no longer shift me from the spot where I am planted by their far-seeing eye for what the past has still to produce. There I stand, scientifically above reproach. To most of them I am an architect—a drawer of bold (if old-fashioned) bows—even though it was the small form which I was the first to compose in our time.[3]

August 19–21, 1923

94

MY BLIND ALLEY
1926

The young composers find my way a blind alley. There is an implicit reproach here—that once, in the days before they knew any better than to copy me blatantly, I sold (or rather gave) them a pig in a poky blind-alley.[1] Measures are needed to stop any more aspiring composers from following me down my blind alley, so I am henceforth shutting off the entry to it with a row of twelve tones. Now they can keep moving round the circle of fifths and need not fear that one of my fundamentals will ever force its way through to them. And vice versa. If now and then they should wonder what the old chap down the blind alley is cooking up, they will find the row standing shoulder-to-shoulder against them. Unauthorized Persons will always find a way in, however—who could stop them?

All the same, until now I always felt more inclined toward a desert island than a blind alley. But since solitude is common to both, I prefer the blind alley of knowing my spiritual property to be common property, even though my participation in the common weal causes me still less emotion than the ending of my solitude would cause me discomfort.

So, back to tonality! (It used to be an artistic means whose advantages I knew how to exploit.) For the young, it is a carousel—why should they not enjoy it? A ride is even cheaper than the pleasure it affords. Grown-ups are admitted, too, and the onlooker also has fun. The young hold the floor, the future is theirs. Who, given a chance in life's carnival, would not prefer a carousel to a blind alley? I never dissuaded anyone from tonality; rather I warned them against the blind alley, which is not for those who want to go round in circles. Nowadays, it is 'après-moi le cul-de-sac'.[2] I blundered into it and shall patiently wait there till my last breath—the breath that still supplies the wind for their miserable carousels. The breakthrough will come no sooner than that!

July 23, 1926

MY PUBLIC
1930

Called upon to say something about my public, I have to confess: I do not believe I have one.

At the start of my career, when to the annoyance of my opponents a noticeable part of the audience did not hiss but applauded, and when the hissers did not succeed in carrying the day against the majority, although hisses sound more striking than applause, then these opponents of mine alleged that those bestowing their approval were my friends and had only applauded out of friendship and not because they liked the piece. My poor friends: as true as few. They were indeed thought depraved enough to be my friends and yet not so depraved as to enjoy my music.

Whether I then had a public—that I cannot judge.

But after the upheaval, there were in every major city those certain few hundred young people with just no idea what to do with themselves. They therefore tried hard to put it on record that they had a philosophy—by supporting all lost causes. About then, when that great variable, their philosophy, included even me—blameless party that I was—optimists asserted that I now had a public. I challenged this; I did not see how people could suddenly have come to understand me overnight. (My works had not, after all, become any more stupid or shallow overnight.) The rapid decline of the radicals—still not knowing what to do with themselves but finding other things to meddle with—justified my view: I had not written anything shallow.

There are many reasons why the great public makes little contact with me. Above all: the generals, who today still occupy the music directorates, are mostly moving along lines that my line does not fit, or else they are afraid to put before the public something they do not themselves understand. Some of them (even though when they admit it they politely look regretful) really regard not understanding me as a virtue. Granted even that is their greatest virtue, I still had to feel surprised the first time a Viennese conductor made it known to me that he could not perform my *Kammersymphonie* because he did not understand it. I was amused, though; why did he have to pick on me in this sudden burst of wanting to understand, and not on the classical works he blithely conducted year in, year out? But seriously, I must say that it is, after all, no honour for a musician not to understand a score, but a matter for shame—many even of my opponents will admit this today, as regards my *Kammersymphonie*.

Apart from these conductors, those who get between me and the public are the many musicians who do not conduct but know other ways to mislead. I have seen countless times that, as regards the main point, it was not the public who hissed: it was a small but active 'expert' minority. The public's behaviour is either friendly or indifferent, unless they are intimidated because their spiritual leaders are protesting. As a whole they are always rather inclined to enjoy something they have devoted time and money to. They come less to judge than to enjoy, and can to some extent sense whether the person appearing before them is entitled to do so. What they are not interested in doing is using their more or less correct judgement in order to display themselves in a better light. This is partly because no single member stands to gain or lose anything (he will either be outnumbered or be swallowed up in the majority); and partly because among the public there are, after all, people who count for something, even without first having to shine by their artistic judgements, and who, without losing prestige, may keep their impressions to themselves, unassessed. One may keep anything to oneself, except expert judgement—for what is expert judgement unless one shows it off? For this reason, I also take it to have been the expert judges, not the art-lovers, who received my *Pierrot Lunaire* with such hostility when I performed it in Italy. I was indeed honoured that Puccini, not an expert judge but a practical expert, already ill, made a six-hour journey to get to know my work, and afterwards said some very friendly things to me; that was good, strange though my music may have remained to him. But, on the other hand, it was characteristic that the loudest disturber of the concert was identified as the director of a conservatoire. He it was, too, who proved unable at the end to bridle his truly Mediterranean temperament—who could not refrain from exclaiming: 'If there had been just one single honest triad in the whole piece!' Obviously his teaching activities gave him too little opportunity to hear such honest triads, and he had come hoping to find them in my *Pierrot*. Am I to blame for his disappointment?

I have to think it possible that the Italian public did not know what to make of my music. But the image of a concert where there was hissing—in twenty-five years I have seen it so often that I may be believed—was always as follows: in the front third of the hall, roughly, there was little applause and little hissing; most people sat unconcerned, many stood looking around in amazement or amusement toward the parts of the hall farther back, where things were livelier. There the applauders were in the majority—there were fewer unconcerned, and a few hissers. But the most noise, both applause and hisses, always came from the standing space at the back and from the galleries. It was there that the people instructed or influenced by the expert judges went into battle against those who were impressed.

And yet I never had the impression that the number of people hissing was particularly great. It never sounded full, like a chord of solid applause entering with precision, but more like an ad hoc group of ill-assorted soloists, the extent of whose ensemble was limited to the fact that their noises told one the direction they were approaching from.

That was how I saw the public, and in no other way, except when, as today with my older works, they applauded. But besides a number of very pleasant letters I receive now and then, I also know the public from another side. Perhaps I may end by relating a few pleasing little experiences. When just drafted to a reserve company during the war, I, the conscript, who had had many a bad time, once found myself treated with striking mildness by a newly arrived sergeant. When he addressed me after we had drilled, I hoped I was going to be praised for my progress in all things military. There followed a blow to my soldierly keenness; surprisingly, the tribute was to my music. The sergeant, a tailor's assistant in civil life, had recognized me, knew my career, many of my works, and so gave me still more pleasure than by praising my drill (even though I was not a little proud of that!). There were two other such meetings in Vienna: once when I had missed a train and had to spend the night in a hotel, and again when a taxi was taking me to a hotel. I was recognized the first time by the *night porter*, the other time by the *taxi-driver*, from the name on the label of my luggage. Both assured me enthusiastically that they had heard the *Gurrelieder*. Another time, in a hotel in Amsterdam, a *hired man* addressed me, saying that he was a long-standing admirer of my art; he had sung in the choir in the *Gurrelieder* when I conducted them in Leipzig. But the prettiest story last: a short while back, again in a hotel, the *lift-man* asked me whether it was I who had written *Pierrot*

98

Lunaire. For he had heard it before the war (about 1912), at the first performance, and still had the sound of it in his ears, particularly of one piece where red jewels were mentioned ('Rote fürstliche Rubine'). And he had heard at the time that musicians had no idea what to make of the piece—the sort of thing that was quite easy to understand nowadays.

It strikes me that I need not alter what I believe about the semi-ignorant, the expert judges; I may continue to think they lack all power of intuition.

But whether I am really so unacceptable to the public as the expert judges always assert, and whether it is really so scared of my music—that often seems to me highly doubtful.

March 17, 1930

11

NEW MUSIC: MY MUSIC
c. 1930

I. IDEAS

Perhaps people as a whole do not sufficiently consider that I am perhaps saying something which cannot be grasped easily or straight away. Consider; if I utter a simple idea, which I base on phenomena that are obvious, then people can easily follow. But if an idea presupposes experiences that cannot have been everyone's, or that are not familiar to everyone, then some people will be quite unable to follow. And, if in expressing such an idea, one uses special resources connected with the subject in question, the difficulties become far worse.

An example, to elucidate this:

Let us assume that I had the chance of talking to someone who lived 100 years ago, saying to him: 'The weather is bad, so we shall need transport to get to the theatre.' This will be clear, straight away, to anyone of the kind. But if I say: 'In weather like this we can't go on the bus, because we should be wet through even getting from the bus stop to the theatre' . . . By now, a man who knows nothing of buses and bus stops will be out of his depth. And as for my saying: 'In weather like this we must take a taxi, but we must set out earlier than usual because the driver will have to drive slowly' . . . Then $[-+-+-+]^1$

All the same, there is nothing particularly profound, nor anything particularly new, about the latter idea, which is sure to be incomprehensible to anyone from before our own time. Just as certainly, uttering it is no achievement. Do we not feel, though, that if a man is anxious to be widely listened to, it is up to him to say something the others *did not know before*, but would be better off for knowing? Something that needs saying, then! Or is a man like that, who believes he knows something of the sort, obliged to keep silent, because he will not be understood? When, for example, a man somehow succeeds in finding out how things look on the moon, is such a man to keep it to himself; will he have to keep it to himself, because the only concise and concrete language in which to express it uses scientific terms? Is such a man to keep quiet, then? Or, if he does after all speak, is he to be abused, because no one can understand him? Is one to be free to abuse such a man, as one pleases? $[-+-+-+]$

In musical terms it looks roughly like this: if my transport, on account of the bad weather, is not a carriage but a minor triad—C minor, for example—, or if I harmonize a melody that uses only notes from C minor and takes good care that the tonic can nowhere be interpreted as anything but the tonic, so that the dominant (its dominant) is all the easier to grasp, then I have a good journey and reach my goal safely: I am understood. There is no denying, all the same, that in the course of such a journey people have been able to think out great, important, previously unexpressed ideas; that was possible, just as it was possible to cover an impressive amount of ground in a carriage or on horseback. But modern methods enable one to cover more ground, and economy is one of the most important principles in art; if the artist gives more for something than prevailing conditions demand, he cannot be as lavish in other directions as is felt to befit the standing of a genius.

But if one writes a sustained chord, b♯–d♯–f♯, in the right hand for the piano, and adds an eighth-note melody, g♯–f♯–e–d♯–c♯–b, this produces horrible, incomprehensible dissonances, and I am glad it was not I who first wrote that sort of thing, but Johann Sebastian Bach.[1] His contemporaries could not understand that. We no longer find it so difficult; we know that the terrible dissonances, b♯–c♯ and b♯–b, are not stopping places on the eighth-notes' route;

that they pass safely by and reach a bomb-proof shelter, an a, whose consonance with the f♯ once again restores harmony.

But if I now put it as follows: consonances are easier to understand than dissonances; and though dissonances are harder to understand, they are not incomprehensible (as the history of music indeed proves) so long as they occur in the right surroundings—then nobody will be able to dispute them.

However, some time ago the streets were asphalted, so that they were really smooth. Now comes a new development: cars skid when the asphalt is wet. So one must either remove the smooth asphalt or learn to drive safely even when the asphalt is wet. The present-day musician's ear has learned to manage without the smoothness of consonances. It has learned to keep quiet about the frequency with which dissonances occur, and indeed they have lost much of their frequency, or, in some cases, all. One recalls, for instance, that in earlier centuries the minor third counted as a dissonance; it was hard to understand. Nowadays one could state it as follows: dissonance may be put on an equality with consonance so far as comprehensibility is concerned. Moreover: the question whether dissonances or consonances should be used, and to what extent, is not a question of beauty, but only a question of comprehensibility. [−+−+−+]

So it can certainly be asserted that not everyone will find dissonances comprehensible; but nobody can deny the existence of ears and brains that find no more difficulty here than our intellect does in jumping from the idea of a car skidding on wet asphalt to the conclusion that one ought to set out earlier, even though the intermediate link is omitted—the need for the car to go carefully.

But the one has no more to do with beauty or taste than has the other. You will, however, certainly have heard that in my music *consonances* do not occur, or only in passing. Can even that be understood? Can one understand sound-combinations if they hang for ever in the air and never settle down; if they never gain a firm footing?

I read somewhere of a device by which aeroplanes refuel over the sea without standing firm anywhere (if so, where?). If that is possible, should one not do it?

2. MELODY

Here is another difficult thing about my music: its melodic steps. The thing hard to grasp is not each and every step; it is their progression. This is inherent, above all, in the harmony—in what I have already said about dissonances. It seems to me self-evident that dissonant combinations of sounds imply a different kind of melodic writing, as against consonant ones. If the harmony is primitive, then the melody must also be so, and vice versa. But accompanying a simple melody with a dissonant harmony, like present-day composers, seems to me as comic as wearing the primitive clothes of a primitive peasant, and rounding it all off with a top-hat and patent-leather shoes.

People must realize that there comes a time when a musician is no longer at ease using the same old interval-progressions. For in matters of melodic novelty and individuality (that is to say, the thing by which the musician establishes his inventiveness, his right to be listened to), interval-progressions are the strongest influence.

But even apart from this:

Do you believe a fencer, a wrestler, a boxer, a tennis-player would remain unbeaten for long if he always employed the same succession of lunges, holds, punches or strokes? Do you not think this would soon be noticed and suitably countered? Of course, a musician who for ever repeats familiar things, whose progression one already knows by heart before it happens, can hardly be countered, or only by losing interest or withdrawing one's attention; that is to say, one becomes bored.

To lay claim to one's interest, a thing must be worth saying, and must not yet have been said.

3. REPETITION

Here is the greatest difficulty for any listener, even if he is musically educated: the way I construct my melodies, themes, and whole movements offers the present-day perceptive faculty a challenge that cannot yet be met at a first hearing.

The causes of this difficulty lie in the following characteristic qualities of the way I write:

1. Substantially, I say something only once, i.e. repeat little or nothing.

2. With me, variation almost completely takes the place of repetition (there is hardly a single exception to this); by variation I mean a way of altering something given, so as to develop further its component parts as well as the figures built from them, the outcome always being something new, with an apparently

low degree of resemblance to its prototype, so that one finds difficulty in identifying the prototypes within the variation.

3. Not only are new sections, as so further developed, linked one to another or juxtaposed or lined up—all in the greatest variety of ways—but, particularly, almost the only aid to one's perception of all these types of combination is logic and an acute sense of form.

To elucidate these factors I should say the following:

In general, music is always hard (not even relatively hard) to understand—unless it is made easier by repetition of as many minute, small, medium or large sections as possible. The first precondition for understanding is, after all, memory: if I have no remembrance of the table, this is enough to prevent my understanding the sentence, 'The man is large', because I do not know what 'large' means. But the precondition of memory is recognition; if I do not recognize what the word 'man' signifies, then I cannot remember him either. If, then, in music, a figure is so constituted, so lacking in character, for example, or so complicated, that I cannot recognize it and remember it, then correct understanding of all that follows—all that results from it, follows from it—is impossible. This is perhaps the reason why, throughout music, as much as possible is repeated as often as possible, especially in simple music. For example, in Strauss' *Blue Danube Waltz* the first phrase is repeated seven times, and that is why the whole melody is so easy to grasp. Minor variations do indeed occur, but they simply ensure variety, a certain diversity, without making it harder to understand.

So one can make the following formulation:

The more easily graspable a piece of music is to be, the more often all its sections, small or large, will have to be repeated. Conversely, the fewer sections are repeated, and the less often, the harder the piece of music is to understand. If one wishes to be easily understood, one must keep harping on the subject in question, and coming back to it: 'I should help him, now?' 'Surely you won't let him down?' 'Yes, but don't forget, he is my enemy, and I should stick my neck out for him?' 'True, but now he needs you.' 'Yes, but how did he behave when I needed him? . . . you keep forgetting that.' Yes, certainly; he keeps forgetting it, although the other man keeps recalling it.

Nothing is any use here; and in music it may also be no use to keep recalling things. But mostly it is some use. The certain thing, though, is the harmful effect of non-recall: one does not know what is being talked about.

Now, if I recall that I confessed to repeating little or nothing in my music, then you will rightly ask, 'Why? Why make it so hard for the listener; why not make things easier for him, in the way he needs; why say once only things that are hard to perceive and remember even when heard repeatedly, so that one completely loses the thread and doesn't begin to comprehend all the things that come later?' To this I have to say: 'I can do it no other way, and it does not work any other way. Only, I did not choose to write like that, I do not go out of my way to write like that, and it would be a relief to feel I might do it differently.'

In the army, a superior officer once said to me: 'So you are this notorious Schoenberg, then.' 'Beg to report, sir, yes,' I replied. 'Nobody wanted to be, someone had to be, so I let it be me.'

Supposing I now asked myself, 'why does somebody have to be?' The only possible answer is, 'I don't know.' But the reason why there is no other way: were I prepared to be as discursive as one must be, in order to be widely comprehensible, my works would all last 10 to 12 times as long, and a piece which now lasts 10 minutes would play for two hours, while a whole day would not suffice to get through a longer one. Were each figure first elucidated by repetition, and each of the resulting small sections repeated at various points, and so on, then I should certainly be easier to follow; but, on grounds of sheer length, people would be less than ever able to follow me through to my destination.

How far would one get, in trying to discuss a house, if one had first to explain what it is, and what it is like? If one had to say: four vertical walls, with windows and doors, and a roof on top—and, eventually, to explain even what walls, windows, doors, roofs, are? When one refers to a house, anyone has a good idea of it and all its important features; if one has more to say on the subject, one can assume of any listener that he has an ever-present image of a house.

That is how music must proceed, if it sets out from complicated figures, to arrive at still more complicated ones. The word 'house' shows how we use terms representing the sum total of a great number of qualities; similarly, this kind of music must operate by putting together complexes whose familiarity is taken for granted, so that other complexes of the same kind can follow, in the expectation that with all their reciprocal relationships, similarities, differences, and so on, they will be so grasped as to be linked in logical succession.

4. OPERA

So far, I have tried my hand three times in the field of opera.[1] The first two: the monodrama, *Erwartung*, composed in 1909; the drama with music, *Die glückliche Hand*, composed about 1913—both would nowadays be called 'short operas', another proof that I was already plagiarizing my imitators fifteen years before they appeared. The common denominator of the two works is something like this: In *Erwartung* the aim is to represent in *slow motion* everything that occurs during a single second of maximum spiritual excitement, stretching it out to half an hour, whereas in *Die glückliche Hand* a major drama is compressed into about 20 minutes, as if photographed with a time-exposure. My third opera, *Von Heute auf Morgen*, is also relatively short; it lasts about an hour, but uses only the customary theatrical methods of condensing and expanding time. Its most important feature as regards the text—and on this point I found the librettist extraordinarily accommodating[2]—is that everything is subordinated to one aim: genuine musical theatre.

In Wagner's music-drama, he placed the drama in the foreground, whereas he had a supporting role in mind for the music. But this became one more case of 'Man proposes, God disposes'; Wagner's music won a victory over the drama, a victory beyond the expectation of any musician, however great his faith. Whereas Wagner's poetry never acquired any influence worth mentioning, the evolution of music went straight along the path he pointed out, and not a single note written by any of the 'new classicists', 'folklorists', 'new objectivists', and 'community-art' musicians would be possible without Wagner the musician.

In evolutionary terms, Wagner's attempt to create a new connection between music and theatre [−+−+−] was indeed a necessity. Had music not learned to carry out scene-changes so quickly, so often, and so clearly—had it not learned to adapt itself quickly and exactly to states and happenings, then our present-day art would lack its wealth of forms, its ability to find an expressive turn in the most limited space, and to illustrate it by characteristic invention.

Wagner could not [−+−+−] make music play a merely supporting role. As a musician he had too many ideas. Too many ideas, even when he applied with full stringency his principle which we no longer need to follow. He had too many ideas, even in passages laid out in such a way that the music, in itself most beautiful and inspired, is pressed into a construction which impedes its development—one that is musically inappropriate. I mean the passages where he makes the orchestra assemble elements of the most heterogeneous kind, forming a symphonico-dramatic subsoil from which the vocal part can no longer grow organically.

That is something we can no longer regard as exemplary, for even when the vocal part does arise organically out of the orchestra, we no longer find that adequate. It is too indirect: first the stage action, the drama, has been cast in a symphonic mould, and from this (indirectly, then) springs the word, the voice, of the performing singer. And yet, in spite of all, this commands the musical field; it is, in spite of all, the most impressive thing there can be in the musical theatre.

I make it my task to arrive at a vocal line that bears within it the text, the stage, the characters, the décor, the music, and everything else that is expressive, while still unfolding purely in accordance with musical laws and musical demands. [—+—+—] Moreover, the whole form, and each of its details, must be an invention of the vocal part, or of the principal voices in the musical theatre.

Today, thanks to Wagner, that is possible. We have learned how to assemble a vocal part from elements which are so flexible, and so amenable to transformation, that we can still always achieve a clear overall form—or, indeed, constant repetition of the same form, as, for example, with a strophic layout, or parallel forms of some other kind. What helps us here is the art of variation— the mentor of our thinking, and of the listener's too.

12

CONSTRUCTED MUSIC
c. 1931

Opponents of constructed music take it principally as the opposite of what they hold art to be: spontaneous music, while the situation expressed in the word 'constructed' is for them a secondary part of its meaning. If one thinks realistically and to the end about 'constructed', rather than just emotionally throwing it about, one can take it to mean a great deal, good and bad. For since music is assembled from notes, i.e. composed, it seems unthinkable that such assembling should not be based on constructional principles. So that perhaps the expression 'spontaneous' music would express more than its opposite does· But constructed music does in fact also seem to exist. And perhaps that is what produced the name constantly applied to mine.

It would not occur to me to deny one of the greatest virtues of my music: that it really is well worked-out, that for all the freedom and for all the wealth of shapes, images, figures, themes, motives, transformations, etc., I am still able to ensure coherence and unity, although there are important form-building elements and aids to comprehensibility that I do not use (key, artificial articulation; performing and expressive-humbug, etc.). But the basis of this is the self-evident nature of my musical logic; I cannot help but think logically and if then, as I build, those well-known symptoms of musical logic show themselves—even in places where I have not consciously put them—that should surprise nobody who has any conception of what musical logic is.

This comes about because in my case the productive process has its own way; what I sense is not a melody, a motive, a bar, but merely a whole work. Its sections: the movements; their sections: the themes; their sections: the motives and bars—all that is detail, arrived at as the work is progressively realized. The fact that the details are realized with the strictest, most conscientious care, that everything is logical, purposeful and organically deft, without the visionary images, thereby losing fullness, number, clarity, beauty, originality or pregnancy —that is merely a question of intellectual energy, which may only be taken amiss by those who themselves possess it and believe themselves entitled to despise it.

Briefly recapitulating:

The inspiration, the vision, the whole, breaks down during its representation into details whose constructed realization reunites them into the whole.

But this other constructed music which I have mentioned, and of which I have already seen examples, is different. It does not set out from the vision of a whole but builds upwards from below according to a preconceived plan or scheme but without a truly visualised idea of the whole, and it works up the basic material anxiously and without freedom.

So whereas I proceed from a vision, working out the details and fitting them out for the purpose they will have to fulfil—and these details do not exist without that purpose—truly 'constructed' music works material up into a systematically arrived-at, synthetically presented whole, which did not previously exist. In the former case it was the details that did not exist before; but in the latter, the whole.

13

ON REVIENT TOUJOURS
1948

I remember with great pleasure a ride in a Viennese fiacre through the renowned Höllenthal. The fiacre went very slowly and we could discuss and admire all the beauty and, even more, the frightening aspects which gave the name to this Valley of the Hell. I always regret that one might never possess nerves calm enough to endure such a slow ride.

At least, when only twenty years later I made a trip by auto through one of the most renowned valleys in Switzerland, I saw almost nothing and my companion on this occasion rather mentioned some of the commercial and industrial aspects this valley offered. In twenty years people had lost the interest to take an eyeful of these beauties and enjoy them.

Of these two cases I had to think, when recently a German—a former pupil and assistant of mine[1]—asked me what he should answer when people demanded from him whether I had abandoned twelve-tone composing, as at present I so often compose tonal music: the Band Variations, Op. 43b, the Second *Kammersymphonie*, the Suite for String Orchestra and several others.

My answer was tuned to the pitch of the two true stories aforementioned, founded upon some historic facts. I said: One should be surprised to find that the classic composers—Haydn, Mozart, Beethoven, Schubert, Mendelssohn, Schumann, Brahms and even Wagner—after Bach's contrapuntal climax, in spite of their in essence homophonic style, so often interpolate strict counterpoint, differing from Bach's counterpoint only by such features as the progress in music had brought about; that is, a more elaborated development through variations of the motive.

One cannot deny that the combination of these two structural methods is surprising; because they are contradictory. In contrapuntal style the theme is practically unchangeable and all the necessary contrasts are produced by the addition of one or more voices. Homophony produces all its contrasts by developing variation. But these great masters possessed such an eminent sense of the ethical and aesthetical requirements of their art that the problem whether this is wrong can simply be disregarded.

I had not foreseen that my explanation of this stylistic deviation might also explain my own deviations. I used to say: The classic masters, educated in admiration of the works of great masters of counterpoint, from Palestrina to Bach, must have been tempted to return often to the art of their predecessors, which they considered superior to their own. Such is the modesty of people who could venture to act haughtily; they appreciated achievements of others, though they themselves are not devoid of pride. Only a man who himself deserves respect is capable of paying respect to another man. Only one who knows merits can recognize the merits of other men. Such feelings might have developed in a longing once again to try to achieve, in the older style, what they were sure they could achieve in their own more advanced style.

It is a feeling similar to that which would give preference over the fast automobile, to the slow, leisurely fiacre; which desires occasionally to dwell in the old, rather primitive living circumstances of our predecessors. It is not that we wanted to nullify all progress, though machinery has eliminated so many crafts: bookbinding, cabinet making, calligraphy, wood-carving and—almost— painting.

When I had finished my first *Kammersymphonie*, Op. 9, I told my friends: 'Now I have established my style. I know now how I have to compose.'

But my next work showed a great deviation from this style; it was a first step toward my present style. My destiny had forced me in this direction—I was not destined to continue in the manner of *Transfigured Night* or *Gurrelieder* or even *Pelleas and Melisande*. The Supreme Commander had ordered me on a harder road.

But a longing to return to the older style was always vigorous in me; and from time to time I had to yield to that urge.

This is how and why I sometimes write tonal music. To me stylistic differences of this nature are not of special importance. I do not know which of my compositions are better; I like them all, because I liked them when I wrote them.

14

MY TECHNIQUE AND STYLE
c. 1950

My technique and style have not been developed by a conscious procedure. Reviewing this development today, it seems to me that I have moved in many roundabout ways, sometimes advancing slowly, sometimes speedily, sometimes even falling back several steps. The most decisive steps forward occurred in the Two Songs, Op. 12,[1] and the Three Piano Pieces, Op. 11. Next to them comes the Suite for Piano, Op. 25. Then comes a turn—perhaps you would call it to the Apollonian side—in the Suite for Seven Instruments, Op. 29. (This answers also your question about autobiographical data.)

As to the development of my personality, I am embarrassed to say that until a few years ago I had not become aware of my age and was still considering myself as the young composer who had not yet ceased to do youthful nonsense. Thus I have not had the chance to watch the development of my personality. According to my subjective feeling I must say: I think I was always the same and I am still unchanged.

But, of course, now I am an old man!

PART II

MODERN MUSIC

1

NEW MUSIC, OUTMODED MUSIC, STYLE AND IDEA
1946

The first three of these four concepts have been widely used in the last twenty-five years, while not so much ado has been made about the fourth, *idea*.

Unfortunately, methods in music teaching, instead of making students thoroughly acquainted with the music itself, furnish a conglomerate of more or less true historical facts, sugar-coated with a great number of more or less false anecdotes about the composer, his performers, his audiences, and his critics, plus a strong dose of popularized aesthetics. Thus I once read in an examination paper of a sophomore, who had studied only a little harmony and much music appreciation, but who had certainly not heard much 'live' music, that 'Schumann's orchestration is gloomy and unclear.' This wisdom was derived directly and verbally from the textbook used in class. Some experts on orchestration might agree upon the condemnation of Schumann as an orchestrator, perhaps even without an argument. However, there might be other experts who would agree that not all of Schumann's orchestration is poor—that there are gloomy spots as well as brilliant or at least good ones; they would also know that this accusation stems from the fight between the Wagnerian 'New-German' School and the Schumann-Brahmsian-Academic-Classicist School, and that the critics had in mind such brilliant parts of Wagner's music as the 'Magic Fire', the *Meistersinger* Overture, the *Venusberg* music and others. Such brilliancy can but seldom be found in Schumann's music. But some experts also know that there are very few compositions whose orchestration is perfectly flawless. More than two decades after Wagner's death, for instance, his orchestral accompaniment covered the singers' voices so as to make them inaudible. I know that Gustav Mahler had to change his orchestration very much for the sake of transparency. And Strauss himself showed me several cases where he had to make adjustment.

Thus, there is not the same degree of unanimity among experts of orchestration as there is between the sophomore girl and her textbook. But irreparable damage has been done; this girl, and probably all her classmates, will never listen to the orchestra of Schumann naively, sensitively, and open-mindedly. At the end of the term she will have acquired a knowledge of music history, aesthetics, and criticism, plus a number of amusing anecdotes; but unfortunately she may not remember even one of those gloomily orchestrated Schumann themes. In a few years she will take her master's degree in music, or will have become a teacher, or both, and will disseminate what she has been taught: ready-made judgements, wrong and superficial ideas about music, musicians, and aesthetics.

In this manner there are educated a great number of pseudo-historians who believe themselves to be experts and, as such, entitled not only to criticize music and musicians, but even to usurp the role of leaders, to gain influence in the development of the art of music and to organize it in advance.

A few years after the first World War, such pseudo-historians acquired a dominant voice, throughout Western Europe, in predicting the future of music. In all music-producing countries, in France, Italy, Germany, Austria, Hungary, Czechoslovakia and Poland, there suddenly arose the slogan:

'NEW MUSIC'

This battle-cry had evidently been created because one of these pseudo-historians had remembered that several times in the past the same battle-cry, or others like it, had furthered a new direction in the arts. A battle-cry must, perhaps, be superficial and at least partially wrong if it is to gain popularity. Thus we may understand Schopenhauer's story of the surprise of one ancient Greek orator who, when he was suddenly interrupted by applause and cheers, cried out: 'Have I said some nonsense?' The popularity acquired by this slogan, 'New Music', immediately arouses suspicion and forces one to question its meaning.

What is New Music?

Evidently it must be music which, though it is still music, differs in all essentials from previously composed music. Evidently it must express something which has not yet been expressed in music. Evidently, in higher art, only that is worth being presented which has never before been presented. There is no great work of art which does not convey a new message to humanity; there is no great artist who fails in this respect. This is the code of honour of all the great in art, and consequently in all great works of the great we will find that newness which never perishes, whether it be of Josquin des Prés, of Bach or Haydn, or of any other great master.

Because: Art means New Art.

The idea that this slogan 'New Music' might change the course of musical production was probably based on the belief that 'history repeats itself'. As everybody knows, while Bach still was living a new musical style came into being out of which there later grew the style of the Viennese Classicists, the style of homophonic-melodic composition, or, as I call it, the style of Developing Variation. If, then, history really repeated itself, the assumption that one need only demand the creation of new music would also suffice in our time, and at once the ready-made product would be served.

This is mistaking symptoms for causes. The real causes of changes in the style of musical composition are others. If in a period of homophonic composition musicians had acquired great skill in creating melodies—that is, main voices which reduced accompanying voices to almost meaningless inferiority in order to concentrate all possible contents in themselves—other composers may well have been annoyed by such a skill, which seemed already to degenerate into a schematic mechanism. They may then have been even more annoyed by the inferiority of the accompaniment than by what seemed to them the sweetness of the melody. While in this period only one direction of the musical space, the horizontal line, had been developed, the composers of the next period might have responded to a tendency that demanded the vitalizing of the accompanying voices also—that is, following the vertical direction of the musical space. Such tendencies might have provoked that richer elaboration of the accompaniment seen, for instance, in Beethoven as compared with Haydn, Brahms as compared with Mozart, or Wagner as compared with Schumann. Though in all these cases the richness of the melody has not suffered in the least, the role of the accompaniment has been intensified, enhancing its contribution to the common effect. No historian need tell a Beethoven, a Brahms, a Wagner to enrich his accompaniment with vitamins. At least these three men, stubborn as they were, would have shown him the door!

And vice versa:

If, in a given period, each participating voice had been elaborated, with respect to its content, its formal balance and its relation to other voices, as part of a contrapuntal combination, its share of melodic eloquence would be less than if it were the main voice. Again, there might then arise in younger composers a longing to get rid of all these complexities. They then might refuse to deal with combinations and elaborations of subordinate voices. Thus the desire to elaborate only one voice and reduce the accompaniment to that minimum required by comprehensibility would again be the ruling fashion.

Such are the causes which produce changes in methods of composition. In a manifold sense, music uses time. It uses my time, it uses your time, it uses its own time. It would be most annoying if it did not aim to say the most important things in the most concentrated manner in every fraction of this time. This is why, when composers have acquired the technique of filling one direction with content to the utmost capacity, they must do the same in the next direction, and finally in all the directions in which music expands. Such progress can occur only step-wise. The necessity of compromising with comprehensibility forbids jumping into a style which is overcrowded with content, a style in which facts are too often juxtaposed without connectives, and which leaps to conclusions before proper maturation.

If music abandoned its former direction and turned towards new goals in this manner, I doubt that the men who produced this change needed the exhortation of pseudo-historians. We know that they—the Telemanns, the Couperins, the Rameaus, the Keisers, the Ph. E. Bachs and others—created something new which led only later to the period of the Viennese Classicists. Yes, a new style in music was created, but did this have the consequence of making the music of the preceding period outmoded?

Curiously, it happened at the beginning of this period that J. S. Bach's music was called outmoded. And, most curiously, one of those who said this was J. S. Bach's own son, Ph. Emanuel Bach, whose greatness one might question if one did not know that Mozart and Beethoven viewed him with great admiration. To them, he still seemed a leader, even after they themselves had added to the first rather negative principles of the New Music such positive principles as that of developing variation, in addition to many hitherto unknown structural devices such as those of transition liquidation, dramatic recapitulation, manifold elaboration, derivation of subordinate themes, highly differentiated dynamics—*crescendo, decrescendo, sforzato, piano subito, marcato,* etc.—and particularly the new technique of *legato* and *staccato* passages, *accelerando* and *ritardando,* and the establishment of tempo and character by specific bywords.

Beethoven's words: 'Das ist nicht ein Bach, das ist ein Meer' (This is not a brook, this is an ocean) constitute the correct order. He did not say this about Philipp Emanuel but about Johann Sebastian. Should he not have added: Who is the brook?

In any case:

While until 1750 J. S. Bach was writing countless works whose originality seems the more astonishing to us the more we study his music; while he not only developed but really created a new style of music which was without precedent; while the very nature of this newness still escapes the observation of the experts—

No, excuse me: I feel obliged to prove what I say, and hate to say it as lightly and superficially as if I were to say: New Music!

The newness of Bach's art can only be understood by comparing it with the style of the Netherlands School on the one hand and with Handel's art on the other.

The secrets of the Netherlanders, strictly denied to the uninitiated, were based on a complete recognition of the possible contrapuntal relations between the seven tones of the diatonic scale. This enabled the initiated to produce combinations which admitted many types of vertical and horizontal shifts, and other similar changes. But the remaining five tones were not included in these rules, and, if they appeared at all, did so apart from the contrapuntal combination and as occasional substitutes.

In contrast, Bach, who knew more secrets than the Netherlanders ever possessed, enlarged these rules to such an extent that they comprised all the twelve tones of the chromatic scale. Bach sometimes operated with the twelve tones in such a manner that one would be inclined to call him the first twelve-tone composer.

If, after observing that the contrapuntal flexibility of Bach's themes is based in all probability on his instinctive thinking in terms of multiple counterpoint which gives scope to additional voices, one compares his counterpoint with Handel's, the latter's seems bare and simple, and his subordinate voices are really inferior.

Also in other respects Bach's art is higher than Handel's. As a composer for the theatre Handel always had the power of beginning with a characteristic and often excellent theme. But, thereafter, with the exception of the repetitions of the theme, there follows a decline, bringing only what the editor of *Grove's Dictionary* would call 'trash'—empty, meaningless, étude-like broken chord figures. In contrast, even Bach's transitional and subordinate sections are always full of character, inventiveness, imagination and expression. Though his subordinate voices never degenerate into inferiority, he is able to write fluent and well balanced melodies of more beauty, richness and expressiveness than can be found in the music of all those Keisers, Telemanns, and Philipp Emanuel Bachs who called him outmoded. They, of course, were not capable of seeing that he was also the first to introduce just that technique so necessary for the progress of their New Music: the technique of 'developing variation', which made possible the style of the great Viennese Classicists.

While Bach thus—as beforementioned—produced work after work in a new style, his contemporaries knew no better than to ignore him. It can be said that not much of their New Music remained alive, though one must not deny that it was the beginning of a new art. But there are two points in which they were wrong. First, it was not musical *ideas* which their New Music wanted to establish, but only a new style for the presentation of musical ideas, whether old or new; it was a new wave in the progress of music, one which, as described before, tried to develop the other direction of musical space, the horizontal line. Second, they were wrong when they called Bach's music outmoded. At least it was not outmoded for ever, as history shows; today their New Music is outmoded while Bach's has become eternal.

But now one should also examine the concept 'outmoded'.

One can find illustrations of this concept in our daily life rather than in the intellectual sphere. Long hair, for instance, was considered an important contribution to a woman's beauty thirty years ago. Who knows how soon the fashion of short hair will be outmoded? Pathos was one of the most admired merits of poetry about a hundred years ago; today it seems ridiculous, and it is used only for satirical purposes. Electric light has outmoded candle-light; but snobs still use the latter because they saw it in the castles of the aristocracy where artistically decorated walls would have been damaged by electric wiring.

Does this indicate why things become outmoded?

Long hair became outmoded because working women considered it a handicap. Pathos became outmoded when naturalism portrayed real life and the way in which people talked when they wanted to finish business. Candle-light became outmoded when people realized how senseless it is to make unnecessary work for one's servants—if one can get them at all.

The common factor in all these examples was a change in the forms of our life.

Can one contend the same about music?

Which form of life makes Romantic music inadequate? Is there no more romanticism in our time? Are we not more enthusiastic about being killed by our automobiles than the ancient Romans were about being killed by their chariots? Are there not still to be found young people who engage in adventure for which they may have to pay with their lives, though the glory they earn will pale with the next day's front page? Would it not be easy to find numerous youths to fly to the moon in a rocket plane if the opportunity were offered? Is not the admiration of people of all ages for our Tarzans, Supermen, Lone Rangers and indestructible detectives the result of a love for romanticism? The Indian stories of our youth were no more romantic; only the names of the subjects have been changed.

One reproach against romanticism concerns its complications. True, if one were to look at scores of Strauss, Debussy, Mahler, Ravel, Reger, or my own, it might be difficult to decide whether all this complication is necessary. But the decision of one successful young composer: 'Today's younger generation does not like music which they do not understand,' does not conform to the feelings of the heroes who engage in adventures. One might expect that this kind of youth, attracted by the difficult, the dangerous, the mysterious, would rather say: 'Am I an idiot that one dares offer me poor trash which I understand before I am half-way through?' Or even: 'This music is complicated, but I will not give up until I understand it.' Of course this kind of man will be enthused rather by profundity, profuseness of ideas, difficult problems. Intelligent people have always been offended if one bothered them with matters which any idiot could understand at once.

The reader has certainly become aware that it is not merely my intention to attack long deceased pseudo-historians and the composers who started the movement of New Music. Though I have used with pleasure the opportunity to write about some of the lesser known merits of Bach's art, and though I have enjoyed the opportunity to list some of the contributions of the Viennese Classicists to the development of compositorial technique, I do not hesitate to admit that the attack upon the propagandists of the New Music is aimed against similar movements in our own time. Except for one difference—that I am no Bach—there is a great similarity between the two epochs.

A superficial judgement might consider composition with twelve tones as an end to the period in which chromaticism evolved, and thus compare it to the climaxing end of the period of contrapuntal composition which Bach set by his unsurpassable mastery. That only lesser values could follow this climax is a kind of justification of his younger contemporaries' turn towards New Music.

But—also in this respect I am no Bach—I believe that composition with twelve tones and what many erroneously call 'atonal music' is not the end of an old period, but the beginning of a new one. Again, as two centuries ago, something is called outmoded; and again it is not one particular work, or several works of one composer; again it is not the greater or lesser ability of one composer in particular; but again it is a style which has become ostracized. Again it calls itself New Music, and this time even more nations participate in the struggle. Aside from nationalistic aims for an exportable music with which even smaller nations hope to conquer the market, there is one common trait observable in all these movements; none of them are occupied with presenting new ideas, but only with presenting a new style. And, again, the principles on which this New Music is to be based present themselves even more negatively than the strictest rules of the strictest old counterpoint. There should be avoided: chromaticism, expressive melodies, Wagnerian harmonies, romanticism, private biographical hints, subjectivity, functional harmonic progressions, illustrations, leitmotivs, concurrence with the mood or action of the scene and characteristic declamation of the text in opera, songs and choruses. In other words, all that was good in the preceding period should not occur now.

Besides these officially authorized 'Verbote', I have observed numerous negative merits, such as: pedal points (instead of elaborate bass voices and moving harmony), ostinatos, sequences (instead of developing variation), fugatos (for similar purposes), dissonances (disguising the vulgarity of the thematic material), objectivity (*Neue Sachlichkeit*), and a kind of polyphony, substituting for counterpoint, which, because of its inexact imitations, in former times would have been held in contempt as 'Kapellmeistermusik', or what I called 'Rhabarber counterpoint'. The word 'Rhabarber', spoken behind the scenes by only five or six people, sounded to the audience in a theatre like a rioting mob. Thus the counterpoint, thematically meaningless, like the word 'rhubarb', sounded as if it had a real meaning.

In my youth, living in the proximity of Brahms, it was customary that a musician, when he heard a composition for the first time, observed its construction, was able to follow the elaboration and derivation of its themes and its modulations, and could recognize the number of voices in canons and the presence of the theme in a variation; and there were even laymen who after one hearing could take a melody home in their memory. But I am sure there was not much talk about style. And if a music historian had ventured to participate in an argument, it could only have been one who was able to observe similar qualities by ear alone. That is what music critics like Hanslick, Kalbeck, Heuberger and Speidel and amateurs like the renowned physician Billroth were able to do.

The positive and negative rules may be deduced from a finished work as constituents of its style. Every man has fingerprints of his own, and every craftsman's hand has its personality; out of such subjectivity grow the traits which comprise the style of the finished product. Every craftsman is limited by the shortcomings of his hands but is furthered by their particular abilities. On his natural conditions depends the style of everything he does, and so it would be wrong to expect a plum tree to bear plums of glass or pears or felt hats. Among all trees it is only the Christmas tree which bears fruits not natural to it, and among animals it is only the Easter rabbit which lays eggs, and even coloured ones at that.

Style is the quality of a work and is based on natural conditions, expressing him who produced it. In fact, one who knows his capacities may be able to tell in advance exactly how the finished work will look which he still sees only in his imagination. But he will never start from a preconceived image of a style; he will be ceaselessly occupied with doing justice to the idea. He is sure that, everything done which the idea demands, the external appearance will be adequate.

If I have been fortunate enough to show some views different from those of my adversaries about New Music, Outmoded Music, and Style, I would like to proceed now to my self-appointed task of discussing what seems to me most important in a work of art—the Idea.

I am conscious that entering into this sphere involves some danger. Adversaries have called me a constructor, an engineer, an architect, even a mathematician—not to flatter me—because of my method of composing with twelve tones. In spite of knowing my *Verklärte Nacht* and *Gurrelieder*, though some people like these works because of the emotionality, they called my music dry and denied me spontaneity. They pretended that I offered the products of a brain, not of a heart.

I have often wondered whether people who possess a brain would prefer to hide this fact. I have been supported in my own attitude by the example of Beethoven who, having received a letter from his brother Johann signed 'land owner', signed his reply 'brain owner'. One might question why Beethoven just stressed the point of owning a brain. He had so many other merits to be proud of, for instance, being able to compose music which some people considered outstanding, being an accomplished pianist—and, as such, even recognized by the nobility—and being able to satisfy his publishers by giving them something of value for their money. Why did he call himself just 'brain owner', when the possession of a brain is considered a danger to the naiveté of an artist by many pseudo-historians?

An experience of mine might illustrate the way in which people think a brain might be dangerous. I have never found it necessary to hide that I am able to think logically, that I distinguish sharply between right and wrong terms, and that I have very exact ideas about what art should be. Thus, in a number of discussions, I may have shown a little too much brain to one of my tennis partners, a writer of lyric poetry. He did not reciprocate in kind, but maliciously told me the story about the toad who asked the centipede whether he was always conscious which of his hundred feet was just about to move, whereupon the centipede, in becoming conscious of the necessary decision, lost his instinctive ability to walk at all.

Indeed, a great danger to a composer! And even hiding his brain might not help; only having none would suffice. But I think this need not discourage anyone who has a brain; because I have observed that if one has not worked hard enough and has not done one's best, the Lord will refuse to add His blessing. He has given us a brain in order to use it. Of course an idea is not always the product of brain-work. Ideas may invade the mind as unprovoked and perhaps even as undesired as a musical sound reaches the ear or an odour the nose.

Ideas can only be honoured by one who has some of his own; but only he can do honour who deserves honour himself.

The difference between style and idea in music has perhaps been clarified by the preceding discussion. This may not be the place to discuss in detail what idea in itself means in music, because almost all musical terminology is vague and most of its terms are used in various meanings. In its most common meaning, the term idea is used as a synonym for theme, melody, phrase or motive. I myself consider the totality of a piece as the *idea*: the idea which its creator wanted to present. But because of the lack of better terms I am forced to define the term idea in the following manner:

Every tone which is added to a beginning tone makes the meaning of that tone doubtful. If, for instance, G follows after C, the ear may not be sure whether this expresses C major or G major, or even F major or E minor; and the addition of other tones may or may not clarify this problem. In this manner there is produced a state of unrest, of imbalance which grows throughout most of the piece, and is enforced further by similar functions of the rhythm. The method by which balance is restored seems to me the real *idea* of the composition. Perhaps the frequent repetitions of themes, groups, and even larger sections might be considered as attempts towards an early balance of the inherent tension.

In comparison with all our developments in mechanics, a tool like a pair of pliers might seem simple. I always admired the mind which invented it. In order to understand the problem which this inventor had to overcome one must imagine the state of mechanics before its invention. The idea of fixing the cross-point of the two crooked arms so that the two smaller segments in front would move in the opposite direction to the larger segments at the back, thus multiplying the power of the man who squeezed them to such an extent that he could cut wire—this idea can only have been conceived by a genius. Certainly more complicated and better tools exist today, and there may come a time when the use of the pliers and other similar tools may become superfluous. The tool itself may fall into disuse, but the idea behind it can never become obsolete. And therein lies the difference between a mere style and a real idea.

An idea can never perish.

It is very regrettable that so many contemporary composers care so much about style and so little about idea. From this came such notions as the attempt to compose in ancient styles, using their mannerisms, limiting oneself to the little that one can thus express and to the insignificance of the musical configurations which can be produced with such equipment.

No one should give in to limitations other than those which are due to the limits of his talent. No violinist would play, even occasionally, with the wrong intonation to please lower musical tastes, no tight-rope walker would take steps in the wrong direction only for pleasure or for popular appeal, no chess master would make moves everyone could anticipate just to be agreeable (and thus allow his opponent to win), no mathematician would invent something new in mathematics just to flatter the masses who do not possess the specific mathematical way of thinking, and in the same manner, no artist, no poet, no philosopher and no musician whose thinking occurs in the highest sphere would degenerate into vulgarity in order to comply with a slogan such as 'Art for All'. Because if it is art, it is not for all, and if it is for all, it is not art.

Most deplorable is the acting of some artists who arrogantly wish to make believe that they descend from their heights in order to give some of their riches to the masses. This is hypocrisy. But there are a few composers, like Offenbach, Johann Strauss and Gershwin, whose feelings actually coincide with those of the 'average man in the street'. To them it is no masquerade to express popular feelings in popular terms. They are natural when they talk thus and about that.

He who really uses his brain for thinking can only be possessed of one desire: to resolve his task. He cannot let external conditions exert influence upon the results of his thinking. Two times two is four—whether one likes it or not.

One thinks only for the sake of one's idea.

And thus art can only be created for its own sake. An idea is born; it must be moulded, formulated, developed, elaborated, carried through and pursued to its very end.

Because there is only 'l'art pour l'art', art for the sake of art alone.

2

CRITERIA FOR THE EVALUATION OF MUSIC
1946

In the best sellers of 150 or 200 years ago there frequently appeared a character —an old cavalier, generally no less than a marquis—whose extreme generosity perplexed and astounded both his fellow characters and the reading public of that day. Whether or not such a character ever really existed, the grandeur of his generosity was impressive. When he met with a slight accident—whether to himself, to his horse, or only to his equipage—he would reward the person who came to his rescue by throwing to him his whole purse, which, of course, contained nothing but gold pieces—small change his hands would not touch. On other occasions he might disperse a few handfuls of louis d'or among a crowd. Such was his generosity in minor accidents.

Imagine then what he might have done in case of a serious accident! He then might have taken the rescuer to his castle and either made him heir to his fortune and title, or offered him his sister in marriage. Even if she were not the most beautiful woman in the world, she was full of charm, and, besides, would have a respectable dowry!

At any rate, as a true nobleman he insisted on paying a price which surpassed the value of the service rendered, and he would have been ashamed to disappoint the faith of lower-class people in the generosity of the nobility. On the other hand, one must not forget that, fictitious or real, this nobleman was convinced of the inexhaustibility of his fortune, was convinced that he need not care what price he paid, and was only afraid to pay less than his social rank required.

What a man! What people! What times!

While the nobleman not only did not ask the price of what he bought, but rather, did not want to know it, we poor people are bound to know prices in advance. All the same, whether we buy a house, a pair of shoes, or an automobile —we must know their value and whether it justifies the price. We must know whether the house has the desired number of rooms, whether the neighbourhood is good, how high the taxes are, whether there is a chance of selling it without too great a loss after some years, and so forth. Similar questions will be asked about the shoes. They must fit, they should not be of an obsolete fashion, the material should be adequate, etc. We would also refuse to pay more for an automobile than it is worth, even if we possessed the money, because, of course, our revenues are not inexhaustible. Moreover, we hate to pay more for a thing than it is worth—if possible, we prefer to pay less. This is—on the average—human nature, and people of all ranks behave similarly. They love to pay less than it is worth.

If we justify such caution in the case of a house, a pair of shoes, and an automobile, merits or shortcomings of which are no secret and do not require the judgement of an expert, how much more is caution justified in the case of art objects, where criteria of evaluation are really only within the domain of the experts and where experts are as rare as a good judgement.

True, the styles of houses, of shoes and of automobiles change, but at least, as they serve a definite purpose, their usability remains the same, and one who judges only that will not fail.

But style in art changes approximately every ten to fifteen years. And almost inevitably evaluation changes with style. One of the safest methods of acquiring attention is to do something which differs from the usual, and few artists have the stamina to escape this temptation. I must confess that I belonged to those who did not care much about originality. I used to say: 'I always attempted to produce something quite conventional, but I failed, and it always, against my will, became something unusual!' How right, then, is a music lover who refuses to appreciate music which even the composer did not want to write!

And is it unreasonable that one who commissions his portrait hates to look as an expressionist painter, whose idea is based on psychoanalysis, thinks it should look? Others, again, do not want to appear as victims of a candid camera's sincerity. It may be the morals, the philosophy, the political viewpoint of a writer to which you are opposed. It may be old-fashioned for an author to come personally to the foreground as Goethe did in *Die Wanderjahre*, when at a certain point he inserts a story without any coherence with the preceding, saying '. . . because we want to prove that we are not lacking in inventiveness'—the inventiveness to produce a nice little story. Strindberg would not have done this; perhaps Balzac would have, or perhaps Shaw—in one of his prefaces but not in the text.

One may wonder, if the great Goethe did it, can it be entirely wrong? And should such a procedure be entirely excluded from art? And, if so, only because it is old-fashioned? Or perhaps because 'to show inventiveness' is no proper reason for inclusion in a work of art, because there should appear only that which derives from and is related to the subject, at least indirectly?

But what if the continuation were to disclose the relation of this story with the subject?

There might still remain the objection to the manner in which it is introduced —'in order to show inventiveness'—which is one of the personal interests of an author, but should manifest itself silently. Then the reader, with enthusiastic admiration, might exclaim: 'What richness of imagination and inventiveness.'

It seems that the man in the street and other uninitiated people have still some access to the evaluation offered by the subject, or the object, or the story of works or literature, painting, sculpture, architecture and other arts. How inadequate such viewpoints are can best be seen in the case of the great number of painters who have already been admitted into the Academy of Immortals: the El Grecos, the Van Goghs, the Gauguins, the Kandinskys, the Kokoschkas, the Matisses, the Picassos.

Since changes of style in the arts do not always mean development, it might be extremely difficult to establish criteria which remain valid in every period of art. But the futility of evaluation deriving from external criteria remains evident throughout the centuries.

At least a wrong evaluation can be based on superficial judgement in the afore-mentioned arts. No such thing is possible in music. There is no story, no subject, no object, no moral, no philosophy or politics which one might like or hate. Rejection of musical works in the last one and a half centuries has been based primarily on features which obstructed comprehensibility: too rich modulation, use of dissonances, complicated formulation of ideas. It was the time when towns were growing into cities, when the development of industrialism was bringing fresh but uninitiated people into the cities. It was the time when concert halls had to become larger and larger, because more people became participants in the audiences.

Before this time audiences had been small and had consisted solely of music lovers most of whom were able to play what they liked, many of whom had at least semi-professional knowledge, if not more. Their judgement was then to some degree based on terms which today only the experts are entitled to use — though also others do. Musicianship of such high degree enables recognition of evaluating criteria. Knowing music meant knowing it—at least partly—from memory. Many persons were able to remember a piece after a single hearing. Do not forget that Mozart wrote down the forbidden music of Allegri's *Miserere* after hearing it only once.

Yes, the role of memory in music evaluation is more important than most people realize. It is perhaps true that one starts to understand a piece only when one can remember it at least partially. But memory must be nursed and given an opportunity to function. Before the first World War I met a man who told me that he had seen *The Merry Widow* twenty times. And during the war, when I con-ducted Beethoven's Ninth Symphony, a man came into the artists' room to tell me that this was the fiftieth performance of the work he had heard from beginning to end. Imagine how well these people knew every note of their favourite music!

127

One could not, of course, expect such capacities of freshly acquired devotees of the arts. While J. S. Bach was allowed to write music of a kind which in its real values only the expert is capable of understanding, very soon the composers in the eighteenth and nineteenth centuries came to feel that their real independence had gone. Even a Beethoven, democratic as he was, must have felt it. But Mozart was told, after the first performance of his *Don Giovanni* in Vienna, by the Emperor Joseph II: 'This is no music for our Viennese.' 'No music for our Viennese?' At that time already it was not the highest quality of art Mozart should produce, but he was supposed to express himself as broadly as popular understanding required.

I would not contend that later composers consciously gave in to these popular demands for comprehensibility—demands which do not correspond entirely to the demands of higher art. But there is no doubt that much in Schubert's melodic construction—his juxtaposition of motives, which are only melodically varied, but rhythmically very similar—accommodated, probably instinctively, to the popular feeling. As a true child of his time, he reflected involuntarily the feeling of his contemporaries. Robert Schumann's style is a further proof of the same kind of accommodation; his extremely frequent repetitions of a rhythmic character indicate this.

Ex. 1 Melodies of Schubert and Schumann

a. Schubert, Scherzo, Piano Sonata in D Major
b. Schumann, *Arabesque*

Accommodations to the popular demands became even more imperative when Wagner's evolution of harmony expanded into a revolution of form. While preceding composers and even his contemporary, Johannes Brahms, repeated phrases, motives and other structural ingredients of themes only in varied forms, if possible in the form of what I call *developing variation*, Wagner, in order to make his themes suitable for memorability, had to use sequences and semi-sequences, that is, unvaried or slightly varied repetitions differing in nothing essential from first appearances, except that they are exactly transposed to other degrees.

Ex. 2 Wagner Sequences

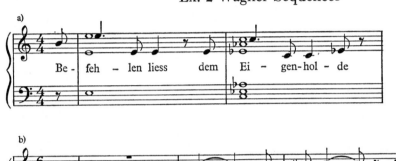

Why there is a lesser merit in such procedure than in variation is obvious, because variation requires a new and special effort. But the damage of this inferior method of construction to the art of composing was considerable. With very few exceptions, all followers and even opponents of Wagner became addicts of this more primitive technique: Bruckner, Hugo Wolf, Richard Strauss, and even Debussy and Puccini.

A new technique had to be created, and in this development Max Reger,

Gustav Mahler, and also I myself played a role. But the destructive consequences did not cease because of that. And unfortunately many of today's composers, instead of connecting ideas through developing variation, thus showing consequences derived from the basic idea and remaining within the boundaries of human thinking and its demands of logic, produce compositions which become longer and broader only by numerous unvaried repetitions of a few phrases.

I have made here the grave mistake of calling a criterion of compositorial technique 'destructive' as if it were now proven for all time to come that such a procedure is worthless.

How can a house differ from every other house and express a definite architectural idea, if there is as little variety in its material—bricks—as there is in the unvaried repetitions of a phrase? Need it be disadvantageous to use motives, phrases, and other units in a manner as uninfluential on the final form as bricks on a building?

Could not the case of Beethoven's *Pastoral Symphony* be considered as one where harmonies are comparable to bricks, because harmonies of only one kind are used? It was very surprising to me, when, listening to the radio recently, I discovered—and later found confirmed in the score—that in the first three movements Beethoven uses almost no minor chords, except in a very small number of cases, when it is impossible, with respect to the natural laws of harmony, to omit minor triads. Even then he uses an escape by leaving many sections in unison, unaccompanied, when the melody is understandable without harmony. Here the intention is clear: in Beethoven's musical vocabulary a minor chord expresses sadness. But he wanted to picture 'the awakening of gay feelings on the arrival in the country.'

I am ready to forget this hypothesis in favour of a different one, the result of a changed standpoint in regard to evaluation. At the beginning of my career, still under the influence of post-Wagnerianism, I wrote sequences like my contemporaries. This seemed justified to me by the model of all great preceding composers: Bach, Beethoven, Mozart, Wagner and even Brahms, who did not avoid true sequences or slightly varied repetitions. Moreover, since a young composer in this period was intent not only on illustrating the mood and all of its changes, but also on describing every bit of action, a special formulation, the Leitmotiv, seemed obligatory. The Leitmotiv, usually a small phrase, did not consume much space because development, apposition of varied phrases, cadential limitations and other establishing technical requirements, which demanded the space of eight to sixteen measures, became superfluous. A phrase of two measures followed by a sequence ordinarily required a liquidating addition of one or two measures. Thus a little independent segment could be produced which also did not require an elaborate continuation, and was, so to speak, open on all four sides. Properly employed, an aesthetic merit is gained by using no more space than the ideas demand, and this is why this technique rather proved a stimulant to the *Neudeutsche Schule*.

It was the Brahmsian school which at this time fought violently against the sequences of the *Neudeutsche Schule*. Their attitude was based on the opposite viewpoint that unvaried repetition is cheap. And, in fact, to many composers sequences were a technique to make short stories long—to make out of four measures eight and out of eight measures sixteen or even thirty-two. It is especially the Russian composers, Rimsky-Korsakoff and Tchaikovsky, who must be blamed for this improper application of an otherwise acceptable technique. And it could have happened that this misuse might have eradicated every higher technical ambition.

Much depends upon the viewpoint whether criteria are judged as merits or as shortcomings. When Schumann speaks of the 'heavenly length' of Schubert's music, one might be led to consider length, heavenly or earthly, a merit. But one is disappointed to learn that Hanslick, Wagner's opponent, blames Bruckner for the length of his symphonies. When Brahms demanded that one hand of the pianist played twos or fours while the other played threes, people disliked this and said it made them seasick. But this was probably the start of the polyrhythmic structure of many contemporary scores. There can be no doubt that those who called Mozart's String Quartet in C major the 'Dissonance-Quartet' intended merely a characterization, just as they called another quartet the 'Drum-Quartet' and still another the 'Hunting-Quartet'. It is perhaps no merit to include drums in a string quartet or to describe hunting pleasures. And it does not contribute a thing to their evaluation.

Certainly calling it the 'Dissonance' quartet includes a criticism on which an evaluation can be partly based. My own experience proves this. A Viennese society refused the first performance of my String Sextet, *Verklärte Nacht*, because of the 'revolutionary' use of one—that is *one* single uncatalogued dissonance.

Ex. 3

The expert is in no position to forget what his education has taught him. His code of honour which, for instance, forbids some dissonances, but tolerates others, demands numerous merits as the basis for evaluation. Thus he values a composition more highly only if its themes and melodies are significantly formulated and well organized; if they are interesting enough to hold the attention of a listener; if there is a sufficiently great number of ideas; if they are well connected so as not to offend musical logic; if they are restricted by subdivision to a conceivable size; if monotony is avoided by good contrasts; if all ideas, however contrasting, can be proved to be only variations of the basic idea, thus securing unity; if a thorough elaboration proves that their inner merits surpass their incidental advantages.

Having evaluated the ideas from these viewpoints, the expert might proceed to problems of style: Is the time-space adequate for the importance or the unimportance of the ideas? Are main ideas distinctly differentiated from subordinate ideas in space by adequate proportions as well as in emphasis, so as always to secure the predominance of the object? Is the breadth of the presentation justified? Is it admissible because of the number of ideas, because of their inescapable consequences, or because of comprehensibility? Is every detail presented in as brief and as condensed a manner as possible?

Does the profundity of the real meaning interfere with the elegance of the presentation and the polish of the surface? Is the material adequate with respect to the medium, and vice-versa? Are heroic themes ascribed to unheroic instruments, such as flute, guitar or mandolin? Is a violin sonata supposed to express passionate emotions adequate for a symphony? Is an instrument as immobile as a contrabassoon required to play a gracious barcarolle? Is musical description stylized tonally and technically to fit the nature of the instruments, as the calls of the nightingale, quail and cuckoo in the *Pastorale Symphony* are suited to the flute, oboe and clarinet respectively? Is the descriptive element incorporated formally and motivally within the basic conditions of the piece? Are states or situations illustrated whose nature is opposed to that of music—as, for instance, expressing repose by slight movement, or silence by sounds, or abstract philosophy by concrete tones? Does the piece elaborate its ideas and material in a technique inappropriate to its style? Are contrapuntal ideas accompanied in a quasi-contrapuntal manner, scarcely producing more than a harmonization? Is the natural phrasing of a homophonic melody confused by the addition of sophisticated counter-melodies, as often happens in popular music? Are dissonances which are not inherent in the tonal content added to simple folk-tunes?

Nor could the expert renounce an examination of the value of the thematic material. He would also have to question the inventiveness of a composer. Was he able to bring forth as much variety as unity and comprehensibility will tolerate and the stimulation of interest demands? Was he able to prove the necessity of the work—that it was forced upon him by an inner urge for creation? Has he been able to produce something which fills a gap in the knowledge and culture of mankind, or, if not that, which at least satisfies a desire for entertainment? In other words, does his product, through novelty, prove to be a desirable contribution? Is this novelty one of essential or subordinate qualities? If derived from essentials, is it of a nature like Beethoven's dramatization of the elaboration, or comparable to the novelty of the structural, emotional descriptive qualities of Schubert's songs? Or is it like Wagner's entirely new way of building, expressing, harmonizing and orchestrating, thus revolutionizing music in all its aspects?

Has this novelty been produced through a new personality rather than through revolutionary changes, through evolutionary developments rather than through frightening outbursts? Did this novelty come from a personality comparable to a Mendelssohn, a Schumann, a Gounod, a Debussy, etc.—artists whose ambition was not that of the reformer, though their originality was rich and distinct enough?

Though originality is inseparable from personality, there exists also a kind of originality which does not derive from profound personality. Products of such artists are often distinguished by a unique appearance which resembles true originality. Certainly there was inventiveness at work when the striking changes of some subordinate elements were accomplished for the first time. Subsequently, used consciously, they achieved an aspect of novelty not derived profoundly from basic ideas. This is *mannerism*, not originality. The difference is that mannerism is originality in subordinate matters.

There are many, and even respectable, artists whose success and reputation are based on this minor kind of originality. Unfortunately, the tendency to arouse interest by technical peculiarities, which are simply added to the nothingness of an idea, is now more frequent than it was in former times. The moral air of such products is rather for success and publicity than for enriching mankind's thoughts.

Some values derive from causes or reasons to which influence on creation should not be credited. Creation to an artist should be as natural and inescapable as the growth of apples to an apple tree. Even if it tried to produce apples in response to the demands of a fashion or of the market, it could not. Thus artists who want to 'go back to a period', who try to obey the laws of an obsolete aesthetic or of a novel one, who enjoy themselves in eclecticism or in the imitation of a style, alienate themselves from nature. The product shows it—no such product survives its time.

There is no essential difference between the criteria of this type of music and the aforementioned. Popular music speaks to the unsophisticated, to people who love the beauty of music but are not inclined to strengthen their minds. But what they like is not triviality or vulgarity or unoriginality, but a more comprehensible way of presentation. People who have not acquired the ability of drawing all the consequences of a problem at once must be treated with respect to their mental capacities; rapid solutions, leaps from assumptions to conclusions would endanger popularity.

This does not mean that in popular music such melodies, rhythms and harmonies as one might expect in higher music must necessarily be excluded. Of course, no such structural problems, no such developments and elaborations as one finds, for example, in Brahms' symphonies, no such contrapuntal combinations like those of Bach can be the object of a popular composer. Nevertheless, listening to popular American music, one is often surprised at what these composers venture with respect to traditional standards. However, for the sake of the popular understanding manifold repetitions, the application of only slight variations and well employed, even if only conventional, connectives are provided.

It seems that friends of popular music have their own code for the evaluation of what they like or dislike. It is not obvious whether a technical or theoretical knowledge is required; probably instinct serves as judge. Certainly a well-functioning instinct can offer a basis for correct judgement.

But most of the aforementioned criteria for the evaluation of higher music are accessible only to the expert, and many of them only to highly competent experts.

Though there is no doubt that every creator creates only to free himself from the high pressures of the urge to create, and though he thus creates in the first place for his own pleasure, every artist who delivers his works to the general public aims, at least unconsciously, to tell his audiences something of value to them.

Ambition or the desire for money stimulates creation only in the lower ranks of artists. 'Money! How can you expect to be paid for something which gives you so much pleasure?'

From the lives of truly great men it can be deduced that the urge for creation responds to an instinctive feeling of living only in order to deliver a message to mankind.

Just as obvious as that music is not created to please, is the fact that music *does* please; that it has an undeniably great appeal to people who 'know naught of the tablature'—who do not know the rules of the game.

On the other hand, to depend on the expert—and on those who usurp the role of expert—may prove disastrous. Wagner in his Beckmesser portrayed one such living expert who knew all of the tablature but failed miserably in applying his knowledge to 'what doth not with your rules agree.' And when Hans Sachs confides more in those who 'know naught of the tablature', his confidence is justified.

It is a well known fact that already in the culture of even primordial peoples music's mysterious appeal to men adorns worship of the divinity, to sanctify cultish acts. With primitive peoples it is perhaps even rhythm or sound alone which casts enchantment. But even the culturally high-ranking Greeks ascribed mysterious effects to simple successions of tones, such as expressing virtues and their contrary. The Gregorian Chant does not profit as much from the meaning of the words as does the Protestant chorale; it lives on music alone.

Considering these facts, one might wonder whether the subsequent higher art forms were indispensable for religious ceremony. Whether or not art of a primitive or higher kind enhances the enchanting effect of music, one conclusion seems inescapable: there is a mystery.

My personal feeling is that music conveys a prophetic message revealing a higher form of life towards which mankind evolves. And it is because of this message that music appeals to men of all races and cultures.

Searching for criteria for the evaluation of music, it seems dangerous to ascribe this mysterious influence to all kinds of music regardless of their standard and value. It would be dangerous to admit that one who is a lover of music and sensitive to its charms has acquired the right and capacity to judge its values. How dangerous the consequences of such conclusions can be was recently proved.

The results of the voting for the Metropolitan Opera broadcasts did not include among the six chosen operas a *Fidelio*, a *Magic Flute*, a *Marriage of Figaro*, a *Mastersinger*, a *Eugene Onegin*, a *Fra Diavolo*, a *Barber of Seville*, etc.[1] Democratic as it is, there is one decisive mistake in such voting. Not going so far as to offer only one candidate, political parties would not go so far as to offer forty-six candidates—the number of operas offered. In practical politics the choice of candidates is made by the leaders.

This is perhaps similar to Schopenhauer's demand that the evaluation of works of art can only be based on authority. Unfortunately he does not say who bestows authority nor how one can acquire it; nor whether it will remain uncontested, and what will happen if such an authority makes mistakes. Mistakes like his own, when he, disregarding Beethoven and Mozart, called Bellini's *Norma* the greatest opera.

My accusation of Schopenhauer may be excused by offering myself to the same condemnation: I confess to be guilty of similar crimes. For a long time I had scorned the music of Gustav Mahler before learning to understand and admire it. I once said: 'If what Reger writes is counterpoint, then mine is not.' I was wrong—*both* were.

On the other hand, in favour of Sibelius and Shostakovitch, I said something which did not require the knowledge of an expert. Every amateur, every music lover could have said: 'I feel they have the breath of symphonists.'

Experts are also human—but this is not the fault of us composers!

NEW MUSIC
1923

I am not really clear what the principles of the new music are (assuming they can be stated in any sort of unified way—and that does not have to be so, nor has it in fact often been so). These young composers need not necessarily have any new principles. Certain dislikes, certain enthusiasms, many ideas, much imagination and ability—there you have a better framework than any principles, however splendid. Nothing collapses so completely as renovation through bad growth. And, on the other hand, all revolutions simply bring reaction out into the open and can threaten what took years to grow. I was never *revolutionary. The only revolutionary* in our time was Strauss!

The first thing to be done in music—purely technically, for the spiritual is incalculable—seems to me the following:

1. To put an end, practically and theoretically, to the apparent (surely only apparent?) extremeness and lack of restraint present in twelve-tone composition, and to look for its laws. Or better, to find the form in which the laws of earlier art can be applied to the new. Five tones have been drawn into composition in a way not called upon before—*that is all*, and it does not call for any new laws.

2. The path to be trodden here seems to me the following: not to look for harmonies, since there are no rules for those, no values, no laws of construction, no assessment. Rather, to write parts. From the way these sound, harmonies will later be abstracted.

3. Gradually one will try to apply this more inclusive sound-material to the old forms. Here there will surely be certain modifications at first, and probably later too. But I am convinced, and have evidence, that *nothing essential changes in all this!*

4. As a reaction against the musical epoch that has just run its course, an epoch which carried to the limit the pathos of subjective feeling, one may expect a more un-pathetic kind of music. Whether it will choose a mode of expression (and perhaps also of vision) that turns against pathos (irony, satire, blasphemy, comment, etc.); whether it will find some other way out, to one side, perhaps

placing humour, harmlessness, indifference or sheer sensuality in the foreground; and whether this foreground is everything, or merely conceals the background— who can recount all the possibilities there are?

In any case, this seems to me the most important thing of all: apart from possible new ideas (new!), it will be more a matter of relatively novel presentations of relatively novel ideas. Five more tones are available; perhaps slightly greater exactness will be possible—or, on the other hand, perhaps it will be necessary to feel one's way for a while.

I hear that the young call their music 'psychological' music. This supposedly means its effect is to be purely on the nerves. But the only changes needed for that would not be in the music, but in the nerves. One cuts them off from the rest of the personality, and henceforth the oldest and newest music alike will merely tinkle in the ears—nobody will have to think about an artist any more. That is easy enough, but I find it correspondingly difficult to think how to produce the necessary music. Imagine the X-rays it will need to use, if its own effect is to be limited to the lower half of the mind. Or, since the complete personality turns away these rays, are they supposed to stop short in monstrous disorder? What sort of parts must one write to achieve this?

I can understand that when a young man says such things, he has something in mind—or, to be more accurate, he feels something. And perhaps the feeling does him so much good that he does not have to care what text he speaks to its melody—that what he says is a matter of indifference to him. If I remember rightly, I too used to be the same once; it was fairly long ago, so I need not be ashamed. For, just as the talented young will some day overcome all that, so (without presuming) have I. Nowadays I make a point of keeping my ideas at a decent distance from the feelings accompanying them.

To say it without more ado: if I understand aright, the young demand that their listeners are no longer to take a musical impression for anything more than it is. They want the sound that goes in at one ear to do nothing, before it goes out at the other, but stimulate the brain or spinal cord at a more or less definite point. (I trust I reproduce this in its full severity.) And it is of their listeners (I repeat) that they demand this—for only the latter are in a position to localize the impression, and even that only if they succeed in making themselves into a body which is, up to a point, non-conductive for music. This is certainly not impossible; joking apart (if without charity), it is not impossible, as one sees from the popular saying that certain dance music goes where it belongs—to the feet. However, whether it goes only there, or merely goes there first, is not stated. Certainly *Forest Murmurs* and the *Moonlight* Sonata do not go to the feet—not, at least as their principal target. It is less hard to imagine someone on whom the waltzes from *Die Meistersinger* and the *Alla danza tedesca* from Beethoven's B-flat String Quartet have such a narrowly 'psychological' effect—but one may not feel obliged to view it as a virtue worth mentioning.

Vienna, September 29, 1923

4

TURN OF TIME
1948

Composition with twelve tones—about fifteen years ago—was contested mainly by reactionaries and commercially-minded craftsmen. Their objections covered a wide scope, but in the main they were identical. They reached from the pre-Wagnerian horror of dissonance to the more romantic and sentimental reproach of cerebralism, that is to the pretence that such compositions were the result of uninspired, dry construction, of a kind of engineering.

One could ignore such criticism because of its sterility. But now opponents of my manner of organization have gained the support of a considerable number of young composers. The situation now presents a different aspect; this is no longer a mere aesthetic fight. These young composers, showing undeniable vitality in musical composition growing out of theories based on these criticisms, bear witness that a change of direction is in the making. Among the avant-garde of this group one meets some real talents, some full-blooded musicianship.

It is not the first time that 'ars nova' has been proclaimed; history repeats itself. The tendency to start on new ways is attractive to the mind of the young. Small causes have thus produced great changes, just as the Telemanns and Keisers paved the way for a Mozart, a Beethoven, a Wagner.

It must be admitted that the mutual inclination for negative criticism between an old predecessor and a young successor is very strong. Thus while I might blame certain young composers for serving the market a little too submissively, they might blame me—and they might be right—for disregarding the market's requirements. Were it not that negative criticism, because it lacks generative power, is wrong ninety times out of a hundred, there would not be much left to the uninitiated, to the non-partisan, in which he could believe, not much in the arts which he could admire.

Voluntarily assuming that I am probably wrong, may I now say that basing new musical expression on 'modal' influences and on the avoidance of 'chromaticism' seems to me a vague concept? First of all, one should not forget that major and minor are also modes: Ionian and Aeolian. That they supplanted the other four modes is due to their greater perfection, distinctness and conformity with nature. Only two of the remaining four modes ever played a role in the imagination of the composers—Dorian and, to a lesser extent, Phrygian. Except for a small number of examples, Lydian and Mixolydian failed to have a real life.

Bach's Toccata and Fugue No. 3 and the first of his Six Sonatas for Violin Solo are supposedly Dorian. But there is certainly nothing in the Toccata and Fugue which could not have appeared in a D minor tonality of Bach; and the harmony of the Violin Sonatas does not differ from that of G minor and its progressions are about the same as those of the Chaconne. Beethoven's Lydian *Heiliger Dankgesang* is distinctly major and its slight fluctuation between F and C could occur also in a piece which claims no modal influence. For instance, the Minuet of Beethoven's Eighth Symphony settles down prior to the recapitulation in the subdominant region (on B-flat), and even recapitulates the first part distinctly in this region. But the preceding *Allegretto scherzando*, instead of ending on the tonic of B-flat, ends on V of the subdominant region (E-flat).

Features reminiscent of the modes can often be found in Brahms' music, endowing such segments with a flavour of the past. But they exert no influence on the harmonic structure. The Tragic Overture, for instance, suggests a mode in its beginning. But whether this is Phrygian, as the progression A to E and the third phrase (which contains the tritone, E-B-flat) indicate, or whether the root progression, D-A (I-V), the ending on D and other features indicate D major-minor is rather difficult to decide. Especially because of the rich modulation which just in the beginning tends toward a minor subdominant region of F—rather far from the Phrygian—a decision is dangerous.

In the contemporary music based on modal principles that I have heard, the use of the modes sounded to me more like a melodic mannerism than like an expression of new tonal configurations. In the main I observed that leading tones were stubbornly avoided even when the harmonic structure did not require it. I am probably wrong to speak of such subtle details when I must gladly admit that some compositions of this style seemed to reveal in a musical language—whether I liked what I understood or not—musical ideas, musical expressions, a musical message.

This might be looked upon as the statement of an old man who no longer understands his time. But this judgement would not be quite true. I know that history repeats itself, and I understand that works produced at a turn of time— that is, when a new period is in the process of development—have always been viciously attacked. I expect history to repeat itself this time also; real merits, if they are present, will not be ignored, will not be forgotten.

5

THE RELATIONSHIP TO THE TEXT
1912

There are relatively few people who are capable of understanding, purely in terms of music, what music has to say. The assumption that a piece of music must summon up images of one sort or another, and that if these are absent the piece of music has not been understood or is worthless, is as widespread as only the false and banal can be. Nobody expects such a thing from any other art, but rather contents himself with the effects of its material, although in the other arts the material-subject, the represented object, automatically presents itself to the limited power of comprehension of the intellectually mediocre. Since music as such lacks a material-subject, some look beyond its effects for purely formal beauty, others for poetic procedures. Even Schopenhauer, who at first says

something really exhaustive about the essence of music in his wonderful thought,
'The composer reveals the inmost essence of the world and utters the most profound wisdom in a language which his reason does not understand, just as a
magnetic somnambulist gives disclosures about things which she has no idea of
when awake'—even he loses himself later when he tries to translate details of
this language *which the reason does not understand* into our terms. It must, however, be clear to him that in this translation into the terms of human language,
which is abstraction, reduction to the recognizable, the essential, the language of
the world, which ought perhaps to remain incomprehensible and only perceptible, is lost. But even so he is justified in this procedure, since after all it is his
aim as a philosopher to represent the essence of the world, its unsurveyable
wealth, in terms of concepts whose poverty is all too easily seen through. And
Wagner too, when he wanted to give the average man an indirect notion of what
he as a musician had looked upon directly, did right to attach programmes to
Beethoven's symphonies.

Such a procedure becomes disastrous when it becomes general usage. Then
its meaning becomes perverted to the opposite; one tries to recognize events and
feelings in music as if they *must* be there. On the contrary, in the case of Wagner
it is as follows: the impression of the 'essence of the world' received through
music becomes productive in him and stimulates him to a poetic transformation
in the material of another art. But the events and feelings which appear in this
transformation were not contained in the music, but are merely the material
which the poet uses only because so direct, unpolluted and pure a mode of
expression is denied to poetry, an art still bound to subject-matter.

The capacity of pure perception is extremely rare and only to be met with
in men of high calibre. This explains why professional arbiters become embarrassed by certain difficulties. That our scores become harder and harder to read,
that the relatively few performances pass by so quickly, that often even the most
sensitive, purest man can receive only fleeting impressions—all this makes it
impossible for the critic, who must report and judge, but who is usually incapable
of imagining alive a musical score, to do his duty even with that degree of
honesty upon which he might perhaps decide if it would do him no harm.
Absolutely helpless he stands in the face of purely musical effect, and therefore
he prefers to write about music which is somehow connected with a text: about
programme music, songs, operas, etc. One could almost excuse him for it when one

observes that operatic conductors, from whom one would like to find out something about the music of a new opera, prattle almost exclusively about the libretto, the theatrical effectiveness, and the performers. Indeed, since musicians have acquired culture and think they have to demonstrate this by avoiding shop-talk, there are scarcely any musicians with whom one can talk about music. But Wagner, whom they like so much to cite as an example, wrote a tremendous amount about purely musical matters; and I am sure that he would unconditionally repudiate these consequences of his misunderstood efforts.

Therefore, it is nothing but a comfortable way out of this dilemma when a music critic writes of an author that his composition does not do justice to the words of the poet. The 'scope of this newspaper', which is always most limited in space just when necessary evidence should be brought in, is always most willing to help out the lack of ideas, and the artist is really pronounced guilty because of 'lack of evidence'. But the evidence for such assertions, when it is once brought out, is rather evidence for the contrary, since it merely shows how somebody would make music who does not know how to—how accordingly music ought in no case to look if it has been composed by an artist. This is even true in the case of a composer's writing criticisms. Even if he is a good composer. For in the moment when he writes criticisms he is not a composer, not *musically inspired*. If he were inspired he would not describe how the piece ought to be composed, but would compose it himself. This is quicker and even easier for one who can do it, and is more convincing.

In reality, such judgements come from the most banal notion possible, from a conventional scheme according to which a certain dynamic level and speed in the music must correspond to certain occurrences in the poem and must run exactly parallel to them. Quite aside from the fact that *this* parallelism, or one even more profound, can also be present when externally the opposite seems to be presented—that, for example, a tender thought can be expressed by a quick and violent theme because the following violence will develop from it more organically—quite aside from this, such a scheme is already to be rejected because it is conventional; because it would lead to making music into a language which 'composes and thinks' for every man. And its use by critics leads to manifestations like an article which I once read somewhere, 'Faults of Declamation in Wagner', in which someone showed how he would have composed certain passages if Wagner had not beaten him to it.

A few years ago I was deeply ashamed when I discovered in several Schubert songs, well-known to me, that I had absolutely no idea what was going on in the poems on which they were based. But when I had read the poems it became clear to me that I had gained absolutely nothing for the understanding of the songs thereby, since the poems did not make it necessary for me to change my conception of the musical interpretation in the slightest degree. On the contrary, it appeared that, without knowing the poem, I had grasped the content, the real content, perhaps even more profoundly than if I had clung to the surface of the mere thoughts expressed in words. For me, even more decisive than this experience was the fact that, inspired by the sound of the first words of the text, I had composed many of my songs straight through to the end without troubling myself in the slightest about the continuation of the poetic events, without even grasping them in the ecstasy of composing, and that only days later I thought of looking back to see just what was the real poetic content of my song. It then turned out, to my greatest astonishment, that I had never done greater justice to the poet than when, guided by my first direct contact with the sound of the beginning, I divined everything that obviously had to follow this first sound with inevitability.

Thence it became clear to me that the work of art is like every other complete organism. It is so homogeneous in its composition that in every little detail it reveals its truest, inmost essence. When one cuts into any part of the human body, the same thing always comes out—blood. When one hears a verse of a poem, a measure of a composition, one is in a position to comprehend the whole. Even so, a word, a glance, a gesture, the gait, even the colour of the hair, are sufficient to reveal the personality of a human being. So I had completely understood the Schubert songs, together with their poems, from the music alone, and the poems of Stefan George from their sound alone, with a perfection that by analysis and synthesis could hardly have been attained, but certainly not surpassed. However, such impressions usually address themselves to the intellect later on, and demand that it prepare them for general applicability, that it dissect and sort them, that it measure and test them, and resolve into details what we possess as a whole. And even artistic creation often goes this roundabout way before it arrives at the real conception. When Karl Kraus calls language the mother of thought, and Wassily Kandinsky and Oskar Kokoschka paint pictures the objective theme of which is hardly more than an excuse to improvise in colours and forms and to express themselves as only the musician expressed himself until now, these are symptoms of a gradually expanding knowledge of the true nature of art. And with great joy I read Kandinsky's book *On the Spiritual in Art*, in which the road for painting is pointed out and the hope is aroused that those who ask about the text, about the subject-matter, will soon ask no more.

Then there will become clear what was already made clear in another instance. No one doubts that a poet who works with historical material may move with the greatest freedom, and that a painter, if he still wanted to paint historical pictures today, would not have to compete with a history professor. One has to hold to what a work of art intends to offer, and not to what is merely its intrinsic cause. Furthermore, in all music composed to poetry, the exactitude of the reproduction of the events is as irrelevant to the artistic value as is the resemblance of a portrait to its model; after all, no one can check on this resemblance any longer after a hundred years, while the artistic effect still remains. And it does not remain because, as the Impressionists perhaps believe, a real man (that is, the one who is apparently represented) speaks to us, but because the artist does so—he who has expressed himself here, he whom the portrait must resemble in a higher reality. When one has perceived this, it is also easy to understand that the outward correspondence between music and text, as exhibited in declamation, tempo and dynamics, has but little to do with the inward correspondence, and belongs to the same stage of primitive imitation of nature as the copying of a model. Apparent superficial divergences can be necessary because of parallelism on a higher level. Therefore, the judgement on the basis of the text is just as reliable as the judgement of albumen according to the characteristics of carbon.

6

THIS IS MY FAULT
1949

In the preface to *Pierrot Lunaire* I had demanded that performers ought not to add illustrations and moods of their own derived from the text. In the epoch after the First World War, it was customary for composers to surpass me radically, even if they did not like my music. Thus when I had asked not to add external expression and illustration, they understood that expression and illustration were out, and that there should be no relation whatsoever to the text. There were now composed songs, ballets, operas and oratorios in which the achievement of the composer consisted in a strict aversion against all that his text presented.

What nonsense!

What is the purpose of adding music to a text?

In the ballet, music should hide the noise of the steps.

In radio it is a substitute for a curtain, when the writers of murder stories are not capable of marking a change of the scenery otherwise. They still could use a bell.

In the movies, besides also serving as a curtain, it is supposed to underscore moods and actions.

But songs, operas and oratorios would not exist if music were not added to heighten the expression of their text.

Besides, how do you make sure that your music does not express something—or more: that it does not express something provoked by the text?

You cannot prevent your fingerprints from expressing you. But your handwriting unveils very much to the graphologist.

I remember how Busoni was the first to claim that music in opera must not express what is expressed by the action.

The opera is principally the product of four factors: the text, the music, the stage and the singer. If one of these constituents is allowed to disregard what the others do, why should they not also enjoy the same privilege? For instance, the singer?

Could not Monostatos ask Sarastro to dance a 'pas de deux' with Pamina? Or could not Lohengrin immediately after his arrival sell the swan to a butcher and start auctioning his gondola? Or would King Mark not better sing his 'Dies, Tristan, mir?' (This, Tristan, to me?) as if he were surprised over a beautiful Christmas present offered by Tristan?

The greatest incongruity with what the text expresses is its contrary. Why not play a pianissimo song to the ride of the Valkyries? Why not play a boogie-woogie when Wotan walks across a rainbow in Valhalla? This at least would make sure that you did not fail and that your music might fit quite well to another opera, but not to your own.

146

I will gladly admit that your tonal and modal products are as expressionless as a poker-face—but why are you trying your bluffs on music?

In the near future there will be machines like the lie-detector, and the craft of the graphologists will be developed and supported by similar devices and gadgets. They will accurately reveal what you hide and tell what you expressed —your bluff will then be called.

7

THE RADIO: REPLY TO A QUESTIONNAIRE
1930

Dear Mr. Ibach:[1]

Quite certainly the radio is a foe!—and so are the gramophone and sound-film. An inexorable foe, irresistibly on the advance; opposition is a hopeless prospect.

Here are the most damaging things it does:

1. It accustoms the ear to an unspeakable coarse tone, and to a body of sound constituted in a soupy, blurred way, which precludes all finer differentiation. One fears, as perhaps the worst thing of all, that the attitude to such sounds will change; until now, one has taken them in, beautiful or otherwise, knowing them to represent the tone peculiar to *one* instrument, and knowing that other sounds also exist—the sounds, that is, of the instrument as it has existed until now. But as they become more and more familiar, one will adopt them as the criterion for beauty of sound, and find inferior the sound of instruments used in art.

2. The boundless surfeit of music. Here, perhaps, the frightful expression 'consumption of music' really does apply after all. For perhaps this continuous tinkle, regardless of whether anyone wants to hear it or not, whether anyone can take it in, whether anyone can use it, will lead to a state where all music has been consumed, worn out. In Busch's time,[2] music was still often (at least, not

147

always!) 'found disturbing', but some day it may no longer disturb; people will be as hardened to this noise as to any other.

'The artist at the transmitter' as 'teacher' is certainly a good idea. It fulfils a demand—if the transmitter can fulfil it: 'the artist as *model*'.

The 'amateur at home, as pupil' will certainly find this useful, particularly if (as optimists like to believe) the people playing at the transmitter are always those who alone can be recommended as models. But what will our poor 'sorely-tried' music teachers have to say about this—even if the radio, which is a large earner but a small spender, gave them the opportunity to put themselves on show as models once or twice a year? (I shall not even discuss singing teachers!)

I do not want to be too pessimistic, for after all, every storm subsides some time; but not too optimistic either, for after all, things will always find a way of getting worse somehow. But one may hope that even the surfeit of music could have one good result: every human being might, after all, some time, somehow, be moved, touched, taken hold of, gripped, by music. As for the models, I hope they will do no more harm than is done by the literature appearing daily in the newspapers. And when I reflect that the discovery of book-printing has resulted in virtual extinction of illiteracy, my optimism returns. On the other hand, when I reflect on the power and influence of many who have just about managed, painfully, to master the alphabet, then indeed my pessimism starts coming back again.[3]

July 31, 1930

8

'SPACE-SOUND', VIBRATO, RADIO, *ETC.*
1931

On the occasion of moving the Berlin Radio (the *Funkstunde*, as it is so charmingly called) to a new building:

In this new building they have again apparently tried something stupid which a few years ago bled to death a gramophone firm, *Ultraphon*. At that time

I myself read of the 'discovery' by which they hoped to improve the gramophone. I believe they called it 'space-sound' (*Raumton*), compared it to the kind of 'two-eyed' reproduction afforded by the stereoscope, and thought a comparable 'plasticity' would come from using (if I remember aright) a double needle, to produce each sound twice within a very short time. A kind of *echo effect*, then.

I spotted the mistake at once: with the stereoscope there were not merely two *different* lines of vision, two *different* distances for the picture, *different* views of light and shade (left and right), but above all: two *different* eyes.

But here, the aim was to produce the same sort of thing with two *identical* sounds, the belief being that in a hall an echo is produced (or several!), and that the living quality of the sound depends on this.

What they are now trying to do at the Berlin Radio seems to come from a similarly wrong idea. (This has to be supposition, for reception is painfully bad: at the moment, they make music badly but transmit it a good deal worse!) They have built a hall that has an 'echo effect', and are apparently very proud of it.

To carry on a long polemic against this nonsense would itself be little more sensible. Indeed I am no longer so sure, as once I was, that (as I always used to say) *'the best way to contradict is with a correct idea'*, for nothing makes headway more laboriously than what is correct, and one has almost more prospect of getting through with a negative polemic than with the idea. All the same I find it more important to note down for once this correct idea (I have already said it to many people, often, but never put it down). So:

The basis of what we feel to be a living, beautiful, warm tone is a certain impurity. Where for once we can see quite clearly, can distinguish beyond all doubt, artistic enjoyment comes to an end, remarkably enough (!). Now, is it that what is pure, the ultimate discovery, is already so clarified that one has to destroy its purity (by admixture) in order to establish any contact with it; or is it that since the material (even, if one may say it, the material of ideas) is faulty, it calls for touching-up, which throws the true relationships into shadow and makes the defects invisible?

In any case, in music the interest in *wholly pure tones* is less great than one ought to suppose. At least, practically speaking—even though theoretically (as I have hinted) one would tend to assume the opposite. Possibly each tone should manifest a certain acuity ('high relief') that makes it stand out, or mildness ('low relief') which makes it recede. Perhaps this is a part of characteristic quality. Just like tone-colour, which is indeed also an adulteration. But, perhaps, here too it is simply a matter of that imperfection of the material which guarantees perspectives—it may be symbolically regarded as adaptation, unification; and it demands a corresponding imperfection.

Here, with reference to 'space-tone', I should mention just two phenomena which so far as I know have *not* been explained (see Riemann): 1. Vibrato. 2. Choral sound.

Both, in my view, are based on the same principle: instead of a 'single', 'pure', 'isolated', 'stiff', 'clear', 'lifeless', 'definitive' tone there appear many tones of assorted pitch ('more colourful', 'louder', 'more rounded'), whose combined effect is 'lively', 'accessible', *'living'*, etc. This mixture (as the whole idea implies) is *impure* in point of pitch, tone-colour, loudness, etc.

First, *vibrato*—it might be best to discuss the violin, since the practical application follows relatively easily here. To even the unpractised ear, there is a striking difference in sound between 'open'[1] and 'stopped' strings. And one can easily establish that some violinists have a 'beautiful', 'warm' tone, while a 'sour' tone, which also sounds 'impure', 'cold', 'unattractive', has no vibrato, or little, or the wrong kind.

But what is vibrato on stringed instruments?

Whereas the 'open' string shuts off its far end with a hard, 'stiff' piece of wood, giving a 'sharp demarcation', in the case of the 'stopped' note this marking-off is done by the 'soft', 'movable' finger, giving less sharp demarcation. So absence of vibrato will not mean a pure tone, because of this indefinite demarcation. The note need not actually be out of tune, but its intonation is unconvincing. There will, in addition, be a vague tremor on the part of the finger. So to touch up the impurity of this lifeless tone one uses vibrato.

Here, with reference to 'space sound', vibrato consists of a rapid and repeated shift of the point of pressure between finger and string, so it varies, *frequently* and in *quick succession*, the *length of the string*, the pitch of the note; thus its effect is that (instead of there being a single pure tone, as with the open string) a number of others, partly higher, partly lower, surround this pure tone, leaving the ear to seek for itself the middle point of this *'simultaneous mass'*—to extract the pitch. This makes the tone 'living', 'interesting', 'lively', 'warm', and all the rest of it.

The situation is rather similar with choral sound—both vocal and instrumental. Each individual violin (each individual voice) has defects: its intonation is impure, it is inexact in point of rhythm and dynamics. In choral sound such defects are lost, just like the virtues that are also present. Here again the combination of pitches sets up for discussion an average pitch, which has its own attractions.

Certainly the doubling of a part (by violins or singers) makes it sound louder. Despite this, it is certain that any music-lover will at some time have been surprised at how disproportionately *loud* a solo violin or a solo soprano sounds after a tutti. Does this not make one wonder whether the principal purpose of doubling is a dynamic one?

Berlin, February 5, 1931

9

MODERN MUSIC ON THE RADIO
1933

The question, whether modern music is suited to radio, and how the one might perhaps be adapted to the other, touches on questions of musical technique, radio technique and taste. I would ask of the radio that it should reproduce everything as it actually sounds. But this particularly affects the highest and lowest registers. Unfortunately, with most transmitters one hears only the upper parts (I call this sort of sound 'a lady sawn in half') and only a few stations, for example those in Britain and Italy, satisfy me in this respect. Modern music is for the most part 'thinly scored'. That should really make it very suitable for broadcasting—more so, than, say, music from the eighties and nineties of the last century. So it is hardly for modern music to adapt itself, particularly since it has another virtue that suits broadcasting conditions—it is mostly quite short.

How could one educate the public for modern music? It will be no more possible now than it ever was to educate the whole of the public for modern, or to put it better, serious art-music. Rightly or wrongly, it is not everyone's business to concern himself with difficult and profound things, just as these things are not thought of with everyone in mind. But the part of the public that is to be won over could and should be won over as soon as possible. The way to do this: many, frequently repeated performances, as well prepared as possible. I have long been pleading that an hour should be given over to modern music, at a time when its opponents will not greatly begrudge it; for example, an hour late at night, once or twice a week, perhaps after eleven. That could be handed over to modern music with no envious reactions.

On the question of concert and musical activity in general, and musical activity on the radio, I find it appropriate to remind the radio of a duty whose moral justification it takes too little into account. Since there is so much music—good or bad—to be heard on the radio, the public is not forced to rely solely on going to concerts. This has certainly played no small part in causing concerts to be so badly attended. The radio should make the most extensive amends to artistic life for this harm done; the harm is not merely material, but in the highest degree artistic! What amazes me about the radio's activities is that it makes so little use of its chance to arrange quite short performances, perhaps of a single piece. In concert life one has to travel a long way to the concert hall, and one will not do that for a single work. But this difficulty disappears in the case of the radio!

The aptness of electrical instruments must doubtless be regarded as, in principle, important. But it has to be said that for the moment their efficiency is still very problematic. The reason for this is not the incapacity of inventors, but the misguided spirit of industry, which does not allow inventions to mature until they are perfect from the artistic point of view, but provides inventors with money only for very dubious purposes—what they are to produce is not an instrument serving art, but something which can be mass-produced and thrown cheaply on to the market, and which can be brought out at least once a year in a new fashionable version that makes the earlier ones valueless, until the whole world loses interest. That is a sad and hope-destroying phenomenon.

10

ART AND THE MOVING PICTURES
1940

When Berlin's UFA made its first successful experiments with talking pictures, about 1928 or 1929, I was invited to record myself in picture and sound. The speech I delivered was an enthusiastic address of welcome to the new invention through which I expected a renaissance of the arts.

The silent film had reached the lowest point of vulgarity at this time, and save for this new invention it would probably have been dead in a few years. Now I expected a renaissance of the word—of thoughts, of ideas—dealing with the highest problems of mankind.

How wrong I had been!

When I expressed these desires, I had in mind the audiences of the Viennese Burgtheater or the Deutsches Theater in Berlin: audiences which consisted mostly of people who knew not only a few quotations, but could recite by heart whole pages of Shakespeare, Schiller, Goethe, Wagner; audiences which did not go to the theatre only to burst into laughter, but which followed the finesses of a dialogue with a fine, quiet smile; audiences which discussed for a long time afterwards the problems of a drama. They also liked their stars, but their real interest centred in the characters—whether they hated or admired, pitied or envied a hero or a villain. No actor could succeed merely by his personal appeal if he did not possess the power of personification—bringing to life a King Lear, a Piccolomini, a Goetz von Berlichingen, or a Wotan—if his use of the word could not overwhelmingly affect the emotions of his audience as well as satisfy its intellectual expectations.

How wrong I had been: a few months afterwards my dream was destroyed by the appearance of the first 'full-sized' film, 'full-sized' also in vulgarity, sentimentality and mere playing for the gallery. It was the first step downward to the lowest kind of entertainment and never since has a step in the opposite direction been ventured with such success. The production of moving pictures abandoned entirely every attempt towards art and remained an industry, mercilessly suppressing every dangerous trait of art.

Astonishingly, after some reluctance, the more highly educated class of people bowed to the facts. Enchanted by the new technical wonders, they renounced superior ideas and found themselves satisfied with a cheap happy ending. I had dreamed of a dramatization of Balzac's *Seraphita*, or Strindberg's *To Damascus*, or the second part of Goethe's *Faust*, or even Wagner's *Parsifal*. All of these works, by renouncing the law of 'unity of space and time', would have found the solution to realization in sound pictures. But the industry continued to satisfy only the needs and demands of the ordinary people who filled their theatres.

There was no compulsion to renounce the demands of the intellectually minded. Though there were always those works which satisfied the whole of a nation, or even of the entire world, like Mickey Mouse, or some of the films of Charlie Chaplin, Harold Lloyd, and the Marx brothers; like some operas of Rossini, operettas of Offenbach and Johann Strauss, and plays by popular poets, like Raimund and Nestroy; or popular music of Strauss, Offenbach, Foster, Gershwin, and many jazz composers; though there existed works which had the same appeal to the more highly educated as to the average citizen, there still remained unsatisfied those minds whose desires were served by the religious spirits of a Calderón, a Tolstoy, or by a Mass of Bach or Schubert; or by Maeterlinck's *Jakob Boehmas*, or Swedenborg's mysticism, or by Ibsen's social and Strindberg's matrimonial problems.

Ignoring the very problems of our times—these religious, philosophical, psychological, social, 'Weltanschauungs', economical, national and racial problems—can one ignore the fact that an Offenbach of our times would not dare to write satirically against a Napoleon III, nor could our Molière venture today to expose our physicians or 'nouveau-riches' to the laughter of an audience? No doubt, a present-day Beaumarchais would not succeed to see his *Barber of Seville* and *Marriage of Figaro* undermining customary privileges of the Grandés. At least not in moving pictures could he see them, unless their tendency, right or wrong, were cut down to that zero point which allows for a happy ending—it can't happen here—remember this. Or rather, it can't happen in the movies, where there is as well no space for the ideas of the fighters for liberal freedom, as presented in *Fidelio*, *Rienzi*, *Sicilian Vespers*, *Massaniello*, or *Uncle Tom's Cabin*, as for the expression of religious ideas like those found in Liszt's *Christus*, or *Saint Elizabeth*, or in Wagner's *Parsifal*, or in my own *Moses and Aron*.

Is it admissible to forget the painter, the artist, who, of course, also produces pictures? In moving pictures one meets only with that which corresponds to the period of realism in art. But one knows that since that time great artists have gone through a number of styles, schools of which never a hint has been made in the films.

So much for poetry and painting. As regards music one need not speak about modern music. With a few exceptions the industry has not yet admitted the classic music from Bach to Schubert, not to mention Brahms, Wagner, Berlioz, Debussy, Richard Strauss, or Mahler.

I do not believe that a great majority of the people as a whole would object seriously against being served occasionally with classic music. There is at least no evidence of that. But there is evidence that the audiences of classic music are growing constantly and that classic programmes are played over the radio several times each week and operas are broadcast from the Metropolitan, coast to coast, and also by recordings from many a smaller station. Would the people do this if there was really the same objection against artistic feeling as producers pretend?

I do not expect that producers will change their attitude towards the arts, nor will they admit that the people can become educated and accustomed to art, to that which they themselves, the producers, cannot be persuaded. And I think there is a different and better way to fulfil the demands of the intellectually minded.

One can assume that, though people of higher ranks may have participated in 'panem et circenses', devoted primarily to the plebs, there might also have existed entertainments devoted to adherents of intellectualism. At least one knows for certain that there exist opera and operetta houses distinctly devoted to the demands of different kinds of people. It may be admitted that operas, in contrast to operettas, were generally not self-supporting. Though I knew also opera theatres whose administration was perfect and accordingly self-supporting. But with moving pictures it can be different.

In Vienna I once met a man who had heard the Ninth Symphony, when I conducted it, only for the fiftieth time. Another man told me he had heard the *Merry Widow* more than a hundred times. When I was twenty-five I had heard operas of Wagner between twenty and thirty times each. The average non-professional music lover in Germany or Austria could likewise claim such a record; he had heard *Butterfly* twenty times, *Tosca*, *Bohème*, and *Cavalleria* eighteen times each, *Aida*, *Carmen*, and *Il Trovatore* fifteen times, *Tannhäuser*, *Meistersinger*, and *The Barber of Seville* twenty times, *Lohengrin*, *The Flying Dutchman*, and *Tales of Hoffman* nine times, *Faust*, *Figaro*, and *Tristan* about eight times each, *Manon*, *Fra Diavolo*, *Magic Flute*, and *Salome* about seven times, *The Prophet*, *Don Juan*, *and Freischütz* six times, *Fidelio* four times, besides lesser known operas once or more.

This investigation was made in a circle of typical music lovers about 1910, and checked somewhat in later years. Twenty-six operas are listed which comprise 285 opera visits. That means that each person questioned attended each of these operas, on the average, more than ten times. Operas which at present are seldom played are not listed. Those listed have been favoured by the regular opera audiences, on the average, for more than four decades, some for more than a century. That means that four generations of opera lovers have seen these works, all told, at least forty times.

But let us assume that each opera has been attended only twenty times. What conclusion can be drawn?

I know only a very small number of people who have seen a movie more than once.

Producers of movies can obtain an attendance of 100 per cent of the movie-going population only in the case of a great success.

Suppose the audience which can be acquired for serious plays and operas is only five per cent of the people (which seems not too exaggerated a hope if one considers how symphony audiences have grown), and in four generations every single person of these audiences would see a work (not ten times, as my account shows) only five times: five times four generations means twenty times for each work. Twenty times five per cent of the population amounts to the same 100 per cent of the population for which the movie industry aims so badly.

Now, my conclusion.

There can, and must be, founded a production of plays and operas to satisfy the demands of the more highly educated, plus the demands of art.

I do not assume that the industry, which at present produces moving pictures, could, or cares to start such a turn towards pure art. This could only be done by men who had not used their talents in the opposite direction. This can only be done by new men.

I, further, do not assume that the theatres which are owned by the industry should be used for such works of art. Art does not need so much pomp. Its own splendour created a scene of dignity, which cannot be surpassed by materialistic profusion.

There are, of course, many problems involved. They need not be discussed at present. There is time enough to do this, especially as the industry might shortly be forced to consider some problems of its own, imposed on it by the advent of television. Perhaps people might come to realize then that art is less expensive than amusement, and more profitable.

PART III

FOLK-MUSIC AND NATIONALISM

1

FOLKLORISTIC SYMPHONIES
1947

Peace after the First World War granted political independence to nations which culturally were far from ready for it. Nevertheless even small nations of six to ten million people expected to be regarded as cultural units, nations whose national characteristics expressed themselves in many ways: in their applied arts, weaving, ceramics, painting, singing and playing and, finally, even composing music. Of course, X-Town might have developed individual habits differing considerably from those of Y-Town, from which it was separated by 3,000 feet of mountains. But both demanded general recognition, and attempted to acquire a 'place in the sun', seeking the opportunity to sell their national products with profit. The balance of trade was the real idea behind their mock-ideals.

Isolation alone does not guarantee fertility. On the contrary, contact, even with inferiority, can be stimulating. On the other hand, inescapable necessities of life, those emotions of love, mourning, nostalgia, etc., will find individual and perhaps original expression. Whether people live in seclusion or not, they may find their own words, their own tunes, and create their own songs. And if those from X-Town differ no more from those of Y-Town than Dorian differs from Aeolian—there will be enough to be proud of.

If songs of the Southern section of West-Parinoxia show Lydian traits in their otherwise Phrygian texture, dances of the neighbouring Northern part of Franimonti may display the opposite: Phrygian influence in Lydian melodies. Such differences constitute individuality to the local connoisseur. There exist such differences, for instance, in the Balkans. Their songs and dances are often overwhelmingly deep in expression and attractive in their melodic configuration; they are beautiful and one must love them. The places of origin of these differences, however, are of interest rather to the specialist than to the undiscriminating music-lover.

In spite of high appreciation of these differences, one has to admit that they are negligible in comparison to the differences between folklore and artistic music. They differ perhaps no more than petroleum and olive oil, or ordinary water and holy water, but they mix as poorly as oil and water. Even a Beethoven could apply only a fugato-like, rather simple treatment to a given theme in the Rasumovsky String Quartet, Op. 59, No. 2. And when he marks this theme 'Thème Russe' one is inclined to believe that on the one hand it is a homage to his aristocratic Maecenas, but on the other hand an excuse to musical experts, who would understand the obstacles connected with commissions. In order to comprehend this problem it is useful to compare this treatment with that of the scherzo of the Ninth Symphony. Here also a semi-contrapuntal treatment is applied; but the second subject is melodically the continuation of the first. The second subjects to the Thème Russe are only incidental accompaniments without combinatory value. Obviously, this theme is founded on a primitive harmonic progression, which is contrary to the requirements of contrapuntal combinations. Furthermore, in its unpretentious constitution there is no problem which suggests development into a theme.

As a folk dance, the Thème Russe is certainly very pleasant. But that there now exists Russian music is due to the advent of some great composers. Were this not the case, great Irish and Scotch symphonies should have been created, because the folklore of these people is of an unsurpassed beauty and full of striking and characteristic traits. On the other hand, some smaller nations whose folk music is not as extraordinary have succeeded in placing in the history of music and into the minds of music lovers representatives such as Smetana, Grieg, Chopin, Liszt, Dvořák and Sibelius. Characteristically enough, Sibelius contends that his music is not based on national folk music, and I guess that Grieg's also is not. Chopin's rhythms are often derived from Polish dances, but harmonically and in part melodically neither his music nor that of Liszt (or much of Smetana's) differ essentially from Western and Central European styles of their day.

Evidently folklore based on extraordinary or exotic scales displays more characteristics, and perhaps even too many. It seems a nightmare to imagine what might have become of music if Japan had succeeded in conquering America, England and finally Germany. The Japanese idea of music has no resemblance to ours. Their scales are not based on a harmonic concept, or, if so, at least it is not ours. Friends of Eastern Asiatic music claim that this monodic music is capable of such variety as to express every nuance of human feeling. This may be true, but to the Western ear it sounds—ah—different. If it is not completely impossible to add a harmonic accompaniment to melodies of this kind, it is certainly impossible to derive it logically or naturally from these scales. For this reason alone it seems they would rather destroy our music than comply with its conditions.

Even Gypsy music, whose characteristic scales have become influential among several surrounding nations in the Balkans, though it is not as foreign to our ears, has been unable to penetrate the wall separating folk music from art. Whenever Brahms incorporates such a melody in a composition the structure ordinarily will not surpass the implications of a set of waltzes or of a quadrille. In works of higher organization he adds only the flavour, the perfume to his own themes. But he is not forced to enter into foreign territory to express unusual melodic types, as is proved by the last movement of the G Major String Quintet. Liszt's Hungarian Rhapsodies are structurally more profoundly organized than those Romanian Rhapsodies and *Zigeunerweisen*. However, they are chiefly pot-pourris, forms of a looser construction than what classic masters from Bach to Brahms call 'Phantasies'.

Much beauty may be credited to natural folklore. No credit is deserved by those 'man-made' pseudo-folksongs, whose popularity is acquired through the mass appeal unfortunately exerted by triviality. Silcher, Abt, Nessler and their like in other countries falsified simplicity by substituting sentimentality for art-lessness and sentiment—they present only the white-collar man's concept of the man in the street. So also do high-standard composers, who never forget their aristocratic superiority when they descend to their 'Im Volkston' songs. They are always at least structurally correct. If one's left leg is too short, one's right leg compensates in that it is too long. But in most of these imitations, there always occur phrases one or more steps too long for which other phrases which are too short cannot compensate. Natural folk music is always perfect, because it stems from improvisation—that is, from a lightning flash of inspiration.

The discrepancy between the requirements of larger forms and the simple construction of folk tunes has never been solved and cannot be solved. A simple idea must not use the language of profundity, or it can never become popular. Everybody will understand the statement that parallel lines are 'in all parts equally distant' (Webster). But the scientific formulation that 'they meet only at infinity' requires too much thinking and imagination to be generally understood and to become popular.

Genuine folk tunes remain within the narrowest compass of a scale and are based on simple harmonic progressions. Changes of the harmony and figuration of the melody such as, for instance, Bach applies to chorales do not produce new material, contrasts, subordinate themes, etc. Structurally, there never remains in popular tunes an unsolved problem, the consequences of which will show up only later. The segments of which it consists do not need much of a connective; they can be added by juxtaposition, because of the absence of variance in them. There is nothing in them that asks for expansion. The small form holds the contents firmly, constituting thus a small expansion but an independent structure.

A motive, in contrast to this, is incomplete and depends on continuations: explanations, clarifications, conclusions, consequences, etc. The opening motives of Beethoven's Fifth Symphony, Example 1, can be understood as E flat without the clarifying harmony in measures 5ff, and a melodic continuation by which the third in *a* is transposed in *a¹* to complete the C minor triad.

Example 2 shows how the motive of the transition is derived from a reinterpretation of the two main notes E flat and F (marked by *)[1] as tonic and dominant of E flat major, surrounded by B flats.

Example 3 shows how the subordinate theme is related to that and to the first statement of the motive (Example 1). This is what I call the 'method of developing variation'.

I cannot remember a single case of deriving subordinate ideas from a folksong by this method. Generally some method is used to make a short story long:

numerous repetitions of a short phrase, varied only by transpositions to other degrees, changes of instrumentation, more recently by addition of dissonant harmonies and by what Hollywood arrangers call counterpoints, i.e., 'unsolicited gifts' of unrelated voices. Thus nothing has been said that was not said in the first presentation of the tune.

A composer—a real creator—composes only if he has something to say which has not yet been said and which he feels must be said: a musical message to music-lovers. Under what circumstances can he feel the urge to write something that has already been said, as it has in the case of the static treatment of folk songs?

A real composer does not compose merely one or more themes, but a whole piece. In an apple tree's blossoms, even in the bud, the whole future apple is present in all its details—they have only to mature, to grow, to become the apple, the apple tree, and its power of reproduction. Similarly, a real composer's musical conception, like the physical, is one single act, comprising the totality of the product. The form in its outline, characteristics of tempo, dynamics, moods of the main and subordinate ideas, their relation, derivation, their contrasts and deviations—all these are there at once, though in embryonic state. The ultimate formulation of the melodies, themes, rhythms and many details will subsequently develop through the generating power of the germs.

Put a hundred chicken eggs under an eagle and even she will not be able to hatch an eagle from these eggs.

Defenders of the use of folk tunes as themes for large forms might see an analogy in the utilization of chorales and other folk songs as themes for variations by classic composers. While Bach often derives the voices which contrapuntally accompany the main voice in his chorale preludes from the chorale melody itself, there is no possibility or necessity of a developing growth. One can admit on the other hand that, in primordial specimens, sets of variations serve rather the virtuoso who wants to be brilliant through his technique. In such variations there is seldom any other development than velocity and no other change than the figuration of the instrumental style. The simplicity of the variation is adequate to the simplicity of the folk melody. In the artistically superior compositions of this kind the 'motive of the variation,' as I called it, is derived through 'developing variations' of basic features of the theme and its motive. Thus, in fact, the same compositorial procedure can be observed here as anywhere else in our established Western music, producing the thematic material for forms of all sizes: the melodies, main and subordinate themes, transitions, codettas, elaborations, etc., with all the necessary contrasts.

A real composer who is accustomed to produce his material in this logical manner—be it by spontaneous inspiration or by hard labour—will only occasionally voluntarily renounce starting his composition in his own way, with his own themes. They will contain many a provocative problem, requiring treatment. There would not be a larger form, were it not that this urgency is present, even in the embryonic state, and cannot be escaped. Thus a real composition is not composed but conceived, and its details need not be added. As a child resembles his parents, so do they correspond entirely to the initial conception. And they break forth in the same manner in which the child's first and second teeth break forth, like all those inconceivable but natural miracles by which creation is marked.

Real folk music could not exist, or survive, were it not produced similarly: spontaneously, as an inspired improvisation. It is well known that Franz Schubert liked to improvise waltzes and other dances when his friends danced. It seems improbable that real folk music has been composed by painfully adding tones to tones and little segments to little segments. Folk tunes have been improvised singing or playing by bards, troubadours and other gifted persons. Knowing that some photographers are capable of forcing better people to pose in a cheap manner—the left hand on the piano, trying to find the tones or harmonies which the pencil in the right hand preserves for eternity—I am always inclined to doubt whether one like this is a real composer, a real creator.

It seems that nations which have not yet acquired a place in the sun will have to wait until it pleases the Almighty to plant a musical genius in their midst. As long as this does not occur, music will remain the expression of those nations to whom composing is not merely an attempt to conquer a market, but an emotional necessity of the soul.

Of course, a soul you have to have!

2

FOLK-MUSIC AND ART-MUSIC
c. 1926

Throughout this earth all the civilized peoples are in unremitting contact with one another, and this inevitably tends to bring about uniformity of conditions, everywhere and in every way. The tendency acts most immediately in, for example, the field of technology—in any city one will find much the same electric railway, the same cars, the same hotels, and so on; or in the social sphere—only a few types of city or forms of law are found; but nobody should be surprised that the same tendency is also at work in art. Any people is aware, though, that if it wants to live at least partly at the others' expense, then it needs to be one idea ahead in as many fields as possible; to produce something the others cannot imitate, or not yet, and therefore have to buy.

Art has long been a most promising export article, particularly so, of course, in the days when craftsmen's great skill still counted heavily. The states most successful in art were not necessarily those still (or at all) in the running for world domination; for those in their initial period of expansion, however, art was a very effective means of propaganda furthering their trading and political interest. Even small defeated states knew how to capture a relatively favourable position by inducing others to adopt their view of art.

Since certain differences between cultures have been ironed out by international contact, it is increasingly true that throughout all the countries that concern us one single view of art is dominant, and one only. In the realm of painting, the French have long since succeeded the Italians in setting the tone; in literature, the English and French were followed by the Germans, then the Russians and recently the Scandinavians—and probably it will soon be the Americans. In music, after the Italians, the Germans exerted the greatest influence, one which even today is still unbroken. But whatever the changes may have been, the number of alternatives was small, limited mainly to west and central Europe, and the dominant view was dominant throughout the whole field. Accordingly, however great the distinctions between the various styles may otherwise have been, they were not such as to prevent each people's playing a certain creative part within the dominant style, even if it lacked the recognizable originality to reach the front rank. But since these peoples were also the colonizers, and in many ways the rulers of most of the non-European states, and were able to impose the advantages of our culture upon them, the European (mainly west- and central-European) view of art is dominant in all these countries too, in so far as they are at all concerned with art in our sense.

As mentioned already, art can figure in the battle of the nations as one way to achieve a place in the sun, and, with this in mind, there have been attempts to create national music on the part of certain people who up to now played no role in the development of art-music, and of others who had to give up their dominant position about a century ago. These attempts reflected a materialistic conception of art, proceeding rather as a gardener would in trying to improve a native plant through grafting a suitable cutting on to it. But there is an important difference here.

This is how their minds worked: the music dominant at any time was always linked to some particular nation in such a way that, of its kind, nothing approaching it in value could be produced by any other people. When occasionally two or more dominant styles existed at the same time, there was still the same national limitation of creative ability. Moreover, no one could fail to notice that in music the national personality emerged in a particularly striking way. So in fact a national quality is an essential feature of national music. How, then, does one produce 'synthetic' national music, how does one breed it? As one breeds horses, or plants—by intermingling or grafting native and foreign products. It was easy to invent a way of doing this; one dug down into the treasury of folk-music, which no people lacks, and which is all the more individual and striking the further removed it has been from the influence of western- and central-European art-music. One dug down and used what one found; these folk-songs and dances were arranged in a western- or central-European way, using all the technique that was uppermost in realms of musical thought which demanded such technical artifice.

Let me add at this point that such attempts took place, for better or worse, in the days of homophonic music. We shall see how this fact influenced matters.

Here one can straightaway point to the first mistake, already hinted at in giving the facts: ideas from folk-art were treated according to a technique that had been created for ideas of a more highly developed kind. The difference between these two ways of presenting an idea was overlooked, and there may even be an underlying difference between two whole ways of thinking. Something can only acquire the feeling of folk-art if everyone can grasp it, i.e., if it is either conceived or expressed so that everyone can understand it; whereas one essential feature of high ideas is that they can scarcely be grasped unless the mind is trained to some extent.

3

NATIONAL MUSIC (1)
1931

Any people can acquire hegemony in art. It seems not even to depend on dominant power in the economic or military field. In the period when Italy was weakest she produced laws for the cultural world; Russia's position among the great powers, when her literature achieved an outstanding reputation, was great but not all-powerful, while that of the Scandinavians, in a similar case, was distinctly slight. So one must conclude that art, unlike other wares, is not the commodity exported by whoever is most powerful at any time, something they can graciously hand on to the smaller people, the colonials. Here there seems to be only *one* power that regulates international success: the power of genius, the power of the idea, the art of representation.

However, as soon as some highly developed national art achieves a position of hegemony, one sees the strong hold exerted on art by race and nationality, how convincingly these are expressed by art, and how inseparably the one is tied to the other; for then, all the rest of the cultural world tries to do just one thing —emulate the national art in question, without stopping to consider whether it is an attainable model, or if so, to what degree. There was painting in the Italian, French, Spanish manner, poetry in the French, English, Russian, Scandinavian manner, music composed in the Netherlands, Italian, German manner, when one nation had come to dominate; and nothing different was thought worthy of recognition, rightly or wrongly, whether it were good or bad, genuine or derivative, new or old.

It is certainly hard to decide whether at such a time of dominance any other art can be good; it would be difficult to reconcile oneself to this idea—that the great fertility of one should bring about the impotence of the others. It is a distressing thought, unworthy of belief; but, alas, it is possible.

It is equally hard to track down the reasons why some particular kind of art should rise to hegemony. The preparatory stages clearly lie far back. For example, say that it was mainly through J. S. Bach (at least it first became clear through him, and irreversible since him) that German music came to decide the way things developed, as it has for 200 years (one may say this, though incidentally there has been a high period of Italian and French *opera*, something that clearly needs separate consideration). Nevertheless, a preparatory period was needed, perhaps 200 years, during which German composers found no predominantly German ways to express themselves and could only practise whatever the Netherlands, Italy and France recognized as art. Indeed—and here there is a certain similarity to our own times—even the turning point toward the homophonic music of the classical composers, the revolutionary movement against the art of the contrapuntal masters, began under the leadership of Latin composers—Italians and Frenchmen.

That movement indeed reached its climax in Germany, and made apparent the position of dominance Germany had reached—but one cannot explain this by saying the homophonic style corresponds to the German nature, for Bach proves the opposite, quite apart from the fact that this art, too, accompanied its first successes with the war-cry 'lightness against heaviness'. Here again there is a similarity to our own times, and we could know on which side heaviness has to lie, since other sides have taken out a permanent lease on lightness. The similarity is so great that it is easy for equally great, historically-trained minds to determine how this movement is to continue. In fact they have already done so, for nowadays historical training does not confine itself to recognizing that conditions are similar—it aims to bring about the similarity of consequences, which can then be used to prove the similarity of conditions.

For these things are, in fact, not at all similar.

The historically trained minds say, 'Harmony has developed to such an exaggerated pitch that now, as at the time of the contrapuntal style, there must be a return to simplicity, i.e. to a harmonically simpler music.' But what the historically trained makers of history overlook is that the real contrast is this: contrapuntal and homophonic art.

But then matters are really as follows:

(a) In Bach's time, contrapuntal art, i.e. the art of producing every audible figure from one single one, had reached such a pitch that in it the transition to a different kind of art is already beginning. Henceforth, the art would be to subject these figures themselves to variation, it no longer being enough to juxtapose them, but rather to show how one gives rise to another. Simultaneously there began a different disposition of musical space: composers began to write a principal part, something there had never been before.

(b) By our own time, the way harmony had developed meant that the use of all twelve tones of the chromatic scale could be moulded in such a multifarious way as not only to bring about a new (harmonic) polyphony but also to make it possible (the total musical space now being more efficiently employed) to let the figures develop in several parts simultaneously.

(c) I have already described the state that now followed, and from a number of different viewpoints:

The new multiplicity of meaning conferred on the tones by new kinds of chords made possible the use of motives in rather the way complex ornaments (*Manieren*) were once used—without regard for dissonant clashes; they explained themselves as the *Manieren* did—from the logic of the figuration as a whole.

Through this preparation and through the broadening of all tonal relationships, musical imagination and creative fantasy were in a position to take the next step, since they were treating dissonances and consonances as exactly alike, so far as grasping them was concerned.

So if at the climax of contrapuntal art, in Bach, something quite new simultaneously begins—the art of development through motivic variation—and in our time, at the climax of art based on harmonic relationships, the art of composing with 'twelve tones related only to each other' begins, one sees that the epochs are very similar. The question is simply whether, and in whose interest, this historical parallel is bound to produce similar results: that is to say, whether the composer's way of writing must again alter from now on, in as unexpected and unforeseeable a way as after J. S. Bach.

Wagner's music was not only the best and most significant of its age—it not only surpassed Berlioz, Auber, Meyerbeer, Bizet, Rossini, Bellini and others—but it was also the music of 1870 Germany, who conquered the world of her friends and enemies through all her achievements, not without arousing their envy and resistance. Here the rise of a people seems to explain not only its predominance, but also the battle against it; what it does not explain is how this uniquely constituted music came about, conceived fifteen years before the rise of the people. On the other hand, its qualities are a fully adequate objective justification of the way it spread.

These qualities, the qualities of the unusual work of art, were arrived at in the usual way: the inspiration of genius. But the resistance came about in a still more usual way: the talented inspiration of those without genius.

It took the highest degree of talent to recognize the export value of art and to place this above its cultural value. Such an assessment furthered nationalist art, brought it about—and it was all it did bring about.

But without this talented inspiration, the musical countries must have confined themselves purely and without contradiction to imitation, and the original, opposed by such bad imitations, must necessarily have increased its influence. But people had realised that the export of a cultural value is good for the export trade as a whole, so the war cry of pre-war musicians was 'liberation from the influence of Wagnerian music'.

The echo this war cry found in Germany is strange and interesting.

4

NATIONAL MUSIC (2)
1931

Here is a remarkable fact, as yet unnoticed: Debussy's summons to the Latin and Slav peoples, to do battle against Wagner, was indeed successful; but to free *himself* from Wagner—that was beyond him. His most interesting discoveries can still only be used within the form and the way of giving shape to music that Wagner created. Here it must not be overlooked that much of his harmony was also discovered independently of him, in Germany. No wonder; after all, these were logical consequences of Wagner's harmony, further steps along the path the latter had pointed out.

It is a remarkable thing, as yet unnoticed by anyone—although a thousand facts point to it, and although the battle against German music during the war was primarily a battle against my own music, and although (as somebody said recently on the radio, not realising or understanding what he was saying) nowadays my art has no line of succession abroad (although I was picked to the bones, or to what people take to be the bones); remarkably, nobody has yet appreciated that my music, produced on German soil, without foreign influences, is a living example of an art able most effectively to oppose Latin and Slav hopes of hegemony and derived through and through from the traditions of German music.

This has remained unnoticed, not only because my scores are hard to read, but, even more, because those sitting in judgement are lazy and arrogant. For it can be seen.

But for once I will say it myself.

My teachers were primarily Bach and Mozart, and secondarily Beethoven, Brahms, and Wagner.

From *Bach* I learned:

1. Contrapuntal thinking; i.e. the art of inventing musical figures that can be used to accompany themselves.

2. The art of producing everything from one thing and of relating figures by transformation.

3. Disregard for the 'strong' beat of the measure.

From *Mozart*:

1. Inequality of phrase-length.

2. Co-ordination of heterogeneous characters to form a thematic unity.

3. Deviation from even-number construction in the theme and its component parts.

4. The art of forming subsidiary ideas.

5. The art of introduction and transition.

From *Beethoven*:

1. The art of developing themes and movements.
2. The art of variation and of varying.
3. The multifariousness of the ways in which long movements can be built.
4. The art of being shamelessly long, or heartlessly brief, as the situation demands.
5. Rhythm: the displacement of figures on to other beats of the bar.

From *Wagner*:

1. The way it is possible to manipulate themes for expressive purposes and the art of formulating them in the way that will serve this end.
2. Relatedness of tones and chords.
3. The possibility of regarding themes and motives as if they were complex ornaments, so that they can be used against harmonies in a dissonant way.

From *Brahms*:

1. Much of what I had unconsciously absorbed from Mozart, particularly odd barring, and extension and abbreviation of phrases.
2. Plasticity in moulding figures; not to be mean, not to stint myself when clarity demands more space; to carry every figure through to the end.
3. Systematic notation.
4. Economy, yet richness.

I also learned much from Schubert and Mahler, Strauss and Reger too. I shut myself off from no one, and so I could say of myself:

My originality comes from this: I immediately imitated everything I saw that was good, even when I had not first seen it in someone else's work.

And I may say: often enough I saw it first in myself. For if I saw something I did not leave it at that; I acquired it, in order to possess it; I worked on it and extended it, and it led me to something new.

I am convinced that eventually people will recognize how immediately this 'something new' is linked to the loftiest models that have been granted us. I venture to credit myself with having written truly new music which, being based on tradition, is destined to become tradition.

February 24, 1931

5

ITALIAN NATIONAL MUSIC
1927

Italian national music, which today is openly written on higher orders (whereas I, in my reactionary way, stick to writing mine on orders from The Most High) —this Italian national music satisfies the requirements of a snobdom of uncomplicatedness, which in no way differs from the snobdom that preceded it; or rather, solely in that here, too, shallowness is to be disguised—but this time by making a display of it. The one as uncomplicated as the other: snobdom and national music. No wonder they appeal to one another. But no wonder, either that such purely national art appeals to the snobs of all the other nations, too.

Take note: were I entitled to say a word in the name of German art (but I am denied such an entitlement), then all the German nationalists must needs agree with me, simply because of the offensively nationalist character of the new tendency in Italy. For indeed the latter is directed against, above all, the Teutonic, heavy, unsensual, at best philosophical but in truth unmusical German spirit in music—and for that reason the German nationalist circles agree with it. Fortunately I have nothing to say there.

But now take note of something else: the funniest thing is (and it adds the finishing touch to the whole rumpus), that the Germans' agreement is justified in a way.

Italian national music aims, indeed, to be no more than music for the comfortable citizens of all nations, to do no more than entertain all those who can think of something more entertaining (and merely begrudge others that less entertaining thing, true art). It seeks nothing more, and it is made to measure. It retains what was essential in German music: the ideas are formulated and then worked over according to the principle of development that was introduced into the art of music by the Germans. Nor is the poverty of its ideas and development anything new; the only new thing is for a nation to lay claim to these methods, this artlessness and poverty of ideas, as something peculiar to itself.

September 25, 1927

WHY NO GREAT AMERICAN MUSIC?
1934

In his article Mr. Henderson is astonished that my 'coming to teach in Boston' made more of a sensation than the performance of a new work by a Boston composer. And he is rightly astonished. For though anywhere in the world the appearance of someone who has already achieved something does in any case make more of a sensation than the work of a composer who has still to prove himself, and though it is quite irrelevant, sensations being ephemeral anyway, how much of one is made by anything, he is, as I said, absolutely right; for such sensations certainly corrupt many of the European artists who came here to give, were obliged instead to make a sensation, and finally found no other way out but to take—to take what America has to give.

It could almost have gone that way with me. But such things break themselves against me; I am old enough and confirmed enough, I am used to giving, unpractised at taking; I intend to pass a portion of my life in this land—if I am wanted—and I shall not grow false to my old habits there: *I shall go on giving*, as before. And in this sense my intervention in an internal matter will perhaps not be resented; I should like here to pass on to you some of my experiences from almost forty years in the battle of art.

In the few months I have been here I have totally altered my opinion of American music. Certainly I find that skill and knowledge, the average level of general musical education, is at times rather superficial and external; I often find people aiming in a wild and mannered way at a target imposed from outside and by its nature neither worth aiming at nor original; I cannot praise such wilfulness; but on the other hand I have recognized an extraordinarily large amount of talent, inventive ability and originality, which in my opinion justify the highest hopes.

But one must have only the highest hopes, and not the second-highest or even lower. Among the second or third highest belongs, above all, the hope of attaining a national art-music by using folk-music. In the polemical foreword to my *Three Satires*, Op. 28, I point to the absurdity of 'trying to apply to the ideas of folk-music, which are primitive by nature, a technique that corresponds only to a complicated way of thinking'. Moreover, Beethoven's *Thème Russe*, Mozart's *Turkish March*, Haydn's *Alla Ongarese* and many other pieces are purely German; Dvořák's *New World* Symphony is (to those who know) undoubtedly Czech; *Aida* is not Egyptian, the *Queen of Sheba* not Jewish, and in Spain, so Spaniards assure me, there is no folk-music resembling *Carmen*. A national masquerade can indeed be mounted in this way, but look at it soberly, the morning after, when the carnival spirit has flown; one knows how such things look then. That Tchaikovsky's way of composing is Russian, folkloristic, aided by Russian folk-songs—that I have to doubt, and I must assert at least that his songs speak an idiom unknown in Europe before him—it may well be Russian, but in any case it is distinguished and very, very unlike folk-music; very aristocratic, at least. The fact that Tchaikovsky's craftsmanship suggests the German school and, let us also add, the French and Italian contributions to the musical make-up of the world in his time—all this alters the national character of his music as little as it did that of Haydn, who was a pupil of the Italian, Porpora, or that of other Viennese classics, who had Salieri to thank for some advanced technical devices. To what extent national music, which can be artificially produced by the mechanical process of using folk-songs, how much longer this can last, is an open question, since attempts of that kind have not yet been in progress for a hundred years, and what is a century in the history of culture?

But on the other hand I seem to hear an American national character speaking very clearly in what I know of American music. Whether this comes from the landscape, the climate, from the spiritual or physical mentality—the musician may safely leave it to the specialists to make false assertions on that point. But a sensitive organism, a musical seismograph, registers the fact that the disturbances caused by American music are different, even when not much is visible in the externals, in the style.

Ah yes, style!

To listen to certain learned musicians, one would think all composers did not bring about the representation of their *vision*, but aimed solely at establishing a style—so that musicologists should have something to do. As far as I myself am concerned, I allow that one can try to detect the personal characteristics of the finished work from the score, from its more or less remarkable figures or turns of phrase. But to overlook the fact that such personal characteristics follow from the true characteristic idea and are merely the symptoms—to believe, when someone imitates the symptoms, the style, that this is an artistic achievement—that is a mistake with dire consequences! A sensitive ear hears characteristics, even invisible ones, where the deaf sees at most style.

Perhaps an attempt will have to be made to move the public to sensitize its ears in this way. Perhaps leading figures will have to acquire influence, in order to persuade the public it is necessary—but leaders who themselves represent an apparatus that functions so sensitively; leaders who can also make value-judgements based on their own knowledge and abilities. The further and natural results of this will be discussed in another connection.

When I speak of American music, I cannot pass over American light music. Who can doubt that it adds up to something American? But who has the right to call it inferior in comparison with the light music of other peoples? We know Wagner despised Offenbach, and, unless I am mistaken Johann Strauss too. And who can say how arrogantly generations of musicians would speak of that light music, had Brahms not been able and sufficiently educated to recognize its purely musical substance and the value of that; had he not had the respect for achievement possessed only by those who know at first hand what achievement is; and had he not added: 'Not, alas, by Johannes Brahms' after the first bars of the *Blue Danube* Waltz? Light music could not entertain me unless something interested me about its musical substance and its working-out. And I do not see why, when other people are entertained, I too should not sometimes be entertained; I know indeed that I really ought at every single moment to behave like my own monument; but it would be hypocritical of me to conceal the fact that I occasionally step down from my pedestal and enjoy light music.

Why a music which entertains the whole nation and also probably is able to move it, even if through sentimentality, why it should not be folk-music—this I do not find quite convincing. Let the farmer's wife, once she has become a grandmother, sing to her grandchildren the songs and dance-tunes she learned from records and the radio—her memory, and later that of her offspring, will already be altering the tunes in ways learned musicians like to find in folk-songs. However, I hope that by then the talented will have resolved to oppose the exploitation of folk-music, and will have decided simply to produce art-music along the generally customary path of genius.

It will come about in this way and no other: a genius will compose and will not worry about what is demanded or expected of national music by the experts; but then, suddenly, all these symptoms, out of which people had been trying to produce an art-homunculus, will be present (though others, too). This, an everyday happening in the history of music, can happen any day. So watch out!

Watch out!—for maybe he has already long been there and has merely not been noticed. And how should he be noticed? Who is there to notice him? Why, in this of all countries, should a genius be noticed as soon as he is there, when throughout the world geniuses are not noticed so long as they are there, but only once they are no longer there? And this brings us to two other questions: by what will he be recognized, and how can he be encouraged?

Since he is after all going to be overlooked, however exactly I describe him, for safety's sake I will first say how he could be encouraged, so that even if overlooked he would still be encouraged.

There is a widespread opinion that the best way to encourage composers is to perform and publish them. I would call these the second- and third-best. I was twenty-five before I was performed for the first time, and thirty-one when I first had a piece published. As if that were not enough: until the year 1911 (I was then thirty-seven) I had, on my word of honour, *ten* performances in all, even though by then I had already made a great sensation abroad—in France, Germany, and England. Something else: about ten years ago everything I had written had already been published or was ready for the press. And despite the spread of my reputation, in many countries my music was as good as unknown.

Nowadays, everywhere in the world, without a doubt, programme-building is inimical to art and to development, more so than in any other age. What would musicians have to play, what would conductors have to show off their conducting, if all the generations before them had behaved as they do? Would Haydn, Mozart and Beethoven have become known and survived if no conductor had ever had the courage and conscience to do his moral and artistic duty? Would they not have remained as unknown as Bach, who was not discovered till fifty years after his death, and then only by one of the true, creative spirits? What would they play, had all their predecessors neglected their duty and had the same exclusive eye to ephemeral success, letting the great masters of their own time perish?

No doubt about it; on an average, half of all programmes ought to be dedicated to the living. And no doubt about it: at least half this space ought to belong to native composers. That is little enough, but it would certainly meet immediate needs, even if it meant performers faced new tasks for which they were inadequately prepared, having neglected to acquire in good time the knack of inwardly performing an unfamiliar piece of music—the important preliminary stage in all performances. That they are still perplexed by the look of scores to which the educated ones have long since become used—that is a judgement on them and removes all mitigating circumstances.

But suppose so much space were given to living and native composers; that in itself is not enough, as experience will soon show. I have read the names of a large number of American composers who were performed this year. But what is achieved, when a few performers buy themselves out of their moral obligations by performing now a work by this composer, now one by another, giving each of them one performance and then never again? Music is only understood when one goes away singing it and only loved when one falls asleep with it in one's head, and finds it still there on waking up next morning. Is that achieved with a single performance? Achievable? No, it is not achievable even with several performances, but in one way alone: the performer must be the *advocate* of the work and of its author. It must be not merely an honour but a pleasure for him to be able to present this music; it must be a need, an imperative urge, to make it known to other people, to convince them of its beauty, to make propaganda on its behalf and to fight for it. For example, think only of two men such as Liszt and Bülow. Who would dispute such men's right to lead a people? But then who could assign it to anyone smaller? In artistic life a leader is never called to answer. A banker who has speculated illegally will be locked up, a political leader will not be re-elected, a general who has lost a battle will be sacked; but the gentlemen who are disavowed in the most pathetic way by artistic developments get, if possible, one more marble monument, instead of a stone round their necks.

But if such a performer were to possess, as a result of his own ability and knowledge, as a result of his well-founded artistic understanding and powers of judgement, as a result of his character, his capacity for self-sacrifice and his incorruptibility, his selflessness and love of art—if, then, such a performer were to possess such authority and had, in addition, a sense of responsibility, not only toward his own time but also toward the future (that is something nobody gives a thought to, unless it be 'Heaven help us!'), then such a man could yet prove a blessing, and all he did, even his least effective action, would work for the good. Such a man will not only know how to encourage music, he will also be in a position to convince the public that his intervention is necessary, for the public is good, very good, and can sooner be won over to the good, the ideal, than against it, or even to the bad. And despite Mr. Henderson's extremely humorous and lively sketch of the various kinds of average man (nowhere in the world are they basically different), I nonetheless believe as firmly in the good instincts of the public as in the bad instincts of those who dominate the public. But a leader of that kind will also be in a position (since he can read music) to discover for himself the worthwhile composer, the genius, the talent worth encouraging. For me, it is beyond doubt that in America there is no lack of such men. I myself have come to know a number and have heard and read the opinions of others. But they have not the power — only, perhaps, the authority.

(Boston). June 28, 1934

PART IV

CRITICS AND CRITICISM

A LEGAL QUESTION
1909

'Must one, on acquiring admission, deposit one's whole personality in the cloak-room?', asks Mr. Liebstöckl in the News Supplement.[1] That is a legal question, he thinks. He would obviously be glad of a law to clear up this legal uncertainty. Something like: 'On (or surely *after*) acquiring a ticket (complimentary?), one is entitled to take one's whole personality into the concert hall and need not deposit it in the cloakroom.' Who would benefit from such legal protection? Someone who has personality cannot deposit it; and we are not concerned, even here, with those who have none. So the only person we are concerned with here would be someone who has none but behaves as if he had—the person who can deposit one personality and pull on another like a dress—the journalist, for whom the question is merely whether he must deposit his *whole* personality or just a part of it. He would also be the only person able to comply with a law demanding the opposite—the deposition of the personality. But since, when we speak of personality, we do not think of it as something that can be deposited, a legal decision that one *need* not deposit it would surely be at least as superfluous and pointless as, say, a legal decision that one *must* have talent.

No: that is no legal question but a cry of pain, a cry of distress. 'A cry of distress from the depths—of the 9th district',[2] uttered by a supplementary (*Extrablatt*) soul: 'May one not surely remain alive to the extent of expressing pain and joy at will (I mean of doing, not what one is pressed to do but what one fancies doing—even when the things going on are by no means to one's fancy)?' It seems that when Mr. Liebstöckl refers to taking his 'whole personality' into the concert hall, he means his intellect. Were he to deposit that in the cloakroom, then only his physical self would be left. He might fairly feel embarrassed to appear in public clad only in that; not that the addition of his intellect helps much in such matters. It strikes me that public order and morality would not be greatly served if people were barred from taking their whole personality into the concert hall, as they are from covering the seats with any other part of their attire. The physical self, freed from the scrutiny and discipline of the intellectual self, would surely react to pain and joy, pleasure and displeasure, in a way that could be intolerable to its neighbours. One might have the misfortune to find oneself sitting next to a full belly or even a sick gut. So it seems indispensable for the whole personality to be taken along, in so far as this implies intellect; indispensable, in order to prevent the physical personality from expressing pain and joy, pleasure and displeasure—as it fancies.

But Mr. Liebstöckl expects just the opposite, if he is allowed to take his whole personality in with him. He expects that one would in fact be all the less inhibited from expressing pain and joy. So he must mean the physical, not the intellectual personality: in other words, the beast. *That* is what he is unwilling to deposit in the cloakroom. The beast must be in on things, on everything; that is the freedom of the personality, as the upstarts (Blue Book) imagine it.

During the interval of a premiere, an acquaintance asked me to point out Liebstöckl to him. I could not spot him; my acquaintance wanted to help me search and asked what he looked like. 'What does the name Liebstöckl suggest to you?' 'Nothing very nice. So what *does* he look like?' 'A lot nastier than that!' And this is the personality Mr. Liebstöckl refuses to deposit in the cloakroom. He, who looks like the incarnation of ill-will—a nightmare become flesh and beard—he, whom one would rather not meet in a dream—*he* is dead-set on showing off his personality in the concert hall!

During the last quartet performance he is said never to have taken his disdainful eyes off me. I sensed this malevolent, loutish gaze and was forced to look back at him a number of times. Is that not punishment enough for a good quartet? No, not in the eyes of Mr. Liebstöckl's colleague, Mr. Stauber! He complains that I sat in the concert hall armed with a stick. Had I not, would he perhaps have had the courage to go for me? He is wrong; for years now I have been in the habit of carrying a thick stick, but not as a protection against him and his like. Against him, at least, I need no weapon—his beard is enough for me!

If only I could make out what this whole personality of Mr. Liebstöckl consists of. One day he defends the names of Beethoven or Brahms with high-flown words. Against whom? Against the most ideal artist of our time—against Gustav Mahler. Comes the transformation, and Mr. Liebstöckl appears as an operetta librettist. He no longer rakes up the names of the great masters, whose works provide such uplift, and is concerned rather to rake in royalties earned in collaboration with very minor masters, of the kind who still uplift their voices in the City of Song. Which is his 'whole personality'?

To cast doubt on someone's idealism, he taxes it with sensation-mongering and mercenary motives. He knows he is lying; but then he and artistic morality have always had a rather prickly relationship — or, since that sounds like a personal reference — marriage. But it is only a left-handed marriage; with his other hand (and he is right-handed) he writes operetta texts!

Neither his left hand nor his right has, indeed, been a resounding success. The thing that does always go down well and brings applause is his ill-will, which forgoes all human decency so long as he is sure of a laugh. If one believes in transmigration of souls, such ill-will can give one the feeling, which all one's experience is unable to dispel, that something can persist from previous incarnations. What, then, might Mr. Liebstöckl's previous incarnations have been? Imagine the picture: Messrs. Liebstöckl, Stauber, Karpath, etc., have been obliged to deposit their (physical) personalities in the cloakroom, and one is obliged to sit in the concert hall alongside their astral bodies! A frightful idea! More frightful than the one in the legend narrated by Mr. Liebstöckl, where the hero, whatever he may hear and see, however terrible, is forbidden to move a muscle. For Liebstöckl, after all, finds an agreeable solution for his hero: 'He makes a fortune' — and (cf. Mr. Liebstöckl's 'whole personality') also a good operetta ending: '*but also* a beautiful wife'. May I propose a different continuation of the legend, one more in keeping with the wish to 'express pain and joy as one fancies': 'Then the king belched (for he had forgotten he was in the concert hall, and thought he was only in his editorial office), saying: . . .'?

But I am still taking Mr. Liebstöckl too intellectually. I must dig deeper, to find the real reason why he wanted, with his 'echoes of the E-flat minor quartet' (my quartet is in F-sharp minor)[3] to spring to the aid of his colleague Karpath. The latter, having first defended himself in every Viennese editorial column, confessed ruefully in the *Leipziger Signal* that he over-reached himself when he 'expressed his joy or pain out loud' in the concert hall. But in the next sentence he again lifts, with a certain amount of pride, his uncertain amount of head and announces that, by a curious logic, his confession now gives him the right to smile upon his attackers. And smile he does. To be precise, he offers to undergo an examination in 'the theory of harmony, form, and the other musical disciplines'—and smiles, because he hopes nobody will take him up on it.

But when I sent every editor an open letter to Mr. Ludwig Karpath, which challenged him to deposit, not his personality, but some such proof, the letter did not appear in one single paper. Enigmatic goings-on! Have the journalistic gentlemen agreed among themselves not to handle the letter? Or is it a case of 'great minds' thinking alike? Telepathy? Or perhaps merely *telephony*? For I have no way of proving that Mr. Karpath called on all the editors in person.

So dog (Mr. Liebstöckl) has once again not eaten dog (Mr. Karpath); on the contrary, he has encouraged a sleeping dog to go on lying.[4] Of course, in any such case there must be a basis of reciprocity. And I am convinced that if Mr. Karpath were to turn a blind eye, Mr. Liebstöckl would help him close the other one too—a more Christian action than that of the late Adalbert von Goldschmied at the performance of my symphonic poem, *Pelleas und Melisande*. On that occasion Mr. Karpath needed no help in closing both his eyes. Adalbert von Goldschmied, who was sitting behind him, woke him with a kick, bringing him back to reality, so that he could then give his opinion of it. And Karpath gave his opinion: 'Although I listened with the greatest attention, I could not . . .', and found fault with my work. I do not know when he had heard it—before sitting his examination, anyway, and probably after sitting down in the hall minus his personality (body). Intellectually, then! So Mr. Karpath, too, knows of a way to 'see with the mind's eye'—in his sleep!

But Mr. Liebstöckl's colleague Karpath has a friend. And this friend is also a lover of music (a great honour for all concerned). And this music-lover (others call him buffoon, though this has always been Mr. Liebstöckl's other name, but I believe he is called Stauber) shouted to Mr. Bösendorfer after the performance of my quartet, 'Now for the Beethoven—let's have some air in the hall!' This cry for some air in the *Bösendorfer-Saal* re-echoed through the entire provincial press. But, bearing Mr. Liebstöckl, Mr. Stauber, Mr. Karpath, in mind, I can imagine a law really decreeing that these gentlemen's whole personalities, once deposited, were to be hung up in the cloakroom—and that the corresponding astral bodies (otherwise and wrongly called souls) were to be there in the hall. A frightful idea! No, Mr. Liebstöckl is right after all: it is a legal question. But the law would have to run rather differently—conversely. And for the time being, pending such a law, one would have to hang up a note in the foyer: 'The depositing of whole personalities is most strictly forbidden here. The compost-heaps and asparagus beds are next door.'[5]

January 16, 1909

2

AN ARTISTIC IMPRESSION
1909

An artistic impression is substantially the resultant of two components. One, what the work of art gives to the onlooker—the other, what he is capable of giving to the work of art. Since both are variable magnitudes, the resultant, too, is variable, so that with the same work of art it can vary from one individual to the next. Thus the effect exerted by a work of art depends only in part on the work itself. The work of art seems rather to be merely the external stimulus that awakens those forces sensed by us (once they come to mingle with the ones given off by the work of art) as an artistic impression; those forces within the onlooker, which are latent at the same intensity, the same tension, with which they explode —magnitudes that are in every respect predetermined, given. So the intensity of an artistic impression depends on the onlooker's ability to receive even as he gives.

An artistic judgement results from the attempt to describe an artistic impression, to pin it down, by comparing it with other artistic impressions. Such comparison need not necessarily lead to an evaluation. But if a value-judgement is to result, meaning one that will be generally valid, then the person judging must satisfy several conditions. If he is to be worthy of credence, he must be in contact, intellectually and morally, with the main line of cultural and ethical development, or at least with one of its necessary offshoots. He must be outstandingly able to receive artistic impressions, to pin them down, compare, and describe them. Anyone else's value-judgement—for example, the kind a creator often passes on a contemporary—usually has mere curiosity interest. The same applies, for the most part, to the judgement of those whose errors were significant enough to serve as a springboard for the minor truths discovered by others. Any other value-judgement is arrogant, since it is not based on what Schopenhauer calls authority.

A real value-judgement, one of general significance, is a very great rarity, then, while the arrogance that disregards all the conditions and tries to drum up generally valid, authoritative judgements unsupported by a personality that is fully developed and to be taken seriously—such arrogance is all the more wide-spread. Indeed, to confer market-value on something, or withhold it, confers on oneself an illusion of power. But market-value is irrelevant to intrinsic value. For example, in a good year for fruit the demand is relatively lower than the supply, so the market-value is low. Yet when ripe fruit is more plentiful it is also, doubtless, *better*. So even here, where the consumer's judgement can be authentic, supply and demand are not criteria of intrinsic value. On the contrary, the latter can be in downright inverse proportion to the market-value.

Unqualified judgement can at most claim to decide the market-value—a value that can be in inverse proportion to the intrinsic value.

Now one is clear how things stand, one realises how indifferent to unqualified judgement the artist is bound to be; how ludicrous he must find it when the very people with the least vocation, the incompetent, the ignorant, sit in judgement on him and try to lecture him. But for the economic factors involved—and here his greater vulnerability constantly presses on him—they would be 'not worth a curse'.

However, on December 21st a new method of determining market-value burst upon the world. It is indeed the custom hereabouts to evaluate without being competent to do so. But to prevent the object under evaluation from being even considered—to bar its entry into the world—to approach an unknown work with one's judgement already prepared: that, surely, is to simplify the juridical process too radically. Even before, it was in most cases a predictably punitive process, with the accused not even allowed anyone to defend him.

My only appeal against this wrong must be an appeal to the non-participants' sense of justice; the non-participants who perhaps have no suspicion how exactly the disturbers on December 21st *knew in advance that they were going to dislike the work*; the non-participants who perhaps do not even suspect (any more, alas, than I can prove) that the crucial thing behind this *a priori* rejection was—dissonances, of a kind absent from my work: dissonances in the politics— not the work—of art. How else is one to explain why music critics—who should, after all, demand to hear a work repeatedly, so as to form a clear impression of it—tried to prevent even this single performance, by shouting 'Stop!'?

I dare not interpret these symptoms. But I shall not let the hubbub intimidate me. My only request would be—off with the masks! Then I could address my opponents in the words which the current view of *Walküre* finds superfluous: 'Where powers are boldly stirring, I counsel open war.'

3

ABOUT MUSIC CRITICISM
1909

Over the past century the value of knowledge has doubtless been exaggerated. 'Knowledge is power', people believed, and answered the question, 'What about error?', with 'It's human', rather than asking conversely, 'What is human?', and replying, 'To err'. And if in fact to err were equal to being human, then knowledge would indeed equal power. But since being human is equal to erring, then knowledge is merely the power that gets in the way of independent realization and examination, and memory takes over the job of providing a substitute for the independent activity of sharpened senses and a mobile intellect. Strindberg says, 'He thought he knew, whereas he merely remembered'—that is one way. And the rest is taken care of by the mental routine that knows how to call analogous cases to mind and, like any routine, to apply existing means with superficially adequate deftness. However, opposition to knowledge based on memory often goes too far, and many a mediocre brain which could not keep going without mental crutches makes a show of despising knowledge and memory—something legitimate only for a quite different kind of person. For it is one thing to do without one's knowledge, one's memory, in order to confront things

191

as if one were the first who ever looked at them; it is one thing to free oneself of all the presuppositions based on one's training and experience, in order to arrive at a new, intuitive realization—and quite another to be without presuppositions from the outset, because one is untrained.

Our times have promoted those who lack presuppositions. The colossal consumption of *Weltanschauungen*, of beguilingly original philosophical and artistic movements, is indeed a product of misunderstood individualism, the individualism of the Philistine, and it leads to an over-estimation of originality, which prevents our reaching the resting points of clear vision and deliberate, considered examination. *In statu nascendi*, any new truth seems to upset everything hitherto believed and gives the impression that it can solve all the riddles which previously kept mankind vainly wracking its brains. And it looks almost as if the older knowledge were a downright hindrance, as if those best able to develop and spread abroad the law were those who know nothing of old-fashioned rules and practices.[1] These new ideas wooed such people, and not in vain. And so they made the layman into a cultural factor that has proceeded to settle the fate of creative forces in a way only slightly less brutal than that of the old guild members.

In the field of art, and particularly of music, contempt for purely formalistic knowledge, though otherwise well-justified, has had a further result: the layman also turned critic. He was not content, as a simple 'man in the street', to be a juryman, he demanded the position and the power of the 'learned judge', and got it too. At first, indeed, this also had its good side. Wagner's work, entirely rejected by guild musicians unable to realize that a new art is not to be measured by the laws of the old, addressed itself to the mass of people on whom words, poetry, the theatre, make an impression. They acquired the faculty of letting the poetic mood work on them; they found it possible to ignore artifice and submit to those elemental impressions released by music, the language of the subconscious. Powers of discrimination also came into play, and people were able to distinguish between originality and imitation. They developed organs as sensitive as the musician's absolute pitch and formal sense—more sensitive, indeed, since they could push ahead and reach the essence, could follow the creator even to the point where for the learned, too, poetry begins and shop-talk has to stop. That was how the 'mood-critic'[2] came into the world.

But the partisans of Wagner, Liszt, Hugo Wolf and Bruckner grew old. Old, above all, in relation to art, which is constantly self-renewing. But then simply senile, too. And they thus formed a closed block, more overbearing, more opposed to developments than their predecessors had been. For these former revolutionaries took their past as the present, destined to suppress the future. And since they remained ignorant, they were not even up to their task of providing a more tangible criterion for aesthetic evaluation than the ephemeral one of mood and poetic content—which remained a criterion only so long as that particular mood could still exert its spell. Thus as new creators appeared, the mood-critic found himself in a far more helpless state than his predecessors.

The natural reaction against Wagner, the theatre-musician, had produced a flowering of so-called absolute music. At first it took the form of song and programme music; later, more and more, of purely symphonic music. This music was unwilling to go on being the serving-maid to poetry; it cut out the detour of first expressing unconscious sensations in the language of consciousness, and then retranslating this translation into the language of the unconscious. At this point the ageing mood-critic was at a complete loss.

But his successors were not young musicians but again mood-critics—this time of necessity. Important musicians with a care for their calling cannot write for our papers. In Paris it is possible, and since Berlioz many, such as Debussy and Dukas, have written daily criticism. But among us a musician goes to a newspaper only when he is unfit to be even a 'professor' of singing or the piano. That was how these emergency mood-critics rose to power. Their calling had been to the remotest fields of reporting, and now they became the chosen ones of art. If a court reporter had once been a choirboy, that was enough qualification to review music. The only excuse for the ensuing lack of standards is the helplessness and insecurity of the ignorant *parvenu*. If they stood singly before you, they made no bones about their ignorance, crawled devoutly, took everything you could possibly tell them as gospel truth, and in their misery begged for consideration only *vis-à-vis* third parties who must, please, not be allowed to see them exposed. Next day one would be amazed to read in the paper the judgements and ideas one had presented to them the day before, pronounced in a tone of self-confidence entirely as their own intellectual property. Then they could once again feel they were the masters, the 'authorities' (as Mahler said), partners in the World Power Company (Limited). One was lectured as if Beckmesser had never existed.

But the lack of standards had to be covered up, and since mood no longer did the trick, knowledge had to lend a hand. Partly out of historical reference books but also with a few technical expressions—counterpoint, instrumentation, ability,[3] dissonance; these were the arsenal of learned weapons against the new. I gave some thought to the question of why precisely these people, who, unlike the guild musicians or the Wagnerians, did not believe themselves the defenders of a culture, threw their weight against the new with such hate. I discovered that, apart from *Schadenfreude* and envy of those with creative potency, it was merely a moral depression that came of being constantly obliged to pretend they understand or like something that is miles above their heads and leaves them entirely cold. Thus one can be sure that when a music critic speaks of an author's 'knowledge', it is more than ever a proof that he has none of his own; when he refers to counterpoint, all he knows is 'the name comes from . . .'; if he wails about dissonances, his ears are incapable of telling them from consonances.

The music of our time presents innumerable problems. But who sees and pays attention to them? One must, in the last event, admit that earlier conservative critics were after all capable of discussing the problem of whether it is effective or admissible for the scherzo to come before the adagio, or whether the second movement may be in F-sharp when the work is in F.[4] Nowadays that is old hat, but one needs to know what the point at issue is. Then one would not simply skirt problems entirely; it would then be impossible for Charpentier, Strauss, Debussy, Dukas to write 'musical prose' with never a word of attention given to it. To be sure, the older critics would have resisted, would have put forth all the aesthetic pros and cons, have proved that it is impossible, even though the masters have shown them that it *is* possible. Much nonsense would have been written, but there would have been the resistance that alone makes a victory worthwhile. Our music critics are in very truth unfit to be even cannon-fodder in the battles of art. They wailed about dissonances while the problem of the one-movement symphony swept by; they wailed about dissonances while new possibilities of melodic development were showing themselves; they even wailed about dissonances when none was there—as when, in discussing a concert of my pupils', one particularly sensitive pair of ears declared a string quartet, whose harmony demonstrably goes only a little beyond Schubert, to be a striking product of my harmful influence.

If one is to be receptive to a work of art, and gain an impression of it, one's own imagination must play a creative part. (I recently found this long-standing idea of mine in letters of Oscar Wilde printed in *Der Fackel*.) A work of art bestows only the warmth one is able to dispense on one's own account, and almost every artistic impression is, ultimately, a product of the listener's imagination. It is indeed released by the work of art, but only if one has available receiving apparatus tuned in the same way as the transmitting apparatus. To convert an artistic impression into an artistic judgement, one must be practised at interpreting one's own unconscious feelings; one must know one's own leanings, and the way in which one reacts to impressions. As for dispensing artistic judgements: one must then be able to compare artistic impressions with each other; either through one's nature, which must not lack characteristic qualities, or at least through one's training (education plus development) one must find a vantage point from which it is possible to gain a closer insight into the nature of the work concerned. One must have a sense of the past and an intuition of the future. Finally, one may indeed go wrong; but then at least one must be someone!

How far from this our critics are! The true cause is, in fact, incompetence, for ill-will can never be so damaging as stupidity. A powerful mind persecuting an artist, perhaps for revenge, will think up everything that is worth fighting against. A stupid man, on the other hand, is harmful even when he is dishonest. For example, he is in favour of simplicity. But if he hears something simple, then he says to himself, 'I understand that, and since it pleases me it must be bad'—and abuse follows. If he hears something he does not understand at all and dislikes very much, then he knows it is something particularly significant—and abuse follows. Or he may indeed praise, but only to annoy a colleague he envies and whose job he would like. Or he is in favour of melody. But if one writes melodiously, then the critic complains of banality, so confessing that he enjoyed it. Not that one tries, but it would be hard to do anything right for them. For they are unaware of their own leanings, or else, they know, if aware, that they are something to be kept carefully hidden, a certain godlike quality being a necessary part of the newspaperman's façade.

Criticism's influence on the public has completely disappeared. Nobody any longer cares about its judgement. For either one is not interested in the whole business, or one is a layman oneself and therefore understands just as much as the editorial gentlemen. Either one was there and knows how it was, or one was not there, so does not know. One can give no credence to reporting—

it sees what it wants to see and not what really happened; makes a success into a fiasco, hisses into applause; projects its own attitude on to the audience—for the critic usually lacks the courage to stand alone with his opinion. If he feels himself in accord with part of the public, even a small part, then he says the whole public was indignant or enthusiastic. If it is quite impossible to misinterpret the audience's attitude, he turns to his colleagues to protect him from public opinion. So the public is now abused along with the artists, now praised along with the critic. But true it hardly ever is; it hardly ever comes out free of distortions and insinuations ('friendship', 'clique'), even on the occasions when the truth would have the same effect as a lie.

The reader attaches little importance to it any more, for one knows the motives at work in nearly all cases; one knows the trends, the personal friendships and enmities that are decisive. But something always sticks, in good or bad: praise and blame—ineffective in themselves, since everyone feels the lack of respect with which they are handed out—are transmuted into more commercially solid values; publicity is made for an artist, or animosity aroused against him, according to the relationship he allows the critic to have with him. And that is a kind of power, if hardly to be compared with the power of the almighty ones of former times, who could bestow and withhold appointments. Nowadays so much is pettier, and this is too—pinpricks where once there was a knife in the back. But it is cumulative; a thousand pinpricks paralyse as surely, perhaps, as a single knife-thrust killed. Perhaps this power is no more dangerous than the old kind, but it is more harrassing. It is more unscrupulous, since the division among many reduces the degree of responsibility; everyone's defence can be, 'Look at him, and him, and him—they're just as guilty as me.' Him and him, and him—one just cannot lay hands on all of them, so that each individual is safe in a way unknown to men who used to throw down their own personal stakes. It takes little courage to join in but a great deal to resist. One is not done away with, but one can go under, disappear, and that is the worst thing of all. No wonder, therefore, that a certain timidity and lack of decision is evident in those to whom this judgement does not apply in its full rigour. Particularly not in Vienna. Although our 'gentle air' cannot improve the way hate and envy look, it does seem not to encourage firmness and decision. All is compromise; caution and refinement are everywhere. Everything has to 'make a good impression'—whether or not it is any good: the *impression* is the main thing.

196

So it would almost be better were there not the few 'decent men'. Were there not these few righteous men in Sodom and Gomorrha, perhaps God would repent of his ways, become angry and make it possible for a new culture to arise out of the salt desert. That is a feeble hope. In Vienna there will always be a few righteous men, but they will have to keep on terms with the unrighteous; a few decent fellows, who keep their disapproval to themselves and so get on in the friendliest way with the corrupt; a few twenty-year-olds with the detachment and composure of men of sixty, able to divert their braver impulses into the grooves of caution and sweet reason; and a few men of forty, as unreliable as fourteen-year-old school-children, as mischievous, with as defective a sense of responsibility, and as lacking in respect for things they are incapable of under-standing.[5]

4

SLEEPWALKER
1912

It is not in a composer's power to do more for the critic than this: to write works, if possible to have them printed, and to persuade people to perform them. Admittedly, since the music critic usually cannot read a score, he gains little from the two first-named ways of meeting him, and if he is to arrive at an impression, or at least make the reader believe he has arrived at one, he has to rely on point three—the performance, and on one thing more—a kind of somnambulistic ability which is hard to understand.

It seems that the critic relies more on this somnambulistic ability than on the performance itself. He 'trusts the author with neither eye nor ear', but solely with his sleep-walking spirit. To that end, going to sleep is an indispensable preliminary; going to the concert is not. Since his spirit is in any case on its travels, the critic can naturally afford not to be at the performance himself; he can safely stay at home, for the main thing is his spirit, and that will sleep-walk without him anyway.

Since the music critic, Leopold Schmidt, was not to be seen during three items of the matinee concert of my music, his spirit was evidently there. For part of the programme Mr. Schmidt was identified by reliable witnesses, while his spirit was noticed by no one. To compensate, his spirit manifests itself in the Tuesday edition. And it seems it was bored—even though it wasn't sitting with Mr. Schmidt. And it lays the blame on the man who gave the concert. But apart from that, it saw and heard things that were missed by everyone who was present in body and spirit. For example, it heard Egon Petri making random noises at the piano, although he is in London. And did not see that the piano pieces were played by Louis Closson—the name was in the programme, which, like everything written in words, would usually be the thing that stimulates the critic most. A remarkable spirit! On the other hand, it heard a song by Maeterlinck being sung,[1] and found it superfluous—superfluous! Indeed, for this is a spirit, a *super*-natural being—to hear Dr. Anton von Webern announce that this piece had to be omitted. Although the hall was as quiet as a mouse! Just as if a spirit were there! Remarkable spirit!

Might not Mr. Leopold Schmidt follow the example of all right-thinking men, who long ago stopped relying on his spirit? Even if the ornaments of 'artistic theory' with which he decorates his little articles turn out in an ever more senile way, he could at least improve the reliability of his reporting by using his eyes more—nobody asks him to use his ears—and looking carefully at the programmes of artists he condemns unheard.[2]

5

THE MUSIC CRITIC
1912

I was not very hopeful of an answer from Mr. Schmidt. But now he has been so rash, I fear he will get into worse trouble than had he kept quiet. He would have done better to console himself with the thought that the public quickly forgets.

His concern that 'such attacks could shake his readers' faith' is baseless—faith such as that will always recover. I have subjected critics to worse ordeals and their readers still trust them across the street. Mr. Schmidt is surely taking me too seriously. Neither his position nor his influence could be in any danger from me, so long as both of us are alive. People will have smiled at him a little, and this time perhaps they will laugh. But his calling will certainly emerge unscathed from the affair, and for this reason: no one has any other idea of a critic's calling than whatever will be left over when this matter is disposed of.

Surely it was incautious of him to take me so seriously. To be consistent, he should have stuck to what he wrote of me when my Sextet was performed for the first time in Berlin—'a dilettante playing with sound-effects'; he should have done as many other people do and ignored what he said in criticizing my symphonic poem conducted by Fried:[1] 'Schoenberg will have to be taken seriously.' Mr. Schmidt should have joined in the laughter, mine and many other people's, at the little joke I permitted myself at the expense of his dignity. The whole matter was treated as the merest side-issue, a few witty remarks were made, and there was no need for him to get even more excited because wit is not a feature of my compositions: it has no place there. Here, on the other hand, it had. For however strongly I may share the reactions of, say, Wagner, to critics in general, I still cannot take individual critics seriously. And whether the nonsense talked about my music comes from Mr. Schulz and Mr. Müller, or Mr. Meyer and Mr. Schmidt, is a matter of such indifference to me that I can only refer to it jokingly, with the humour that Mr. Schmidt finds lacking in my compositions.

But if Mr. Schmidt is determined to take me quite seriously, he could have found other and better opportunities. A fair number of my works have appeared in print. Mr. Schmidt is doubtless as versatile as he is influential, and if out of all the activities he practises, all the many things he teaches, he can actually do even half, then one may safely assume he can read music. Were he to do so, and look at the works which were indeed printed to just that end, then he would not need to describe as 'a dilettante playing about' the work of someone whose score shows a very practised hand even at a casual glance. But let us assume that he is even shorter of time than of ability; there is nothing for it, then, but to go conscientiously to the concerts in which artists he wishes to take seriously perform their works. Otherwise one will have to doubt his seriousness, or his ability to take anything seriously. But—and to me this is the main thing I was trying to say in those jokes Mr. Schmidt feels as a personal attack—when I give a concert, then he, Schmidt, has to be there. Not for my sake, for I am quite indifferent to what is written about me. I have proved this over a period of fifteen years. But for the sake of 'his readers' faith', about which he is so concerned, and for the sake of the post his boss has given him, without anyone's having so far had a chance to confirm that God also made *His* necessary contribution.

And the fact that Mr. Schmidt did not hear the whole concert, but hardly the sixth part of it, that is clear to everyone who was there, from his sentence— 'No such announcement (of the omission of the Maeterlinck song) occurred during my presence in the hall.' Since this cancellation occurred only a few moments before the start of the fourth item on the programme, when the hall was quiet as a mouse, and since it must have been heard by all those present, then Mr. Schmidt was not in the hall for that item. In my first article I did not dare make this accusation, nor did I need to, since he did not mention that particular item. But after the confession that is to be read between the lines, I would almost take the risk, did I not prefer to investigate something else that is also there between the lines. Mr. Schmidt skirts with suspicious care the question whether he heard my piano pieces—he writes such things as 'Arnold Schönberg, and him I did hear.' (Yes, as he himself says, eight or ten of the twenty songs that were performed. But what about the other songs and the piano pieces?) Mr. Schmidt feels 'obliged to characterize as dishonourable such a way of fighting.' (I am not fighting, I merely made a joke.) But what word would he use for *this* way of fighting, that picks its way round an open confession by using ambiguous sentences designed to divert attention from the facts? It is, after all, not open to doubt that had Mr. Schmidt heard all the songs and the piano pieces, he could simply write the sentence, 'I heard the piano pieces.' He could do that, without sacrificing his personal stylistic touch, in one pure, simple sentence. Why doesn't he? What name does one give this way of fighting?

I do not want to be as malicious as Mr. Schmidt, nor as offensive as stylistic incompetence always becomes. So I will give it a name: helplessness!

Helplessness; Mr. Schmidt lost all his presence of mind. And that makes me so sorry for him, that I will believe his naïve explanation that in his programme the name Closson was crossed out and Petri written over it in ink. And I will also bear in mind that the gentleman is no longer rightly capable of defending himself against the associations that crowd in upon him, so that when he refers to authors he has to list every name known to him. And I will grant him that, as he asserts, he 'could have listed still more authors'. I take him at his word.

But really, what is one to call such incompetence, such inability to tell which associations are still relevant to the subject under discussion, and which not?

Mr. Schmidt says I am 'clinging to inessentials to divert attention from the main issue.' But he is wrong; I am clinging to inessentials to make the main issue clear: the nonchalance with which critics play with lives, even when they have recognized that they will have to take an artist seriously.

These same people who mark up against an artist his slightest oversight, should they chance to notice it, are incapable of carrying out in a blameless way the ludicrously easy and insignificant work their job demands. So strict with others, they ask for the greatest allowances to be made for themselves and take as a personal attack the resistance of someone who has already been exposed to attacks of the crudest and most offensive kind.

This Mr. Schmidt knows just as well as do I, and every right-thinking person, that I am right. And, for all that, he calls my way of fighting dishonourable.

So I had better stop.

For it seems I have, after all, descended to a level that is beneath me.

Prague, February 25, 1912

6

MUSICAL HISTORIANS

c. 1915

Musical historians need not really concern themselves with contemporary problems. There is enough material for them in fields where scholarship has already handed out its opinions. Moreover, their bird's-eye view means they see the facts in the blurred way demanded by historical insight, whereas in the bright light of the present day, events blind their eyes—they could never pick out a grain of corn. So it would take a bird-brain view to be able to assert that a historian has a panoramic view of anything more, or sees clearly. Nor is it any help here to use foreign words, however uncharacteristic they may be. If a musical historian describes my style as 'poly-ody', that is something there was no need for; and he should not have been lured by his publishers, 'in order not to neglect the present, either', into discussing all manner of things he does not understand. Otherwise, complications ensue such as this: the same musical historian quotes five bars by me, using them to point out that 'in the individual instance' my style descends almost to 'rudimentary sticking-together of parts'. 'The individual instance'! And in order to arrive at this—in order not to lose the over-all view because of all the other individual instances, no matter how character-istic—in order, in a word, to produce the blur the historian needs so that his short-sight can count as clairvoyance, the 'researcher' addressed me with a request (that is how people research nowadays) to write out for him, from my works, a few passages characteristic of my polyphony. I did him the kindness, and by way of thanks he makes a fool of himself. I was almost obliged to try to save his reputation, in order to clear myself. But it is too difficult. I do indeed realize that for a historian the idea of artistic creation tends to touch off the asso-ciation 'sticking-together' (for how could a mass of notes turn into a book un-less they were stuck together with something?)—but only if he would not, in turning to the most recent composers, go on to refer to incompetent botchers of the kind who have always pushed themselves to the fore in times of stylistic transition. For another historian (who nowadays concerns himself less with the past than with the future—that of his son—and twists present and future events to suit his son's requirements) could not miss the opportunity, even if he were an unnatural father (which fortunately he is not), of opening the road to the most distant future by quoting the said authority to clear the most talented younger composers out of the way.[1] In a dilution that so exactly fits the needs of the broad public, even the science of history, otherwise harmless, becomes poison. To hinder the spread of the poison, one must induce as many people as possible to convince themselves, by reading the book right through, that this science is harmless. I am not reading it: I have to stay unenlightened, since I am partly to blame; I should not have sent the scrap of paper with the 'individual instances' on it. I realize this, beg for punishment, and shall learn from it.

Berlin, Südende, c. 1915

7

THOSE WHO COMPLAIN ABOUT THE DECLINE
1923

The main thing impressing the decline or downfall of our art and culture on all these Spenglers, Schenkers, and so forth, has been an awareness of themselves as totally lacking in creative talent. A natural and very simple reaction to such findings would have been contempt for themselves, not even for others comparably impotent. For that to happen, though, their realization would have had to be *clear* and conscious. But such people are outstandingly good at suppressing everything of the kind; their self-preservative instinct triumphs, everyone else can decline, so long as it helps *them* to get to the top and stay there. Nowadays, according to such prophets — the only ones 'with honour' in everybody's country — the creative disposition no longer exists; what does exist, plentifully, is critical trash such as themselves, and these are the only ones still to have ideas, to possess creative gifts, even — the only geniuses, then! So there are no more geniuses, only critics. But if the latter are geniuses after all, then geniuses *do* exist; if they are not, then there is no reason to give them credence, for anyone knows as much as non-genius! The difference between the two kinds of person lies precisely in what they know or don't know: secret science.

The Fatherland extends to these false prophets an incomprehensible amount of credit — it is downright inexhaustible! Fiasco follows fiasco, on the largest scale, yet the words written by these men, who can do less than anybody, stay in business, in the same old way, alongside works whose value they have contested. Simply as curiosities, of course, and only thanks to the existence of the works they oppose. All the same, the tendency to start believing them again is always there. But the remarkable thing (or, rather, the characteristic thing) is that, in my case, respect for Spengler or Schenker never lasts very long! And it is too stupid of me, to let myself be impressed anew, time and again, by these loud-mouths. Although I see they are merely thrashing about with tasteful turns of phrase (Hauer does the same), although I see through their arbitrary clockwork mechanism, I fall for it every time; those who shout the loudest win the day.

At least I never *praised* Spengler, but I am genuinely sorry for what I have said about Schenker. I so enjoy paying due tribute, or tempering criticism by dwelling on whatever there is to praise—but I almost believe that here I am in the wrong, and that this case calls for action with a firm hand, or even, perhaps, foot.

Mödling, June 9, 1923

PART V

TWELVE-TONE COMPOSITION

1

TWELVE-TONE COMPOSITION
1923

In twelve-tone composition consonances (major and minor triads) and also the simpler dissonances (diminished triads and seventh chords)—in fact almost everything that used to make up the ebb and flow of harmony—are, as far as possible, avoided. But this is not because of any natural law of the new art. It is, presumably, just one manifestation of a reaction, one that does not have its own special causes but derives from another manifestation—which it tries to contradict, and whose laws are therefore the same, basically, as its own. At the root of all this is the unconscious urge to try out the new resources independently, to wrest from them possibilities of constructing forms, to produce with them alone all the effects of a clear style, of a compact, lucid and comprehensive presentation of the musical idea. To use here the old resources in the old sense saves trouble— the trouble of cultivating the new—but also means passing up the chance of enjoying whatever can *only* be attained by new resources when the old ones are excluded!

A later time will perhaps (!) be allowed to use both kinds of resources in the same way, one alongside the other, just as recently a mixed style, partly homophonic, partly polyphonic, permitted these two principles of composition (which in fact differed far more) to mix—although it would be stretching a point to call it a happy mixture.

The weightiest assumption behind twelve-tone composition is this thesis:

Whatever sounds together (harmonies, chords, the result of part-writing) plays its part in expression and in presentation of the musical idea in just the same way as does all that sounds successively (motive, shape, phrase, sentence, melody, etc.), and it is equally subject to the law of comprehensibility.

This law, which I was the first to utter and accord its true significance, has the following results:

(a) in homophonic forms, for the sake of the principal part's development, a certain economy governs the harmony, thanks to which it is in a position to exert a decisive influence on the development of the structure (contrasts, climaxes, turning-points, intensifications, variations).

(b) in polyphonic music, motivic shapes, themes, phrases and the like never succeed in stretching beyond a certain length (that is how the same sort of economy applies here), and are never developed, never split off new shapes and are seldom varied: for all (almost all) development takes place through alteration of the mutual relation to each other of the various components of the idea. These are not merely present within one part, but from the outset the idea consists of several parts, each containing a quite definite component of the idea. And as the mutual relationship of the simultaneous sounds alters, the components not only can remain unaltered but even must, since otherwise there is no assurance that a wholly new relationship (the new derivation from the idea as treated) will come about!

(c) in twelve-tone composition one need not ask after the more or less dissonant character of a sound-combination, since the combination as such (ignoring whether its effect creates a mood or not) is entirely outside the discussion as an element in the process of composition. This combination will not develop, or, better, it is not *it* that develops, but the relationship of the twelve tones to each other develops, on the basis of a particular prescribed order (motive), determined by the inspiration (the idea!). So here a consonant opening chord would not be a hint of a tonal region, nor would a dissonant one bring with it a resolution. (But then what sense is there in using such chords, if the formal consequences they lead to are not followed, because not felt?)

In twelve-tone composition the matter under discussion is in fact the succession of tones mentioned, whose comprehensibility as a musical idea is independent of whether its components are made audible one after the other or more or less simultaneously. But perhaps (or even, certainly) the further development and the tempo of the presentation depend on whether in its first form it was sufficiently comprehensible, or, on the contrary, whether it was perhaps too comprehensible (laws of popular expression!).

May 9, 1923

HAUER'S THEORIES
1923

I

All the laws so apodictically set forth by Hauer—laws based on the principle I expressed—are wrong. These laws which he leaves so mystically unproven, and behind which he would like to keep cosmic causes and occult parallels hidden— whether they are present or not: he does not know them and I certainly have more inkling of them than he has, otherwise I could not have expressed the principle. That is to say, these laws are wrong insofar as it is important for the musician.

It is not a matter of inventing kinds of form that will make it possible to accommodate the twelve tones without repetition; this is merely a means to an end, a new means to an old end.

With the renunciation of the formal advantages inherent in tonal cohesion, presentation of the idea has become rather harder; it lacks the external rounding-off and self-containedness that this simple and natural principle of composition brought about better than did any of the others used alongside it. At least, none was able to achieve so much simply by its presence: rhythmic relatedness could not do anything similar, nor could motivic repetition, nor any of the more complicated ones (which are indeed more apt to disrupt than to further cohesion— sequences, variation, development, etc.). For in a key, opposites are at work, binding together. Practically the whole thing consists exclusively of opposites, and this gives the strong effect of cohesion. To find means of replacing this is the task of *the theory of twelve-tone composition.*

May 8, 1923

II

Hauer looks for laws. Good. But he looks for them where he will not find them. I say that we are obviously as nature around us is, as the cosmos is. So that is also how our music is. But then our music must also be as we are (if two magnitudes both equal a third . . .). But then from our nature alone I can deduce how our music is (bolder men than I would say, 'how the cosmos is!'). Here, however, it is always possible for me to keep humanity as near or as far off as my perceptual needs demand—I can inspect it from in front, and from behind, from right or left, above or below, without or within; if I find there is no other way of getting to know it from within, I can even dissect it. In the case of the cosmos all this would really be very hard to manage, if not impossible, and no success in cosmic dissection[1] will ever earn it any particular respect!

May 9, 1923

III

J. M. Hauer's essay in *Die Musik*[2] (16th year, vol. 2, November 1923) prompts me finally to state my attitude to Hauer firmly. I can point to certain things that have happened in the past—directly, in particular, to many polemical passages in my *Harmonielehre* (revised edition, 1922, pp. 487–8); indirectly, to the basic principles of musical composition in general, as positively formulated in this work. But it will be advisable to sum up here the most important points, or in some cases to present them anew.

I find above all that the expression, 'atonal music', is most unfortunate—it is on a par with calling flying 'the art of not falling', or swimming 'the art of not drowning'. Only in the language of publicity is it thought adequate to emphasize in this way a negative quality of whatever is being advertised. ('Untearable picture-books', for example: should one not recommend the pictures or the text, rather than what they are printed on?) Otherwise a musician will still call his music *Tonkunst* even if it renounces the use of tones (*Töne*). And should it all be without dynamic variation, he will still think he has written music, and should it be without melody, or at least be found so, his term for it will still be 'endless melody'. The expression is certainly unfortunate, then. But it is no such great misfortune, for one may reckon that in a short while linguistic conscience will have become so dulled to this expression that it will provide a pillow, soft as paradise, on which to rest.

In the aforementioned polemic in the *Harmonielehre* I also show that this expression is *wrong*: with tones only what is tonal, in keeping with the nature of tones, can be produced; there must at least be that connection of tones based on the tonal, which has to exist between any two tones if they are to form a progression that is at all logical and 'comprehensible; an opposite, 'atonal', can no more exist among tones and tone-relationships than can an opposite 'aspectral' or 'acomplementary', among colours and progressions of colours. (For what follows, see the *Harmonielehre*, pp. 487–8). Moreover the expression, atonal, cannot be taken seriously as an expression, since that was not how it first came about; a journalist derived it by analogy from *amusisch*,[3] as a means of over-aggressive characterization—such, at least, was the context in which I first noticed it. That could also explain why it is an exaggeration, and why it is inexact; journalism needs gesticulating expressions, which do not strike dead-centre, because it must be able to withdraw everything next day; all these things said 'without obligation!'. But expressions in aesthetics must sit better, should not originate in satire (*Geusen*!),[4] nor should they scream as publicity does.

Just as this expression is imperfect, so, I find, is everything in Hauer's theories. He starts from the statement which already appeared in the first edition of my *Harmonielehre* (1911): 'For I have noticed that tone-doublings, octaves, seldom occur. This is perhaps explained by the fact that the tone doubled would become predominant and so turn into a kind of tonic, which it may scarcely be.' (Note the hypothetical form of this sentence and compare it with Hauer.) Hauer uses this sentence in his pamphlet, *Vom Wesen des Musikalischen* (*Of the Essence of the Musical*), 1920: 'Its *nomos* lies in the fact that within a certain succession of tones no tone may be repeated and none may be left out.' (May!!) 'Primal law of all melody, that no tone should take on physical predominance (the sense of a dominating tonic), not even . . .' It is obvious that this idea lies unspoken in mine (p. 469). My reasons for keeping it unspoken lay partly in the greater delicacy with which I go about things (p. 470: 'I refrain from further description'), but partly in the fact that this side of the idea is not to be realized just like that. For while it is quite possible to avoid octave-doublings, it is completely impossible to refrain from tone-repetition in such a way that the omission has an effect and can be pointed out—unless one uses some primitive, constantly perceptible, wholly unconcealed, openly visible pre-existing scheme, from which at any time and without any effort on one's own part the fact of non-repetition can be perceived. But naturally it cannot come about, to the degree Hauer intends, in an artistic way—the way, for example, that motivic working-out needs to be concealed and yet effective, basic yet also felt on the surface. For in only one case is the return of each tone delayed until all twelve others have occurred—that is, when the same succession of tones is used all the time. But insofar as one does not do this, the gaps become completely irregular and there must even be times when the shortest is used: immediate repetition. A purely external counting-system will be unable to make this construction in any way effective, and one that was noticeable would necessitate formal construction of a primitiveness appropriate only to primitive ideas at the lowest stages of the spirit's development.

That is the problem as it stands, something I have seen long and clearly. And when in the summer of 1921 I believed I had found a form that fulfils all my requirements of a form, I nearly fell into an error similar to Hauer's: I too believed at first that I had 'found the only possible way'. Things went better for me than for Hauer; he had found one possibility, but I had found the key to many possibilities—as I very soon realized! Hauer's mistake I find very illuminating; the fact that he made it and that he had to make it. He sought his solution in the cosmos. I limited myself to the human brain available to me; what was to be discovered here would necessarily correspond to the cosmos, if brain and cosmos have anything at all in common with each other. Either we are tied to universal laws, in which case they are also at work within us, or our brain creates independently of the cosmic laws, in which case it is superfluous to search among the latter, since we can neither comprehend nor perceive them. But I believe that our brain (to the extent that we can comprehend the cosmos with it and with our other comprehending faculties—intuition, feeling, etc.) certainly functions according to the laws of the cosmos, even if it is not identical with it, and permits us to comprehend and perceive only whatever is the cosmos. So why such zeal? A musician is always more likely to discover the secrets, if not of the cosmos, then at least those of tones, along 'tonal' paths, than to be able to apply even fairly appropriately the laws of the universe discovered more or less correctly by astronomy. (The intellects concerned would answer for those with their lives; but on the other hand, none of them would risk anything on behalf of what an educated present-day man has gathered ready-made from his schooldays, and still less for the conclusions drawn by an amateur from such extracts and compilations!). I understand nothing of astronomy, but I know what great nonsense even great intellects come up with when they move into territory foreign to them. Into musical composition, for example. Astronomers impress me less than astronomy; there are certainly as few able and informed people here as in the field of counterpoint. But: before one who knows it as I do counterpoint, before this one man, I should be glad to know myself on safe ground, and should be sorry to make a fool of myself. And I believe that is all one can hope for here.[5]

begun November 9, 1923

3

'SCHOENBERG'S TONE-ROWS'
1936

Mr. Richard S. Hill's article, 'Schoenberg's Tone-Rows and the Tonal Systems of the Future', shows a highly astonishing amount of work of research based on much ability and knowledge to find out what he was looking for. I myself, who was sometimes forced by bothersome inquiries to analyse the way in which I used the rows in certain parts of a work—I myself know how difficult it is often to get a result. No wonder I admire very much as well the sagacity and shrewdness which enabled him to resolve these problems with such a security that he can use his results as a basis to criticize them, but appreciate not less the steadiness and diligence applied for such results. But perhaps because I am more a composer than, as Mr. Hill calls me, 'an able and ingenious theorist', I find this diligence applied in the wrong place.

At the very beginning, when I used for the first time rows of twelve tones in the fall of 1921, I foresaw the confusion which would arise in case I were to make publicly known this method. Consequently I was silent for nearly two years. And when I gathered about twenty of my pupils together to explain to them the new method in 1923, I did it because I was afraid to be taken as an imitator of Hauer, who, at this time, published his *Vom Melos zur Pauke*.[1] I could show that I was on the way to this method for more than ten years and could prove so by examples of works written during this time. But, at the same time, already I did not call it a 'system' but a 'method', and considered it as a tool of composition, but not as a theory. And therefore I concluded my explanation with the sentence: 'You use the row and compose as you had done it previously.'[2] That means: 'Use the same kind of form or expression, the same themes, melodies, sounds, rhythms as you used before.'

213

What I feared, happened. Although I had warned my friends and pupils to consider this as a change in compositional regards, and although I gave them the advice to consider it only as a means to fortify the logic, they started counting the tones and finding out the methods with which I used the rows. Only to explain understandably and thoroughly the idea, I had shown them a certain number of cases. But I refused to explain more of it, not the least because I had already forgotten it and had to find it myself. But principally because I thought it would not be useful to show technical matters which everybody had to find for himself and could do so. This is also the error of Mr. Hill. He also is counting tones and wants to know how I use them and whether I do it consequently.

At first I have had to recall that consequence is not an exigency of art. That is wherein art and science differ principally. While science has to demonstrate its problems perfectly and completely without any omission and from every point of view, and has therefore to proceed systematically, logically and consequently, art presents only a certain number of *interesting* cases and strives for perfection by the manner of presentation. Therefore art is more inclined to choose its cases according to variety rather than to system, according to structural qualifications rather than to consequence. To mention such commonplace wisdom should appear superficial, were it not that the theorists always fall into the error of believing their theories to be rules for composers instead of symptoms of the works, rules which a composer has to obey, instead of peculiarities which are extracted from the works. Of course, these rules ask for consequence, for logic and systematic procedure.

4

COMPOSITION WITH TWELVE TONES (1)
1941

I

To understand the very nature of creation one must acknowledge that there was no light before the Lord said: 'Let there be Light.' And since there was not yet light, the Lord's omniscience embraced a vision of it which only His omnipotence could call forth.

We poor human beings, when we refer to one of the better minds among us as a creator, should never forget what a creator is in reality.

A creator has a vision of something which has not existed before this vision.

And a creator has the power to bring his vision to life, the power to realize it.

In fact, the concept of creator and creation should be formed in harmony with the Divine Model; inspiration and perfection, wish and fulfilment, will and accomplishment coincide spontaneously and simultaneously. In Divine Creation there were no details to be carried out later; 'There was Light' at once and in its ultimate perfection.

Alas, human creators, if they be granted a vision, must travel the long path between vision and accomplishment; a hard road where, driven out of Paradise, even geniuses must reap their harvest in the sweat of their brows.

Alas, it is one thing to envision in a creative instant of inspiration and it is another thing to materialize one's vision by painstakingly connecting details until they fuse into a kind of organism.

Alas, suppose it becomes an organism, a homunculus or a robot, and possesses some of the spontaneity of a vision; it remains yet another thing to organize this form so that it becomes a comprehensible message 'to whom it may concern'.

II

Form in the arts, and especially in music, aims primarily at comprehensibility. The relaxation which a satisfied listener experiences when he can follow an idea, its development, and the reasons for such development is closely related, psychologically speaking, to a feeling of beauty. Thus, artistic value demands comprehensibility, not only for intellectual, but also for emotional satisfaction. However, the creator's *idea* has to be presented, whatever the *mood* he is impelled to evoke.

Composition with twelve tones has no other aim than comprehensibility. In view of certain events in recent musical history, this might seem astonishing, for works written in this style have failed to gain understanding in spite of the new medium of organization. Thus, should one forget that contemporaries are not final judges, but are generally overruled by history, one might consider this method doomed. But, though it seems to increase the listener's difficulties, it compensates for this deficiency by penalizing the composer. For composing thus does not become easier, but rather ten times more difficult. Only the better-prepared composer can compose for the better-prepared music lover.

III

The method of composing with twelve tones grew out of a necessity.

In the last hundred years, the concept of harmony has changed tremendously through the development of chromaticism. The idea that one basic tone, the root, dominated the construction of chords and regulated their succession—the concept of *tonality*—had to develop first into the concept of *extended tonality*. Very soon it became doubtful whether such a root still remained the centre to which every harmony and harmonic succession must be referred. Furthermore, it became doubtful whether a tonic appearing at the beginning, at the end, or at any other point really had a constructive meaning. Richard Wagner's harmony had promoted a change in the logic and constructive power of harmony. One of its consequences was the so-called *impressionistic* use of harmonies, especially practised by Debussy. His harmonies, without constructive meaning, often served the colouristic purpose of expressing moods and pictures. Moods and pictures, though extra-musical, thus became constructive elements, incorporated in the musical functions; they produced a sort of emotional comprehensibility. In this way, tonality was already dethroned in practice, if not in theory. This alone would perhaps not have caused a radical change in compositional technique. However, such a change became necessary when there occurred simultaneously a development which ended in what I call the *emancipation of the dissonance*.

The ear had gradually become acquainted with a great number of dissonances, and so had lost the fear of their 'sense-interrupting' effect. One no longer expected preparations of Wagner's dissonances or resolutions of Strauss' discords; one was not disturbed by Debussy's non-functional harmonies, or by the harsh counterpoint of later composers. This state of affairs led to a freer use of dissonances comparable to classic composers' treatment of diminished seventh chords, which could precede and follow any other harmony, consonant or dissonant, as if there were no dissonance at all.

What distinguishes dissonances from consonances is not a greater or lesser degree of beauty, but a greater or lesser degree of *comprehensibility*. In my *Harmonielehre* I presented the theory that dissonant tones appear later among the overtones, for which reason the ear is less intimately acquainted with them. This phenomenon does not justify such sharply contradictory terms as concord and discord. Closer acquaintance with the more remote consonances—the dissonances, that is—gradually eliminated the difficulty of comprehension and finally admitted not only the emancipation of dominant and other seventh chords, diminished sevenths and augmented triads, but also the emancipation of Wagner's, Strauss's, Moussorgsky's, Debussy's, Mahler's, Puccini's, and Reger's more remote dissonances.

The term *emancipation of the dissonance* refers to its comprehensibility, which is considered equivalent to the consonance's comprehensibility. A style based on this premise treats dissonances like consonances and renounces a tonal centre. By avoiding the establishment of a key modulation is excluded, since modulation means leaving an established tonality and establishing *another* tonality.

The first compositions in this new style were written by me around 1908 and, soon afterwards, by my pupils, Anton von Webern and Alban Berg. From the very beginning such compositions differed from all preceding music, not only harmonically but also melodically, thematically, and motivally. But the foremost characteristics of these pieces *in statu nascendi* were their extreme expressiveness and their extraordinary brevity. At that time, neither I nor my pupils were conscious of the reasons for these features. Later I discovered that our sense of form was right when it forced us to counterbalance extreme emotionality with extraordinary shortness. Thus, subconsciously, consequences were drawn from an innovation which, like every innovation, destroys while it produces. New colourful harmony was offered; but much was lost.

Formerly the harmony had served not only as a source of beauty, but, more important, as a means of distinguishing the features of the form. For instance, only a consonance was considered suitable for an ending. Establishing functions demanded different successions of harmonies than roving functions; a bridge, a transition, demanded other successions than a codetta; harmonic variation could be executed intelligently and logically only with due consideration of the fundamental meaning of the harmonies. Fulfilment of all these functions—comparable to the effect of punctuation in the construction of sentences, of subdivision into paragraphs, and of fusion into chapters—could scarcely be assured with chords whose constructive values had not as yet been explored. Hence, it seemed at first impossible to compose pieces of complicated organization or of great length.

A little later I discovered how to construct larger forms by following a text or a poem. The differences in size and shape of its parts and the change in character and mood were mirrored in the shape and size of the composition, in its dynamics and tempo, figuration and accentuation, instrumentation and orchestration. Thus the parts were differentiated as clearly as they had formerly been by the tonal and structural functions of harmony.

IV

Formerly the use of the fundamental harmony had been theoretically regulated through recognition of the effects of root progressions. This practice had grown into a subconsciously functioning *sense of form* which gave a real composer an almost somnambulistic sense of security in creating, with utmost precision, the most delicate distinctions of formal elements.

Whether one calls oneself conservative or revolutionary, whether one composes in a conventional or progressive manner, whether one tries to imitate old styles or is destined to express new ideas—whether one is a good composer or not—one must be convinced of the infallibility of one's own fantasy and one must believe in one's own inspiration. Nevertheless, the desire for a conscious control of the new means and forms will arise in every artist's mind; and he will wish to know *consciously* the laws and rules which govern the forms which he has conceived 'as in a dream'. Strongly convincing as this dream may have been, the conviction that these new sounds obey the laws of nature and of our manner of thinking—the conviction that order, logic, comprehensibility and form cannot be present without obedience to such laws—forces the composer along the road of exploration. He must find, if not laws or rules, at least ways to justify the dissonant character of these harmonies and their successions.

V

After many unsuccessful attempts during a period of approximately twelve years, I laid the foundations for a new procedure in musical construction which seemed fitted to replace those structural differentiations provided formerly by tonal harmonies.

I called this procedure *Method of Composing with Twelve Tones Which are Related Only with One Another*.

This method consists primarily of the constant and exclusive use of a set of twelve different tones. This means, of course, that no tone is repeated within the series and that it uses all twelve tones of the chromatic scale, though in a different order. It is in no way identical with the chromatic scale.[1]

Ex. 1

Example 1 shows that such a basic set (BS) consists of various intervals. It should never be called a scale, although it is invented to substitute for some of the unifying and formative advantages of scale and tonality. The scale is the source of many figurations, parts of melodies and melodies themselves, ascending and descending passages, and even broken chords. In approximately the same manner the tones of the basic set produce similar elements. Of course, cadences produced by the distinction between principal and subsidiary harmonies will scarcely be derived from the basic set. But something different and more important is derived from it with a regularity comparable to the regularity and logic of the earlier harmony; the association of tones into harmonies and their successions is regulated (as will be shown later) by the order of these tones. The basic set functions in the manner of a motive. This explains why such a basic set has to be invented anew for every piece. It has to be the first creative thought. It does not make much difference whether or not the set appears in the composition at once like a theme or a melody, whether or not it is characterized as such by features of rhythm, phrasing, construction, character, etc.

Why such a set should consist of twelve different tones, why none of these tones should be repeated too soon, why, accordingly, only one set should be used in one composition—the answers to all these questions came to me gradually.

Discussing such problems in my *Harmonielehre* (1911), I recommended the avoidance of octave doublings.[2] To double is to emphasize, and an emphasized tone could be interpreted as a root, or even as a tonic; the consequences of such an interpretation must be avoided. Even a slight reminiscence of the former tonal harmony would be disturbing, because it would create false expectations of consequences and continuations. The use of a tonic is deceiving if it is not based on *all* the relationships of tonality.

The use of more than one set was excluded because in every following set one or more tones would have been repeated too soon. Again there would arise the danger of interpreting the repeated tone as a tonic. Besides, the effect of unity would be lessened.

Justified already by historical development, the method of composing with twelve tones is also not without aesthetic and theoretical support. On the contrary, it is just this support which advances it from a mere technical device to the rank and importance of a scientific theory.

Music is not merely another kind of amusement, but a musical poet's, a musical thinker's representation of musical ideas; these musical ideas must correspond to the laws of human logic; they are a part of what man can apperceive, reason and express. Proceeding from these assumptions, I arrived at the following conclusions:

THE TWO-OR-MORE-DIMENSIONAL SPACE IN WHICH MUSICAL IDEAS ARE PRESENTED IS A UNIT. Though the elements of these ideas appear separate and independent to the eye and the ear, they reveal their true meaning only through their co-operation, even as no single word alone can express a thought without relation to other words. All that happens at any point of this musical space has more than a local effect. It functions not only in its own plane, but also in all other directions and planes, and is not without influence even at remote points. For instance, the effect of progressive rhythmical subdivision, through what I call 'the tendency of the shortest notes' to multiply themselves, can be observed in every classic composition.

A musical idea, accordingly, though consisting of melody, rhythm, and harmony, is neither the one nor the other alone, but all three together. The elements of a musical idea are partly incorporated in the horizontal plane as successive sounds, and partly in the vertical plane as simultaneous sounds. The mutual relation of tones regulates the succession of intervals as well as their association into harmonies; the rhythm regulates the succession of tones as well as the succession of harmonies and organizes phrasing. And this explains why, as will be shown later, a basic set of twelve tones (BS) can be used in either dimension, as a whole or in parts.

The basic set is used in diverse mirror forms. The composers of the last century had not employed such mirror forms as much as the masters of contrapuntal times; at least, they seldom did so consciously. Nevertheless, there exist examples, of which I want to mention only one from Beethoven's last String Quartet, Op. 135, in F major:

Ex. 2

Beethoven, String Quartet, Op. 135, 4th movement

The original form, *a*, 'Muss es sein', appears in *b* inverted and in the major; *c* shows the retrograde form of this inversion, which, now reinverted in *d* and filled out with passing notes in *e*, results in the second phrase of the main theme.

Whether or not this device was used consciously by Beethoven does not matter at all. From my own experience I know that it can also be a subconsciously received gift from the Supreme Commander.

Ex. 3

Kammersymphonie, Op. 9, E major

The two principal themes of my *Kammersymphonie* (Chamber Symphony) can be seen in Example 3 under *a* and *b*. After I had completed the work I worried very much about the apparent absence of any relationship between the two themes. Directed only by my sense of form and the stream of ideas, I had not asked such questions while composing; but, as usual with me, doubts arose as soon as I had finished. They went so far that I had already raised the sword for the kill, taken the red pencil of the censor to cross out the theme *b*. Fortunately, I stood by my inspiration and ignored these mental tortures. About twenty years later I saw the true relationship. It is of such a complicated nature that I doubt whether any composer would have cared deliberately to construct a theme in this way; but our subconscious does it involuntarily. In *c* the true principal tones of the theme are marked, and *d* shows that all the intervals ascend. Their correct inversion *e* produces the first phrase *f* of the theme *b*.

It should be mentioned that the last century considered such a procedure cerebral, and thus inconsistent with the dignity of genius. The very fact that there exist classical examples proves the foolishness of such an opinion. But the validity of this form of thinking is also demonstrated by the previously stated law of the unity of musical space, best formulated as follows: *the unity of musical space demands an absolute and unitary perception*. In this space, as in Swedenborg's heaven (described in Balzac's *Seraphita*) there is no absolute down, no right or left, forward or backward. Every musical configuration, every movement of tones has to be comprehended primarily as a mutual relation of sounds, of oscillatory vibrations, appearing at different places and times. To the imaginative and creative faculty, relations in the material sphere are as independent from directions or planes as material objects are, in their sphere, to our perceptive faculties. Just as our mind always recognizes, for instance, a knife, a bottle or a watch, regardless of its position, and can reproduce it in the imagination in every possible position, even so a musical creator's mind can operate subconsciously with a row of tones, regardless of their direction, regardless of the way in which a mirror might show the mutual relations, which remain a given quality.

VI

The introduction of my method of composing with twelve tones does not facilitate composing; on the contrary, it makes it more difficult. Modernistically-minded beginners often think they should try it before having acquired the necessary technical equipment. This is a great mistake. The restrictions imposed on a composer by the obligation to use only one set in a composition are so severe that they can only be overcome by an imagination which has survived a tremendous number of adventures. Nothing is given by this method; but much is taken away.

It has been mentioned that for every new composition a special set of twelve tones has to be invented. Sometimes a set will not fit every condition an experienced composer can foresee, especially in those ideal cases where the set appears at once in the form, character, and phrasing of a theme. Rectifications in the order of tones may then become necessary.

In the first works in which I employed this method, I was not yet convinced that the exclusive use of one set would not result in monotony. Would it allow the creation of a sufficient number of characteristically differentiated themes, phrases, motives, sentences, and other forms? At this time, I used complicated devices to assure variety. But soon I discovered that my fear was unfounded; I could even base a whole opera, *Moses and Aron*, solely on one set; and I found that, on the contrary, the more familiar I became with this set the more easily I could draw themes from it. Thus, the truth of my first prediction had received splendid proof. One has to follow the basic set; but, nevertheless, one composes as freely as before.

VII

It has been mentioned that the basic set is used in mirror forms.

Ex. 4

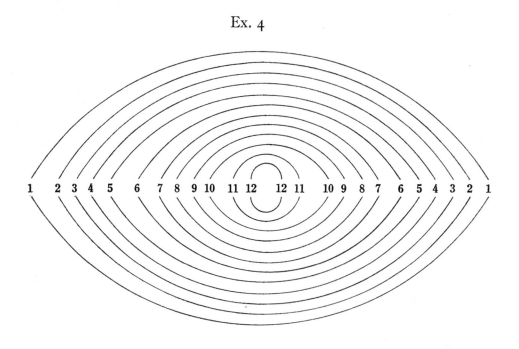

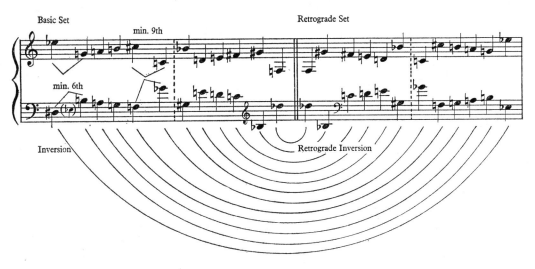

BS means Basic Set; INV means inversion of the Basic Set; INV 8, INV 5, INV 3, INV 6 means inversion at the 8ve, 5th, minor 3rd, or major 6th from the beginning tone.

From the basic set, three additional sets are automatically derived: (1) the inversion; (2) the retrograde; and (3) the retrograde inversion. The employment of these mirror forms corresponds to the principle of *the absolute and unitary perception of musical space*. The set of Example 4 is taken from the Wind Quintet Op. 26, one of my first compositions in this style.

Later, especially in larger works, I changed my original idea, if necessary, to fit the following conditions: (see page 236) the inversion a fifth below of the first six tones, the antecedent, should not produce a repetition of one of these six tones, but should bring forth the hitherto unused six tones of the chromatic scale. Thus, the consequent of the basic set, the tones 7 to 12, comprises the tones of this inversion, but, of course, in a different order.

In Example 5 (page 227), the inversion a fifth below does not yet fulfil this condition. Here the antecedent of the BS plus that of the INV 5 consists of only 10 different tones, because c and b appear twice, while f and f♯ are missing.

VIII

In every composition preceding the method of composing with twelve tones, all the thematic and harmonic material is primarily derived from three sources:

the tonality, the *basic motive* which in turn is a derivative of the tonality, and the *rhythm*, which is included in the basic motive. A composer's whole thinking was bound to remain in an intelligible manner around the central root. A composition which failed to obey these demands was considered 'amateurish'; but a composition which adhered to it rigorously was never called 'cerebral'. On the contrary, the capacity to obey the principle instinctively was considered a natural condition of a talent.[3]

The time will come when the ability to draw thematic material from a basic set of twelve tones will be an unconditional prerequisite for obtaining admission into the composition class of a conservatory.

IX

The possibilities of evolving the formal elements of music—melodies, themes, phrases, motives, figures, and chords—out of a basic set are unlimited. In the following pages, a number of examples from my own works will be analysed to reveal some of these possibilities. It will be observed that the succession of the tones according to their order in the set has always been strictly observed. One could perhaps tolerate a slight digression from this order (according to the same principle which allowed a remote variant in former styles)[4] in the later part of a work, when the set had already become familiar to the ear. However, one would not thus digress at the beginning of a piece.

The set is often divided into groups; for example, into two groups of six tones, or three groups of four, or four groups of three tones. This grouping serves primarily to provide a regularity in the distribution of the tones. The tones used in the melody are thereby separated from those to be used as accompaniment, as harmonies or as chords and voices demanded by the nature of the instrumentation, by the instrument, or by the character and other circumstances of a piece. The distribution may be varied or developed according to circumstances, in a manner comparable to the changes of what I call the 'Motive of the Accompaniment'.

X

The unlimited abundance of possibilities obstructs the systematic presentation of illustrations; therefore, an arbitrary procedure must be used here.

In the simplest case, a part of a theme, or even the entire theme, consists simply of a rhythmization and phrasing of a basic set and its derivatives, the mirror forms: inversion, retrograde, and retrograde inversion. While a piece usually begins with the basic set itself, the mirror forms and other derivatives, such as the eleven transpositions of all the four basic forms, are applied only later; the transpositions especially, like the modulations in former styles, serve to build subordinate ideas.

Ex. 5

Example 5 shows the basic set (with its inversions in the octave and fifth) of my *Wind Quintet*, Op. 26.

Many themes of this work simply use the order of one of the basic forms.

Ex. 6

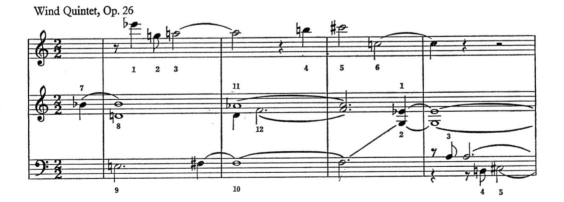

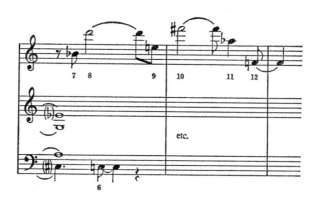

The main theme of the first movement uses for its first phrase the first six tones, the antecedent; for its second phrase, the consequent of the BS. This example shows how an accompaniment can be built. As octave doubling should be avoided (see p. 233), the accompanying of tones 1–6 with tones 7–12, and vice versa, is one way to fulfil this requirement.

Ex. 7

Example 7 proves that the same succession of tones can produce different themes, different characters.

Ex. 8

Example 8, the principal theme of the Rondo of this Quintet, shows a new way of varying the repetitions of a theme. The production of such variants is not only necessary in larger forms, especially in Rondos, but useful also in smaller structures. While rhythm and phrasing significantly preserve the character of the theme so that it can easily be recognized, the tones and intervals are changed through a different use of BS and mirror forms. Mirror forms are used in the same way as the BS. But Example 9 shows a more complicated procedure.

Ex. 9

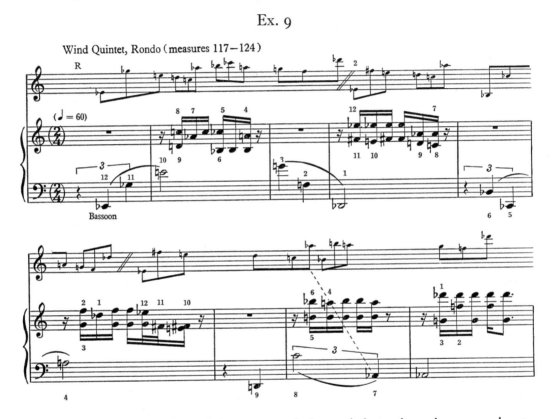

At first a transposition of the retrograde is used three times in succession to build melody and accompaniment of this subordinate theme of the Rondo from the same Quintet. The principal voice, the bassoon, uses three tones in each of the four phrases; the accompaniment uses only six tones, so that the phrases and the sets overlap each other, producing a sufficient degree of variety. There is a definite regularity in the distribution of the tones in this and the following Example 10, the Andante from the same Quintet.

Here also the form used, the BS, appears three times; here also, some of the tones appear in the principal voice (horn) while the others build a semi-contrapuntal melody in the bassoon.

Ex. 11

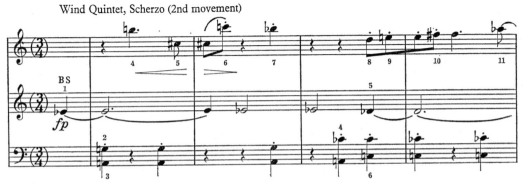

In the Scherzo of the same work (Example 11), the main theme starts with the fourth tone after the accompaniment has employed the preceding three tones of the BS. Here the accompaniment uses the same tones as the melody, but never at the same time.

In Example 12, inversion and retrograde inversion are combined into a contrapuntal unit which is worked out in the manner of the elaboration of the Rondo.

Ex. 12

Wind Quintet, Scherzo (measures 88–94)

XI

Obviously, the requirement to use all the tones of the set is fulfilled whether they appear in the accompaniment or the melody. My first larger work in this style, the *Piano Suite*, Op. 25, already takes advantage of this possibility, as will be shown in some of the following examples. But the apprehension about the doubling of octaves caused me to take a special precaution.

Exs. 13 and 13a

The BS as well as the inversion is transposed at the interval of a diminished fifth. This simple provision made it possible to use, in the Praeludium of this Suite, BS for the theme and the transposition for the accompaniment, without octave doubling.

Exs. 14 and 14a

Suite, Op. 25, Intermezzo

But in the Gavotte (Example 14) and the Intermezzo (Example 14a) this problem is solved by the first procedure mentioned above: the separate selection of the tones for their respective formal function, melody or accompaniment. In both cases a group of the tones appears too soon—9–12 in the left hand comes before 5–8. This deviation from the order is an irregularity which can be justified in two ways. The first of these has been mentioned previously: as the Gavotte is the second movement, the set has already become familiar. The second justification is provided by the subdivision of the BS into three groups of four tones. No change occurs within any one of these groups; otherwise, they are treated like independent small sets. This treatment is supported by the presence of a diminished fifth, db–g, or g–db, as third and fourth tones in all forms of the set, and of another diminished fifth as seventh and eighth tones. This similarity, functioning as a relationship, makes the groups interchangeable.

Exs. 15 and 15a

Suite, Op. 25, Menuet

Ex. 15a   Suite, Op. 25, Trio

In the Menuet of the *Piano Suite* (Example 15) the melody begins with the fifth tone, while the accompaniment, much later, begins with the first tone.

The Trio of this Menuet (Example 15a) is a canon in which the difference between the long and short notes helps to avoid octaves.

The possibility of such canons and imitations, and even fugues and fugatos, has been overestimated by analysts of this style. Of course, for a beginner it might be as difficult to avoid octave doubling here as it is difficult for poor composers to avoid parallel octaves in the 'tonal' style. But while a 'tonal' composer still has to lead his parts into consonances or catalogued dissonances, a composer with twelve independent tones apparently possesses the kind of freedom which many would characterize by saying: 'everything is allowed'. 'Everything' has always been allowed to two kinds of artists: to masters on the one hand, and to ignoramuses on the other. However, the meaning of composing in imitative style here is not the same as it is in counterpoint. It is only one of the ways of adding a coherent accompaniment, or subordinate voices, to the main theme, whose character it thus helps to express more intensively.

XII

The set of my *Variations for Orchestra*, Op. 31, is shown in Example 16.

A work for orchestra must necessarily be composed of more voices than one for a smaller combination. Of course, many composers can manage with a small number of voices by doubling them in many instruments or in octaves, by breaking and doubling the harmony in many ways—sometimes thereby obscuring the presence of a content, sometimes making its absence clear. It must be admitted that most orchestral combinations do not promote what the artist calls unmixed, unbroken colours. The childish preference of the primitive ear for colours has kept a number of imperfect instruments in the orchestra, because of their individuality. More mature minds resist the temptation to become intoxicated by colours and prefer to be coldly convinced by the transparency of clear-cut ideas.

Avoidance of doubling in octaves automatically precludes the use of broken harmonies which contribute so much to the pleasant noise that is today called 'sonority'. Since I was educated primarily by playing and writing chamber music, my style of orchestration had long ago turned to thinness and transparency, in spite of contemporary influences. To provide for the worst seems better wisdom than to hope for the best. Therefore, I declined to take a chance, and, by making some slight changes, built the basic set so that its antecedent (see p. 225), starting a minor third below, inverted itself into the remaining six tones of the full chromatic scale.

Exs. 16 and 16a

Besides, I used in many places a device, derived from double counterpoint of the tenth and twelfth, which allows the addition of parallel thirds to every part involved. By transposing BS a third up (BS3) and INV a third down (INV3), I obtained two more basic forms which allowed the addition of parallel thirds.

Ex. 17

In the First Variation (Example 17) I used this device often, but not as often as I had expected. Very soon I recognized that my apprehension was unnecessary. Of the following examples, chosen at random to illustrate other peculiarities, none shows the addition of parallel thirds.

After an introduction successively revealing the tones of the BS and its INV3, the 'Theme' of the Variations appears (Example 16). Built as a ternary form, it uses the tones of the BS and its three derivatives in strict order, without any omission or addition.

The motive of the Fifth Variation is based on a transposition of the INV (INV8). Here are six independent parts built from only one set, comprising only the first two beats; the continuation carries on this system and finds ways to produce a satisfactory amount of variety (see Ex. 18).

The motive of the Sixth Variation is built from another transposition of the INV (INV6). It is composed of a contrapuntal combination of two melodic parts, using some tones of INV6 in the upper and others in the lower voice. This combination allows a great number of forms which furnish material for every demand

Ex. 18

Ex. 19

of variation technique. New forms result through inversion of both voices (Example 20) and other changes of their mutual positions such as, for instance, canonic imitation (Example 20a).

Exs. 20 and 20a

One should never forget that what one learns in school about history is the truth only insofar as it does not interfere with the political, philosophical, moral or other beliefs of those in whose interest the facts are told, coloured or arranged. The same holds true with the history of music, and he who guilelessly believes all he is told—whether he be layman or professional—is defenceless and has to 'take it', to take it as they give it. Of course, we know their guesses are no better than ours.

But unfortunately our historians are not satisfied with rearranging the history of the past; they also want to fit the history of the present into their preconceived scheme. This forces them to describe the facts only as accurately as they see

them, to judge them only as well as they understand them, to draw wrong conclusions from wrong premises, and to exhibit foggy visions of a future which
exists only in their warped imaginations.

I am much less irritated than amused by the critical remark of one Dr. X,
who says that I do not care for 'sound'.

'Sound', once a dignified quality of higher music, has deteriorated in significance since skilful workmen—orchestrators—have taken it in hand with the
definite and undisguised intention of using it as a screen behind which the
absence of ideas will not be noticeable. Formerly, sound had been the radiation
of an intrinsic quality of ideas, powerful enough to penetrate the hull of the
form. Nothing could radiate which was not light itself; and here only ideas are
light.

Today, sound is seldom associated with idea. The superficially minded, not
bothering with digesting the idea, notice especially the sound. 'Brevity is
essential to wit'; length, to most people, seems to be essential to sound. They
observe it only if it lasts for a comparatively long time.

It is true that sound in my music changes with every turn of the idea—emotional, structural, or other. It is furthermore true that such changes occur in a
more rapid succession than usual, and I admit that it is more difficult to perceive
them simultaneously. The Seventh Variation (Example 21) offers just such obstacles to comprehension. But it is not true that the other kind of sonority is
foreign to my music.

The rapid changes of the sonority in this Seventh Variation make it difficult
for the listener to enjoy. The figure in the bassoon part continues for some time,
while the instrumentation of the harmonies in eighth notes changes rapidly and
continuously.

Ex. 21

Variation VII

Ex. 22

Variation VIII

Ex. 23

Finale (measure 332)

Ex. 24

Finale (measure 396)

Examples 21–24 show that a great multitude of thematic characters can be derived from one set. Various methods are, of course, applied. It may be worth while to mention that in Example 25, as an homage to Bach, the notes B-flat, A, C, B, which spell, in German, BACH, were introduced as a contrapuntal addition to the principal thematic developments.

Ex. 25

Finale (measure 435)

The main advantage of this method of composing with twelve tones is its unifying effect. In a very convincing way, I experienced the satisfaction of having been right about this when I once prepared the singers of my opera *Von Heute auf Morgen* for a performance. The technique, rhythm and intonation of all these parts were tremendously difficult for them, though they all possessed absolute pitch. But suddenly one of the singers came and told me that since he had become familiar with the basic set, everything seemed easier for him. At short intervals all the other singers told me the same thing independently. I was very pleased with this, and, thinking it over, I found even greater encouragement in the following hypothesis:

Prior to Richard Wagner, operas consisted almost exclusively of independent pieces, whose mutual relation did not seem to be a musical one. Personally, I refuse to believe that in the great masterworks pieces are connected only by the superficial coherence of the dramatic proceedings. Even if these pieces were merely 'fillers' taken from earlier works of the same composer, something must have satisfied the master's sense of form and logic. We may not be able to discover it, but certainly it exists. In music there is no form without logic, there is no logic without unity.

I believe that when Richard Wagner introduced his *Leitmotiv*—for the same purpose as that for which I introduced my Basic Set—he may have said: 'Let there be unity.'

ADDENDUM (1946)

In the course of about the last ten years, some of the strictness of the rules concerning octave doubling and prominent appearances of fundamental chords of harmony have been loosened to some degree.

At first it became clear that such single events could not change the style of non-tonality into tonality. There remained still those characteristic melodies, rhythms, phrasings and other formal devices which were born simultaneously with the style of freedom of the dissonances.

Besides, even if the negation of a tonal centre's domination would have been temporarily undermined, this need not have destroyed the stylistic merits of a composition.

I have to admit that Alban Berg, who was perhaps the least orthodox of us three—Webern, Berg and I—in his operas mixed pieces or parts of pieces of a distinct tonality with those which were distinctly non-tonal. He explained this, apologetically, by contending that as an opera composer he could not, for reasons of dramatic expression and characterization, renounce the contrast furnished by a change from major to minor.

Though he was right as a composer, he was wrong theoretically. I have proved in my operas *Von Heute auf Morgen* and *Moses und Aron* that every expression and characterization can be produced with the style of free dissonance.

5

COMPOSITION WITH TWELVE TONES (2)
c. 1948

The method of composing with twelve tones purports reinstatement of the effects formerly furnished by the structural functions of the harmony. It cannot replace all that harmony has performed in music from Bach—and his predecessors—unto our time: limitation, subdivision, connection, junction, association, unification, opposition, contrast, variation, culmination, declination, ebbing, liquidation, etc. It also cannot exert influences of similar ways on the inner organization of the smaller segments, of which the greater divisions and the whole work consists.

But in works of Strauss, Mahler and, even more, Debussy, one can already observe reasons for the advance of new formal techniques. Here it is already doubtful, as I have shown in my *Harmonielehre*, whether there is a tonic in power which has control over all these centrifugal tendencies of the harmonies. Certainly, there are still methods employed to establish a tonality, there are even cadences concluding sections which move into the most remote relations of a tonality. But the problem is not whether this number of tonalities can still admit unification, but whether they are controlled by a centre of gravitation which has the power to permit their going astray because it has also the power of recalling them. It is quite obvious to the analyst that here compositorial methods have been in function which substitute for the missing power of the harmony.

This proves that harmony also in times preceding these masters never had the task of accomplishing all these structural techniques alone, by its own power. There were always several powers at work to produce themes, melodies, and all the larger sections of which a composition consists: the manifold forms of crystallization of intervals and rhythms in their relation to accented or unaccented beats of the measure.

This also proves that many composers working with twelve tones are mistaken when they expect too much from the mere application of a set of twelve tones, or of Hauer's 'Tropen'. This alone could not create music. Doubtless these other formative forces which produce the configurations and variations are even more important. And the history of music shows that harmony was the last contribution to music at a time when there was already great development in existence of melody and rhythm.

The construction of a basic set of twelve tones derives from the intention to postpone the repetition of every tone as long as possible. I have stated in my *Harmonielehre* that the emphasis given to a tone by a premature repetition is capable of heightening it to the rank of a tonic. But the regular application of a set of twelve tones emphasises all the other tones in the same manner, thus depriving one single tone of the privilege of supremacy. It seemed in the first stages immensely important to avoid a similarity with tonality. The feeling was correct that those free combinations of simultaneously sounding tones—those 'chords'—would fit into a tonality. Today's ear has become as tolerant to these dissonances as musicians were to Mozart's dissonances. It is in fact correct to contend that the emancipation of the dissonance is at present accomplished and that twelve-tone music in the near future will no longer be rejected because of 'discords'.

The other function is the unifying effect of the set. Through the necessity of using besides the basic set, its retrograde, its inversion, and its retrograde inversion, the repetition of tones will occur oftener than expected. But every tone appears always in the neighbourhood of two other tones in an unchanging combination which produces an intimate relationship most similar to the relationship of a third and a fifth to its root. It is, of course, a mere relation, but its recurrence can produce psychological effects of a great resemblance to those closer relations.

Such features will appear in every motif, in every theme, in every melody and, though rhythm and phrasing might make it distinctly another melody, it will still have some relationship with all the rest. The unification is here also the result of the relation to a common factor.

The third advantage of composition with a set of twelve tones is that the appearance of dissonances is regulated. Dissonances are not used here as in many other contemporary compositions as an addition to make consonances more 'spicy'. For the appearance of such dissonant tones there is no conceivable rule, no logic, and no other justification than the dictatorship of taste. If dissonances other than the catalogued ones are admitted at all in music, it seems that the way of referring them all to the order of the basic set is the most logical and controllable procedure toward this end.

In using Hauer's *Tropen*, one could not even postpone the reappearance of a tone for as long as possible. Hauer mixes *Tropen*, that is sets of six tones, according to his own taste or feeling of form (which only he himself possesses); there is certainly no such function of logic as in the method described here. Besides, Hauer calls his technique that of *atonality*. This is probably a mistake.

This seems to be the appropriate opportunity to tell about the way I arrived at my method.

Ever since 1906–8, when I had started writing compositions which led to the abandonment of tonality, I had been busy finding methods to replace the structural functions of harmony. Nevertheless, my first distinct step toward this goal occurred only in 1915. I had made plans for a great symphony of which *Die Jakobsleiter* should be the last movement. I had sketched many themes, among them one for a scherzo which consisted of all the twelve tones. An historian will probably some day find in the exchange of letters between Webern and me how enthusiastic we were about this.

My next step in this direction—in the meantime I had been in the Austrian army—occurred in 1917, when I started to compose *Die Jakobsleiter*. I had contrived the plan to provide for unity—which was always my main motive: to build all the main themes of the whole oratorio from a row of six tones—C-sharp, D, E, F, G, A-flat. These were probably the six notes with which the composition began, in the following order: C-sharp, D, F, E, A-flat, G.

When after my retirement from the University of California I wanted to finish *Die Jakobsleiter*, I discovered to my greatest pleasure that this beginning was a real twelve-tone composition. To an ostinato (which I changed a little) the remaining six tones entered gradually, one in every measure. When I built the main themes from these six tones I did not bind myself to the order of their first appearance. I was still at this time far away from the methodical application of a set. Still I believe that also this idea offered the promise of unity to a certain degree. Of course, in order to build up a work of the length of *Moses und Aron* from one single set, a technique had to be developed, or rather the fear that this would not succeed had to be conquered. That took several years.

Before I wrote my first strict composition with twelve tones—in 1921—I had still to pass through several stages. This can be noticed in two works which I had partly written preceding the *Piano Suite*, Op. 25—partly even in 1919, the *Five Piano Pieces*, Op. 23, and the *Serenade*, Op. 24. In both these works there are parts composed in 1922 and 1923 which are strict twelve-tone compositions. But the rest represent the aforementioned stages.

In my workshop language, when I talked to myself, I called this procedure 'working with tones of the motif'. This was obviously an exercise indispensable for the acquisition of a technique to conquer the obstacles which a set of twelve tones opposes to a free production of fluent writing. Similarly, as in the case of *Die Jakobsleiter*, here also all main themes had to be transformations of the first phrase. Already here the basic motif was not only productive in furnishing new motif-forms through developing variations, but also in producing more remote formulations based on the unifying effect of one common factor: the repetition of tonal and intervallic relationship.

It is quite easy to repeat a basic set in one or more voices over and over again. There is no merit in writing canons of two or more voices, because the second, third, fourth, and further voice has only to begin two or more notes later and there will never occur parallel octaves. And who cares about parallel fifths?

I believe canonic or other imitation should serve only in order to base accompanying voices, which make the sonority fuller, on a more intimate relation to the main voice. Even the writing of whole fugues is a little too easy under these circumstances. Composing of these forms in which the highest achievement has already been reached by composers whose form of expression was that of contrapuntal combinations—composing of these forms should only be undertaken for some special reason. For instance, if a composer feels he must calm down a sort of nostalgic longing for old-time beauty; or because in the course of a huge work—an opera, an oratorio, a cantata, etc.—one of the parts must be in old style. There are certainly few reasons which might oblige a composer to compete with those *hors-concours* achievements of such great masters, whose native language was counterpoint.

6

IS IT FAIR?
1947

It has become a habit of late to qualify aesthetic and artistic subjects in terms borrowed from the jargon of politics. Thus mildly progressive works of art, literature or even music might be classified as 'revolutionary' or 'left wing', when they only evolve artistic possibilities. On the other hand, old-fashioned products are called 'reactionary', without any clarification of what its antonym might mean in contrast.

No wonder, then, that there are people who call the method of composing with twelve tones 'bolshevik'. They pretend that in a 'set of twelve tones', upon which such compositions are founded, since there is no tonic nor dominant, every tone is considered independent, and consequently exerts equal functions.

This is wrong in every respect; yet it is curious to note that even the exact contrary has been contended. The German composer, Paul von Klenau, during Hitler's time, composed a whole opera in twelve-tone style. After a successful performance, he published an essay in which he 'demonstrated' that this method is a true image of national-socialist principles! This, of course, also is politics—though of the opposite colour.

As a matter of fact, the structural independence of the single tone is rather limited in a set of twelve tones, because every tone is bound unchangeably to a definite place. For example, observe the following set:

In a 'fascist' interpretation, the basic set accordingly would represent the leader, the Duce, the Fuehrer, on whom all depends, who distributes power and function to every tone, who also is the originator of all the three mirror forms, and who is responsible for all the subsequent transpositions of the basic set and its derivatives—to function as sub-Fuehrer in minor affairs.

Whether this concept is an advantage or a handicap to the composer or to the listener, certainly it has nothing in common with 'Liberty, Equality and Fraternity', neither with the bolshevik, fascist, nor any other totalitarian brand.

Most important: is it an evaluation?

December 2, 1947

PART VI

THEORY AND COMPOSITION

1

THEORY OF FORM
1924

A theory of form would have to aim, first and foremost, at showing the significance of all artistic forms—the fact that they try to endow the artistic product (whose shape is conditioned by a material extrinsic to ourselves) with an external and internal constitution permitting us to recognize it as something that corresponds to the qualities of our intellect. Through its relationship, analogy with, similarity to other things we think, feel and sense, we are able to grasp it as similar to us, appropriate to us, and related to us. So one must show how the material, against or in accordance with its own aim, is forced by art—by fulfilling the demands of comprehensibility—to adapt itself to such conditions.

I am just reading in a criticism of my *Georgelieder* that I 'do not shrink from doing violence to nature'. What is meant is doubtless that I do not feel the need to write anything banal, conventional, obsolete. For it must be apparent, in view of what I have just said, that one must, on the contrary, in all circumstances, use force on nature, on the material—sounds: that one must force them to keep to a direction and succession laid down by us. One has to force nature—the material—by means of nature—our way of thinking—to work naturally according to our nature; otherwise we can either not grasp it or else, if one lets the sounds run as they please, it remains a children's game, like electrical experiments with elderberries or tobogganing or the like. Every more developed game comes about because the course of nature is modified by a force from outside. Thus in nine-pins the task is not merely to hurl a ball, but to knock down nine-pins with it, and in billiards the cushions and countless other more or less arbitrary, artificial conditions restrict the natural aim of the stroke to such a degree that it can be taken as meaningful and successful only in terms of a very modified goal. One of the most primitive games, dice (primitive because its intellectual conditions are very simple and their number very small), is content to increase the interest of the question, 'which side will be up?', giving the various sides differing values—winning values, to appeal to our lowest instincts! Accordingly, the higher an artistic idea stands, the greater the range of questions, complexes, associations, problems, feelings and so on it will have to cover, and the better it succeeds in compressing this universality into a minimum of space, the higher it will stand. The further presentation of the idea will indeed proceed according to the same laws, but will use a more popular or a stricter manner of expression, presentation and development, depending on the hearer to whom it addresses itself. And yet one will have to designate as the highest forms those in which the presentation is concise, comprehensive and exhaustive, the richness of discovered relationships to the subject impressive, the elimination of inessentials carried through consistently and uncompromisingly, and yet the presentation suited to taste, and no harder to grasp than the state of the subject demands.

Since in our age of pathos the author, standing temporarily aside from his work, has learned how to inspire respect for his person, such an age will also wish to see enumerated the qualities that set a standard for this. But it should not be forgotten that the only man able to make himself noticed here will be the one found interesting by the fashion of the moment. And that varies too much to be able in itself to become the standard. Don't forget: if, for example, at present it is the one who knows how to scream loudest, or softest, most interestingly or most atmospherically as each pain jars him, before long it could again be the one who under no circumstance moves even a muscle. But once one accepts that this factor is a variable quantity, and since, despite what we think at the moment, one can even imagine it no longer there, then it is not hard to find a standard for this too. One may ignore whatever directly caused the artist to give tongue, since this is important mainly to him, and take as one's criterion the intensity with which mental and spiritual excitement is represented and reproduced; but here, in assessing the credibility of what he says, one would be forced to rely almost exclusively on feeling. However, none of the more measurable qualities mentioned above are determined to more than a very small extent by taking thought either. The majority, and often the more important ones, are a matter of feeling anyway, for a true artist. A true artist's inborn emotional and intellectual gifts have, by self-cultivation and culture, become a faultlessly functioning apparatus that does not need the spur of conscious thought; he is as much at home in the world of the intellect as in the world of emotions, and it is this that distinguishes the true artist from the others. It is fair to say of such a man that everything is granted him as a pure matter of feeling. The world of feelings is quite inseparable from the world of the intellect; the two are always felt as one and the same. So one may take it that the intellectual is just as much a criterion as the emotional, and that if a work has any measurable intellectual qualities (if one finds in it lofty qualities of intellect) one may reckon also to find in it emotional things that are equally worth-while. And vice versa—where there is dearth, it is just as much a dearth of true and worthwhile feelings as of true intellect. For there is but one source!

Mödling, January 29, 1924

2

TONALITY AND FORM
1925

I read in a newspaper that a group of modern composers has decreed that tonality must be restored, as, without it, form cannot exist. That tonality must be re-established, I do not believe, but I think it is possible that it will be done. For the belief in technique and its material accompaniments is so deeply rooted that the 'Faiseurs' would certainly sooner move mountains than risk adventures in more mental regions.

That the harmonic alone is form-determining is a widely spread delusion, probably just because I have already refuted it in my *Harmonielehre*. It can certainly be drawn upon as an aid to form; but music that does not consist of joints and parts is to be attained by a very different method.

My pupils will be able to confirm the fact that, in teaching, it was my chief endeavour to make clear to them the difference between the formative poten-tialities of principal and secondary subjects, introductions, transitions, and codas; and they will remember that I always maintained that most of the composers of today are able to write only introductions, able only to place one thing next to another.

The art of giving a true and varied expression to a musical thought is very little known. Today the majority strive for 'style, technique and sound', meaning thereby something purely external and therefore merely striking in character, for the sake of which all the old culture displaced in presenting a thought is neglected. And yet we need only take, for example, an older novel of Dickens and note the complex structure and treatment, the cleverly woven threads, and we become conscious of the knowledge that is really necessary for a work of art.

This primitive art of presenting thoughts belongs wholly to the uneducated, who can only relate in orderly succession things just as they happen, who have no grasp of the whole, who can therefore neither anticipate nor go back nor connect one sentence with another except by means of the copula 'and' . . . 'And then I said . . . and then he said . . . and then we laughed . . . and . . . and so on.' The narrative goes on only because the story that is being told goes on, because a continuous action drives the story-teller on. The climax is then naturally only dynamic, as its cause is merely extraneous.

It would, however, be a mistake to think that a more artistic expression is only a matter of using a certain technique. I have worked for more than ten years on this, to settle these differences theoretically, and am so far successful that the work in question will soon be written. But I can say that it is really in the mental realm—where musical thought must be rich in variety—that an artistic expression is possible. The unthinking do not demand it, do not even allow it, and would only feel doubtful if they did. But they simply do not think.

In my youth a feeling for form was still very much alive; this, without theoretical explanation, told one how a principal subject was to be formed. 'This sentence rambles', was a criticism one might often hear. Brahms was not the last one who possessed this art. Mahler and Strauss also have inherited it. Most of those who follow are not even conscious of what it is all about.

In my *Harmonielehre* I also analyse the function of tonality and show what the tasks of a composer are who wishes to make use of this medium. Tonality does not only serve; on the contrary, it demands to be served. And that is not so simple as the decreeing committee thinks. I am probably the last of the modern composers who has occupied himself with tonal harmony in the sense of the oldest masters. That this circumstance is not heeded nor understood is not my fault. Those who examine in my First String Quartet or in my *Kammersymphonie* the relation of the keys to each other and to the incident harmony, will get from them some conception of the demands that are made, in the modern sense, on the tonal development of a harmonic idea. Perhaps they would also understand why a step must be taken from thence onwards, which the critics in question would gladly reverse.

Why does this clique make decrees? I, if I wanted to write with profit on tonality, should neither decree it nor write about it—but to reverse it! Were I compelled to write such a work, I would write it first and then perhaps—No! not even then. Listeners must have ears, and ears to detect the difference between music and shibboleths.

When I hear these particular tonal pieces in which are avoided all possible tonal non-relationships, or at least those not developed to the end (or similar passages, many of which might be taken for codas) through an F-sharp or C-major triad—according to the mood, then I always think of those savage potentates who wear only a cravat and a top-hat.

The form of a composition is achieved because (1) a body exists, and because (2) the members exercise different functions and are created for these functions. He who from the outside forces through some function on them all reminds one of the bad craftsmen who, to hide faults of construction, over-upholster, over-daub, over-lacquer, cover with nickel and so on.

Who can say today how a principal subject must be built up? What must one do that it may hold together, so that one does not find oneself suddenly on the wrong track? Who can say how a fluid form is solidified, how an introduction or a development must be evolved? He who can do these things and knows will not be in doubt as to whether or no tonality must be restored to achieve form.

I know that the majority are incapable of accomplishing this with the simplest harmony. And I know that construction, formation, super-structure—in one word, artistic expression does not depend on any technical trick, but lies rather in musical thought itself. He who really thinks, and thinks deeply, will, with different musical ideas, produce different expressions.

All honour to these composers in their desire for form! but they have to look yet further afield in the resources of the art of music when they aspire to higher forms.

3

OPINION OR INSIGHT?
1926

Tonal or atonal: by now, the question whether one or the other is justified, admissible, possible, necessary or indispensable, has already taken on a more manageable form—it has become a matter of opinion. This is an advantage, since those confronted by the question can ignore all the objective points on which decisions are based and can follow their own inclination, whim, feelings and the various points to do with self-preservative instinct. If they do so, they know they are covered by a more or less numerous body of other people who share their omission to think, their inclination, whim, feelings or foresight. A party matter.

Parties rely on adherents, whom they recruit with slogans. But these never strike dead-centre, but well to one side, in the space that has to be left for the partisans. For the latter need to develop, to find success. But how are they to do so if their path is laid down by strict laws which come from a foundation of deep insight and show that the Way of the Cross indeed exists, but no cross-roads; and that to have reached a 'parting of the ways' is a sure sign that one has already strayed out of the world of art?

A few of today's composers still find a few tonal triads sufficient, even now (that is part of their private life where, to some extent, anything goes); however, most of them have noted what has been done by the works of Wagner, Strauss, Mahler, Reger, Debussy, Puccini, etc., and they have drawn certain conclusions about harmony, whose outcome is recognizable as the emancipation of the dissonance. But this has placed the tonal centre of gravity in jeopardy (something already perceptible in Wagner), and problems have arisen which are not to be solved by partisan belief, but only through insight. Belief is sweet, and it makes for happiness, but religions themselves develop, since their tendency is to come ever nearer to perfect insight into the Divine Essence. So if belief views the ultimate truth as a variable, why should it be entitled to pronounce judgement, in art, against living certainties?

Many modern composers believe they are writing tonally if they occasionally introduce a major or minor triad, or a cadence-like turn of phrase, into a series of harmonies that lack, and must lack, any terms of reference. Others hope the use of ostinati and pedal-points will do the same thing for them. Both are acting like believers who buy an indulgence. They betray their God, but remain on good terms with those who call themselves His attorneys. They use accidentals and key-signatures to fit the key that would like to hold sway, as if putting on a Christian-German mantle for loving their neighbour (something they rarely used to wear), to cloak their secret, sinful converse with dissonances. Perhaps this has not much to do with art. But I should like to show why.

Tonality's origin is found—and rightly so—in the laws of sound. But there are other laws that music obeys, apart from these and the laws that result from the combination of time and sound: namely, those governing the working of our minds. This latter forces us to find a particular kind of layout for those elements that make for cohesion—and to make them come to the fore, often enough and with enough plasticity—so that in the small amount of time granted us by the flow of the events, we can recognize the figures, grasp the way they hang together, and comprehend their meaning. The easiest deviations to grasp are those that can most easily be related back to the underlying tonic. These are grasped immediately in cases where their resemblance to it is at a maximum, less immediately where more remote formations can only be felt as logical if one relates them to another, or several others, lying in-between. The farther removed the formations, the greater the deviation, the more intermediaries are needed if one is to work out the connection, and the harder it is to grasp the progression and the sense. So this is the true reason for the marked development of tonality: to make what happens easily comprehensible. *Tonality is not an end in itself, but a means to an end*, and its close accord with nature offers great advantages to those who use it. That is why until our own time composers were always extremely cautious about how the succession of harmonies was arranged, at times even carrying things to the point of using only harmonies whose relationship to the tonic and their 'accessibility' to it (further underlined by convention) was easy to grasp. But the appearance of *vagrant* chords (as I call them in my *Harmonielehre*)—phenomena whose greatest value lies in their ambiguity—so greatly widened the field of events accessible from a tonic, that to an ever increasing extent the tonic could merely be proved, intellectually, to be in command, while it became steadily harder to hear. Or in other words: just as all roads led to Rome, so there is always a road leading back to the point of departure—the tonic; but anyone who went astray in the labyrinth could put the blame on a coloured thread, on which contact between entrance and interior now exclusively depended. Moreover, the proportion of elements pointing to the tonic became ever smaller, as against those pointing away from it; the 'natural preponderance of the tonic' was henceforth out of the question, and the resistance to the music of Wagner and his successors can easily be understood, since he sacrificed the immediate 'accessibility' which still gave a touch of folk-music to Beethoven and Schubert. And yet another element added to its impetus, the tendency towards 'music as expression', which appears with the greatest intensity in Beethoven. Initially limited to elements of performance (tempo, character, variability, etc.) and of dynamics (accents, crescendi, diminuendi, abrupt alternations, etc.), it increasingly used harmony as well—particularly its surprising side—for the same purpose. This led to sudden and surprising modulations, expressive turns of phrase, strange chord-progressions, interesting chords, and later to new hitherto unexploited melodic steps, unusual progressions of intervals and other such things, not to mention the element of rhythm and of variations in articulation, in movements' form, and in the way the smaller thematic components (phrases, motives, etc.) were welded to each other. It is clear that all these tendencies, which exert an eccentric pull, worked against the desire to fix, make sensorily perceptible, and keep effective an harmonic central point, and that the composers who succeeded Wagner were soon obliged to make fast their forms in a way different from that practised until then. (This is the point to mention that the appeal to the 'text' in operas, songs and symphonic poems must be regarded as one attempt at producing cohesion among the heterogeneous elements, and to recall that in my essay, 'The Relationship to the Text', in *Der Blaue Reiter*, 1912, I was perhaps the first to turn away from expressive music—theoretically, for the time being—very soon after my first steps in a new territory where I had still been using expression to the fullest extent, even if unconsciously.)

'The emancipation of the dissonance.' That is to say, it came to be placed on an equal footing with the sounds regarded as consonances (in my *Harmonielehre* the explanation of this lies in the insight that consonance and dissonance differ not as opposites do, but only in point of *degree*; that consonances are the sounds closer to the fundamental, dissonances those farther away; that their comprehensibility is graduated accordingly, since the nearer ones are easier to comprehend than those farther off). This was an unconscious process; it was assumed that the comprehensibility of the dissonance can be ensured, given certain favourable circumstances. In so far as one's aural sense could not, on its own, recognize and comprehend connections and functions, these circumstances had to do with expression and also with something not greatly regarded until then—timbre. At this time impressionism was in full flower, and indeed it used the same extra-musical resources, to the same end, as the classics and romantics had used. Today, one or two masters of that epoch would rather disown the works which most helped the evolutionary process, but their achievement and influence have firmly established for all that, and one is grateful remembering their courage, their strength and the single-mindedness of their youthful ardour.

In the emancipation of the dissonance there was a final step that could be taken, and it has frequently been condemned—a step, as I myself believe, which has exluded consonances from music for only a short period, but one which I have shown to lie along the path followed by the evolution of music, through the works of our greatly revered predecessors. I should now explain this last step as a supplement to remarks made earlier in my *Harmonielehre*; here, as in the earlier part of this article, I am supported by the principles and methods of observation contained in a work entitled 'The Musical Idea and Its Presentation', on which I have long been working.[1]

1. Tonality's function begins to exist if the phenomena that appear can, without exception, be related immediately to a tonic, and if they are arranged so that their accessibility is a matter of sensory perception; or else if one uses the kind of methods that allow those farther away to become accessible.

2. The effect of tonality lies in this: everything that occurs in the harmony is accessible from the tonic, so its internal relationships are given suitable cohesion; and a piece of music so constructed is sure, in advance, of a certain formal effectiveness, whether or not it is constructed with the same logic and cohesion in respect of its other functions.

Tonality is not an end in itself, then; it is one of the technical resources facilitating (but not guaranteeing) unity in the comprehension of tone-progressions.

3. To isolate one or two of the resources which work toward unity if all of them are present, and then to mix them in a purely superficial way, will by no means assist the eventuation of form, but will have merely the effect of 'style',

of veiling the true relationships for reasons of taste. Anyone who wishes to use tonality's cohesive function appropriately can do so with only one end in view: a reliable and effective form. But if one does it merely out of a liking for tonality, ignorant of how to use it to its true end, and no other (rather than as a means of creating atmosphere, or to comply with party principles), one commits a grave sin and acts as ludicrously as if one were to paint a marble slab with lacquer. If, even so, a work of that kind is formally effective, it is because of extra-musical influences—performance, character, etc.—some of which are mentioned below.

4. There is no reason in physics or aesthetics that could force a musician to use tonality in order to represent his idea. The only question is whether one can attain formal unity and self-sufficiency without using tonality. The appeal to its origin in nature can be refuted if one recalls that just as tones pull toward triads, and triads toward tonality, gravity pulls us down toward the earth; yet an airplane carries us up away from it. A product can be apparently artificial without being unnatural, for it is based on the laws of nature to just the same degree as are those that seem primary. But I have moreover shown that there is nothing new about the state in which music finds itself when it ceases to seek help from tonality; that, on the contrary, music has been in this state ever since Wagner, and one must simply use a new and strong enough cohesive force to bring all that happens to a common denominator; I have already argued that the 'expressive' musicians and impressionists did exactly that.

5. In my first works in the new style I was particularly guided, in both the details and the whole of the formal construction, by very powerful expressive forces, not to mention a sense of form and logic acquired from tradition and well developed through hard work and conscientiousness. These forms became possible because of a limitation which I had been unconsciously imposing on myself from the very outset—limitation to *short* pieces, something which at the time I explained in my own mind as a reaction against the 'extended' style. Nowadays I know a better explanation: renunciation of traditional means of articulation made the construction of larger forms temporarily impossible, since such forms cannot exist without clear articulation. For the same reason, my only extended works from that time are works with a text, where the words represent the cohesive element.

6. I cannot give a single physical reason justifying the exclusion of consonant chords, but I can give a far more decisive artistic reason. It is in fact *a question of*

economy. My formal sense (and I am immodest enough to hand over to this the exclusive rights of distribution when I compose) tells me that to introduce even a single tonal triad would lead to consequences, and would demand space which is not available within my form. A tonal triad makes claims on what follows, and, retrospectively, on all that has gone before; nobody can ask me to overthrow everything that has gone before, just because a triad has happened by accident and has to be given its due. On this point I prefer if possible to start right and continue in the same way, so far as error is avoidable. Every tone tends to become a tonic. Every triad to become a tonic triad. If I were to draw even this one conclusion from the appearance of a triad, then the idea could inadvertently be forced aside on to a wrong track; but sense of form and logic have so far saved me. Immediately, in my first attempts, I felt this, and I justified it in my *Harmonielehre* on the grounds, among others, that the consonant chords sound empty and dry alongside those containing many tones. But even standing where I do at the present time, I believe that to use the consonant chords, too, is not out of the question, as soon as someone has found a technical means of either satisfying or paralysing their formal claims.

From the very beginning, this was clear in my mind: tonality's aids to articulation having dropped out, one must find some substitute, so that longer forms can once more be constructed. Length is relative and yet is one of music's dimensions; pieces of music can therefore be either long or short, so short pieces can be only an occasional way out. Starting from that premise, I arrived at twelve-tone composition. Some day I shall explain the paths and detours I followed and the reason why I needed a number of important insights about the musical idea and its presentation before that became possible; but first there are a few problems still to overcome, which I am on the verge of solving.

I still owe an answer (or, surely, I only seem to) to the question whether one is justified in writing tonally or atonally, or whether the one or the other may even be necessary or impossible. First I should like to point out that in my *Harmonielehre* (3rd edition, p. 487), I reject the expression 'atonal'. Nowadays this method of composition is, alas, generally so referred to; if one has to give it a name, I can think of only one which is not a slogan and is therefore unsuitable for a party banner, thank goodness: 'Composition with twelve tones related only to one another.' But as for the question itself: you neither must, may write tonally, nor must you, may you, write atonally. Write or don't write, but in any case don't ask, but do what you can. If you can do something pure, you will be able to do it tonally or atonally; but those who think impurely—that is to say, those who do what anyone can—may go ahead and form tonal or atonal parties, and for that matter make a noise about it. They will certainly shout us down, we who give ear to our destiny; and they will surely be heard, soon and in full measure, by those who are in favour of everything ambiguous but against everything genuine. If *we* address ourselves to those people, it is only out of acoustical necessity, since a literally empty concert hall sounds even worse than one full of 'empty people'.

Many of those who went along with me for a time have by now thought better of their atonal aspirations. It is not to these young lions of atonal music, who have now found a more comfortable den in a musical renaissance, that I refer when I say at this point that I have great esteem and respect for many who still adhere to tonality, or who have returned to it. There are true and genuine talents among them, and they have a very important task. The leap from a method of composition that emphasized key to mine was very swift and sudden. For a long time to come, the listener's ear must still be prepared before he finds dissonant sounds a matter of course and can comprehend the processes based on them. It seems to me that such composers' activity is very much the thing to ameliorate this. The idea is timeless, so it can perfectly well wait; but the language must make haste!

4

FOR A TREATISE ON COMPOSITION
1931

Taking a sober view, one can explain certain poetic forms in the following way:
Through the juxtaposition of various events, observations, impressions and the like, one can compare them, become aware that they are similar; next, the thing by which each most resembles all the others, their common factor, is em-

phasized, underlined, i.e. brought to the fore; then their kinship will leap to the eye with the force of an axiom.

The couplet with its recurring refrain; the rondo with its strophe that makes itself heard time and again; indeed, even rhyme, whose origin was, doubtless, that roots and relationships 'rhymed', i.e. repeated themselves—all these do the same thing, as does much else in related fields ('For Brutus is an honourable man'), to the same end already mentioned: to throw light on how everything else can be related to the basic facts. All this provides a way of using exact repetition as an effective artistic form.

The rondo in music allegedly arose in imitation of the poetic form so named (of course, Riemann says it 'obviously' did). That is neither impossible nor unlikely, even though music, being what it is, could have produced such a form of its own accord. After all, the alleged imitation lies in the fact of repetition; but repetition plays such a leading role in the way music is given shape, in its whole formal technique, that the deviations from it are what might require special pleading, if anything does. Music in its primal condition consists of most primitive repetitions; and the element which functions as a unifying factor in the higher forms to which it has developed, the element which guarantees that one may be able to relate all the sections to each other—the motive—can manifest its presence only through repetition. The more artistic forms do indeed obscure this fact in a great variety of ways; but since even today it is impossible to mould a form with plasticity, and in an easily comprehensible way, unless one uses repetition (even if the result is not to be a rondo)—that is to say, since up to the present we have found no other basic principle for giving shape to music—it is a justifiable thesis that repetition is the initial stage in music's formal technique, and variation and development its higher developmental stages.

To compare is not to equate but to point out similarity. Moreover, the best imitation is less good than a moderately good original. The repetition of various sections in the two forms was held to constitute similarity, but that was insufficient reason to downgrade the musical rondo to the status of an imitation; and it was glaringly obvious that such an imitation would be inferior, because of the formal significance of the sections repeated in the respective forms. There is such a difference here that the musical form would be meaningless unless judged according to its own laws.

One can say that, in one case the idea is the rondo theme, in the other it is the refrain. Then the strophes, which are not repeated, are indeed subordinate to the refrain, which is repeated; they are illustrations which develop it and are added to it.

Now, the musical idea, the rondo's principal theme, is indeed also repeated, but for a *different reason*: repetition is the only way to develop it, whereas in the poem the idea is developed by the strophes, which are not repeated. For it is *they* that prove the aptness of the refrain and give expression to its core of meaning: the fact that *different things* can be *equal*, *similar*, or *related*. (Incidentally, a more popular, generally comprehensible mode of presentation; for in the higher forms there are less obvious, less generally comprehensible ways of doing that. The axiom appears only once, at the beginning or the end or at some other point.)

But repetition in music, especially when linked with variation, shows that *different things* can arise from *one* thing, through its development, through the musical vicissitudes it undergoes, through generating new figures—though this happens in a convincing way only in the higher forms.

And something more:

Whereas in the poem the strophes, the non-repeated parts, test the meaning of the refrain, in the musical rondo there is a different point to those sections which are seldom or never repeated. They are subsidiary and incidental ideas, whose point and purpose is digression, linking, introduction, transition, preparation, interruption, etc.—and contrast, which banishes the danger of monotony arising from so much repetition. The point of all these is purely functional and promotes the aims of the principal theme. That is their importance, and the degree of need to repeat them is in keeping with it, as also with their development. They serve their purpose at once, on the spot. And just as in our body blood is present throughout, whereas eyes, arms, legs, etc., occur merely twice, so here, too, the subordinate status of the merely auxiliary organs is expressed in the form of less prolific repetition.

So if musical rondo form were really supposed to be modelled on the poetic form, it could only be so very superficially; and since any good imitation is a bad one, Riemann's 'obviously' could in fact be accepted—that is, if one conceives this modelling process as having a purely ornamental significance.

But such a conception is an insult to the spirit of great musicians. If such a man writes a 'Spring' Sonata, then it is not an imitation but perhaps a premonition of spring, and when one hears it, spring must come to mind; a fugue does not imitate the way one voice chases another, like cops and robbers; an echo does not aim to be such a cut-and-dried imitation of an echo as the latter is of an original; and a musical rondo, even one composed to a rondo text, fills out this form according to its own style of being, for all that it may fit the prescribed outline.

This is something different from imitation; and the use of tried and trusted experiences and methods, such as a scheme for musical organization, is also something different. But it is not only more deserving to discover, to invent, to work out anew every time, that a hundred times a hundred equals ten thousand —it is also more correct, truly more correct. For, as we have said, if correctness is merely taken over, then the only reason why all is correct is that nobody has checked on the ways in which it might have been different.

Schemes of musical organization, too, should be invented only after one has used them, even if they were conveniently in existence before. The way the theory of composition is expressed, however, is as enigmatic as the way it was discovered.

Anyway:

If a musician, feeling not that he must, but that he ought, should be inclined to write a piece whose expression is to be popular, i.e. generally comprehensible, let him reflect on the following:

1. One understands only what one can take note of.
2. One can easily take note of something only if it is
    (a) clear (characteristic, plastic, sharply contoured and articulated);
    (b) frequently repeated;
    (c) not too long.
3. Any digression makes comprehensibility harder.
4. Any digression that rapidly and convincingly demonstrates its kinship with the main point makes comprehensibility easier.
5. The unarticulated is harder to comprehend than the articulated; articulation makes for character.
6. Over-elaborate articulation leads to confusion.
7. Segments that are different should look different; but what is identical must be strikingly identical.
8. Widely-ranging development is digression, which makes comprehensibility harder.

9. Depth of development must not destroy the smoothness of the surface.

10. The quicker the tempo of the tones and rhythms, the slower must be that of the figures, the motives and their development, i.e. the tempo at which the idea is presented.

11. The greater the distinctions between the individual figures, the motivic transformations, themes, etc., and the more loosely such things are juxtaposed, the greater the difficulty in comprehending the way in which things are being expressed.

12. A plastic mode of expression, however, will introduce subsidiary ideas of the kind that help the main idea to stand out.

Countless rondos have been written which resemble each other only in general outline, for all that their pattern is schematically the same. But even though this form fulfils the above conditions better than most others do, it is still a fact that the only people who can write in a popular and generally comprehensible way are those born with an inventive talent, turn of mind, and mode of presentation that are popular. The best examples are Johann Strauss and Nestroy.

But: flexible and clear self-expression is an art which one should be able to teach.

5

PROBLEMS OF HARMONY
1934

Modern music has centred interest on two problems: that of tonality, and that of dissonance. It cannot be said that the conflict regarding these questions is new, nor that it is waged with new weapons. On the contrary: just as all the battle-fields of world history are constantly the scene of renewed strife, so, too, is this one; this also is a battlefield in the historic sense.

Of course, it is not necessary for me to cite as proof the well-known precedents from the musical past. It is enough to recall the 'Dissonance'-Quartet of Mozart and Hans Sachs' lines:

Ihr schlosset nicht im gleichen Ton,
Das macht den Meistern Pein;
Doch nimmt Hans Sachs die Lehr' davon;
Im Lenz wohl müss' es so sein.

[Your closing key is not the same,
This gives the masters pain;
But Hans Sachs draws a rule from this;
In Spring it must be so, 'tis plain.]

In Spring!

We can say that in the development of art, it must always be as it is in Spring! One does what is necessary, though it cause somebody else pain; one does what the situation demands, unconcerned about the approval or disapproval of others.

And the cause of music demands, as the history of art-battles shows, that the secret of the sounding tone be always pursued anew. The development of music is more dependent than any other art upon the development of its technique. A truly new idea—at least as musical history reveals—is hardly imaginable without significant changes in musical technique. The material of music offers inexhaustible possibilities; but every new possibility in turn demands a new kind of treatment, because it presents new problems or at any rate demands a new solution of the old one. Every tonal progression, every progression of even two tones, raises a problem which requires a special solution. Yet the further such tones are brought into relation and contrast with each other and with rhythm, the greater is the number of possible solutions to the problem, and the more complex are the demands made on the carrying out of the musical idea.

In no art, properly speaking, can one say 'the same thing', the same thing which has been said once before, least of all in music.

An idea in music consists principally in the relation of tones to one another. But every relation that has been used too often, no matter how extensively modified, must finally be regarded as exhausted; it ceases to have power to convey a thought worthy of expression. Therefore every composer is obliged to invent, to invent new things, to present new tone relations for discussion and to work out their consequences. It is for this reason that the technique of music must develop so quickly and so persistently. In a methodic progression from the more simple

269

to the more complex, one would hardly be aware of the inevitable changes in technique. But imagination does not ask about method, nor does it invent according to a graduated scale. Differences in technique therefore appear far more abrupt than they are in reality. When we realize that today the difference in the technique of the early Beethoven from that of the later is apparent only to the connoisseur, we can no longer understand the cry from the gallery at the premiere of Beethoven's *Eighth Symphony*: 'Es fällt ihm schon wieder nichts ein.'

As I have said, the battle today, as always in music, is fought for the cause of dissonance and tonality, around concepts that are not even now clearly enough defined. For the phenomena which they are intended to reveal have been in continuous development since the beginning of music. This compels us always to conceive them in a new way. Therefore we shall try in the main to define them in relation to our time, according to present conditions, without claiming eternal validity.

Let us first examine the concept of tonality.

This coincides to a certain extent with that of the key, in so far as it refers not merely to the relation of the tones with one another, but much more to the particular way in which all tones relate to a fundamental tone, especially the fundamental tone of the scale, whereby tonality is always comprehended in the sense of a particular scale. Thus, for example, we speak of a C-major tonality, etc.

If, however, we wish to investigate what the relation of tones to each other really is, the first question that arises is: what makes it possible that a second tone should follow a first, a beginning tone? How is this logically possible?

The question is more important than it seems at first; nevertheless to my knowledge it has not previously been raised. Although all imaginable and far-reaching problems have been considered, no one has yet asked: How, after all, can two tones be joined one with another?

My answer is that such a juxtaposition of tones, if a connection is to be brought about from which a piece of music may be the result, is only possible because a relation already exists between the tones themselves.

Logically, we can only join things that are related, directly or indirectly. In a piece of music I cannot establish a relation between a tone and, let us say, an eraser; simply because no musical relation exists.

To elucidate the relationship between tones one must first of all recall that every tone is a compound sound, consisting of a fundamental tone (the strongest sounding one) and a series of overtones. We may now make the statement, and to a great extent test and prove it, that all musical phenomena can be referred to the overtone series, so that all things appear to be the application of the more simple and more complex relationships of that series.

Considered singly these relations are as follows:

1. The major scale is to be explained as nothing else than the addition of the tones of the three main triads on the I, IV and V degrees. In C-major they are, on the I degree: c-e-g; IV degree: f-a-c; V degree: g-b-d. But these tones again are nothing other than the fourth, fifth and sixth overtones of the three main fundamentals of a scale, (dominant, tonic, sub-dominant) which the following table demonstrates:

I	2	3		4	5	6		7	8	9	10	11	12	13
C	C	G		c	e	g		b♭	c	d	e	f♯	g	a♭
F	F	C		f	a	c		e♭	f	g	a	b	c	d♭
G	G	D		g	b	d		f	g	a	b	c♯	d	e♭

[cfg eab gcd]

The origin of the main fundamental tones is explained by the fact that each one occurs as the third overtone of the one lying a fifth below it. So that C is the third overtone of F, just as G is the third overtone of C. In this manner G:C = C:F. And it is evident that C attracts the tones related to it through G, just as F and its related tones do with the complex of C.

The natural origin of these fundamentals of the main degrees of the three main triads constructed on them, and of the resultant major scale from these components, as well as the circumstance that we actually to some extent hear and to some extent feel this relationship in every sounding tone, makes it possible for us to combine the tones of the major scale with one another.

2. But if we note the more distant overtones (up to the thirteenth) of these same fundamental tones, F, C, G (see the table above) we find the chromatic scale. Thus there appear:

b♭ as the seventh overtone of C
f♯ ,, ,,   eleventh   ,,   ,,   C
e♭ ,, ,,   seventh   ,,   ,,   F and thirteenth of G
d♭ ,, ,,   thirteenth ,,   ,,   F and eleventh of G
a♭ ,, ,,   thirteenth ,,   ,,   C

Of course the lower overtones that lie nearer the fundamentals are more easily perceptible than the higher, more distant ones. It is certain that the more perceptible overtones sound more familiar to the ear than those it hears but faintly; these last therefore remain strange to it. For that reason the chromatic scale is a somewhat more complicated tonal form than the major. And since, moreover, the chromatic scale levels the differences in the intervals, a fundamental tone can hardly be regarded as implied at the outset. On the contrary the significance of the tones changes in accordance with the manner in which one or the other is artificially made the fundamental. In each case we have seven other major scale tones and five other non-diatonic tones. In the major scale the relation of the tones to one another is firm and constant through their relation to the fundamental, but in the chromatic scale the relation of the tones is variable and dependent entirely on whether one of the tones is regarded as a fundamental.

But let us bear in mind that the chromatic scale flows from the same source as the major: from the elements which are the constituents of every tone. The difference is only that the one imitates the natural sound up to the sixth overtone, while the other reaches about twice as far, to the thirteenth overtone; in other words, the chromatic scale brings the more distant overtones within the possibility of relationship.

And here is the answer to our question regarding the possibility of interconnection of the tones. It is founded on the fact that in the sounding tone and its nearest relative, the union and the companionship of the tones is continuously demonstrated to our ear, so that we do nothing more than imitate nature when we make use of these relations.

In the major scale the ear follows a clearly perceptible pattern. Other scales, as for example the minor and the church modes, I regard as art products. The church-modes represent, namely, previous attempts to find the true fundamental tone and its laws, whereas the minor scale has its particular characteristic less in the minor third than in the artificial imitation of the cadence, by means of a half step, which is found in the major scale.

The chromatic scale, as the result of the more distant overtones, raises the question whether, and by what means, one of its tones following or opposing its nature, may be made a fundamental; and we can only answer that the means must be the same as those employed in the major, which we shall examine more closely later. Of course, any tone of the chromatic scale can be made a fundamental if the succession of tone and chord combinations gives emphasis to such meaning. Each tone can pass for a fundamental if its most important characteristics are strengthened, for example, if its major third and its perfect fifth are reinforced, if the major triad which is lightly sounded in the overtone series be stressed, be awakened to life.

Not every succession of diatonic tones or chords unequivocally expresses a key, that is, the predominance of a fundamental tone. Every major triad by itself belongs to at least three major and three minor keys (and here we are not considering transitional dominants and the like). For instance the triad g-b-d belongs to C, G and D-major as well as to A, E and B-minor. [See below, Example 1.]

A succession of two chords, for example, v–i in C major belongs to four keys (C and G-major, E and A-minor). [Example 2.]

But v-iii in C-major belongs to six keys, namely C, G and D-major, and A, E and B-minor. [Example 3.]

Even a succession of four chords may belong to four keys, for instance, the succession iii, vi, v, i of C-major belong to C as well as to G, but also to E-minor and A-minor. [Example 4.]

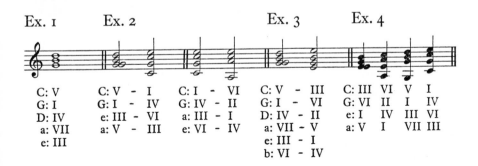

Ex. 1   Ex. 2   Ex. 3   Ex. 4

C: V	C: V - I	C: I - VI	C: V - III	C: III VI V I
G: I	G: I - IV	G: III - II	G: I - VI	G: VI II I IV
D: IV	e: III - VI	a: III - I	D: IV - II	e: I IV III VI
a: VII	a: V - III	e: VI - IV	a: VII – V	a: V I VII III
e: III			e: III - I	
			b: VI - IV	

Anyone well versed in harmony knows that there are even more complicated instances and that tonality is often so endangered that one can only say 'the last prevails'. But in contradiction even to this, let me point to the B-flat Allegretto of Beethoven's *Eighth Symphony*, where even the last does not prevail, for undoubtedly the piece does not end as it should in B-flat major, but rather on the v of E-flat major.

And this in spite of some of the cadences.

Cadences are successions of chords so chosen and arranged that a key appears to be set off from those it most resembles, and that its fundamental tone is significantly strengthened by being placed at the end.

But if the cadence were really a definite means to establish a key, we would not find, in the midst of a piece of music, cadences to various keys or degrees, the so-called modulations. And the classicists would not have been obliged to add many such cadences together if their feeling for form had not indicated that a key is not definitely established through a cadence. Therefore the familiar endings, consisting of a number of cadences of various combinations are often further extended through repeated successions of v-i, and concluding in several repetitions of i. Thus 'the last prevails', a method of procedure which Wagner, as is known, ironically characterized as grandfatherly in 'Papa Haydn'. But unjustly so; for Haydn knew how difficult it is to set up a key definitely and how necessary such persistent emphasis was for apperception by his audience.

Even in the relatively simple forms, those most nearly related to the fundamental tone, which employ chords and chord successions that are very near the key, tonality does not appear automatically, of itself, but requires the application of a number of artistic means to achieve its end unequivocally and convincingly.

The question of endangering tonality becomes acute at that stage, where, in addition to the diatonic, key-determining chords, an excessive number of chords occur within a composition, whose use the key at best permits but which no longer definitely refer to it.

This danger manifested itself rather early in musical history. In my *Harmonielehre* I have shown how every diminished seventh chord and every augmented triad belong to all major and minor keys and, what is more, in many a different sense. This is probably the place to point out that J. S. Bach in many 'Introductions', for example, and especially such pieces or parts labelled 'Fantasia' prefers a disposition of the harmonic structure which neither in its entirety nor even in its detail can be easily referred to a key. It is not uninteresting that in just such instances these old masters use the name 'Fantasia' and unconsciously tell us that fantasy, in contradistinction to logic, which everyone should be able to follow, favours a lack of restraint and a freedom in the manner of expression, permissible in our day only perhaps in dreams; in dreams of future fulfilment; in dreams of a possibility of expression which has no regard for the perceptive faculties of a contemporary audience; where one may speak with kindred spirits

274

in the language of intuition and know that one is understood if one uses the speech of the imagination — of fantasy.

To recapitulate:

1. Every isolated major triad can of itself express a key.

2. If no contradiction is added it may be taken for a tonic-chord.

3. But every succeeding chord contests the feeling for this tonality and pleads for others.

4. Only a few very special kinds of chord-successions permit the conception that any one of the used chords, chiefly the last one, is the fundamental chord of a key.

5. But even this designation is only final if nothing contradictory follows.

6. Without the application of very definite art-means a key cannot be un-equivocally expressed.

For example: the last movement of Beethoven's quartet, Opus 59, No. 2, is in E-minor. We know this principally because it ends in E-minor. But it begins in C-major with a theme which uses every means to establish this key. After a few measures it turns to the key which Beethoven decides to make the main tonality of the piece. I beg you to give due consideration to this case: by every ingenious means C-major is at first stressed in the harmony and in the melody; and the subsequent turn to E-minor can be taken even at that point as the third degree of C-major. How unconvincing is a key under certain conditions, if such a group can still be taken as the main theme of a movement in E-minor! I could cite many such instances in Beethoven, Brahms and other masters, where, in an extremely fine and ingenious manner, the ambiguity, that is, the indefiniteness of a key is made apparent.

We must conclude that neither at the beginning nor at the end, nor in the middle is the key automatically present. On the contrary at every point firm measures of art are required to give the key unequivocal expression.

Now then, since tonality is not something which the composer unconsciously achieves, which exists without his contribution and grows of itself, which would be present even if the composer willed the opposite; since, in a word, tonality is neither a natural nor automatic consequence of tone combination and therefore cannot claim to be the automatic result of the nature of sound and so an in-dispensable attribute of every piece of music, we shall probably have to define tonality as the art of combining tones in such successions and such harmonies or

275

successions of harmonies, that the relation of all events to a fundamental tone is made possible.

Thereupon the second question presents itself: Must tonality be uncon-conditionally present in every piece of music?

To answer this, one might say that tonality could not be sacrificed

1. if it accomplished the indispensable;
2. if no other substitute could be created for what it accomplishes.

Let us see what tonality accomplishes.

Even here the development of music can point the way. It is difficult to imagine that music could have pursued a road different from the one taken. Naturally at first the successions of the more directly related tones were obtained: the triad inherent in the tone, the major scale, the diatonic triads. It was natural also that these closely related results should be the first to be combined into forms.

But even here we find an inconsistency, a side-jump. For, strange to say, the near relationships were not realized immediately at the start, but only by the devious route of the church-modes. These reveal a remarkable phenomenon: the key of the underlying tonal series of which they are composed is different from the key in which the piece really exists. If, for example, a piece is written in the Doric mode on D, the tones of which it is composed are those of C-major. But in this mode the tones d,e,f,g,a,b,c, should be related to the fundamental D, and all endings, all semi-cadences and all else that expresses the key should refer to this D. Naturally these tones, which are fixed by their intervals, with the leading tones e-f, and b-c, are without a doubt in the C-major tonality. As is well known, these seven tones are the material of other modes on E, F, G, etc. This contra-diction was first resolved when the two principal modes used today were evolved out of the church-modes into a predominant position. Up to that time music can scarcely be regarded as tonal, in the present sense of the word. On the contrary we must concede that the church-modes do not at all conform to the law of tonality.

I have ventured to characterize the role played by the ear in the following statement: the presence of a fundamental tone was felt, but, since it was not known which of the scale tones possessed this quality, all tones were tried. How-ever the opposite point of view might also be justified: it was felt that a fundamental could be present, but, since the necessity of allowing the claims of a particular tone was not demonstrated, all tones were tried. And, as a matter of fact, exactly this proved to be possible!

Let us hold to the essential results of the foregoing consideration:

1. Music at that time was without tonality as we understand it.

2. The tones of our major scale could be referred to different fundamentals from those predicated by our idea of tonality.

3. We arrived at our present-day tonality by a very roundabout process.

As the ear advanced to the major and minor tonality it was already inspired with the certainty that it was possible to add other tones to the seven diatonic ones generally used. The ear knew that in the series c,d,e,f,g,a,b, no matter what the mode, almost all the missing half-steps could be used as accidentals, namely: c-sharp and b-flat in the Dorian mode, g-sharp in the Phrygian, b-flat in the Lydian, f-sharp in the Mixolydian, and g-sharp in the Aeolian—all the tones except d-sharp, which appeared only later in transpositions. The major and minor tonalities were not based, as might be expected, from the beginning on seven diatonic tones, but included also the four or five non-diatonic tones, which not only served the chromaticism of melodies, but also the development of closed tonalities on the individual degrees, as I call them, or, as they are otherwise known, modulations to the nearest keys.

From the beginning major and minor tonalities were interspersed with non-diatonic elements tending to form opposition to the fundamental tone yet compelling the application of strong means in order to verify the tonality, to paralyse eccentric effects. This was evident even before Bach's time. The conflict becomes more acute in the Romantic period following the Classical. The increasing attraction exerted by foreign harmonies made them more and more a significant element of expression. I shall not adduce all the known facts, for everyone is familiar today with the road that led from Schubert through Wagner to Reger, Richard Strauss, Mahler, Debussy and others. It is more important to state that this development began almost simultaneously with the realization of the major and minor tonalities, and that the art of music was never really in possession of a tonality wholly limited to the seven diatonic tones of the scale.

Though the development of tonality was by leaps and bounds, though it has not signified the identical thing at all times, its function has, nevertheless, been one and the same. It has always been the referring of all results to a centre, to a fundamental tone, to an emanation point of tonality, which rendered important service to the composer in matters of form. All the tonal successions, chords and chord-successions in a piece achieve a unified meaning through their definite relation to a tonal centre and also through their mutual ties.

That is the unifying function of tonality.

Just as important is its other, the articulating function, by means of which parts that previously were unified by a different application of the same means are limited and separated. If, for example, a phrase in A-flat may on the one hand, be regarded as belonging to C-major, on the other, this A-flat is somewhat kindred to the original tonality, and its relationship though distant is nevertheless well balanced; in this manner it helps to produce what is required in every exposition of an idea: coherent contrast.

The degree of relationship allows a graduated removal of individual parts away from the tonal centre, according to the degree of their meaning: more remote digressions can thus be characterized differently from ideas that are closely related.

Not only the position of the parts but their form can be fixed by assistance of tonality. Whether something be principal or subordinate idea, introduction or transition, episode, bridge, connecting link, embellishment, extension or reduction, whether independent or dependent, and, further, at which moment it begins or ceases to express one of these formal characteristics — all this is possible for masters of form to make manifest through harmony. Characteristic kinds of beginnings and endings, basic and concentrated or resolving and liquidating dispositions of the harmony and many other means of art have accomplished that great clarity necessary to formal ends.

I perceive in both these functions, the conjoining and the unifying on the one hand, and on the other the articulating, separating, and characterizing, the main accomplishments of tonality. The resulting advantages to the composer and audience are as follows: through the unity of relationships, the listener of a certain degree of comprehension must inevitably perceive a work so composed to be a unit, to be a totality. On the other hand the impression on his memory is deepened by the articulating function which characteristically builds the whole and its parts as well as their relation to one another, thereby facilitating the comprehension of fugitive events. For instance the listener with a schooled musical ear will recognize the reprise of the theme through the return to the original key;

he will also feel that so long as foreign keys are present the main theme is less likely to recur, but rather secondary themes or developments. Such trained listeners have probably never been very numerous, but that does not prevent the artist from creating only for them.

It is evident that abandoning tonality can be contemplated only if other satisfactory means for coherence and articulation present themselves. If, in other words, one could write a piece which does not use the advantages offered by tonality and yet unifies all elements so that their succession and relation are logically comprehensible, and which is articulated as our mental capacity requires, namely so that the parts unfold clearly and characteristically in related significance and function.

Without a doubt there are means of accomplishing this; certainly it would not be impossible to mention and to explain at least a few. But our question, if we put it negatively, is easier to solve, and the answer can be given in a general, relevant form. Let us ask then: do unity and coherence depend exclusively on tonality? A few well known facts will quickly elucidate this question.

Everyone with a knowledge of music is aware that each piece has certain parts, the smallest, which always recur: the so-called motives. Though it is not always possible or easy to follow the function of these motives in the most modern compositions, there is no doubt that it can almost always be done in the classics. The meaning of the elaboration of motives can only be uniformity (the more of an art-form the composition is, the more far-reaching the application): it is always the same material which is being handled; every form no matter where or how it appears may be traced back to these motives, the same idea is at the base of everything. Hence we shall find in the classics, besides the unity of tonal relations, that at least the same end of coherence is attained with at least the same amount of carefulness, through the unity of configurations, the unity of ideas.

Tonality is thus seen to be not the only means of producing the unity of a piece. It could, moreover, be easily shown that a work might have tonal unity, but nevertheless might still be confused in content, incoherent, superficial, external, yes, even without sense. It is apparent that it would not be difficult to apply to the harmonic structure of any sonata movement of Beethoven—incoherently and without any connection—themes from his other works. That such a product would be sheer nonsense is obvious. It must of course be conceded that to attempt the reverse, to build a structure, moreover, artistic in its motive forms, but on a foundation harmonically senseless, would probably lead to just as unintelligent results.

But here I have been trying not to show how the greatest nonsense can be achieved, but rather, that harmony alone, while contributing essentially to unity and articulation, cannot fill these requirements, since it needs other active art-means co-operating in the same direction. I am rather inclined to believe that one may sooner sacrifice logic and unity in the harmony, than in the thematic substance, in the motives, in the thought-content. Without doubt, in a genuine work of art, from the point of view of the ideal, there can be no serious consideration of the question as to whether one of the elements which compose it has less meaning than any other. Yet we know that dross is found in many a significant work. And if I reiterate that I do not regard tonality as the natural requirement of a piece of music, it will be understood in what sense I make the following statement:

It is difficult to conceive that a piece of music has meaning unless there is meaning in the motive and thematic presentation of ideas. On the other hand a piece whose harmony is not unified, but which develops its motive and thematic material logically, should, to a certain degree, have intelligent meaning. A message written in the worst orthography, with the grossest grammatical errors can nevertheless convey a clear, comprehensible report. On the other hand we know certain stylists, poets, who in recounting an incident are unable to state clearly, whether the lover shoots the husband or the wife, or whether the wife one of the others.

We have said that a meaningless harmonic foundation may support a structure artistic in its motive forms. If, even in this case, a certain effect cannot be denied the whole, how can it be denied when the harmony is not without meaning, when only the sense of the harmony is not easy to recognize, because, for example, certain requirements (tonality) are not fulfilled, or because it consists only of unresolved dissonances? It is obvious that such harmonies may appear irrational to an untrained ear which can just about receive the conventional. But there is no proof as yet that such a harmonic scheme lacks tonality, and it is easy to imagine that the concept of tonality will be so extended as to include all sorts of tone-combinations.

What detracts from the impression of tonality, according to my observation, is not so much the absence of the conventional formulae, the usual succession of degrees, that is, not alone the flow of these harmonies, but rather the appearance of a greater number of such tone successions and chords, the relation of which is difficult to account for, especially when their relation to a fundamental tone is not particularly emphasised.

This is the moment to consider the unresolved dissonances whose key relationship is not expressly fixed.

Up to a few decades ago only such chords were written as tended toward a key. These chords as a rule refer clearly to a fundamental, or they are made up of tones that have the melodic tendency to resolve like a leading tone, a half-step up or down; as, for example, the fourth-chords, which I have discussed in my *Harmonielehre*.

Distinct from these two groups is a great number of more-than-five-tone chords, the resolving tendencies of which have not yet been systematically investigated. It can be maintained neither that they belong to a tonality, nor that they point toward one. And conversely neither can the opposite be held; no proof has yet been brought that these properties are entirely lacking. But something else can be proved. If, with the simplest triads, such as I have shown in the example above, we can produce short phrases which do not definitely determine a key, we can also take chords, not too complicated, such as are used in Wagner's harmony, and make rather extensive examples in which no unresolved dissonance occurs, all of which by themselves may refer to a key but which *in toto* leave no doubt that no tonal centre exists and therefore no modulation. (Example 5)

Ex. 5

Then, too, conversely, we can take such chords as well as more complicated ones, that in no manner refer to a key, and join them to diatonic triads, and similar successions, in this manner creating, *a posteriori*, an impression that the preceding dissonances, no matter how unprepared and unresolved, referred to this key. (Example 6)

Ex. 6

N.B.—Which of the two examples is tonal, which atonal?

Strange to say, the ear accepts the final chord here just as it does a tonic and it might almost seem as if the preceding dissonances were really standing in legitimate relation to this tonic. The law mentioned before is again made manifest: 'The last prevails.'

One thing is certain: all chords, that in any way turn to a key, no matter how dissonant they may be, fall within the domain of the old harmony and do not disturb tonality.

It might further be said:

Tonality does not depend on the number of dissonances used, nor on their eccentric effect, but rather

1. on whether these chords may be referred to a key; or

2. whether these relations are convincingly enough worked out.

Dissonances, even the simplest, are more difficult to comprehend than consonances. And therefore the battle about them goes on throughout the length of music history. The number of consonant chords is limited; in fact, it is rather small. The number of dissonances is so great that it would be difficult to systematize the relation of even the simplest ones to all the consonances and to each other, and to retain them in the memory. With the majority of dissonances the ear meets a new and unknown situation, often a situation for which there is not the slightest analogy. How difficult it was even with the four and five-tone dissonant chords for the hearer not to lose the sense of coherence! But as soon as the ear grew accustomed to such sounds and tonal combinations, recognizing old acquaintances, it learned also not to lose the coherence, even though the solution of the problem was revealed not immediately but later.

It is easier to recognize and define three different, simultaneously sounding tones than five or six; it is easier to follow and to perceive the succession of three, than of five or six. But is the use of polyphonic chords therefore unjustified because they are more difficult to apprehend?

The criterion for the acceptance or rejection of dissonances is not that of their beauty, but rather only their perceptibility. The recognition of coherence, logic, conclusiveness is one of the most important conditions for the apprehension of what occurs, and one can only understand what one has retained in memory. If *a* plus *b* equals *c*, I can conceive *c* in the sense of *a* and *b* only if I remember *a* and *b*; only thus can I sum them up as equal to *c*. Since the presence of complicated dissonances does not necessarily endanger tonality, and since on the other hand their absence does not guarantee it, we can ask now, what are the characteristics of that music which is today called 'atonal'? Permit me to point out that I regard the expression atonal as meaningless, and shall quote from what I have already expounded in detail in my *Harmonielehre*. 'Atonal can only signify something that does not correspond to the nature of tone.' And further: 'A piece of music will necessarily always be tonal in so far as a relation exists from tone to tone, whereby tones, placed next to or above one another, result in a perceptible succession. The tonality might then be neither felt nor possible of proof, these relations might be obscure and difficult to comprehend, yes, even incomprehensible. But to call any relation of tones atonal is as little justified as to designate a relation of colours aspectral or acomplementary. Such an antithesis does not exist.'

I am usually not a coward; but if I should be asked to give this phenomenon a name, I would prefer—to avoid it entirely. But a habit has arisen of regarding music first, not with the ears by listening, second, not with the eyes by playing and reading it, and third, not with the mind but according to some technical peculiarity, for which there is a suitable slogan, a most striking term. 'This symphony is impressionistic!' Yes, but has something occurred to the writer? 'This song is expressionistic!' Yes, but does the composer know anything? 'This piano piece is atonal!' Yes, but does it contain an idea? And how is it accomplished? And what does the composer say that is new? or worth while saying?

If audiences and musicians would ask about these more important things and attempt to receive answers by listening, if further they would leave the idle talk and strife rather to the school-masters, who also must have something to do and wish to make a living, I, who have the hope that in a few decades audiences will recognize the *tonality* of this music today called *atonal*, would not then be compelled to attempt to point out any other difference than a *gradual* one between the tonality of yesterday and the tonality of today. Indeed, tonal is perhaps nothing else than what is understood *today* and atonal what will be understood in the *future*. In my *Harmonielehre* I have recommended that we give the term 'pantonal' to what is called atonal. By this we can signify: the relation of all tones to one another, regardless of occasional occurrences, assured by the circumstance of a common origin.

I believe, to be sure, that this interrelationship of all tones exists not only because of their derivation from the first thirteen overtones of the three fundamental tones, as I have shown, but that, should this proof be inadequate, it would be possible to find another. For it is indisputable that we can join twelve tones with one another and this can only follow from the already existing relations between the twelve tones.

Now let us briefly recapitulate the assertions already advanced. Tonality has been revealed as no postulate of natural conditions, but as the utilization of natural possibilities; it is a product of art, a product of the technique of art. Since tonality is no condition imposed by nature, it is meaningless to insist on preserving it because of natural law. Whether, for artistic reasons, tonality must be retained depends on whether it can be replaced. Since, as I have pointed out, the logical and artful construction of a piece of music is also secured by other means, and since the lack of tonality only increases the difficulty but does not exclude the possibility of comprehension; and since further proof of lack of tonality has not yet been adduced but as, on the contrary, probably much that today is not regarded as tonal, may soon be so accepted; and since dissonances need not in the least disturb tonality, no matter how increasingly difficult they may make the understanding of a work; and inasmuch as the use of exclusively tonal chords does not guarantee a tonal result, I come to the following conclusion: music which today is called 'tonal' establishes a key relationship continuously or does so at least at the proper moment; but music which is today called 'not tonal' never allows predominance of key relationships. The difference between the two methods is largely in the emphasis or non-emphasis on the tonality. We further conclude that the manner of composition of a piece abandoning tonality in the traditional sense must be different from that in which tonality is followed. From this angle tonality is seen as *one of the means* which facilitates the unifying comprehension of a thought and satisfies the feeling for form. But since this means alone does not achieve the goal, it may be said that tonality accomplishes but a part of the purpose. If the function of tonality be dispensed with, but the same consideration be given to unity and feeling of form, this effect must be achieved by some other function. Obviously music so contrived can hardly be easy to grasp at the present time.

To prove the correctness of an idea no special method of order and construction in its presentation is demanded. The effort of the composer is solely for the purpose of making the idea comprehensible to the listener. For the latter's sake the artist must divide the whole into its parts, into surveyable parts, and then add them together again into a complete whole now conceivable in spite of hampering details. Experience teaches us that the understanding of the listener is an unstable quantity: it is not permanently fixed. Fortunately! It gradually accommodates itself to the demands made on it by the development of art. How otherwise would it have been possible, in scarcely more than sixty years, to follow the leaps and bounds of musical development that have led us from Wagner through Mahler, Reger, Strauss and Debussy to the harmony of today. Many are still living who can recall the difficulties presented to their sense-perception by the dissonances of Wagner. Certainly there must still be many today who only a short time ago found Mahler, Strauss, Reger and Debussy incomprehensible; yet today these composers must appear to them, at least in their manner of expression, self-evident. No longer does one lose the thread in their compositions—in so far as one holds it at all—because of incomprehensible harmonic passages. Nothing now hinders the understanding of their thoughts, the recognition of their melodies, of the flow and construction of their works. What at first appeared harmonically incoherent, wild, confused, arbitrary, eccentric and hideous is today felt to be beautiful.

If we imagine that the perceptive faculties of audiences will advance nearly as far in the near future as in these past years, then we must have faith that we shall achieve a true knowledge of the ideas presented today and an understanding of their beauty. The difficulty here is, in the first instance, to recognize and to feel in the polyphonic dissonant sounds, the capacity to be joined successively;

to see in them elements of form and construction in the same manner as in the simple chords, and to feel also their relative measure of weight and significance just as in the older harmonies. Theoretical knowledge here is not the most essential need. Wagnerian and post-Wagnerian music was understood for a number of years before the derivation of certain chords and their relation to the key were theoretically established. Probably habit is all that is required; for it is able to prevent the recurrence of shock and the resultant lapse of presence of mind. He who is frightened is seldom in a position to follow exactly what is happening. Should such a one be accepted as witness, or rather one who does not lose presence of mind and remains calm, is enraptured or stirred only through the power of the idea and the emotion?

I do not assert that from now on there will be no more works of art which stress tonality; on the contrary, I believe that this is possible in more than one way. First, a popular art can exist beside pure art-music. Furthermore, works can be written occasionally 'in the old style'. But I cannot deny the possibility that as often in the musical past, when harmony has developed to a certain high point, a change will occur which will bring with it entirely different and unexpected things. The best example of this we find in J. S. Bach, whose manner of composition was regarded as out-moded by his son, Philip Emanuel, and in whose time, directly at the apex of the contrapuntal style, the homophonic-melodic of the classical period began.

How such a new method of composition is to be contrived, I am as little in a position to say as probably Bach in his day. I hope it will not be held against me, if I confess that I have no faith in such an end—though I hold it to be possible. For the parallel is not entirely sound. Bach was, to be sure, the first and only one to found and develop a domain of contrapuntal writing. He carried over perfectly —a fact not yet discovered—the secret of the old contrapuntal art of former periods, from the church-modes to major and minor, from seven to twelve tones. This art had no predecessor and no successor and probably herein lies the explanation of the sudden turn toward a new goal; namely that the goal of the contrapuntal style had been perfectly realised! But the music of today is developing a field which must at first appear entirely new to us. And here probably is the difference: the field must first be cultivated. It is virgin soil. We are not at the high-point of an old art but rather at the beginning of a new one. It seems improbable to me that this is already the moment for departure; I do not believe

286

we can afford to call a halt on work that is hardly begun; but naturally I am not able to dispute this.

6

CONNECTION OF MUSICAL IDEAS
c. 1948

The technique of the connection of musical ideas is as manifold as the same technique in our language; one would, accordingly, best proceed along the line of *grammatical* principles. There exists only the difficulty of applying grammatical concepts directly to music without metaphorical circumscription. Such *connectives* as the word 'and' admit addition only if one does not try to add six apples and five pears, i.e. if there is enough in *common* to permit addition. 'On the other hand' or 'in contrast to that' and 'however' suggest the contrary: ignoring the *absence* of a common factor which might, or might not, show up, but only later.

Fluency depends greatly on the right connective in both literature and music, notwithstanding the fact that simple *juxtaposition* often functions satisfactorily. It is not necessary to think of the 'general rests' which Bruckner so often uses as an opening for a new idea. But the highly dramatic general pause of Beethoven is of a different kind. While in the first case the part before the pause serves principally to diminish the obligations in which it has engaged, Beethoven's general pause furnishes time and space to take a deep breath before, like an explosion, a profound truth bursts forth. It is a moment of tension, enforcing what arrives as its consequence.

Tonality and rhythm provide for *coherence* in music; *variation* delivers all that is grammatically necessary. I define variation as changing a number of a unit's features, while preserving others. The change of features serves as an *annihilation* of former *obligations* and eventually as a gradual introduction of the new qualities that will make up the characteristics of the subsequent idea. The preservation of features constantly secures logic, and upon the presence or absence of these *connectives* is based the greater or lesser degree of *fluency*.

One of the most important functions of the changing of features is the production of *liquidation*. By producing at least a preliminary end to a section it makes the appearance of a new idea a reasonable, if not necessary, event. A liquidation is often carried out unto the entire elimination of all features. No wonder that in such a case the entrance of a terrifically strong *contrast* does not violate the feeling of balance. It is as if everything began anew.

A liquidation can, at one point or another, cease to eliminate; instead it can begin to develop and add new features. It then will have changed into a *transition*. A transition must have a goal. Like a bridge it leads from one bank of the river to the other. Between them an abyss might preclude communication.

7

OLD AND NEW COUNTERPOINT
1928

One can say that in the old art (and probably also among the Netherlanders) the ultimate aim of all contrapuntal skill is to produce parts in such a way that they give a 'comprehensible' total sound (my terminology!) in many (or all) of the positions in which one puts them together. From a different point of view, the necessary condition for this is that every relationship of simultaneity between two or more parts should allow each part to continue in whatever way one wishes (upwards, downwards, stationary), so that there is no question of *dissonance treatment* such as appears in the old theory of counterpoint—for none of the dissonant intervals is under any obligation, and each sound-combination of that kind can be resolved in *all possible ways*. I often explained this similarly to my pupils (and was the first to do so in our time), and also to some extent gave them the means with which to do it (they are not to be found in any book, and have, since the Netherlanders, evidently been known to only J. S. Bach and myself).

But looking at this matter in yet another way, we find that there is, strictly speaking, no essential difference between the way dissonances are regarded in our day and the treatment of dissonance in old music—I mean as regards the practical effect, which is that the fact of non-consonant intervals' sounding together has no perceptible outcome in the way parts subsequently move.

It is very interesting to see that my standpoint—'the harmony is not under discussion' (which represents merely the application of the old contrapuntal principle to the new technique)—has its counterpart in the dissonance's 'lack of influence' (no obligation)!

Vienna, June 10, 1928

8

LINEAR COUNTERPOINT
1931

I was always clear about the existence of something looking and even sounding like counterpoint, which is not in fact counterpoint. Namely, *linear counterpoint.*

A line can join two points—two, perhaps that are counter-points; but a point and a counter-point can never be linear, never resemble a line. Even semantically.

Counterpoint—the word—derives, ostensibly, from the name given the first species of exercises by which this art is learned (point *counter point*: a whole-note against a whole-note).

That is perfectly possible.

But a combination of knowledge and intuition tells me that the masters of counterpoint were very fond of expressing themselves through symbolic and mystical word-play. On this I base the hypothesis that, whatever the origin of the word (see above), the deeper sense alone defines the true essence of this art. That is, that counterpoint means an 'opposing point' whose *combination with the original point* is needed if the idea is to exist. The opposing point may contain the completion: $(a+b)(a-b) = a^2 - b^2$, so that $a^2 - b^2$ means, as it were, the idea represented by the point $(a+b)$ and opposite point $(a-b)$. Or things may be in the manner of diophantine equations, where there are many solutions, many ways to bring together point and opposing point (polymorphous canon; polymorphous texture)—here point and opposing point are placed as if right and left of the 'equals' sign, hinting at many possible solutions, or sound-combinations. Or their relationship may be something like that of subject and predicate— though in this case, whereas someone wishing to express different things without literally 'changing the subject' has, then, to change the predicate, in music it is enough to change the layout (in space and time).

Anyway, whatever one's views about the pleasure that can lie in conducting each part in polyphony independently, melodiously and meaningfully, there is a higher level, and it is at this level that one finds the question which needs answering in order to arrive at the postulate: 'Whatever happens in a piece of music is nothing but the endless reshaping of a basic shape.' Or, in other words, there is nothing in a piece of music but what comes from the theme, springs from it and can be traced back to it; to put it still more severely, nothing but the theme itself. Or, all the shapes appearing in a piece of music are *foreseen*[1] in the 'theme'. (I say a piece of music is a picture-book consisting of a series of shapes, which for all their variety still (a) always cohere with one another, (b) are presented as variations (*in keeping with the idea*) of a basic shape, the various characters and forms arising from the fact that variation is carried out in a number of different ways; the method of presentation used can either 'unfold' or 'develop'.)

It should by now be clear that from this point of view linear counterpoint is nonsense, or at least a distortion of sense. Merely for safety's sake let me add the following:

1. In a contrapuntal piece the idea is compressed in the form of a theme whose constituent elements, sounding together, form a kind of 'point of departure'.

2. This 'point of departure', this theme, contains all the possibilities for future redeployment of the elementary material.

3. In the course of the piece, the new shapes born of redeployment (varied forms of the new theme, new ways for its elements to sound) are unfolded, rather as a film is unrolled. And the way the pictures follow each other (like the 'cutting' in a film) produces the 'form'.

If, then, a contrapuntal idea is based on a combination of several parts, what can there be about it that is linear?

Now, however:

Linear: Here I must interpolate that I have not read E. Kurth's book *Der lineare Kontrapunkt*,[2] and hardly know more than the title and the odd things I have heard or read. Even my pupils could not tell me anything about it. So, like Jean-Paul's 'Little Schoolmaster Wuz', I am obliged to write my own book to fit the title, construct my own theory to fit this slogan. I must say at once, though, that so far as I can see any such possibility, it is from certain angles which are highly important and necessarily far from Mr. Kurth's way of thinking; they originate with me, in the structure of my theory, and I doubtless go far, far beyond anything he could have thought.

So: *linear*—one must not regard *independence* of the parts as meaning merely that, so far as their horizontal flow is concerned, they do not depend on one another—which means that parts:

A. (a) never move (carry out) in parallel for long;
    (b) do not have to work with the same motive;
    (c) if they work with the same motive, develop it differently;
    (d) are independent rhythmically, in fact ought to contradict each other;
    (e) ought to have different dynamics, performing indications, climaxes, cadences;

but must take it to mean also that parts ought to be independent of each other even in their harmonic relationship. This means:

B. (a) that in sounding together they need not be related to a common harmony;
    (b) that no sort of 'registerable' harmony has to result from the way they sound together;
    (c) that if possible they should produce dissonances when they sound together (to show how little they are worried);
    (d) that there need be no attempt to produce harmonic *progressions* ('registerable') ones, such as cadences or any other identifiable fundamental-progressions, and that such progressions are no criterion of the parts' function;

291

(e) that so far as possible one should avoid any articulation such as can arise from the coincidence of parts in articulating 'steps'.

So by 'linear' one can imagine a number of parts, each of which has its own development, and none of which worries in any way about the others.

This poses the following questions:

1. What, then, makes these parts belong together at all? That is to say, as regards their content?

2. How is one to grasp the 'combination' of sounds which, all the same, such parts produce?

3. Why do they *sound together*, and why at the particular times the composer has indicated?

One can begin by making a concession:

For practically any truly new creation the sole criterion is the formal sense possessed by the author, who can say to himself: 'My formal sense, tested in so many cases, trained by the best masters, and the logic of my thinking, which for me is beyond all doubt, and about which I have convinced myself—these guarantee me that whatever I unconsciously write will be correct in form and ideas, even when I renounce the aids given the intellect by theory and convention.'

That is how I proceeded! That is how I argued it afterwards!

But (here I must again interpolate) that was not what the people did who built on Kurth. Rather, in order not to lose all safety, building on sand, they chose ruins as their foundations; they claimed to be turning back to 'old forms'. Claimed—for those were not forms but, at the most, manners, methods, styles, ways of acting and behaving. They wrote toccatas and the like, 'à la Handel', in a 'running' or motoric way; they assumed a 'cantata-*tone*', a 'concerto-grosso-*tone*'; favoured canons in fifteenth-century style, or inexact ones, and a new imitative style appeared, which I had to call 'imitation-imitation'. This is how it looked: their toccatas consisted of one or more rapidly-moving parts, so independent and on their own that, as well as no longer worrying about the others, each part did not even worry too much about itself and its own appearance. In fact, even on their own they really made no sense either, chattering or stuttering for no apparent reason, at best chattering like a weekly column or however else people talk; when stuttering, they were more determined, like village idiots. But they were able to make a certain effect through a certain primitive formal sense, and a piece of good luck: jazz, with its rhythmic and other drolleries, had just appeared; drolleries whose effect one could acknowledge simply as drolleries. Now, whatever in these toccatas 'worked' formally came from the formal sense of a jazz-arranger, and whatever in them was 'daring' came from the drolleries. But an overall sound (basically tonal, in all other respects confusing and irregular) produced by unheard and mutually irrelevant parts is in fact not particularly droll—any more than jazz, sharing the same state of mind, was entirely comprehensible. Do not forget: these toccata-boys knew how to finish—like the jazz-boys, throwing in a surprising, cheeky tonic, hardly to be justified by anything in the body of the piece.

It is much the same with the concerti grossi, where the only exception was the adagios. These stood out through their *exaggerated slowness* and lived on the advantages it offered: in music, if everything happens slowly enough, anybody can follow up to a certain point. And since I am not alleging that the authors of such pieces were entirely ungifted (I find, to the contrary, that many a musical talent was led astray by just this), it cannot be denied that these pieces could make a certain effect—the more so as certain clichés of adagio-cantabile and adagio-mood were at work, lending their support. The abrupt succession of a series of these was felt to be a virtue, to be modern.

One hardly need waste words on the canons—they bear witness to the most utter ignorance, so far as understanding the essence of contrapuntal composition is concerned.

But about this time the 'imitation-imitation' style proved an ideal way of seeming to 'consolidate'. In reality the *imitation* found here was nothing but a substitute for sequence. Just as sequence *creates cohesion through repetition* and aids *comprehensibility*, so does two- to five-fold imitation.

Let us pass over what the other parts, the accompanying parts, had to add. What could they do? Imitate—inexactly, like the stuff found in junk-shops.

But a piece that sent two 'themes', or several, rolling down one after another in this way, occasionally repeating a phrase, perhaps superimposing two such themes (what can one not superimpose, given such lack of scruple?), and even making one further concession to great art by devising some sort of 'motivic relationship' between the themes (not an innate one!)—a piece like that made a certain formal effect which the masters of this style were clever enough to enhance by allowing a key (appropriate to the purpose, or as likely not) to glimmer through, or simply by administering a half-cadence or some arbitrarily cobbled-on tonal triad.

Far be it from me to deny that certain genuine talents, such as Hindemith or Krenek, have by an indisputable inventive talent and strong musicality produced things on a far higher level, and in their best moments even good and beautiful music. But neither can I deny that very often their unconcern strikes me as lack of conscience and bears witness to a disturbing lack of responsibility. Here I have in mind, for example, Krenek's 'basses', which he doubles (in octaves) on the bass-instruments, as if they were *fundamentals* (and in such conventional part-writing they will really sound like fundamentals, too), although the 'harmony' above them has *nothing whatever to do with them*, and the 'progressions' just as little. Or Hindemith's folk-song arrangements in the book of folk-songs where mine also appear.[3]

And I readily admit that this criticism is a little influenced by what I find the unsympathetic mentality of most of the young composers of the present-day — by their mania for success, their publicity, and their skill in using their elbows. I also readily admit that criticism by a contemporary, especially by someone a good deal older, is relatively inconclusive. All the more so as I feel I could bring some sense into the aesthetic and theoretical nonsense that accompanies their activity as composers — perhaps I could even draw up a complete and sufficient theory of these methods; but I do not yet find myself mature enough to assess their value.

For it is quite conceivable to apply the following procedure to the formulation of ideas, the development of ideas, and to formal construction (also bearing in mind what I know, or have noticed, about the so-called 'new tonality'. I still have to deal with this). The themes could be organized according to the following principle, as for a new tonality, or else by chromaticism, in which, however, a tonal centre would be provided.

(N.B. *New Tonality* was explained to me as follows: everything is derived from the seven tones of a series (major? minor? some other kind?), but after that one need pay no further heed to the sound as a whole, so that any note may occur together with 1, 2, 3, 4, 5 or 6 others; nor does one pay any heed to parallels (not even to octaves, apparently). But since 'the modern composer feels the need for dissonances', still other notes are introduced at certain points (??). I immediately raised the objection that the complete lack of modulation would mean monotony, at least if one limited oneself strictly to the seven tones. This objection remained unanswered. But I think I noticed in Hindemith's oratorio[4] that he has a way of encircling the main key with certain other keys, and in so doing he seems to organize his cadences in a way which does in fact perform a certain articulating function—hinting, in the melody or other parts, at elements that are to appear at the cadences, also by displacements in the lay-out, and by replacing the tonic and dominant with other degrees of the scale.)

Barcelona, December 2–3, 1931

9

LINEAR COUNTERPOINT: LINEAR POLYPHONY
1931

These two expressions—one stemming from Professor Kurth,[1] the other from his acolytes—form one of the bases of present-day musical theory. I know few expressions so hollow and irresponsible (and there are many—'loosened harmony', etc.). I take it that Kurth said 'linear polyphony'. This is supposed to mean a plurality (multiplicity) of parts, in which the criterion of admissibility is no longer the sum total of the sound, but exclusively the individual line—that is to say, the horizontal, and no longer the vertical.

It is a fair assumption that Mr. Kurth arrived at this expression through wrongly grasping certain personal qualities in my music. 'Wrongly', for the following reasons. My earlier works did not yet come within the scope of my remark, 'The harmony (or "the total sound"—but that was wide of the mark) is not under discussion'; it applied only to those from the time of twelve-tone composition. It can easily be shown that in the earlier works the chords are designed to have at least an accentual, articulating and colouring effect, and that their mutual conduct is full of regard for the relationships of the parts as they move. However, what is even here not under discussion—not, at least, in the way found in the *Harmonielehre*—is the harmonic *progression*. This, however, was never under discussion in counterpoint; but still one must pay a certain amount of attention to chordal progression, insofar as there is a prevalent tendency to avoid tone repetition as much as possible, or to disguise it. However, in twelve-tone composition harmony is no longer in any sense under discussion, nor even is progression, since both are subordinate to a different law.

But has it occurred to Mr. Kurth and his followers that there must be some bond of cohesion between a number of parts intended to be heard simultaneously and meaningfully, and that this bond can cohere only in some other direction than the linear? It seems that here we have to think of motivic cohesion, since that of tonality and even organized barring is discarded by the followers. An assumption such as this would also apply to my own works, and obviously no objection could be raised against it.

But what is just as obvious is that the expression, 'linear polyphony', is then entirely wrong. For the individual line explains nothing about the whole and gives no indication why this one line should appear at the same time as others. Or, at most, negatively; the line would in itself be incomplete, inadequate. (So the idea is in fact not linear enough!—not enough of a *single* row (*Reihe*).) Only the relationship of several rows one to another, the vertical aspect of the line, gives them their significance! So this polyphony, polylinery (horrible new word!) is based on a relationship of cohesion between the individual lines, which does not necessarily lie in anything tonal, chordal, or in any other way corresponding to the older harmonic theory. In particular, the most important thing is missing: the treatment of dissonance and the prohibition of parallels (for the clumsy).

But now it is clear that *linear counterpoint* is a contradiction in terms. For *counterpoint* signifies, even in the view of school masters and historians, who lack any feeling for word-play, the relationship of one 'point' (note) to (or against— 'contra') another point—that is to say, *relationship* in a *direction other* than that of the *line*. Here let me also set down what I have probably set down elsewhere[2] —that I believe 'counterpoint' to be a play on words (I lack the philological equipment to explain this fully) and gather from it the following: the art of counterpoint, of 'against-notes', those notes or note-progressions which can be set in opposition and magically possess a relationship to each other that fulfils the principle of cohesive contrast. What these notes and note-progressions are, that could form a counterpoint, seems to have been a secret for a few initiates. I have always thought so, and I recently came across some supporting evidence. Naturally it was through Riemann, quoting an older theorist (Marpurg, if I am not mistaken) who doubts this secret science. Mr. Riemann, naturally, then does the same; Mr. Riemann, who doubts everything his particular old hat will not fit. As opposition to this Riemann, who teaches counterpoint by adding 'ornaments'—passing notes and suspensions—to harmonic textures, one could even approve of a formulation like 'linear counterpoint'! But only then.

So, even were my assumptions unprovable, counterpoint is in all circumstances the relationship of two or more rows one to another. But 'linear' surely means that the entire significance resides in the line, in itself!

So: linear counterpoint $=+-+-$ a piece of nonsense.

10

FUGUE
1936

Fugue is a composition with maximum self-sufficiency of content. The more such self-sufficiency is manifest in the form of unity of material, the more all the shapes stem from one basic idea—that is to say, from a single theme and the way it is treated—the more artful it is. In its highest form, which may perhaps be a merely theoretical construction, nothing would claim a place in a fugue unless it were derived, at least indirectly, from the theme. To this extent—and also in many other ways—it also employs the principle of variation in the formulation of two or more forms of the theme (*Dux* and *Comes*), as also in the production of countersubjects and material for the episodes. But the theme's everchanging 'way of accompanying'—through other parts, through transposition of invertible combinations, through the various types of canon, and also through harmonic re-interpretation—all this, too, is best regarded as variation. Here its way of thinking shows its identity, in comparison with the classical art of homophony where, again, new figures produced from a basic figure (*Bilder*) are welded into a whole in an effective way.

August 5, 1936

11

ABOUT ORNAMENTS, PRIMITIVE RHYTHMS, *ETC.*, AND BIRD SONG
1922

The second half of the nineteenth century dealt summarily with ornaments. The battle against tradition, opened by Schumann's Band of David against the Philistines, was continued with relentless severity and consistency by Wagner and his successors. A process of that kind was entirely in keeping with the ideals of the time; it realized demands imposed in the civil sector by the French Revolution, demands that made people aim at equality in the field of art, putting forward only ideas the masses could understand, with content or presentation suitably adapted. But this *mass art* outgrew concert-halls and music-rooms; there being so many listeners, one had to build larger halls, and the music played in them had then to be louder. But since everyone needed to understand, too, one had to express oneself more slowly. Style became broader; repetitions (sequences) regained the upper hand; quicker notes (fluidity) dropped out as far as possible; one limited oneself to main points; wherever possible, ornaments were regarded as minor points and so mostly left out.

There is proof that this desire for simplicity did really result from the demand of the day for maximum comprehensibility: namely, that the same thing has again come about in our own day, and for similar reasons. Such ideas are Utopian. If something is art, then it will not be understood by the broad mass, however broadly it is expressed; but if it can be so broadly expressed, then it is something liable to be understood only to the extent that men's unison choral singing is understood.

Art for all—it took much time and many sacrifices for this ideal to be recognized as Utopian. And certainly the people to suffer are those who knew better all along, who long ago realized that the laws of art work in a way that contradicts the way the popular mind works. Such people take no pleasure in doing penance for ideals which they have opposed with the severest mistrust; all the less so, as they have already been blamed for the fact that art and the masses entirely refused to be united with each other. But I think these people are used to paying, for to pay, wherever others have had the pleasure, suits their *noblesse oblige*, their sense of position. They will not shrink from this duty. They will be proud to pay off the debts of the chronic scroungers who have already wormed their way into a new hostelry, for, having done them that service, one may at least despise them—so much is clear even to those whose moral sense makes life somewhat gloomy for them.

But one thing is certain: this simplifying process has led to ignorance, insofar as it was not the result of ignorance. It is certainly to blame if nowadays we no longer know how to play the so-called ornaments in the works of our great masters. It is certain that not everything so called is an ornament; not all that glisters is mere gold, deprived of the right to count as anything more in the work of art; that in a work of art, *glitter* is meant to attract attention to the *main idea*, and that in true works of art nothing is an ornament in the sense that one could leave it out.

What was the reason for concluding that ornaments are dispensable minor points? One single fact, unsatisfactorily enough: these melodic particles are notated differently from the rest, in a way which soon nobody understood any more, since it was passed on purely by word of mouth. It may be assumed that by J. S. Bach's time there were already differences of opinion about how to interpret various markings. This is seen not only from the fact that J. S. Bach began, against his contemporaries' practice, to write out his fioriture in full, but also from the fact that C. P. E. Bach found it necessary to write an 'Essay on the true art of playing keyboard instruments'. By then people no longer knew for certain; but rather than proving that nobody *ever* knew (as was later assumed), this proves almost the contrary: no sooner did people notice that they had lost the tradition than they began to look for an artificial substitute; doubts set in, people tried to formulate rules to cover what had earlier been self-evident, and part of it had to be left to taste, in the form of exceptions. Only a part, though—

whereas the modern view of the subject is based on the erroneous premise that all fioriture, in their entirety and in every detail, were left to the performer. But if that is the premise, then one may fairly arrive at the conclusion that the ornaments can be left out entirely; this, however, is taking the argument to an extreme—much too far, certainly.

However, in my view *the performer's freedom was by no means so inconceivably great* as it now seems to us to have been. Above all, it was *relatively speaking hardly any greater than we are nowadays* forced to grant the performer on many points, and wherever our notation is in any case inadequate. In tempo and its modifications; in dynamics, in accents and phrasing, in colouration—in all these fields we are still far from able to indicate perfectly what it is we want. For example, we use the same sign to indicate phrasing and legato, and have thoroughly inadequate methods of showing the distinction between short notes (détaché) and thrown and struck staccato, or between portato and 'staccato within the same bow'. We have not yet even thought of indicating in any way how a tone is to end, and yet a great deal depends on just that; nor do we possess a sign for gradation, suspension and displacement of accent—this leaves far too much room for 'interpretation', especially in solving the innumerable and far-reaching rhythmic displacements in Beethoven. In time to come, people will want more exact information about all this, for the same reason that prompts us to inquire about the performance of ornaments; the tradition will no longer be familiar; or instruments will have altered; or there will once again be a new (or old and resurrected) ideal of sound, performance and expression. And then it will be incomprehensible that we could fail to indicate all this. Let us hope that people will then not make the same mistake and assume we deliberately left it all to the performer, so that he might have a chance to display his interpretation! Rather, they will (one hopes) assume:

1. That many differentiations were unknown to us.

2. That a whole series of others were, partly, not sensed clearly enough, and, partly, impossible to depict because we lacked suitable notation.

3. That we omitted to fix anything of the kind, because we could assume that in any case everybody would know what was meant (e.g. when the trombone is marked *pp* and the flute *ff*, something that will perhaps some day be incomprehensible), but could have no idea what would later alter, and in what respects, and in which direction.

4. That a certain unexpressed residue in the work of art must be added to make it complete, not so much through exactness as through the performer's talent; this is so even when there is the best imaginable mechanism at work, setting down the definitive version, since even such a mechanism becomes obsolete, and our ear changes and becomes ever more acute.

But the performer's freedom was probably *not absolutely greater than it is today, either*. Using the metronome as often as we do, we have sharpened our powers of sensing and remembering the exact division of time, to the point where we can recognize and depict the slightest deviations from every division. And yet we do not in fact do so; rather, we leave a good deal just as it would be if the strictly measured tempo carried on exactly. Note the following, for example: nearly all musicians combine a change in dynamics, consciously or unconsciously, with a change of tempo; a crescendo is usually accompanied by an accelerando, a diminuendo by a rallentando. Whether this is making a virtue of necessity, or corresponds to psychic conditions, or is in the last analysis just a traditional performer's mannerism: in any case, it does happen, and changes of pitch and dynamics are also linked to some extent. It is, at least, almost universal practice to make a crescendo in a melody that rises, and there is no way of indicating that this is to be avoided—one can only use the decrescendo sign. Again, it is very customary to swell out and die away again on held notes. If one wants the performer to refrain from doing so, one is helpless: there is no available marking. Or, sequences are almost always performed as a 'build-up', dynamically as well as in tempo. In the classical forms a technique has developed for making the architecture explicit. For example, one stresses the fact that material is of an introductory nature by sharply separating the sub-sections, which are mostly juxtaposed in a disconnected way; in transitional passages, on the other hand, one achieves connection rather through supple modifications in tempo, while dwelling on, or confirming, the dominant (e.g. before the second subject) is most often indicated by a ritardando. On the other hand, the second subject (even when it is not a 'cantabile' theme) is usually performed at a different tempo, rather slower for the most part. All these performing methods are liberties, for the composers did not indicate most of them. And what they *did* indicate—how does that stand? Any musician knows how to play *cantabile*, *dolce*, *grazioso*, *espressivo*, and so on. Nobody has yet attempted to say how it should be done in each individual instance.[1] One sees that the cases where the score can provide only very incomplete performing indications are far more numerous than is generally assumed.

So there is no denying that different musicians have different ways of realizing all these indications, which are mere stimuli; the various ways differ just as widely as the musicians' talents differ in kind and degree; such differences reach the point where one should call them a matter not of taste but of lack of taste; yet, despite all this, it is true that the reasons for leaving all this to the performer are those I have already adduced. I should however, point out one or two such differences. Nowadays the execution of certain alterations in tempo has reached the point where 'exaggeration' is a fair description. Here too it is the necessity of addressing a discussion of fundamentals to a mass of people with limited powers of comprehension in a large concert-hall (and nobody now does otherwise), which imposes a monumental plasticity on one's way of expressing oneself. Clearly, to be understood even from far away, all the points of light have to be reproduced more brilliantly, all the shadows more deeply, all the climaxes more obtrusively, all the caesuras more decisively. Nowadays, a tone with a fermata will not have its length doubled, as the rule demands, but is sure to be four times as long. It is in the case of ritardando and accelerando, where there are no rules, that one can find the greatest differences, though. Most musicians move into a tempo half or twice as quick with hardly an intermediate stage, while others think that either modification has to happen 'flowingly', gradually, as an even acceleration or slowing-down. But the greatest need for clarification is on the question of how slow or fast the tempo may become in the course of this. Are these merely matters of taste? Nietzsche calls Schiller 'the moral Trumpeter of Säckingen', and yet his pathos is certainly just as great as Schiller's, so one must become clear in one's mind whether in a given case the pathos lies in the performance and the manner of speaking, or in the idea itself. Beethoven's pathos can certainly be reproduced in many varying degrees, even if one may find that the milder among them certainly do not suit such a fiery spirit. In any case, a lack of pathos which might seem fitting to Mozart will leave us unsatisfied in Beethoven. But no matter how far pathos is 'thematic', the differences arising from temperament do still produce such far-reaching differences in performing style that one can by no means speak even here of a guaranteed performance, unified by correct interpretation of what is written down.

The fact which more than any other speaks for the assumption that earlier musicians were more lax than we are in formulating their markings is that their *inexactness*, unlike ours, affects more than merely the performance, such points as tempo and dynamics; *the performers are given considerable, almost incalculable freedom as regards the relationship of the notes to each other in the matter of pitch.* Here I am thinking not merely of the many ornamental notes, which could be introduced (or even had to be) without any indication on the author's part (e.g. appoggiaturas); nor of cadenzas and other free additions of that kind; nor even of accidentals, for which there may have been rules; but particularly of the well-known method of *continuo*, by which the performers were indeed left so seemingly great an influence on the eventual sound that hardly one present-day composer would be able to bring himself to do anything similar. I shall find some other opportunity to show that even this freedom only seemed to be especially great, but was in reality less significant than people of our time can possibly imagine. For relatively speaking, and bearing in mind the type of formal moulding appropriate to the polyphonic style, the expression of the idea, its marking-off and working-out, happened so precisely and exactly within the notes written down, that whatever the continuo player may have added, be it too much or too little, had no influence, since it merely took up the space outside the idea, around it, like a better- or worse-fitting suit of clothes such as any craftsman can run up to the best or worst of his ability. As comprehended by people of earlier times, a work of art's meaning did not change in any essential respect, any more than a man becomes someone else when he has different clothes on. There was no question of its being distorted and unrecognizable—the change of outward apparel could rather come to be regarded in a comparable way, as an attractive variation, like the obviously intentional alteration of their appearance which people go in for if they are worth looking at: an additional attraction! Although freedom is here found once again to be hardly greater, in proportion to the prevailing view of art, to the power of comprehension and to formal structure than that allowed in our own time, one can still go on to prove something else—that here again it was hardly intended as freedom, and that its aim was not to facilitate 'interpretations'. Remember the unpredictable volume of sound produced by the accompanying instruments available for any particular performance (organs of all dimensions, harpsichords, clavichords, and the like). Such things are even nowadays an obstacle, despite all the schools and the efforts to ensure unity, because different players have a bigger or smaller tone, different expressive capabilities in point of dynamics, and, particularly, varying taste and other hindrances to clarity. But in those days the obstacle was even greater. Remember, too, that in a texture of only two or three worked-out parts (which, however, contain everything needed in the way of ideas) the continuo player is given the chance to adapt, to accompany as loudly or softly, in as full or as light a way, as prevailing circumstances demand; and that nowadays, even given the greatest powers of instrumentation and the existence of but a small and unified number of orchestral instruments, it is only seldom that the necessary dynamic levels can be reliably written down, once and for all. It will be clear that all this is a great deal harder still with organs of differing sizes and intonation and varying acoustical conditions, and it will have to be admitted that here, too, people of olden times were placed very much as they were in the cases discussed earlier, and that their notation represents neither an open invitation to the virtuoso nor deliberate laxity.

I believe I have shown that we are not justified, when a type of notation strikes us as inadequate, in coming to any conclusion about the artistic significance of the parts of the music not included in the notation—any conclusion which would make it permissible to leave them out. I think the best way of summing this up is by the following formulation: in old works, when parts of the texture and melody are not expressly notated, one may by no means simply leave them out but must heed them just as one does certain inadequacies of notation that appear with equal frequency in modern works. They are left to the performer's interpretation only because we have lost the tradition that clarifies them beyond ambiguity.

This tradition was bound to be lost in proportion to the growth of notation, since the latter was forced to develop in a mathematically simple way, whereas performance could correspond to the most complicated numerical relationships.

Certainly people have failed to acquire from elements that are familiar an idea of how music was made in earlier times and of how it was possible to play together before any elaborate notation existed. How else could they have come to the incomprehensible, grotesque conclusion that before European music no real polyphony existed? It is assumed that a rich variety of instruments existed, playing partly in the same register, but certainly at different dynamic levels and with differing expressive possibilities; and all these were given the same thing to play at the same time.

Play? What else could they do? If there was no real polyphony, what can the unreal kind have been like? Surely this is a false assumption. Either the instruments played the same thing, or some of them played something else, and in the latter case there can only have been real polyphony, unless one assumes that there were groups separated in space and time, but monophonic, alternating with each other. But this seems unlikely when there were so many of them— enough to make it likely that the spaces involved were large, for surely there would not have been more musicians than listeners present. And it seems improbable that all these musicians there on the spot were barred from playing together at least occasionally—it is not in keeping with such colourfully festive occasions, and it offends, in a psychologically implausible way, against the laws of economy which very much dominate the human race. So one may assume that they all played and that real polyphony, therefore, already existed. No written transcriptions of polyphonic compositions exist, but this proves nothing, or only that it was thought unnecessary to write down anything so obvious as the accompanying parts. There is no understanding why people make such basically wrong assumptions about all this—why they categorically assume that people of earlier times were so basically different from those of the present day, and present-day people so infinitely superior, on so far higher a level, thanks to our achievements, that between our ideas and theirs no parallels can be drawn. And yet it is so rewarding and easy to acquire a correct idea of the past, if one assumes that everything, except for the discoveries which make us feel so arrogant, was exactly as it is nowadays. But unfortunately we learn as soon as we go to school to exaggerate the value, the supremacy of our own day, and so we cannot imagine everything that has already existed in earlier times.

In our case one very easily gets a satisfactory idea how polyphonic music can exist without being tied down to a written version, if one recalls the way gypsy musicians practise their new pieces. The principal fiddle, or the composer, plays the main melody to them, the others either listen or try straight away to find a suitable accompaniment; the less skilful may even have their parts played to them. For each piece, moreover, all the instruments have what amounts to a scheme within which each part moves, so that each individual is soon oriented, can play his part from memory, and the ensemble can play. Here, then, there is polyphony in two ways: harmonies in various rhythmic patterns, and counterparts which elaborate on the basic character. That, to some extent, is polyphony, even if not in our sense (which implies a high level of combination and economy). But as regards this procedure—clearly, it not only could have been the practice in earlier times, but one can hardly imagine such a well developed procedure only coming into existence since Europe became aware of harmonic theory. Here we have this basically wrong assumption—that one composes according to theory. But people forget that, in so far as disposition and natural talent play a role in art, these can lie only in the fact that, thanks to his powers of hearing, true knowledge of sounds and good memory, a musician is able to do correctly, without study, precisely the thing no theory has yet thought possible. And that is the only basis for the assumption that no true polyphony existed before that in Europe—the fact that apparently no theory exists to cover the harmonies used.

Here it may be safely assumed that in producing the polyphony of gypsy music, there is again no lack of rules which are merely passed on by word of mouth, stemming from experience and practice, and perhaps applying only to individual cases. This state of affairs, incidentally, is matched elsewhere, as in the way many parts of our harmonic theory (e.g. the theory of tones foreign to the harmony) are treated from a purely practical, routine point of view, or in counterpoint teaching, which entirely lacks any theory. This shows that the way to perform a given task may be common knowledge to all the musicians of a particular period, even without their arriving at it via any explicit and detailed theory.

Continuo playing is, then, basically very similar to the method practised by nature's musicians, the adaptation of an accompaniment to a given melody, as they feel it; the similarity being so great, one can regard continuo as simply a more complete version of these methods.

This should be plain to anyone who wants to see in such things simply what is truly there—not a higher or lower aesthetic stage, for that is governed by other factors, but simply attempts at solutions, usable, in keeping with prevailing conditions and to be evaluated only from the standpoint of usefulness. This can be shown by many examples. Anyone who knows Bach's musical handwriting knows that it is the practical script of a man who did not care whether he wrote more or less, but a man glad to do just what was required, not without taking care and pleasure in it. This script—these groups of eight-, sixteen-, and thirty-second notes which mark out the melodic line, the exactness of the vertical line-up, the constant writing-out of parts that are doubled—none of this gives the impression that Bach wanted to save himself work. So it was not for any such reason that he left the continuo part unwritten. There must have been other reasons for this, and perhaps, among others, those already mentioned, concerning adaptation to halls and instruments. It is also noticeable that in the choral works all the choruses are given a fuller accompaniment, and not merely through two or more of the louder instruments doubling each part; the number of parts is greater, far greater, too. The arias and duets, on the other hand, seldom show more than one or two written-out parts doubling the voices, over and above the figured bass, and often none at all. Now even though one may assume that a fuller instrumentation also makes necessary a greater number of parts, no such reasoning applies in the arias, and yet one often finds these are accompanied by from one to three obbligato parts (*even at times by the full orchestra*). One can conclude from this that the choruses are indeed accompanied a good deal more fully than the arias, but not, basically, in a more polyphonic way, and that in the arias there is a smaller number of obbligato parts which are not written down, because the continuo player, being adaptable, has no need of them—he knows artistic ways to make the texture polyphonic without its being prescribed. The orchestral musician, on the other hand, needs his part exactly prescribed. Here, perhaps, pleasure and utility combine; a full, even if small, orchestra can naturally give way less easily to the singer than can a small chamber-music ensemble, but the continuo player can certainly do it best of all, and the fewer others there are playing at the same time and hampering him, the better. In Bach's case we also know for certain that he played the continuo part himself and was thus in a position to meet every demand in matters of sound, counterpoint, and harmony, just as he could those of character. When he did so, it was no doubt less a matter of leaving himself freedom (since he had ensured that for himself from the very outset), than of his simply ignoring the fact that somebody else would someday wish to play this part, or be allowed to, or have to; for, in his time, could anyone imagine that musical works would still be performed once the fashion had changed? The composer had written this part for himself, and for no one but himself, and it did not occur to him that it could ever provide anyone else with a warrant to take greater liberties than he himself took: after all, he had taken no liberties but had most strictly carried out the author's wishes!

The only difference when one turns to the art of the present day is that although the performers have no more right to take liberties, they still take them. Though of course, as we know, reproduction is inconceivable without liberties of that kind. For one can represent on music paper only so small a part of the musical idea that, unless a performer knows how to read between the lines, he never gets down to the content at all. So one must expect liberty of that kind, and perhaps one will never get by without it. Why, then, should our predecessors' notation, because of its relative inexactness, be thought to provide proof for the assumption that ornaments can be left out? Will future generations similarly leave out of our present-day music everything they cannot immediately understand? Probably. But are they also going to regard it as quite in order to do so? The answer, again, is probably yes, which means there is all the more need to make things clear.

Surely people began to leave the ornaments out at a time when they still recognized them as subsidiary notes. It can also be shown that particularly in polyphonically written works the construction is based on the principal notes, and the subsidiary notes are subordinated to those, though in a way that is systematic, emphasizing meaning and furthering character. That is to say, rather in the way every house has its structural walls and to that extent differs little from other houses of the same category. But it only becomes some particular house, belonging to some particular person with particular demands and habits, through all those thousand familiar things which are of course subsidiary from the structural point of view and yet are the only things that can in fact be of principal importance, looked at in terms which define more exactly the structure's purpose. For example, if the owner is satisfied by everything else about a house, the fact of its having a structural fault which he does not notice may leave him indifferent (for a time, at least; but a structural fault tells in the long run, and then one knows about it!). Nobody would leave out the coat of arms, the doors, and the windows, unless he were ignorant of their purpose or had forgotten it!

But be that as it may, the ornaments were left out—or simplified, which is as bad—and we no longer know what they were like. So now I want to indicate a path along which one might well seek, and even find.

As we know, there is some dispute as to whether short appoggiaturas should be played on or before the beat, and whether with an accent or without ♪ or ♪. In recent times it has looked as if playing them before the beat, and definitely without accent, were about to become the generally valid way. In my time, on the other hand, one was still taught (as far as I know) to play them as coinciding with the beat, and so, in my view, necessarily accented. However, there is an objection to playing the appoggiaturas as an anacrusis, particularly with long appoggiaturas: the point of writing them 'outside' the barring is that this is said to indicate the underlying harmony more clearly than if they were written out.

But that strikes me as correct and probable. For after all, the main source of information about the harmony should be the figured bass. Diagnosis is perhaps made easier if the melodic line is taken into account, but in such cases the appoggiatura is, after all, so short that the score will leave no more uncertainty about the correct harmony than would a section of passage-work, which often enough occupies the same amount of room and certainly has a more confusing effect with its 'tones foreign to the harmony'. Moreover, in the latter case the tempo may perhaps be quicker. This explanation may possibly apply to long appoggiaturas, since there is no other justification at all for these—they probably represent merely an 'un-ornament', a most ill-mannered imitation of the short, good appoggiatura's relatively good manners. But if the latter were to be played before the beat, it could easily be shown by using dotted notes:

So there is no reason to write it in a more complicated way:

However, the matter looks different if one takes the oddness of this notation as a sign of some notational difficulty and assumes that since the oddness is a rhythmic one, the difficulty had to do with rhythm. And in fact it is not possible, simply by using dotted notes, to represent appoggiaturas in an entirely satisfactory way:

We should have written this as at (a). But formations like (b) and (c) almost coincide with (d) and (e), respectively, and differ only in that the copyist does not bother to calculate the appoggiatura's value exactly, since he knows that the player will also measure it only approximately, rather as a knight takes a certain number of copper coins from the purse at his knee, uncounted, and throws them to a beggar. We may safely assume that this gesture is no more of a risk for him than a similar one is for a musician and is no more likely to be regretted: it has been well practised! And just as the knight is, after all, well aware how often he may repeat this gesture and how much he may empty his purse each time he does so, the musician is aware what proportion of the available time he has consumed and how much still remains. And all this without our pedantically exact calculation and the notation it implies.[2]

On this point, it has perhaps never yet been noticed that with most, if not all, peoples, nature's music, as we call it, (probably that, too, is a considerable exaggeration!) far surpasses art-music in matters of rhythm. Let me straight away juxtapose this fact with another—that something similar undoubtedly occurs in bird-song—and then venture the hypothesis that the cause lies precisely in the reduction to simple relationships that is necessary in art-music, forced on us by our determination to write music down, so that we renounce all complicated relationships and have to be content with the kind of simplification which, for example, leaves nothing of the living essence of a philosopher beyond Diogenes' 'Get out of my sun!'.

Surely one can say the most important thing distinguishing our art-music from nature's music is that, in so far as our powers of differentiation and the art of notation are able to draw attention to structural relationships, the latter are laid down in a definitive and economical way which is conditioned by notation and made possible only by notation. All the remaining differences result of their own accord from this economy; nature's piece of music is condemned to a certain stagnation because of its rhythmic, motivic, and perhaps also tonal complexity; it must either remain short, or repeat itself incessantly; the idea, once formulated, remains as it is; on the other hand, a piece of art-music can extend in all directions, unfold, develop and work out its ideas. This is what the laws of comprehensibility demand. But as a further result, nature's music (since it indeed neglects the unfolding of all other elements) has the chance to build distinctive forms out of the few elements it *does* develop ,with no loss of comprehensibility.

The example of the pedal-point will show this clearly. In the art-music of the past century its formal function is retardation. The harmony is held back to prevent development, and this makes for well-defined articulation, e.g. in the case of introductory characters or before the entry of a new idea or the recurrence of an old one—that is to say, at the end of transitions and introductions and leads-in, so that the idea entering with the new chord is clearly marked off as new. Here its main purpose is to increase tension, but it can also be used as a 'final resonance', to release tension, at the final point of a build-up, for example. The pedal-point can only fulfil all these functions because it momentarily halts the flow of the harmony, so that the latter's other functions are put out of action. But even when the basis of primitive music is not simply a pedal-point (as it mostly is), it is never a well-planned, widely-ranging harmony, whose mobility aids the form; rather is it the kind which, at best, goes round and round a limited circle, for ever returning home, but which is for the most part static. Clearly, all the other biological functions can assume more complicated forms when the relative stagnation of the harmony allows our senses to concentrate entirely on the phenomena left outstanding. The harmony having been demoted so that it means no more than a conventional turn of phrase, one pays it no more attention than one pays any conventional turn of phrase. Thus it is by no means surprising that the music of so many primitive or early peoples, inferior in all other respects, has attained a higher level as regards the development of its single main part than has been possible in our music.[3]

Here we must also take into account that at the moment when notation was thought of, people must also have thought of it as becoming progressively more exact. Something else must be borne in mind here; our musical notation is disposed so that nearly all the characteristics involved are notated only relatively or approximately: pitches, rhythm, loudness, etc. Even this low degree of exactness can be achieved only because a system of inexactness, in the form of approximation, is made the basis of a convention—because all the true relationships are tempered, all the recurring decimals rounded off. All the rhythms, pitches and tempi in nature are more manifold or complicated. Recall, for example, the way the waves of the sea move, the rushing of a river or brook, the way rain falls, or the noise of a railway train, even.

November 21, 1922
copied December 30, 1922

12

ORNAMENTS AND CONSTRUCTION
1923

This morning Görgi[1] asked me why ornaments are so rare in modern music. I could not give him a satisfying answer. That people suddenly or gradually lost the taste for them—which is certainly true, at least in part—is, at best, a symptom; but it is probably nothing more than the formulation (for and by the ignorant) of the true (hidden) cause.

The process could in reality have been as follows:

In contrapuntal forms, the basic combination occurs almost exclusively between the *principal* notes. The subsidiary notes serve partly to take the edge off certain 'harsh' occurrences, partly to make them possible at all, without infringing the laws of counterpoint. But, in particular, they are placed so that, harmonically and rhythmically, there is more than one way of grasping them (function of 'puzzling' changing-notes). Apart from this contrapuntal aim, their task is to invest with 'material', with living substance, with flesh, the naked constructive facts, the bones, the framework of the construction—to cast these dry facts in a pleasing form and give them, through additions and a broader presentation, the shape which alone fulfils the demands of comprehensibility.

Just as the contrapuntal technique is displaced by homophony, so this method too falls into disuse. In homophonic art, in which the essential thing is the *development* arising from the basic motive, the crystallizing-out of *new* motives (and therefore relatively simple ones, easy to comprehend), there will have to be a rather slower rate of succession among the notes, even for reasons of comprehensibility. In any case, 'overloading' will especially have to be avoided at the opening, since otherwise comprehensibility and possible development are endangered. Where once there was the *figure*, made *more expressive* by decoration with subsidiary notes, there is now *performance* (espressivo!) of the theme, made *more expressive* by dynamics and many varied types of accompaniment.

Traunkirchen, July 20, 1923

GLOSSES ON THE THEORIES OF OTHERS
1929

In the last *Anbruch* (October 1929) there's a fair round-up of them, the theorists of the new music (some of them my friends, rather sceptical about me, as they usually are), and the only ones missing, more's the pity, are the seven other gentlemen, *Melos* to the fore—Strobel, Mersmann, etc.

Slow decadence or no slow decadence, there is still the occasional new wave, and, as each one comes, I labour (not that it gets me anywhere) to demonstrate the theoretical instability of these programmes. Hardly have I finished than the crest of the wave is already long past, the foam has dispersed (for that's all it was), and the depression in the trough of the wave bring out one's fellow-feelings, setting one's mind at rest about these little revolutions.

In particular, there is a fragment 'from the foreword to *paul hindemith's* (sic!) *lehrstück*'[1] in among the advertisements. It says, among other things that 'omissions of the teaching-pieces and transpositions are possible. Whole musical numbers can be left out, the dance can be omitted, the scene for the clowns can be shortened, or left out, other musical pieces, dances and readings can be interpolated, if necessary (what? necessary? full of necessity?—my comment!)—and if the pieces interpolated do not upset the style (!!! style!!!) of the work.' And in the same volume, *Krenek* says the design of an opera must be like that of a potpourri.

If music is frozen architecture, then the potpourri is frozen coffee-table gossip, instability caught in the act, a parody of all logical thinking. It is justified, to any degree at all, only as a harmless travesty; it behaves as people behave when they get together socially—jumping from one thing to another, so that an egg-recipe suggests Columbus, a match a risqué story, and the decline of the world a boxing match—all involuntary associations against which primitive brains are defenceless, to which they succumb, being able to link them only by the word 'and': A and X. Potpourri is the art of adding apples to pears; its law applies without being able to divide, and it multiplies through non-repetition. It is an accumulation, a mass of things adding up to nothing. It has parts but no articulation, combination but no cohesion. A pen-knife is sewn on to a nose, and a town clock on to the knife, and a mood on to the lot.

Now, if Krenek's operas, as he himself assures us, are laid out in this way—if his productive self, when it places one piece after another, knows no stronger or deeper reason, this could indeed mean merely that his theorizing self is over-ready to verbalize about his conception of the work. Conceivably, one of his left hands does not know what the other left hand is doing—but it does not know merely, while nevertheless doing the right thing. That is to say, the creator's potential could be sufficiently strong to ensure the work's adhering to its 'status nascendi' sufficiently long—the creative act's being sufficiently extended—for there still to be an awareness, when individual sections were interchanged, of the formal requirements resulting from previous and succeeding sections. In that case, even transpositions and new interpolations would satisfy the will to form, in accordance with the original conception. For obviously an opera (even if it is reworked a hundred times, merely to improve it so that it is more in keeping with the conception—since usually the latter is not quite realized by the work as carried through)—an opera is a whole, conceived unitarily. It comes about as does any fruit of the womb—an apple, a pear, or a child—as a whole, in a single act of procreation. A wasp may lay its eggs in an unripe apple, a pregnancy may be disturbed, one grape may get more sun than another, or the year may be a bad vintage: all this can alter the final result. But no apple tree ever yet tried to produce apples with prune stones, or shaped like grapes. I have no way of telling whether the vine views its grapes as a potpourri. But if it does, that is certainly a quite subjective opinion on its part, for they are not a potpourri. Certainly one should not throw everything into the same pot. If one does so all the same, and on Sunday cooks up everything one threw in during the week, such a potpourri may still turn out as a palatable dish. No need to inquire too closely after its logic and constitution, since cooking—cooking together—is in any case one of the legitimate combinatory methods in preparing food. But I doubt whether the French peasant throws all the week's left-overs into one pot, anyway; surely he throws certain things away. I do not doubt that, even here, half an eye is kept on the effect of the end-product and that it influences the way things are put together. The least of Frenchmen has that much taste.

So I believe Krenek has merely gone astray in his officialese—and in that kind of language, which he seems to have copied over the shoulder of a drafter of police reports, anyone can go astray. Admittedly, I often have the feeling, when his double-bass parts are made to play a wrong bass, that he is cooking up *Räucherspeck mit Ananas*.[2] These, however, are details—ugly details, perhaps, but they do not preclude an unconscious plan underlying the whole, a plan from which the author, for all his conscious superficiality, cannot cut loose.

It is another and far more serious matter with *Hindemith*, on this occasion. Were it he himself who carried out the alterations he permits, then the thing that is all-important (to him) could still be preserved: the work's style—since he must be able to recapture at any moment his bygone will to form. But he allows anyone to make such alterations, however far-reaching. There is only one word for this: nonchalance, going beyond the limits of a genius' audacity, and reaching into the realms of deficient conscience.

What, then, is this *Lehrstück* supposed to teach us? How to chatter senselessly, brainlessly, incoherently, unselectively, tastelessly, formlessly? Surely people can do that just as well without him; surely one should prevent them, not teach them?

How does he compose such a piece? How does he himself put it together? How does one make something whose every part can be replaced or omitted? How are such parts made up? Why does he compose it if someone else is allowed to make any and every part? To this mass of questions no serious reply can be given, and really there is nothing more to say.

Then we have *Mr. Hans Gutmann*, a heavy manual labourer, who writes a horny-handed style, expressive of the difficulties the manipulation of a pen offers someone accustomed only to swinging a heavy hammer. One is for ever having to go back and think—something also true of Wiesengrund, unfortunately—in order to find out what he means, and then one fails to see why he does not say it straight away, since it's so simple.

Although I have given an indication, in the *Anbruch* Yearbook,[3] of the part that *extra-musical elements* can play in moulding form, he can't put two and two together. He indeed borrows my terminology, without acknowledgement (as do all of the *Anbrecher*[4]). He writes: '*We* have made a clean sweep of the legend about valid norms of beauty.' (He 'broke in' to my *Harmonielehre* to find that.) But he thinks there is some obstacle—goodness knows what—preventing exact *criticism of composition*, whereas the only reason why they go hungry is their own ignorance and eccentricity.

Does Mr. Gutmann think that a composition teacher is not practising composition criticism? Not, admittedly, of an exact kind (or not always) but merely intuitive. There are many, though, who rely on laws—these may be true or false but are principles anyway. But leaving that aside, he could at least gather from my shorter articles that an exact basis for the criticism of composition does exist. Admittedly I left my essay 'Criteria of Musical Value'[5] in a first draft and have not published it. But I have let so much of what I know percolate through in small doses that if these gentlemen stopped being content to 'break into' my works and steal—if they thought on, instead of babbling their polemics, then they could already have discovered a good deal.

I have, above all, repeatedly pointed out the *purpose of all forms*: a layout which guarantees comprehensibility. I have then shown what are the conditions that go with comprehensibility; how it is a question of the kind of listener one is writing for (and, in so doing, defined the difference between light and serious music, something else that troubles him); how there is always a manifest relationship between an *idea's difficulty* and the way it is presented, so that an idea which is hard to grasp demands a slower and broader presentation than does one which is easy to grasp; the role played here by *tempo*, so that when the notes move quickly, things must unfold more slowly. How, for example, when the harmonies are hard to grasp, the tension must be lower in other directions—and other things of the same kind. Obviously one cannot formulate this kind of consideration of material without *psychology*, since the material is destined to affect the psyche and only comes into consideration at all *through this function*.

PART VII

PERFORMANCE AND NOTATION

1

FOR A TREATISE ON PERFORMANCE
1923 or 1924

I

The highest principle for all reproduction of music would have to be that what the composer has written is made to sound in such a way that every note is really heard, and that all the sounds, whether successive or simultaneous, are in such relationship to each other that no part at any moment obscures another, but, on the contrary, makes its contribution towards ensuring that they all stand out clearly from one another. Every composer of any experience arranges his notes in that way, whether he is writing for a solo instrument, a small chamber ensemble, or for orchestra. It is the precondition of all music making, and anyone who fails to satisfy it will never succeed—even with all the performer's other resources, however life-like—in satisfying a knowledgeable and sensitive listener.

It should not be denied that in making the author's ideas and their flow comprehensible, a good deal can be done through a certain liveliness in rhythm and tempo, a certain emphasis in the delivery of phrases, in contrasting, opposing and juxtaposing them, a certain build-up in tempo and dynamics, a purposeful distribution of *espressivo* and its opposite. Indeed it seems that the naive, less cultivated listener can more easily be convinced by this obtrusive and gesticulating type of performance than by reproducing the relationships of the ideas in a subtle, carefully considered manner.

But, on the other hand, an outstanding soloist (Kreisler, Casals, Huberman, among others) has a way of working at his part; he tries to make even the tiniest note sound, and to place it in correct relationship to the whole. . . . [unfinished]

II

The more exact performing indications become, the more imperfect. Instead of simply presenting one's idea, complete in every detail of content and construction, one is tempted to use liveliness of performance, in order to place it out of reach of the fashionable need for interpretation. This temptation is too great to be resisted, to any but a steadily decreasing degree, by a composer who wants to express himself with the clarity needed to ensure that *he*, at least, always understands. For a later age, though, this way of marking will in its turn be too strict, or too vague, and will have to be either complemented, or modified, or ignored. All the same, the path, once trod, cannot simply be abandoned; we cannot return to the economy of markings found in Beethoven and Mozart, or even in Bach. The question, whether we hear more than our predecessors did, or are merely willing to leave the performers less freedom than they did—that question may be left unanswered, all the more so since the answer can claim only qualified credence.

2

TODAY'S MANNER OF PERFORMING CLASSICAL MUSIC
1948

Today's manner of performing classical music of the so-called 'romantic' type, suppressing all emotional qualities and all unnotated changes of tempo and expression, derives from the style of playing primitive dance music. This style came to Europe by way of America, where no old culture regulated presentation, but where a certain frigidity of feeling reduced all musical expression. Thus almost everywhere in Europe music is played in a stiff, inflexible metre—not in a tempo, i.e. according to a yardstick of freely measured quantities. Astonishingly enough, almost all European conductors and instrumentalists bowed to this dictate without resistance. All were suddenly afraid to be called romantic, ashamed of being called sentimental. No one recognized the origin of this tendency; all tried rapidly to satisfy the market—which had become American. One cannot expect a dancer who is inspired by his body and narcotized by his partner to change tempo, to express musical feelings, to make a ritardando or *Luftpause*.

Music should be measured—there is no doubt. As an expression of man it is at least subject to such changes of speed as are dictated by our blood. Our pulse beats faster or slower, often without our recognizing it—certainly, however, in accommodation to our emotions. Let the most frigid person be asked a price much higher than she expected and feel her pulse thereafter! And what would become of the lie-detecting machine if we were not afflicted by such emotions? Who is able to say convincingly 'I love you', or 'I hate you', without his pulse registering? Why are happy endings attached to movies if not because of the sentimental feeling of the audience?

Does one smile only because of the customer, or even the photographer?

Will music composed without emotion not show the lack of it?

Why is music written at all? Is it not a romantic feeling which makes you listen to it? Why do you play the piano when you could show the same skill on a typewriter? Why do you sing? Why play the violin or the flute?

Change of speed in pulse-beats corresponds exactly with changes of tempo. When a composer has 'warmed up' he may feel the need of harmonic and rhythmic changes. A change of character, a strong contrast, will often require a modification of tempo. But the most important changes are necessary for the distribution of the phrases of which a segment is composed. Over-accentuation of strong beats shows poor musicianship, but to bring out the 'centre of gravity' of a phrase is indispensable to an intelligent and intelligible presentation of its contents. This may or may not involve emotional expression, though it is done mainly by dynamic changes: crescendi, decrescendi, sforzati, etc. To people who have never heard those great artists of the past who could venture far-reaching changes of every kind without ever being wrong, without ever losing balance, without ever violating good taste—to such people this may seem romantic.

It must be admitted that in the period around 1900 many artists overdid themselves in exhibiting the power of the emotion they were capable of feeling; artists who considered works of art to have been created only to secure opportunities for them to expose themselves to their audiences; artists who believed themselves to be more important than the work—or at least than the composer. Nothing can be more wrong than both these extremes. Natural frigidity or artificial warmth—the one not only subtracts the undesirable additions of the other, but also destroys the vital warmth of creation, and vice versa.

But why no true, well-balanced, sincere and tasteful emotion?

To make a perfect ball of clay solely with the hands is extremely difficult. What one presses away on one side will stick out on the other side. Using mechanical devices immediately eliminates every problem.

At the age of forty I still wanted to be a conductor—especially when, as often happened, I heard a poor performance. But after studying the work in question thoroughly and trying to formulate my feelings in conformity with those of the composer, I found myself facing so many problems that I cried out, 'How fortunate that I do not have to perform this work now!' When subsequently I heard a performance of this work, it seemed to me as if the conductor had taken a wet sponge, erasing all traces of problems by playing whole movements in one stiff, inflexible tempo.

3

THE FUTURE OF ORCHESTRAL INSTRUMENTS
1924

I

Very probably only the most usable instruments will be preserved in the long run. History shows this: the viola d'amore, oboe da caccia, oboe d'amore, gamba, the various types of lute, the natural horn, natural trumpet and many others have disappeared, partly because they were less usable, partly because they could not be further developed. All these instruments have a beautiful or characteristic sound, but this beauty did not keep them above water. How, for example, is one to use a viola tuned in D major, on which most keys are difficult, and where one must go into at least third position to play the ninth from the open d to e, and where the octave g'–g'' can be played only as a double-stop fingered as for a normal tenth—an instrument on which, as with the lute, 'one spends a great proportion of one's life looking at the part?' Or the natural horn and trumpet, where the necessity of hand-stopping rules out rapidity, the playing of even scales, and homogeneous sound. It is probable that the natural horn had a more beautiful sound—but not certain, for our horn-players now have such technical fluency that they probably also have a more beautiful tone. In any case one does not notice that the present-day horn is less beautiful than the natural horn, and that is really the decisive point. The greater certainty afforded by the more easily playable instruments leaves the player time to concern himself with producing his sound.

II

Brahms is supposed to have said he would have liked to write more for the horn, but for the natural horn, not the valve-horn. Certainly our horn players are sorry he did not put a more liberal construction on the example provided by Beethoven, who was one of the first to use the new instrument. On the other hand, in his orchestral works and in the Horn Trio Brahms naturally used the valve-horn, and so contributed his tithe to the evolutionary process by which the perfected instrument is helped to victory over traditional beauty—for the benefit of a new beauty. The valve-trombone, on the other hand, has not yet succeeded in driving out the (nobler sounding!) slide-trombone. The latter is indeed not so imperfect as the natural horn. But for all that, it is amazing that 'serious' composers have to make do with relatively immobile (brass) or thin (double-bass and woodwind) bass instruments, while their un-serious colleagues, when writing for military band, enjoy command of full-sounding bass instruments with virtuoso mobility. Another victory for beauty.

III

Most musicians are unable to do without a multiplicity of colour; they lack the ability. But they forget the string quartet; does anyone feel a lack of colour there? For colour is in fact produced not just through variety of instruments, but through their varied use. And in particular: not by the craft of scoring, but by the craft of composing.[1]

IV

The modern orchestra has developed to great complexity through a misunderstanding of the colour-richness of the organ. The latter's multiplicity of stops is conditioned by a technical point; a powerful forte can not be attained by stronger wind pressure, nor by adding more pipes of the same kind, but only by adding heterogeneous sounds. Also, for the main part to stand out, a more piercing colour is needed, since there are no individual dynamics. In the orchestra, the latter on their own are enough to meet most needs.

V

Will an orchestra lacking the airy flute, the chaste oboe, the comic (always comic?) bassoon, the lamenting cor anglais, the blaring trumpet, the solemn trombone—will such an orchestra sound less airy, chaste, comic, lamenting, blaring and solemn? A genius can express a prayer or the rage of battle on a mouth-organ, should he really need to. And a non-genius either can do it too, or else he simply imitates.

VI

In reality colours serve to make the train of thought more apparent, to make the main points stand out better and the secondary ones recede better. In an epoch which started from dance pieces and folk-song and set itself the task of expressing feelings and sensations, a danger finally arose, in impressionism, that characteristic quality would come to be the main point. Here, even imperfect instruments could satisfy, insofar as at any given moment they were able to produce a characteristic effect. Satiation banished this danger. The idea, which had still been dominant at the start of this epoch but had gradually sunk to the level of a second main point, again comes into its rights, and 'from now on knows only the main points—only itself'.

VII

The orchestra of the future will certainly consist only of instruments that are all equally capable in technical respects. There will probably still be no lack of differences in loudness and colour, but one will hardly be content to preserve instruments of insufficient compass or technique, merely because their colour or their way of producing sound is interesting. So one may take it that all instruments incapable of evolving will fall by the wayside. Instrument-makers and instrumentalists do indeed tend to increase instruments' capabilities. But insofar as they think merely of more beautiful, fuller tone, they are not on the right path. For the greatest and most palpable defects are in dynamics, compass and mobility. Here the instrument furthest behind is the oboe. Its tone is as beautiful as its usefulness is rare. The relationship between its softest and loudest notes is very unfavourable, its crescendo limited, its compass hardly more than two and a half octaves, its mobility inadequate. The flute is indeed more mobile, but its tone is so deficient that one would have to set from two to six flutes against one violin if the flute were really to play with an equivalent range of dynamics—whereas at the moment it plays almost exclusively between *mf* and *f* in order to penetrate, except in its topmost register. The bassoon constantly lets one down in point of dynamics. Almost all fast runs are played at less than *forte*. The bottom is too loud, the top, if one thinks of the cello's loudness and penetration, thin and unrewarding. The harp suffers from the greatest difficulties in tuning and lacks a chromatic scale. This makes it practically useless in modern music. The celesta serves only for special effects—it has the defects of the piano, but not the same advantages, as regards its touch for example. The piano, however, can do almost all the harp and celesta can! The trumpet's compass is too small (two and a half octaves), and in this it is far surpassed by the horn. The slide-trombone, even with a big technique, remains clumsy and the bass tuba even more. So too the double-bassoon.

VIII

Among the winds only the clarinet and horn can be given a favourable prognosis on the basis of their present state. The clarinet is almost as perfect as the violin, if not so versatile. It lacks only a few intervals and a really good staccato. Clarinets in E-flat and D, but particularly in A-flat,[2] will have a great future, as soon as leading players begin to have more to do with them. The bass clarinet, though rather weak in tone, is at least as mobile as the bassoon and has a rather greater compass. But the horn has the best prospects. It has a compass of at least three and a half octaves, and if it becomes possible, for example, to make the outermost registers more reliable by adding a fourth-valve at each end (high and low B-flat horn), then it will no longer rank behind the woodwind in point of mobility.

IX

All the foregoing is not meant to deny that improved construction and expanded technique (especially as regards dynamics and expressiveness) could develop even currently imperfect instruments to make them wholly usable. But this must be said: in their present state the clarinet and horn have a lead so significant that beauty of tone, on its own, will hardly be able to preserve technically imperfect instruments. For beauty passes, but virtue lasts.

4

MECHANICAL MUSICAL INSTRUMENTS
1926

Mahler was at the height of his career as an interpreter when he said, 'I consider it my greatest service that I force the musicians to play exactly what is in the notes.'

And indeed, among a thousand musicians scarcely one will be found who has the will and ability really to decipher and play what is in the notes. Almost exclusively they play as quickly or slowly, as short notes or as long, as loud or as soft—yes, almost as high or as low—as the instrument allows them to without discomfort. For this reason only, mechanical production of sounds and the definitive fixing of their pitch, their length and the way they relate to the division of time in the piece would be very desirable. For the true product of the mind—the musical idea, the unalterable—is established in the relationship between pitches and time-divisions.

But all the other things—dynamics, tempo, timbre and the character, clarity, effect, etc., which they produce—are really no more than the performer's resources, serving to make the idea comprehensible and admitting of variations. In a quick tempo, for example, the distinctions of dynamics must differ from those in a slower one. It is said of Beethoven that in his later years he took everything slower than before, in order that it should be easier to understand. But I have observed the opposite in myself—nowadays I take everything in my works a basic degree quicker than at the earliest performances, when, partly for technical reasons (difficulty and inadequate dynamics), partly to obtain flexibility, I consciously and unconsciously took everything much too slowly. At the first performance of works whose ideas are not superficial, correct tempi can, for the most part, not be taken at all, because this would make everything too hard to understand, and too unusual. Thus I could not understand Mahler's First Symphony until I heard it under a mediocre conductor who got all the tempo relationships wrong. All the tensions were alleviated, banalized, so that one could follow. For, as a listener, even the best musician is no less slow to comprehend, no less in need of a helping hand, than is the layman. But that the best interpreter, even when he is the author, holds a variety of interpretations to be possible, indeed necessary (since any realization of what has been conceived in the abstract falls short of what has been noted down), this could be supported by another remark of Mahler's. After the first performances of his Seventh Symphony he said to me: 'I don't know which you find more important. In the first performance I achieved more precision, in the second I got my tempi across better.' So in the first performance Mahler could not get his tempi across, but he did not himself decide which had been the better performance. And yet another Mahler anecdote. Once when at the Court Opera he had a guest Sarastro who took everything very broadly, much more slowly than suited Mahler's conviction, he went along with that throughout the work, modifying all the tempi accordingly, and so gave the whole performance a unity of character. (But for that, one needs a sense of form!)

The sound-relationships established by means of notation need interpreting. Without interpretation they are not understood. Not only does each age have different tempi and make different demands on performance (faster-slower, heavier-lighter, more pathetic-less pathetic, more tender-rougher—such things as these fluctuate in an irregular way), but even the demand for greater or less clarity in the constitution of the texture alters. Just think, for example, how in our time people have been content to play only the theme of a Bach fugue in an audible way, keeping everything else as unobtrusive as possible, while perhaps in Bach's time *no* part was allowed to stand out. But for an interpretation to be in keeping with our technique one must expect to hear *all* the parts with equal prominence. Think how, in the days when Wagner was new, singers used to declaim rather than sing, whereas now everyone tries even in Wagner to fulfil the demands of *bel canto*. Think of the broad pathetic style which in Wagner's time affected even the performance of classical works, then set against it the atmosphere of comedy in which *Die Meistersinger* is now given, and the tender lyrical tone which is allowed to make itself felt in most present-day performances of *Tristan*. Realizing that all this was necessary and can again become necessary as soon as a new age forces performers to satisfy new demands, one will understand that interpretation is indispensable, and to what extent.

Were there among a thousand musicians just one with the will and the ability to discover from the score what is true and eternally constant, to present it and to make it fit the needs of a contemporary listener, then for the sake of this one man, the Sodom and Gomorrha of false interpreters, aiming only to glorify themselves at the music's expense, would deserve to be spared. Interpretation is necessary, to bridge the gap between the author's idea and the contemporary ear, the assimilative powers of the listener at the time in question. As an interpreter of his own works, the composer sets a standard more through the way his performance alters than, for example, through the tempi he is supposed to have taken. (For nobody remembers all of them, not even the man who notices them, and there is hardly any tempo in which a talented player cannot make music rightly, or an untalented one wrongly.)

So, insofar as the mechanization of music (a rather infelicitous expression, unfortunately) states as its main aim the establishment, by composers, of a definitive interpretation, I should see no advantage in it, but rather a loss, since the composer's interpretation can by no means remain the finally valid one. But insofar as it is a matter of making performances independent of the performer's inadequacy—which nowadays, because of the distaste for rehearsing, threatens to make unperformable everything that offers any but the most conventional problems: insofar as it is a matter of definitively settling the basic relationships within the musical ideas and of ensuring the production of sounds and their correct relationship to each other, freeing them from the hazards of a primitive, unreliable and unwilling sound-producer—to that degree the use of all mechanical musical instruments could be of the greatest advantage. That was what I had in mind when I advanced the idea more than ten years ago, and I still hold it to be a valid idea.

A proposal of this kind understandably touches off resistance among instrumentalists; their interests do indeed appear to be threatened by it, whereas in reality their activities would not become superfluous even if mechanical instruments were to be widely used. For no one is ever likely to become a musician, to practise and develop hearing and rhythm, by learning to play the barrel-organ, but only by doing it himself, learning to command an instrument. But the objections touched off by the rather provocative expression 'mechanization of music' collapse when one realizes how much mechanization has taken place in our most important instruments. Do not merely compare the piano with the violin: on the piano, even apart from the mechanism proper, the system of levers, the tones themselves are ready-made and unalterable, whereas on the violin each tone, according to its pitch, has first to be produced. Or compare the organ with the horn. On the organ the player in reality carries out a manual movement which has nothing whatever to do with sound-production, merely giving the signal for it to happen. But think simply of the clarinet's keys, the horn's valves, the harp's pedals, the guitar's frets, and finally the very scroll of the violin, and then decide whether we can do without the mechanical element in our tools for producing sound and whether it has made music worse. It is sentimental to wail about mechanization and unthinkingly to believe that spirit, so far as it is present, is driven out by mechanism; only very small spirits suffer at every turn if they are not given enough room. Wailing room. Bach's spirit would not be expelled by any improvement in organ-mechanism, and even alongside the piano's keyboard and the horn's mechanism Beethoven's spirit has found quite an adequate amount of room.

Imagine a musician attendant on a mechanical instrument which he commands. This is what he has to do: he needs an exact knowledge and understanding of the work he is to perform, and has to influence the reproducing apparatus so that in the matter of dynamics the performance attains the degree of clarity and expressiveness matching his insight and taste. He is in a position to draw for this purpose upon every means of altering the tempo and the sound. Like an organist, he does not himself produce the sound, but that makes his position no worse than that of a pianist who can alter nothing after the key has been depressed. So far as rhythmic relationships are concerned he will still be able to effect as many modifications as a good musician requires. But one need not allow him to indulge a taste for playing things successively when they should be simultaneous, since flexibility can be more perfectly achieved by dynamics and colour. (I have in mind the kind of piano-playing in which the hands are not together.) One need not even waste words on the tendency to do the opposite— to play things simultaneously when they ought to be kept separate.

Naturally, as soon as there were such instruments many instrumentalists would become superfluous. Twenty years ago I should still have said: 'All the better, for then only the best ones will make it, and not, as today, the bad and mediocre ones.' Today I know that the same people will be in a position to make music then as now. But that is no reason to begrudge them and us better instruments.

5

INSTRUMENTATION
1931

In the instruments of our orchestra there is too much individuality (of colour, sound, technique, etc.) for groups of equivalent instruments (with the *possible* exception of the trumpets and trombones) to be strong enough to hold their own against accompaniment by the rest of the orchestra.

Let me say at once that even the trumpets and trombones can only do so in favourable conditions. For example, when they have rapid notes to play, they are much less able to. Moreover, the reason why the ear is particularly liable to react to these instruments and immediately pays attention to them is that on the whole they are, even today, used less in the quieter passages than are the others—since they are not always qualified to join in. Their entry is still *always striking*, I believe, because of their colour, which still seems unusual, rather than their loudness.

If our orchestra consisted of a smaller number of colours, then it would straightaway be possible, with this handful of 'individualities', to maintain at least something approximating the dynamic balance of the string quartet. There, each of the four players (three colours!) is in a position to make his part come through, so long as he is using a register of his instrument which is relatively favourable (favourable in relation to the other players); the others need only have the obvious consideration for the principal part that may reasonably be expected anyway.

So if our orchestra consisted, for example, of two kinds of woodwinds, brass, strings, and perhaps piano, harp, celesta (which all have octaves)—the higher-pitched ones in each case corresponding in compass to the violins, and the lower to the cellos; and there were then one extra group for each of the extreme registers (piccolo and double-bass registers), it would be possible to score an octet of that kind so that the relationships are as in the string quartet. For example:

(6) 12 high woodwinds	(6) 12 high brass	(10) 20 violins
(6) 12 low woodwinds	(6) 12 low brass	(10) 20 cellos

(4)   8 instruments in piccolo register

(6–10) 12–20 instruments in double-bass register (according to their loudness; e.g., if they are helicons or bombardons far fewer will be needed than if they were double-basses or contra-bassoons).

As you can see, the smaller orchestra could manage with 60 players.

But the fatal flaw in this idea is that no woodwind yet exists with anything like the violin's compass (g–c'''', even without harmonics or the very highest notes); nor are there any such brass instruments. (With the latter, things are rather astonishing; whereas the horns have an extreme compass of

and, even so, move by no means easily in certain parts of it, the trumpets have one which is still smaller, by almost an octave and a half:

Two and a half octaves. If the trumpets had the same compass

they could go up nearly as high as the violins, while at the bottom they would approach the cellos. This would be superfluous, for if one did without the possible (weak) low notes, one could certainly produce instruments with a better command high-up. It is the same with the clarinets: the lowest note on the E-flat clarinet

is indeed the same as on the violin, but while the A-clarinet commands

what should be possible on the E-flat clarinet,

one can scarcely demand more of the E-flat clarinet high up than of the A-clarinet! An incomprehensible and impossible state of affairs!)

Here I must mention a possible flaw in this idea of producing an orchestra through 6–10-fold doubling of perhaps eight types of instruments—a doubt I have always harboured as a criticism of the organ: that the organ uses so many different colours (a hundred or more) because (this is what I suppose, and physicists should test it) no individual tone-colour can be intensified beyond a certain degree (what degree?), and in any given register one can produce still louder sounds only by mixing in a different tone-quality.

If this supposition were found to be correct, one would have to fear—and this too should be investigated by the physicists—that the same will apply to the instruments of the orchestra, so that heavy doubling would help very little in the matter of loudness.

I have another supposition, as follows, about the aim and effect of doubling: the effect is not so much of loudness (as one can observe with massed choirs and monster concerts) as of evenness, which makes for the disappearance, the self-effacement, of the individualities, with their defects—intonation, particular weak registers, etc.—and also their virtues. The music thus sounds very 'homogeneous'. (Indeed, that is also why a solo violin stands out so strongly from the orchestra. Individuality, a personal kind of variation between different notes, of intonation, of coloration, in contrast to the mixed sound where everything averages out.)

However, in the orchestra even 6–10-fold doubling would produce a mixed sound, where weaknesses of a particular instrument would be relatively unimportant, while loudness would in any case be cumulative. And an instrumentation of this kind would offer the advantages mentioned at the outset: *each individual group could easily hold its own against the rest, without the help of 'foreign bodies'.*

But our orchestra, as made up at present, is based on the principle of the organ: *loudness is achieved through mixture.*

Naturally this instrumentation offers many attractive possibilities through the use of manifold soloistic groups, and it seems almost inexhaustible in point of colourfulness, if one recalls that one has two types of flute, 2–4 types of oboe (oboe, cor anglais, oboe da caccia, oboe d'amore), E-flat, A- and bass-clarinets, and basset-horns, bassoon, contra-bassoon, horns, tenor tubas, tenor horns, trumpets, cornets, flugelhorn, trombones, bass tuba, four strings and piano—that is to say, some 30 different types (add to that all the kinds of mutes!). In a texture of from three to five parts all this has produced countless possibilities of solo scoring; and then one has to add scoring with two or more instruments on one or all parts (even ignoring the possibilities of combining several instruments of the same kind). As against all this, the orchestra consisting of a mere eight types of instruments seems very meagre.

All the same, it seems to me quite certain that with such an orchestra one will be able to represent everything imaginable, in sufficient variety.

Remember, first of all, that the piano can make no distinction of tone-colour whatever, and that the string quartet manages on three individualities. Yet the literature of both possesses unparalleled richness of figures, and one almost doubts whether there is a greater wealth of sound-figures in the orchestra than in the media whose economy has forced composers to make the fullest use of prevailing conditions.

But then one must reflect on the following point:

If coloration had no deeper significance than that of a crude, naïve pleasure in sheer colour, it would be something on a very low level—perhaps that of a child who enjoys striking matches, or the rather more primitive pleasure uncultivated peoples, or sections of the populace, derive from explosions and shooting—and it could scarcely have a claim to consideration.

333

But if one's approach is that colour serves to underline the clarity of the parts, by making it easier for them to stand out from one another, then one must reflect for a while, and moderate one's views.

Any painter will know that he can not in fact paint *light*, but only differences of brightness, as effects of a source of light not included in the picture. Colour is indeed only a part of decomposed light. For the same reason he cannot, at the other extreme, paint darkness. Total blackness is absence of light, and therefore absence of colour; there can be semi-darkness, even if the fractional amount of light can then hardly furnish our eyes with colours.

But here we also know at once that objective representation can be achieved in all its plasticity even without colour, simply through distinctions of brightness. More than that, a certain plasticity can be achieved—in line-drawings— even without distinctions of brightness, though perhaps not without a certain unconscious co-operation from the memory and the imagination, which have already identified some familiar object that is only hinted at; and here it would seem doubtful whether the object could be identified if it were unfamiliar or only slightly familiar.

Applied to the orchestra, to instrumentation, this would mean that the objects, the parts, obviously stand out one from another with greater plasticity, the more they are distinguished from each other in all respects, including colour. But over and above that, black-and-white drawing again allows one to distinguish the parts with complete certainty, so long as they differ from each other in essentials—in movement, in rhythm, in the space allotted them.

Let us remind ourselves at this point that there are not only elements meant to stand out from each other, but others that are meant to mingle, dissolve into one another, as, for example, harmonies mostly do if they move evenly and simultaneously.

Moreover, one must now point out another reservation by asking, 'To what end, after all, does one aim to perceive and follow separately all the parts that work together?' Here the only reasonable answer can be, 'What is played, what is composed, must be amenable to perception.' And vice versa, 'Whatever can not be perceived should not be written.' As a formulation that is only a shade too severe—only, that is, in so far as the 'co-operation' of elements which are not all individually perceptible need not be flatly ruled out. But there is another objection to raise. It is justifiable to demand that, perceptibility being there, the way things stand out should still be graded according to their degree of importance. This objection will be particularly justified in homophonic music and in a certain kind of pseudopolyphony. In truly contrapuntal music there are only main points: that is to say, the whole. For the factor represented at any moment is the specific, mutually-opposing layout (horizontal and vertical, in simultaneity and succession); *not* the way in which a principal part is accompanied by subsidiary parts. The demands of *plasticity* would here be replaced by the demand for transparency. Only a transparent texture allows the ear to check whether at any moment the 'individual' sound of the elements' 'layout' ('stratification') is perfectly in keeping with the strictness here applicable in the shape of thematic-motivic exactitude. Whether it is free of falsification, deviation, softening, watering-down of the idea—whether, that is, the idea has been strictly and exactly adhered to. Whether the new sound, the new figure in the unfolding succession of pictures does not 'fall out of the picture'. Whether, in fact, a strict further development of the idea is present.

This interest could in principle be satisfied without colour, and therefore clavichord and organ were rightly the principal instruments of contrapuntal art. And, in fact, the moment one has a theme played by different instruments, one is forced to alter the performing indications, the phrasing, the dynamics. Certainly it can not be said that the idea is then a different idea; but that a different colour, different bowings, different phrasings, different dynamics very easily represent a different stage of the idea—this possibility is by no means to be automatically excluded. But one may assert that a composer with a sense of form will do no such thing unless he has taken it into account in his construction, if only unconsciously.

And, as already remarked, the organ uses varied colours, though without being forced to modify phrasing and mode of attack. Much more could be added here, but I shall confine myself to a brief statement of the degree to which a certain colourfulness is appropriate even in contrapuntal music. To be specific: transparency of sound can be more fully achieved when the elements used are heterogeneous rather than homogeneous. Similar colours, particularly similar tone-colours, melt too easily into one another, forming chords, and it is then certainly harder to follow the construction of the texture (e.g. when parts cross!).

It will surely have been noticed that very often I even give chords, and also chordal progressions of simultaneous parts, to heterogeneous instruments. Though that only happens within homophony.

Barcelona. November 23–25, 1931

6

THE FUTURE OF THE OPERA

1927

The *Neues Wiener Tagblatt* asks about 'the future of the opera'.

The future of the opera depends on the future of the drama, and both have new ways forced on them by the fact of the cinema, which can offer all the theatre offers except speech.[1]

The future of the drama can therefore rest only with speech. The coming drama will be a *verbal* drama.

It is self-evident that the highest art can never address itself to the many. To be understood by many, ideas need expressing in a particular way. Nature decrees that the essence of any such mode of expression must be a basic decrease in the tempo at which things happen. Clearly one may not leave gaps in the action, during which many of the audience would have to think out for themselves what was missing. All the conclusions that the listener is to draw must be explicitly stated, clearly and at length. Endless time would have to be spent on this, and one could hardly spend so much time in order to arrive at certain extreme conclusions that follow from complicated and deep ideas. So it is self-evident that art which treats deeper ideas can not address itself to the many. 'Art for everyone': anyone regarding that as possible is unaware how 'everyone' is constituted and how art is constituted. So here, in the end, art and success will yet again have to part company.

The erosion of the theatre began as the emotions of the people acting on the stage came to absorb more and more of the audience's interest. The result of this, and of the attempt to interest as many people as possible in the emotions

336

concerned, was that the characters represented necessarily became even more ordinary, their emotions even more comprehensible to all. The result is that nowadays one sees on the stage almost exclusively the kind of philistines one also meets in life, whether they are supposed to represent heroes, artists, or men-in-the-street.

The opera is in a comparable situation. It has less to offer the eye than the film has—and colour-film will soon be here, too. Add music, and the general public will hardly need to hear an opera sung and acted any more, unless a new path is found.

Fortunately it is so expensive to make a film that producers will not be able to renounce widespread popular appeal. This again makes clear the need to seek some individual form for the newest art.

The minority that can understand deeper things will never let itself be satisfied wholly and exclusively by what everyone can understand. This minority will always want art to match its power of comprehension. So the desire for higher art would persist even if there were no authors able to satisfy it. But there is little likelihood of the human spirit's ceasing to explore the depths where riddles lie. It is unlikely to give up the attempt to recognize and solve the riddles: their magnetic power is too great for that.

So the drama of the future and the opera of the future cannot be art for the masses; and if the drama is to be a verbal drama, then the opera will have to be an opera of *musical ideas*.

How will it look? One cannot say—one can only do!

Cannes. December 24, 1927

7

OPERA: APHORISMS
c. 1930

I find that:

It is for the opera to turn toward a public who live in music, who experience music so powerfully as to make all other thoughts and feelings secondary, not surrendering themselves as to a narcosis or some other intoxication, but receptive, with senses alert and ready to receive.

After the first note of music, everything external is lost on such a public; action of any kind vanishes, or is, at most, taken in. For such a public all the action that follows is purely *musical* action, and everything else that goes on — movement, staging, sounds, speeches, colours, lights, etc.—is less significant, secondary to the most insignificant musical accompaniment—even the oompah-pah of a waltz.

I find, moreover:

If I place a singer high up, while the orchestra is down below, then even on acoustical grounds the main part can only go to the singer. The more visible the singer is and is meant to be, the more audible he will be. Anyone who wants to treat the orchestra as the main thing will have to put it on the stage and let it take part in the action. But then the singer would have to go into the orchestra pit.

In painting, one puts the main things in the foreground, the minor ones in the background. The orchestra can only be background. Anyone who shifts it to the foreground does wrong. Certainly the background may help to blend the things in the foreground, so contributing to unity. Certainly one is entitled to guarantee the proportions sometimes, but the rule can only be as follows:

Let the singer sing the main part.

I find, moreover:

Let the singer sing!

He is not to declaim but to sing. When he sings, the word ceases. From that moment on, there is only the music and the voice singing it; the word is a mere accompaniment.

So a vocal part must be moulded as the art of singing demands. Speech-song is not song plus speech. It is neither song nor speech.

I find, moreover:

A singer on the musical stage is not like an actor in the verbal theatre. He is not seen to perform. He is heard to perform.[1] The music does the acting for him; his acting may at most accompany the music and must never aim at a prominence over and above that of the music, never aim to be stronger than the music, as we feel it—not even for the benefit of the tone-deaf.

This shouting theatre, now customary, is only for deaf people—people with coarse nerves who can not react to more subtle things, whom one must hit on the head so that they notice they are being addressed, and who then ask in surprise, 'Did someone say something?'

When I drink a glass of wine, I get the full taste of it on my palate, with all the details but no single detail standing out specially. But what a variety of things are at work in a glass of wine; more important still, what a variety of causes were needed to set them working! I receive them all at once, involuntarily, in a single sense-impression, and their presence makes itself felt only as the characteristic quality that distinguishes wine from everything else.

While enjoying wine, one could obviously think of all these causes—the splendid landscape in which it grew, the sun that made it fiery, the work of the vintners and all those who made it into wine; the chemical processes, too, and the merchants from whom one bought it; one could think of them. But: does that make the wine taste any different? Does the taste stand in need of my remembering all that?

I find:

The impression given off by the musical theatre must have a comparable makeup. In it, all the causative factors would have to exert their effect, unnoticed. But then the emergence of any single productive element would clearly be seen as a bad thing—as it were, the highly-recommended merchant taking a bow, and asking to be praised, or the man who prepared the wine—the 'arbiter of taste'.

Here I have in mind the efforts of the production team, who tend to aim for effectiveness on their own, apart from the total impression; the contortions of conductors, who can put themselves on show; the top notes of singers, who see their chance to be heard; the humour, or feeling, of many a performer, who will not let us pass by unaffected.

No. All that can be mentioned in an analysis or criticism. The verdict may be that the total impression consisted of this and that, but anything which stands out on its own, anything which ceases for even a moment to be subordinate to the total impression, is superfluous and harmful.

PERFORMANCE INDICATIONS (DYNAMICS)
1923

Rules should be laid down for *fp*, *sfz*, *marcato* and the like. Some of this is straightforward, but there are problems at times!

Suppose one said: *sf* is an absolute dynamic, always meaning, for example, *ff*; then it could not be used when *ff* had already been reached. So it is simpler to say: *sf* is a relative dynamic, meaning that the note so marked (and *that note only*) is to be played one degree (or how many?) louder than everything immediately before and after, unless there is a different marking for the latter. It differs from *marcato*, which it otherwise very much resembles (in both, the intensification is not an accent, to underline the phrasing, but is there simply for reasons of dynamics—characteristic quality, tone-painting, expression of feeling, and also for the sake of dynamic stress, one of a number of parts being made to stand out and be more obtrusive) in that with *sf* the contrast with the foregoing dynamic level is the main aim, and therefore has to be particularly striking, whereas in *marcato*, as befits the meaning of the word, it is only a means to an end, and so may be slighter, more discreet, so long as there is any other way of achieving the aim. It should be noted that in *sf*, as in *fp* and *marcato*, it is never the whole length of the note that is played louder—on the contrary, it is a rule that one falls back into the old dynamic level as quickly as possible, so that the intensification takes up the smallest possible proportion of the note's duration.

In any case, *fp* should be used solely as an *absolute* dynamic marking. This is supported by the example of Mozart, who often writes *mfp*, and also of modern composers, who write *fpp*, and *ffp* and *ffpp*.

It is very necessary to clarify these questions!

(N.B. Would not the inclusion of my accent-signs, ⌐ and their removal ⌣, make the use of *marcato* superfluous? It really has very great resemblance to these. But my signs are more practical because they also can be used for metric indications. Though ⌐ differs from *marcato*, it does not differ very much. Essentially it differs only in interpretation, though in reality the realization is very much the same.)

Traunkirchen. July 16, 1923

9

MUSICAL DYNAMICS
1929

In indicating loudness, part of what the author writes is meant *absolutely*, part *relatively*. At times, that is to say, it is a matter of 'however loud *forte* means on your particular instrument's scale of dynamics, play that loud' (from the point of view of the instrument, an absolute dynamic). But at other times the same *forte* will simply mean 'loud compared with what is going on around you' (as loud or louder; absolute in relation to the sound as a whole, then, but relative as far as the instrument is concerned).

Now, it would be best to indicate a degree of loudness for the total sound, since on individual instruments the degree of loudness is a variable factor, not only from one player to another but also changing to match technique and also the taste of the time or country.

A marking of this kind (such as I myself have used for the most part) matches the kind found in the classics and arose, in the latter, from the erroneous belief that loudness will remain forever the same. In my music, however, the basis is a desire always to use the particular instruments on which the prescribed loudness fits correctly into the total loudness. A marking of this kind has the disadvantage that if my procedure is not adhered to, and also if loudness alters, the conductor is obliged in each case to give the player special instructions about loudness.

Perhaps the following is a way out:

To show, in one's markings, whether the total loudness is meant or the instrument's own degree of loudness.[1]

April 5, 1929

ABOUT METRONOME MARKINGS
1926

Conductors hold forth about metronome markings as if, whether successful or misguided, these offended their most sacred right—the right to make of the work what they succeed in getting out of it, and no more. Admittedly, one may not demand of an interpreter more than his talent enables him to do. Admittedly, over-strict prescriptions make life hard for him, just as other strict laws do for those they apply to. But then one must also admit that no one has ever objected to the punishment of larceny when he had no intention of stealing, and that the life of such a person is made no harder—easier, rather—by laws, however strict.

Interpreter's rights; are there not also author's rights? Does not the author, too, have a claim to make clear his opinion about the realization of his work, even though no conductor of genius will neglect to override the author's opinion when the performance comes? Has not the author at least the right to indicate, in the copies of the work *he himself* publishes, how he imagines his ideas should be realized? Is that too immodest? And should one not rather chalk it up as immodesty that he makes clear what are the notes the poor conductor has unfortunately to conduct, rather than that he makes clear the tempo of the notes? Were I a modern conductor, that would be my main grudge against composers, since the dances the modern conductor performs before a spectacle-loving public do not need notes, nor rhythms, nor tempo, nor metronome markings. That is why so many present-day conductors conduct from memory; to look at the score could only disturb and hinder their display of the mimetic arts which they command to so high a degree. However, from this point of view I still do not understand why they make an onslaught on metronome-markings; there is, after all, such an easy cure—conduct from memory! Nor am I sure they should not make up their minds to dispense entirely with looking at the score, long before the concert!

Anyone who has learned at his own expense what a conductor of genius is capable of, once he has his own idea of a work, will no longer favour giving him the slightest scrap more freedom. For instance, if such a man has got into his mind a 'powerful build-up', which means he has found a place where he can begin too slowly and another where he can finish too fast, then nothing can hinder him any longer in giving rein to his temperament. 'What cares he for phrase or line? If they are hungry, let them go and beg.'[1] He laughs at the hungry quarter- and eighth-notes; there is no room for them in his *al fresco*. Dynamic markings, rhythms, inner contrasts and the like are as nothing, set against his grand design. He knows his goal and everything else . . . everything else, true enough, he does not know. So he is not bothered by metronome-markings either. He knows what can be 'made' out of the piece! But the trouble is, they are there in the score, and some churl who knows and understands them could be there taking notes. When it merely says 'adagio', one can indeed do what one likes. In the Adagio of the Ninth Symphony, Beethoven writes M.M. ♩ = 60. That's awkward. But fortunately people have already discovered that all Beethoven's metronome-markings are wrong. So nobody plays it at 60 quarter-notes a minute, but, at the most, at 30. Obviously Beethoven's marking is correct, though. And only bunglers with no inkling of what is involved if one is to bring out the calm and the cantabile of this movement *without* such a slow tempo—only they, being bunglers, are forced to take a slower tempo; and even so they are unable, when the tempo later quickens, to avoid an allegretto character. But I take it as a duty to adhere throughout to the given tempo and to preserve the cantabile at all times, never falling into scherzando, as has been the case at most of the performances I have heard.

October 25, 1926

11

TRANSPOSITION
1923

Seligmann's argument about transposing instruments is not compelling enough.[1] It could be better demonstrated as follows:

Nowadays the following instruments (and all the others, not named, for which the same holds good) are no longer to be regarded as 'transposing': clarinet, cor anglais, horn, trumpet, tuba, guitar and the like—indeed, all the ones that can play chromatic scales made up of equivalent notes, without this involving any particular difficulty that enforces limitations (avoidance of some keys).[2]

A chromatic instrument is no longer 'in' some particular key—otherwise one would have to regard and treat all trombones as in B-flat or E-flat, violins as in G or D, and all other instruments as in a key conditioned by the open notes.

Why are *these particular instruments* 'transposing' in the first place? In answering this question one learns something about whether they will need to go on being so.

Formerly all these instruments could produce not every note of the chromatic scale, but at most some of them, and often only one, or even, with quite a few instruments, only the overtones of one single note. So for each, or almost each, key, one had to use a different instrument (or else retune the same instrument—tuning the violin higher, or putting a *capo tasto* on the guitar, or crooks on the horns and trumpets).

Had one written down for each instrument the actual notes it was to sound, then the instrumentalist would have had to learn from three to twelve different fingerings. Since these instruments were very imperfect, they were not regarded as main instruments, only a short time was spent on learning them, and the standard reached remained, on the average, relatively low—lower than on other instruments, anyway. For this reason, too, composers usually made no particular demands. Thus it was possible to learn to play a horn- or trumpet-part in a very short time. Otherwise something better would have been demanded even then: that the musician be given absolute pitches to read, since his sense of absolute pitch can, in any case, leave him in no doubt as to what he is playing. The more advanced, more practised musician, at least, almost always has absolute pitch, and he is really not going to believe that what he is playing on the E-flat clarinet is a B—he knows perfectly well it is a D, because he can hear it!

Such a man is, in fact, forced precisely by 'transposing instruments' (!) to transpose! But that was what people wanted to avoid!

This is how it is for all the instruments mentioned. Nowadays, all the chromatic notes can be played in all combinations—some are indeed harder, but this is just the same on stringed instruments: F-sharp major is harder than C major, and in A-flat minor some things are practically unplayable which would give no trouble in A minor. Indeed, even on the piano not all stretches in all the keys are equally difficult; take the tenth, d to f-sharp, which is much harder than c to e! In fact the latter, a major tenth, is easier than the minor tenth, f-sharp to a, or g-sharp to b. (So is not the piano *an instrument in C*? And are there not, in fact, *transposing pianos*?!)

Since the instruments mentioned can now play all the chromatic notes, they are no longer to be treated as transposing instruments. Rather, teaching should begin (particularly on instruments which have in any case remained fairly unique of their kind, such as the cor anglais, the F-horn, the F-, B-flat- or C-(!) trumpet —one should decide which it is to be and stick to that—and the C-clarinet) by giving the notes their right names, regardless of *fingering*. On the horn one may obviously still begin with the 'open' notes of F major, but also *call it* F major (not C). One will then learn (since the effect of trumpet and horn crooks on intonation led to their disuse) to transpose—just as up to now, only more intelligently, which is why I call these instruments 'intelligent-horn and intelligent-clarinet'.[3] Anyone who has learnt such an instrument will also have become able to work out that by doing so he has spared himself a transposition!

May 12, 1923

12

VIBRATO

c. 1940

In my youth vibrato was called tremolo, a fitting expression since tremolo means trembling. It was one of the ways of giving life to a note that was dying out or losing its colour—one could strike it over and over again, as in the case of the *Bebung*, also of the mandolin; or, in the case of a broken tremolo on piano or strings, one could repeat it as rapidly as possible; or, as in flutter-tongueing, break it down into a large number of single short attacks. Lastly one should also include here the trill, which indeed serves the same purpose.

All musical instruments except the organ have difficulty with a sustained note. Whether it is the length of breath, or of the bow, or its steadiness, evenness, or the shortness of the note itself (as on the piano, harp, guitar, etc.)—the musician is constantly concerned to divert attention from the imperfection of the sound. In many cases dynamics are enough; swelling out and dying away, or one of the two. One may forgive it in the case of trumpets, horns, trombones, saxophones and most woodwind instruments, for the same reason, even though it does harm to a certain 'worthiness', chastity, clarity, and unsentimentality and objectivity in the sound of these instruments. A tremolando of that kind is entirely ludicrous on instruments of the organ family, since there the wind-strength can be maintained without limit.

Many of the vibrations produced by tremulant stops resemble the vibrato of strings and singing voice. As with trills, here too the main note, the true note, alternates with one or more subsidiary notes. But whereas the trill uses subsidiary notes that are in themselves pure, the subsidiary notes in vibrato are from every point of view impure.

Vibrato has degenerated into a mannerism just as intolerable as portamento-legato. Even though one may at times find the latter unavoidable, and admissible for purposes of lyrical expression, its almost incessant use even for intervals of a second is as reprehensible technically as from the point of view of taste.

But I find even worse the goat-like bleating used by many instrumentalists to curry favour with the public. This bad habit is so general that one could begin to doubt one's own judgement and taste, did one not occasionally have the pleasure, as I did recently, of finding oneself supported by a true artist. I listened on the radio to Pablo Casals playing the Dvořák Cello Concerto. Extremely sparing vibrato, exclusively to give life to long notes, and carried out with moderation, not too quickly, not too slowly, and without detriment to intonation. *Never* that sentimental portamento. Even intervals not easy for the left hand to join smoothly are bridged without adventitious help, simply by the artistry of his bowing. And when the occasional portamento does occur, it is only to lend a lyrical *dolce* passage the tender colouring that expresses the mood of such a passage all the more piercingly.

346

About the same time I heard on the radio a French woman singer performing Gluck's *Orpheus* perfectly, as I had never heard it before. It would be wrong to try to characterize this ideal performance in any other way than by the word 'perfect'. Such a performance places the inferiority of technical palliatives in its true light and, at the same time, shows who is able to do without them.

13

PHRASING
1931

It occurs to me that in his critical work on phrasing (in new editions, revisions, and also apropos of Riemann's kind of nonsense) Schenker insists, unless I am mistaken, that the phrasing must be shaped so as to make motivic structure clear; at least, I recall his proving a phrasing justified on the ground of a motivic relationship.[1]

I do not know exactly what other people do about this. Nor (momentarily having no music at hand) do I know exactly what the classical composers did. Anyway, in my opinion (and I believe my memory serves me right) neither Beethoven nor Mozart phrases in this way.

Here is what I think:

Phrasing has to do solely with *performance*. In that sense one is justified in expounding motivic relationships to the listener ('performing' them for him), in so far as it genuinely helps him to understand a piece. It is, certainly, not in all cases a matter for controversy, and it certainly can and should be usable in the kind of form where the motivic working-out is on a low level. There, however, it is as unavoidable as it is superfluous, for in lower forms comprehensibility is ensured anyway by primitive repetition, while 'overlapping' of motivic figures seldom occurs.

But in Mozart things are nearly always very different—there is an almost unbroken succession of the most far-reaching variations, dissections, simplifications, enlargements, reductions, overlappings, displacements, lengthenings, contractions and the like. To try and define exactly where a motive begins and ends would be labour lost.

Let me say at once that I am more inclined—unconsciously, for sure, and often even consciously—to blur motives, a tendency that will certainly meet with the approval of those who feel in music 'life on several levels' and who therefore prefer to hear a kind of 'counterpoint' between motive and phrase: a complementary opposition.

But I have still a good deal more to say against the idea:

1. Phrasing must suit the instrument (so must vary!).

2. The character of the piece is influenced to no small degree by phrasing; but a motive can appear with the utmost variety of character.

3. However, joining or dividing the notes (legato or non legato) does not even settle the phrasing beyond all doubt. Conversely, it is always possible to bring out a phrase in very much the same way regardless of legato or non legato: for

4. The way the notes are joined is less important than where the centre of gravity comes or the way the centre of gravity shifts.

December 7, 1931

14

THE MODERN PIANO REDUCTION
1923

I

A piano reduction comes into being, not like a work of art—from unknown causes, but like a useful object—for known reasons, for a particular purpose.

II

The reduction differs from the score: it is a reduction—something extracted from it. But a piano reduction is (1) a reduction and (2) for the piano. However, a reduction is not the whole, only a part. And to write orchestrally for the piano is just as bad as to write pianistically for the orchestra.

III

A sculpture can never be seen from all sides at once; despite this, all its sides are worked out to the same degree. Almost all composers proceed in the same way when handling the orchestra; they realize even details that are not under all circumstances going to be audible. Despite this, the piano reduction should only be like the view of a sculpture from *one* viewpoint.

IV

The attempt to make a useful object equally usable for a variety of purposes is usually the way to spoil it completely; it is no good for anything. Is a piano reduction to be used for reading, or for playing? For playing to others, or for accompaniment? Should it be a reduction, transcription, arrangement, paraphrase, or re-arrangement? How is it to be all these things at once?

V

The layman is very unlikely to praise something that exercises consideration for his abilities and inclinations, because he will certainly be unable to recognize any such consideration. But the expert is far more ungrateful still; he is equally certain to criticize consideration or lack of consideration, calling the one vulgar, the other incompetent. So all that is left is consideration for the thing itself.

VI

Most authors of modern piano reductions limit themselves to transposing for piano the various parts that the score at any point contains, placing them one on top of the other. These people resemble a cook who instead of serving up dishes, serves up the ingredients from which they should be prepared.

VII

Anyone writing for piano should bear constantly in mind that even the best pianist has only one pair of hands, though he also has a pair of feet, unfortunately, which now get in the way of his hands, and now help them on their way. The feet sometimes know (as and when required) what the hands are doing; and

349

while on other occasions they take no notice of it whatever, they still give monotonous and reliable support to the main aim of all present-day piano playing: the suppression of any possibility of a clear, pure sound. These feet, together with the pedals appertaining to them, make piano-playing more and more into the art of concealing ideas without having any. As remarked, this fact must be taken into account by anyone who wants to write for the piano. And the only way is to write as thinly as possible: as few notes as possible.

15

ON NOTATION
1923

It seems I stand alone (except, obviously, for my pupils, who do as I do) on the question of repeating or omitting accidentals (natural, sharp, flat). I believe that there are only two alternatives here, so long as there is no 12-tone notation (I did, however, recently make a draft for such a notation).[1] One says either:

A: 1. The notes c,d,e,f,g,a,b, etc., are *always* written *without* any accidental, regardless of whether the sharpened or flattened version immediately proceeds, or even occurs simultaneously.

2. The notes c-sharp, d-flat, d-sharp, e-flat, f-sharp, g-flat, etc., are *always* given the appropriate flat or sharp, however often they appear. (If this principle is strictly applied, one will soon find certain difficulties are unavoidable —if, for example, a chord is to contain the notes g, g-sharp, a, b-flat, b, so that one cannot manage without the natural sign, and is often liable to lose clarity. But in other respects this would be the purest way, and the one most full of possibilities.)

Or B: 1. The rule that the accidental applies throughout the bar, while not abolished, would be used *most sparingly*.

2. The notes c,d,e,f,g,a,b would in general always be given the natural sign, without pedantic exaggeration, i.e. when it is also clear in some

other way, then the simpler alternative is followed, for in modern music it is difficult to keep in one's mind, throughout a long bar, whether some note has already occurred with a sharp or a flat. This rule is only at all sensible and justified in music where, the modulation rate being slow, a melody is nearly always built on one of the familiar scales. There one would not usually expect, within a single bar, anything but the same version of a note (except for made-up figures).

3. However often they occur, the notes c-sharp, d-flat, d-sharp, e-flat, e-sharp, etc., are (again without pedantry) provided with a sharp or flat; this usually applies even when they occur a second time in the bar, unless things are made absolutely clear in some other way.

This method B is more difficult but more logical, more reliable, and not pedantic, nor does it mistake what the rule is there for.

Bartók's and Krenek's procedures are inadequate and pedantic.[2] They lead to contradictions, consequently cannot be applied consistently, and make a demand on the memory that is *unjustified* and *illogical*. The only possible task of any pictorial notation is to make its effect purely through the *picture*, without using abstractions of any kind. Even when the picture, simplified in some way, has become a symbol—in fact, precisely then—it may not be any further modified.

Traunkirchen. June 26, 1923

16

PICTORIAL NOTATION
1923

It is my opinion that in musical notation one should express as little as possible with letters, or even words, and make ever-increasing use of signs (if possible, pictures) which have nothing to do with letters. Accordingly I recommend the following signs which I myself shall use in my next work:[1]

pizzicato: a picture of a finger, plucking. In *print* it would look rather like a certain 'pointing hand', as realistic as possible:

when *written*, it could then look like this,

basing itself on the attempt to find a convenient copper-plate form; further development would then decide which of the copper-plate forms would be the final one (this obviously also applies in the appropriate ways to the remaining proposals).

arco: a picture, perhaps simplified, of the violin bow, with the wood to the right:

col legno, bowed: the bow reversed and without the hair —the wood to the left:

col legno, struck: the reversed bow and, instead of the hair, the wavy line used for arpeggios (cf. spiccato):

spiccato: like arco, but instead of the hair, the line used for broken chords:

con sordino: a picture of the mute:

senza sordino: the picture of the mute crossed out:

sul ponticello:

sul tasto:

Mödling. November 10, 1923

REVOLUTION—EVOLUTION,
NOTATION (ACCIDENTALS)
1931

It is remarkable that my most revolutionary steps (I always thought them evolutionary) have never had a destructive effect. What could be preserved (and what was important could always be preserved; what had to go was only the incidental, the fashionable) I always preserved. This is interestingly shown by the following example.

In our seven-tone system of notation my harmony can only be written down by using many accidentals. Nearly all those who followed me in using such harmonies departed from previous rules of notation: some by abolishing the natural sign, so that in the same bar three different notes could follow one another on the same line—d-flat, d and d-sharp, for example; the middle one (d, but with no 'natural' sign) thus broke the rule that any accidental applies throughout the bar; others, on the contrary, by being over-orthodox and exaggerating the rule, as when, for example, the last eighth-note was b-flat and the next note in the same part (first eighth of the next bar) was b, written without the natural sign; still others, by using various hybrid forms—but all either altering or exaggerating a rule.

Generally speaking, all I ever did was to use any accidental as often as deemed necessary in order to exclude all doubt; a procedure entirely in keeping with the older practice.

Now it has reached the point where many 'prominent' men who once accompanied me along my path have turned back, mostly toward tonal harmony, and now face the problem that they have spoiled musicians by their new rules, intended for a music which today they oppose!

This is a very good illustration of the difference between self-will and necessity.

January 18, 1931

A NEW TWELVE-TONE NOTATION
1924

The inadequacy of our musical notation has made itself felt and is widely admitted. Its defects, to formulate them exactly, are as follows: it is a seven-tone notation based on C major, which treats the remaining five tones as occasional alterations of the principal tones and thus all other keys as subordinate keys. All pitch-relationships can, indeed, be expressed by means of this system, particularly now most composers have made up their minds that each note is to have its own sign, some of them giving every note an accidental, whilst others do away with the natural-sign and indicate only sharps and flats. The main reason why no general agreement has so far been reached is that some composers are as pedantic in contradicting the old rule, according to which accidentals apply throughout the bar, as others are in adhering to it. Either way is very inadequate: hard to read, for lack of a proper visual image (a fault found in no other system of 'pictorial notation'); even harder to write, copy and engrave; and virtually impossible to proof-read so that the result is even approximately free from error. Apart from this, insuperable difficulties arise with, for example, the whole-tone scale, or in the kind of case where the following way out (which strikes me as not very satisfactory) has been found:

Ex. 1   Ex. 2

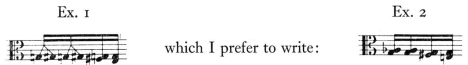

which I prefer to write:

Far be it from me to misjudge or forget the virtues of our notation. Above all, its basis in nature; the fact that its wealth of characters richly compensate for a certain difficulty in grasping it; that it is a product of evolution; that it suits instruments as well as they, finally, suit it; that it can accommodate a great deal in a small space; and particularly that till now nothing really better has been found.

This last reason should not be underestimated. The need for a new notation, or a radical improvement of the old, is greater than it seems, and the number of ingenious minds that have tackled the problem is greater than one might think. Previous attempts, so far as I have come across them, relied on the keyboard as a model.[1] This idea is of little use, since other instruments do not have black and white keys, but is justifiable insofar as it accords with our system for naming the tones.

I am very aware that a reform of our notation would have to be accompanied by a reform in the way we name the tones. In this article I am advancing a novel proposal, but I am under no illusion that I have discovered anything definitive, nor do I assert that my proposal could be enacted immediately, even if automatic resistance were not a certainty. But I believe my solution clarifies the question in one important respect, because it shows, on the one hand, that it is possible to depart from the natural scale without sacrificing 'characters' and comprehensibility (the defect of the Janko keyboard), while on the other hand it takes up hardly any more room than the old system, even though it gives each tone its own position and is thus a genuine twelve-tone notation.

Perhaps its good use of space is the characteristic that strikes the eye, so the exposition of the system will also start at this point.

A slanted 'ledger-line' will make it possible to write three different tones in each space, instead of the single one possible up to now. The first (above the line) will lie under the (slanted) ledger-line; the second on it, the third above it:

Ex. 3

This makes it possible to represent an octave within three lines, whereas in our musical notation at least four are needed, and even then not every note has its own position:

Ex. 4   So this is how   Ex. 5
an octave looks:

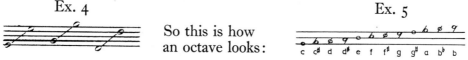

For the tones e-flat, g and b the ledger-lines could be left out with no loss of clarity (but this advantage will only make itself felt when the system comes to be used for writing at full-speed) (a):

Ex. 6

It could perhaps also be left out, but hardly so easily, with c-sharp, f and a.
Then three successive semitones would look as in (c) or (d), and an octave:

Ex. 7   Ex. 8

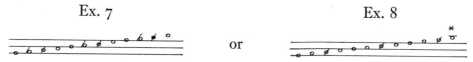

or

But I believe it will be best to omit the line only for one of the two signs, otherwise there would have to be a ledger-line at a different point (8*), and the distance
between the lines would also have to be greater. To represent more than one
octave, one would use: (1) ledger-lines, of the kind found in old notation; (2)
clefs, which would merely indicate the octave-register, since in this notation,
as in many other attempts, tones of the same name always occupy the same
position on the staff, regardless of whether they belong to a higher or lower
octave (see Ex. 17); (3) the coupling of two or more staves in different ways
(Exs. 11 and 12).

Ex. 9 shows that even when ledger-lines are used, one obtains forms that are
characteristic and easy to write (by no means harder than those now customary).
It also shows that the ones below the staff stand out very distinctly from those
above the staff, while at the same time (* in Ex. 11) they link up with tones of
identical pitch in a lower staff in the same way as between treble and bass clefs
at present.

Ex. 10 shows that three octaves can be accommodated in a relatively small
space, using merely seven ledger-lines; and ten lines in all. In old notation eleven
lines were needed. A layout of this kind will be useful for instruments of small
compass.

Ex. 11 shows a way of linking two staves to give (with ledger-lines—at *) a
compass of five octaves. This can be used for the celesta.

In Ex. 12 two staves are coupled without interruption, giving four octaves.
Two such double staves linked together cover the entire compass of the piano.

Ex. 9

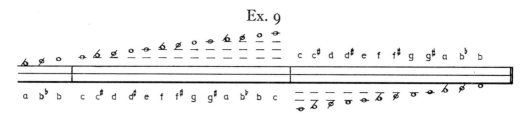

Ex. 10

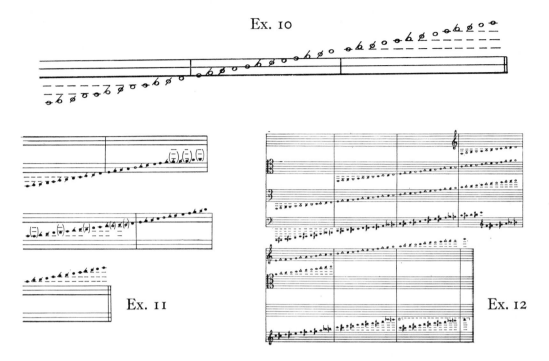

Ex. 11

Ex. 12

In the foregoing examples the lowest line of each staff is reinforced, to make it easier to tell the various types from one another. One can also experiment with a top line consisting of dots and a middle one of dashes, as in Ex. 13, or use one of the other means of distinguishing them, as shown in Exs. 14, 15 and 16.[2]

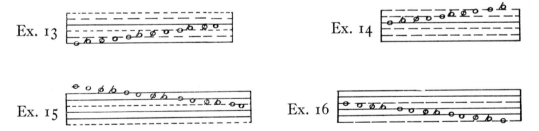

Ex. 13

Ex. 14

Ex. 15

Ex. 16

The clefs which were shown in Ex. 12 also uses the clefs demonstrated in Ex. 17:

Ex. 17

They are double clefs whose form has been chosen because it allows one to cover two octaves in a characteristic way, as can be seen from Ex. 18 (practical application of the clefs).

Ex. 18

Since two staves are always superimposed here, we have a series of examples showing how the clefs can delineate the various octaves. Here the clefs are not to be taken as G, F, or C clefs, but only as pitch-indications for the octaves they span.

This also shows a possible way of adapting to the compass of voices or instruments without using too many ledger-lines. Here the relationship of each clef to its lowest line is taken as constant, so that, for example, this line in the treble clef means the C above middle C, in the alto clef middle C, and in the bass clef the C below middle C. Using one staff of three lines and two sets of ledger-lines, one can adapt as well as possible to the compass of orchestral instruments, according to whether the clef is placed on a full or a ledger-line staff.

From Ex. 19 one can see that (particularly in engraving) a wide shift of register is matched by a change from a simple to a double staff (Ex. 19a), but (19b) that a change of clef can be used just as graphically.

Ex. 19a *Pierrot Lunaire*, No. 19

Ex. 19b *Pierrot Lunaire*, No. 2

One of the main virtues of this proposal is that the new notation has no difficulty with something that has become fairly frequent, i.e. groups of several simultaneous notes a semitone apart. Ex. 20 shows this:

Ex. 20

Chords of this kind are perhaps no easier to write than they were in the old notation, but they certainly need less looking at and are easier to decipher. After a few attempts, even writing them becomes quite easy, and once they have stamped themselves on the mind, they are unlikely to give very much trouble.

There is no doubt that definitive forms will emerge only through practical use. At first, perhaps, one will write only on a large scale, and will be able to write smaller only once handier shapes have evolved through practice in writing fast. But, I believe, it is not even as hard as that; if a few composers decided to use this notation, and a few instrumentalists learned it, then the tempo would soon speed up.

I cannot refrain from drawing attention to the N.B. in Ex. 21b of the accompanying transcriptions. Here a note is tied over from the previous bar and from the previous page without sharp, flat, or natural sign, and yet there is no doubt that it is an *a*, not an a-flat or an a-sharp!

Ex. 21a   *Suite für Klavier*, op. 25

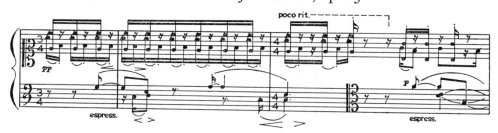

Ex. 21b *Pierrot Lunaire*, No. 18

When preparing these hand-written examples I did not make any attempt at calligraphy, but tried to write as quickly and flowingly as possible. This notation suits engraving or expert copying very well. The only doubt (though no longer in my own mind) is at most its legibility when written quickly.

Now, finally, an assurance: I am not of the opinion that all the music so far printed and written will have to be reprinted and rewritten, any more than every single book has been rendered into shorthand. But just as any schoolchild can read and write cursive and italic script, and any Russian, Bulgarian, Serb, Turk, Arab, Chinese or Japanese knows not only italic (and perhaps even cursive) but also his far more varied national script, so the ability to master two different musical notations equally well will have to be acquired.

Postscript 1

In order to introduce this notation I propose:

1. To found an association to which shall belong

(a) Composers, who undertake to publish at least one work in this new notation;

(b) Instrumentalists, who undertake to study and perform at least one of these works.

2. That a number of prominent composers, members of the association, shall also publish a small volume of short compositions written for this purpose in the new twelve-tone notation.[3]

3. The renaming of the tones demanded by logic is to come about by a free imitation of the model of 'do-re-mi'. (In the transitional period, however, one may still use the old system based on only seven tones.) For a continuation of letter-names to 'n' would hardly be possible (one hates to imagine a tenor singing a top 'm'), without confusion or illogicality; and 'do-re-mi' would be hard to extend further. To prevent these new tones from creating a Babel of confusion like the old ones, for which people throughout the world used the same signs but naming-systems that varied in a number of ways, it is probably best to fit them out with their names at the very start and to choose the kind that will meet with sympathy throughout the musical world. They should bear the names of twelve of the outstanding living musicians of a modern turn of mind. To this end I shall invite a number of the best-known composers and instrumentalists to join the association. The first twelve, in the order in which I receive their acceptance, will each give a suitable syllable of their Christian or surname as a name for one tone of the scale.

Postscript 2

In the meantime it has emerged that even for piano music two staves (six lines in all, then), are adequate. So, there being no time left for engraving, I have re-transcribed Ex. 21a.

Ex. 22   Op. 25

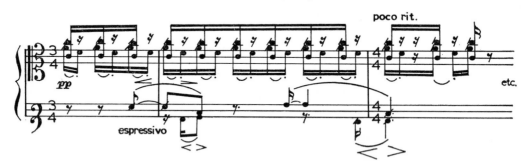

Mödling. November 1924

PART VIII

TEACHING

1

PROBLEMS IN TEACHING ART
1911

I believe art is born of 'I must', not of 'I can'. A craftsman 'can': whatever he was born with, he has developed, and so long as he wants to do something, he is able to. What he wants to do, he *can* do—good and bad, shallow and profound, new-fangled and old-fashioned—he *can*! But the artist *must*. He has no say in the matter, it is nothing to do with what he wants; but since he must, he also can. Perhaps he was not born with something; then he acquires it—manual dexterity, command of form, virtuosity. Not other people's, though: his own. This ability developed from within, under compulsion, this ability to express oneself differs fundamentally from the craftsman's ability, which in fact really expresses someone other than himself. The craftsman can make what the artist had to create. With his dexterity and adaptability he can apply, as an artistic method, something the creative spirit did unconsciously, when it forced from the material the effects that matched a need for expression.

So the genius really learns only from himself, the man of talent mainly from others. The genius learns from nature—his own nature—the man of talent from art. And this is the weightiest problem in teaching art. The art teacher believes he should pass on only artistic methods and aesthetics. Normally he mixes the two in a proportion that depends on his degree of insight; when he can get no further with the one, the other had better come to the rescue. When there are no more artistic methods to make available, then good taste, formal sense, sense of beauty must help out. So long as he provides artistic methods, thus remaining positive, it may in fact work. But when he turns to functions of feeling and sensitivity he becomes nebulous, unclear, and loses control. At that point his best course would be to turn straight to his talented pupil and simply ask him to find out for himself. But if the pupil can find out for himself—if he may be left in the lurch, thrown back on his own resources at precisely the most important, the hardest point, then what is the good of easing him over what are, after all, the much easier preliminary stages? If he could solve the harder point, he would surely do very well indeed with the easier one.

The customary line is rather different: 'You must be able to walk before you learn to dance.' But it is a false comparison. For a teacher can show how to dance but not how to be inspired or how to invent an exceptional method for an exceptional case. And the exceptional case, calling for the exceptional method, at every moment confronts the man who produces art. The man who has to dance, on the other hand, is confronted by the everyday case; the effect he is to produce is of a purely formal nature and has relatively little to do with his personal leanings and needs. Art, though, answers only to these, and everything merely formal is contingent—regular contingencies, perhaps, but hardly the main thing.

So what is the point of teaching how to master everyday cases? The pupil learns how to use something he must not use if he wants to be an artist. But one cannot give him what matters most—the courage and the strength to find an attitude to things which will make everything he looks at an exceptional case, because of the way he looks at it. Here, artistic methods are more liable to do harm than good. To use them means to generalize them, and then they are no longer artistic methods but artistic tricks, craftsman's tricks. A carpenter must explain to his apprentice the reason why he has to saw straight, and show him the best way of holding the saw for that purpose. But it can be superfluous or downright dangerous to force someone to compose symphonic forms if his expressive needs are later going to seek out the path of lyricism. Merely for the sake of culture, of education?

It is said of many an author that he may have technique, but no invention. That is wrong; he has no technique either, or he has invention too. You don't have technique when you can neatly imitate something; technique has you. Other people's technique. If one is in a position to look closely, one must realize how fraudulent technique of that sort is. Nothing really works, everything is just neatly glossed over. Everything is approximate, none of the joints fit properly, nothing holds together; but from a distance it looks almost genuine. Technique never exists devoid of invention; what does exist is invention which has still to create its technique. But the art teacher's aim is to give his pupil this technique. He urges him to model himself on art, instead of nature, and shows him that one can say something even without the compulsion an expressive need exerts.

366

The basis of this is a fallacious insight. Outward symptoms tell us what is going on inside. Only, symptoms are not always causes; they are often effects of what is going on. Thus Strindberg inclines to the view that germs accompany rather than cause illness. One man will think a fever is the illness, the evil to be fought, while another takes it for the healing process, which is to be encouraged. Similarly here. Is technique a cause or an effect, a by-product? Expressive content wishes to make itself understood; its upheaval produces a form. A volcano erupts, the devastation makes an ornamental effect; a steam-kettle explodes, and the objects it strews around fall at points one could exactly calculate on the basis of relationships of tension, weights, distances and resistances. One can, however, also lay the same objects out, so that they imitate an explosion's sense of order, and the temperament implied by the distances and weights. But there is a difference after all. Just as at some point a nobleman's pedigree raises him above a plebeian, so here it makes some difference whether an ornament has as its author the explosion of a steam-kettle or the arranging hand of an interior decorator. There are two obvious equations: 'Similar treatment of material must achieve similar effects', and, 'If one produces similar effects, one must have similar feelings.' We are dealing with three unknown quantities, so a third equation is still to come. This one, however, is: 'Similar feelings express themselves through dissimilar treatment of material.' The facts of art prove this, and not the opposite, though people would like them to. So the third equation, instead of producing the solution, upsets the first two.

There is no point in arranging the indices of a volcanic eruption, for the expert will see at a glance that nothing more than a spirit-burner has been raging. And it is ludicrous for simple, pleasant people to withhold their due contribution —a clear statement about what really goes on inside them—preferring to play out a Hero's Life before us. We are to admire them as Don Juan, for Don Juan is the masculine ideal, and always good for a bit of literature. They simply must lay a masterful hand on life—it happens to be the modern thing to do. Rogues in the grand manner, or heroes in the grand manner—they won't be seen in public without their grandeur. But they would do us and themselves more of a service if they told a little truth about the sad state they get into whenever life is too much for them. We grow up with ideals, harbour mistaken notions about love, about women, about truth, about falsehood, about trust, about everything that matters. But we are met by ever more literature, and for all its realism and naturalism it is, as always, blue-eyed, blonde and bearded, is poet, sculptor, or at the very least, professor, and masters life or philosophizes Nietzsche. Disappointments are an end in themselves, though; to suffer them, one needs the same difference of potential that is the spur to production. And the enlightenment found in art and literature is neither a shield against disappointment nor a comfort. It is an illusion to think that insight gives comfort or that other people's experience has any value for us except to confirm what we, too, have undergone. If today's unoriginals talked of what really preoccupies them, then they would in fact be talking about the real thing, instead of its illusory image. But for them the main thing is the illusion, the 'beautiful illusion'. Such a thing is undeniably given off by art, and that should be enough; but they want art itself to be this beautiful illusion, and that is a confusion fraught with calamity.

The kind of contribution the talented can make is best seen when they are forced to stick to the point. I once browsed among the documents in the library of the Patent Office, and was amazed at the wealth of well-conceived, ingenious ideas there. Admittedly an important discovery, one of genius, has more in it than have a hundred such small ones, and often makes them superfluous. But these ideas are something in themselves. Something small, perhaps, and dispensable; and yet genuine results, which proceed from the point at issue. Here is 'inspiration', mind-work, achievement. There is no style to carry one through, no ornament to give a lift; pomposity is out of the question, and fraud too. This is morality; an idea makes its appearance for what it is worth—no less, but no more either.

This shows me the direction in which a true teacher of art would have to guide his pupils—toward this severe matter-of-factness which, more than anything else, is the distinguishing mark of everything truly personal. So doing, a teacher of art could help even the talented to reach the point where they can give voice to the kind of utterance that fittingly expresses a personality. Belief in technique as the only salvation would have to be suppressed, and the urge for truthfulness encouraged. Then it would even be permissible to call in examples from art and to pass on the methods of art. They would be recommended for imitation, but in a different sense. The pupil would have to gather from them the *fact* that one must come to grips with all the problems—not *how* to. Technique, too, could be demonstrated—but only as the grammar of a language might be. In the latter, one can find meaning, spirit—the spirit of a nation. But the ideas, the feelings—these are one's own contribution. One may let oneself be carried by language, but it carries only the man who would be capable, if it did not exist, of inventing it himself. 'Language, mother of the idea,' says Karl Kraus—as wrongly as if he had said the hen is there before the egg. And as rightly. For that is how it is in the real work of art: everything gives the impression of having come first, because everything was born at the same moment. Feeling is already form, the idea is already the word.

It should be the art teacher's aim to bring ideas like these over the horizon of his pupil's mind. Then, perhaps, even the talented pupil will find some necessity within himself, and the chance of being able to do something he alone can do, even though there are others greater than he.

2

MUSIC
(from 'Guide-Lines for a Ministry of Art' edited by Adolf Loos)
1919

PRELIMINARY REMARK

I wrote this little essay immediately after the war had been lost, when the possession of five rational senses was threatened right and left by Bolshevism; when the whole world looked only to suicide for help, and only to its fantasy for a new, better reality, building bomb-proof castles in the air, intended to protect the brain from the assaults of hunger; when it could cost a man his head to refrain from saying the things that would satisfy the parties!

No reasonable spinner of fantasies can hope to see his dreams come any truer than by having his article reprinted. For that reason, it is hereby permitted.

January 1924

I

The most important task of the music section is to ensure the German nation's superiority in the field of music, a superiority which has its roots in the people's talents. These may stem from the fact that in former times the German elementary school teacher was nearly always also a music teacher; in even the smallest village he carried out that function and so created a reservoir great enough to supply the topmost strata. With the establishment of the modern elementary school, music teaching was reduced to a barely sufficient instruction in singing. Another hundred years, and this superiority will have been lost.

The best thing would be to reincorporate music teaching in the elementary school curriculum. This, however, would be hard to organize and too costly, so the following is recommended:

Music schools will be divided into three classes: elementary, secondary and high schools. These differ partly in the level of education aimed at, partly in the difference in the time taken to reach it. The lower schools, as with schools in general, could to some extent be regarded as a preparation for the higher. But in any case talent is the sole qualification for the higher schools.

It must be possible for all, even the poorest, to attend. To this end school fees will be graded in as many classes as are needed to match social circumstances as closely as possible. The decision as to which fees are payable will then be based on tax assessment, and, as with the latter, special circumstances (large family, etc.) can be borne in mind.

II

Concert life must gradually cease to be a commercial business. Given the right organization, that will avoid all middlemen, arrangers and the like, and address itself directly to the public, it should easily be possible to do everything needed for the furtherance of art, even without state assistance.

The basic fault in public concert-life is competition (concert rivalry). One gives concerts for two reasons. The first, pure reason: one or more people make music, recite, sing; others anxious to share this experience are permitted to listen. The second, petty, impure reason: art wins prizes. Many people want to win prizes, and the highest goes to the winner. So now he has to win, whereas once he merely had to sing. Thus competition, the need to win, brings pettiness into the business of art.

Once the correct relationship is re-established through direct contact with the public (which will then no longer be the high-handed judge, deciding between hunger and laurels)—the relationship: 'There is a performance: those who want to listen are allowed to,' it will be possible to find a way of paying artists appropriately while still holding adequate rehearsals.

III

Rights in intellectual property would have to be put in every respect on a par with rights in all other property, especially as regards inheritability. With this kind of property more than with any other it is justifiable to recognize permanently inheritable rights, since it is precisely here that the heirs realize, through the fact that they still receive something, that the estate really was someone's property. On the death of the last heirs the inherited rights should pass half to the state and half to an association for personal publication, to be mentioned in the next section. The copyright would have to be non-transferable, and its purchase forbidden, punishable and void by law.

IV

In present-day artistic life the real artist not only suffers from misunderstanding, has not only to watch the worldly victory of all that is not art, but he must also pay for the cost of propagating the kind of bad art by which he is driven out. To the publisher, the author who sells well is the better-selling ware that covers the losses arising from incautious purchase of wares that sell less well. Thus the true artist, whose works as a rule attain a higher market-value only after his death, receives so little in his lifetime that he is in no position to apply all his working energy to creation.

This situation could be ameliorated as follows:

1. The assignment of copyright would have to be declared inadmissible as stated in section III.

2. As regards copyright acquired in works already published or still to be published, they would have to be expropriated in return for moderate compensation to the publishers (matching their risks and outgoings), and the property reassigned to the author.

3. Authors would have to combine in forming an association for personal publication, with direct approach to the public, avoiding all unnecessary expense and providing an author with the entire proceeds of his works, since it will deduct merely its own expenses and a certain percentage as a kind of insurance premium against losses from other publishing ventures.

V

Musicians' social position must be improved. The oboist or horn-player who has to play a solo in the evening is an artist who in his own field needs a higher degree of infallibility than do most top civil servants in theirs. His studies demand diligence, perseverance, seriousness, they last so long and require so much talent that he should be numbered among the truly elect on the social ladder.

VI

As regard the musical theatre, I agree with Adolf Loos' proposals, though with certain reservations arising from musical necessities.[1]

The reservations are as follows:

1. One does not know music after hearing it once. The music lover, and especially the artist who has to reproduce music, must hear it often. So there will still not be enough performances, even of a small number of works, particularly if, as Loos proposes, these works will not be repeated for some years.

2. If this theatre had the best resources at its disposal and there were perhaps a second or a third theatre to meet the artistic demand mentioned above, then if this possessed more limited means one would unfortunately still be unable to hear sufficiently frequent and good performances of masterpieces.

On the other hand, I approve strongly of the idea of touring theatres, for which a repertoire of two or three works could well suffice. At the same time I would put in a plea for the formation of touring orchestras and professional choirs to the same end.

VII

An Arts Council could be formed under the following conditions:

1. A section will be founded for each branch of art and will have two types of members:

    (a) Those whose importance is also recognized abroad, who will be appointed for life;

    (b) Those whose importance is recognized only at home, who can belong to the Arts Council until their fiftieth year.

2. Each section will advise and decide on matters concerning it. However, to become valid, the decisions taken will need ratification by a council to be formed of members of class (a) of all sections.

VIII

Finally I should like to point out that the way of paying school fees for music lessons, proposed in our first section, can also be applied to the educational system as a whole. There is no need for the children of the rich to attend elementary school free of charge, nor, at secondary schools or University, for them to pay the same as the less-affluent and the poor.

3

ON THE QUESTION OF MODERN COMPOSITION
TEACHING
1929

Any ox can certainly tell hay from grass, and one may assume that in summer he prefers grass, perhaps even to the point of rejecting hay. In the same way even the least educated musician can tell a modern work from a non-modern one; for him, as for the ox, the season is the main thing. For an ox, it is a criterion, if only because his decision depends purely on time; in winter he appreciates hay, without rejecting grass. But the uneducated and untalented musician is timeless; he knows only trends, and rejects one in exactly the same offhand way he accepts another.

One would think it possible to enlighten such a musician, to show him what is lasting and what ephemeral, what of value and what worthless, what is fashionable tinsel and what has substance, what is genuine and what imitation. But, as I said in a similar case, 'you learn only the things you can do anyway'. Were it otherwise, how could musicians ostensibly understand Bach and then write mood-picture fugues and a dreary, empty polyphony that lacks the spirit of counterpoint; praise Mozart's light touch, and string together two-bar phrases; have heard about Beethoven's logic, and go in for brainless note-spinning; know of Brahms' motivic art, and model themselves only on his superficially 'conservative' attitude; equate Handel and Bach or Gluck and Mozart?

Be for or against tonality and atonality, regardless of the idea presented and its value?

Whereas the ox chooses its fodder realistically, the rootless musician lacks natural judgement, so his daily diet does not nourish him.

Many people take as a sign of the times the hopeless lack of criteria shown in the judgements of music critics and musical assessors. But looking back over a few decades, one knows otherwise. Didn't the 'new German' musician recognize the 'Brahmin' by a failure to use chromatic progressions and 'interesting' harmonies? Did he not reject self-contained accompaniment figures of the old-fashioned kind, free of bombast, and turn against everything 'formalistic', such as variations? Vice versa, did not the Brahmins pour scorn on static basses, sequences, general pauses? And did not one composition teacher even poke fun at a 'new German instrument', the cor anglais? At the time of the symphonic poem, did not everyone say 'interesting', and at the time of expressionism, 'powerful, deeply-delving, overwhelming, significant', and so on? What did people gather from my music except that it sounded mixed-up, and did they not praise or blame accordingly? So is it any worse today, if matter-of-fact, deliberately expressionless music is called 'musikantisch, fresh, untroubled, unromantic'—all of which are assessments basically in terms of expression?

Composition, though, is above all the art of inventing a musical idea and the fitting way to present it. And however surely the 'how', the presentation, is a symptom of the 'what', the idea itself, one should still be able to take for granted in a professional musician a certain ability to recognize an idea in itself. Were that so, people would not be in the habit of rejecting ideas, perhaps ideas for the whole of humanity, without recognizing them as such, merely because they are delivered in an expressive, pathetic or romantic way. (Only a moron could believe that someone endowed with important ideas would produce unimportant ones—that Alekhine would make weak moves because they were easier for everyone to understand, or even that Einstein's theories are looking for a way to reconcile themselves with everyday obtuseness.)

The feeling for what is truly new about an idea and its presentation can never be lost, so long as one refuses to stop at the mere externals of the manifest form; nor will one become dulled to its effect. I can say that in all great masterpieces I feel at countless points the thrill of novelty, scarcely less strongly than it must have been felt at the time the work first appeared. For example, in Mozart's

Dissonance Quartet I feel it over and over again when there is that daring contradictory entry of the first violin on A, directly after the A-flat just left by the viola. Or at the bass' B-natural passing against the B-sharp in Bach's C-sharp minor Prelude (Book I). Or in the expressive power of the third, A-flat to C-flat, at Ortrud's lamenting cry of 'Elsa'. For what is truly new remains as new as it was on the first day.

But the 'how', the art of presentation, is apparent not only in phenomena that stand out conspicuously by their novelty, but even more in deeply hidden traits that have always escaped the theorist's notice: indeed, in the kind of trait that has never yet crossed his mind. It is easy for mannerists to produce the uniform, thin layer that conceals everything, even when there is nothing worth concealing. And imitators know how to string together the symptoms of an idea, to imitate its style of presentation and to use this baseless 'how' to divert attention from the idea. But nobody can give voice to an idea unless he could also think of it, and the true art of composition (like true science) will always remain a secret science. It already counted as such at the time of the Netherlanders, for all the doubting scorn of graceless historians. It has to be so, not just because the initiated are forbidden to make it known, but, particularly, because the others are unable to grasp it.

For example, Bach, who doubtless had an incredibly profound knowledge of the nature of the composer's art and was made acquainted with the secret paths along which sounds are led to combine or co-exist—a man like Bach could certainly have written a treatise on composition. We know he did not write one; but that he should not have given away some of the essential secrets by word of mouth to his pupils, his sons, is hard to believe. What success did such teaching achieve, though? This: it was just *his* art, even his own work, that fell into oblivion, and his admittedly gifted son Philipp Emanuel quite expressly turned away from his father's outmoded art to write in the new style.

For me, it is certain that the laws of the old art are also those of the new art. If you have correctly perceived and correctly formulated them, and if you understand how to apply them correctly, then you no longer feel the need for any other, any new teaching. A piece, an idea, its presentation are assessed in the same way as at any other time, by those truly informed. What was a discovery is still a discovery today, its logic has not changed, its beauty has stayed the same; but forms continue to arise, in keeping with the demands of the idea and the manner of its presentation, which depends on the initial inspiration. Methods of delivering the idea may change in their external form. One will say something now more briefly, now at greater length. One will further comprehensibility now by a greater expressiveness, now by a lesser. One will leave things out or emphasize them, sometimes bring out the plasticity of the motive, at others that of the theme rather; one will articulate more sharply or more by overlapping, let things follow or oppose each other, or simply let them arise. What does it all mean to someone who grasps merely the means but not the end that alone sanctifies them?

So even a new way of teaching composition, to be of use to many people, would simply teach again, as I have already said, how it's done, not what it is! And so I believe there are problems for the modern composition teacher, but none demanding a *new* way of teaching composition; rather the kind that demand an *old* one.

4

TEACHING AND MODERN TRENDS IN MUSIC
1938

That a young man composes in the style of the time, should not be surprising. It is as natural as using all the other facilities offered by the progress and the developments of the epoch in which one lives.

There would not exist the style of Louis XIV if he had liked to live in the style of Louis XIII. And thus Louis XV and his successors were conscious of their own time and abhorred living in a second-hand style.

But the attitude of a teacher has to include some intricate considerations. Often, a young man who wants to study with me expects to be taught in musical modernism. But he experiences a disappointment. Because, in his compositions I usually at once recognize the absence of an adequate background. Superficially investigating I unveil the cause: the student's knowledge of the musical literature offers the aspects of a Swiss cheese—almost more holes than cheese. Then I ask the following question: 'If you wanted to build an aeroplane, would you venture to invent and construct by yourself every detail of which it is composed, or would you not better at first try to acknowledge what all the men did who designed aeroplanes before you? Don't you think the same idea is correct in music? Don't you assume that there exists already a number of sound solutions to all the problems concerning a young composer? You might perhaps be afraid to lose your originality if you were to take advantage of your predecessors. But how can you know whether your ideas are original if you are not in the position to compare them to what the others wrote? Maybe everything you consider your own creation has been in general use—or even abuse—for decades. Maybe it is even already antiquated instead of original.'

Only a thorough knowledge of the styles makes one conscious of the difference between 'mine and thine'. And accordingly one cannot really understand the style of one's time if one has not found out how it is distinguished from the style of one's predecessors.

Modernism, in its best meaning, comprises a development of thoughts and their expression. This can not be taught and ought not to be taught. But it might come in a natural way, by itself, to him who proceeds gradually by absorbing the cultural achievements of his predecessors.

June 30, 1938

5

EARTRAINING THROUGH COMPOSING
1939

I

Suppose someone paid a visit to the ancient buildings of Rome or the famous pictures in the Louvre in Paris, or read a poem by Goethe or an involved mystery story by Poe. What would his reactions be?

In Rome he might dream of the mighty Roman empire, of the slaves who

377

built its monuments, the citizens who attended the public games. At the Louvre he might again surrender to his imagination. A religious painting would remind him of Biblical stories, mythological sculpture would turn his thoughts to paganism. Reading the poem by Goethe, he would associate it with the life of this great man. Remembering the *Sorrows of Werther*, he would go on to think of the opera, *Werther*, by Massenet—who also wrote *Manon*, which he likes better.

A nice dream!

And he would be quite right not to resist the temptation of his imagination. But would the same attitude be advisable while he was reading a mystery story? Dreaming of more or less related subjects, interesting or beautiful though they be, could he absorb and remember the details which simultaneously hide and reveal the murderer?

It is not too serious *not* to discover the solution of such crimes. But if the first examples did not show the point I am about to make, then the case of the detective story must have made it clear: one cannot do justice to a work of art while allowing one's imagination to wander to other subjects, related or not. In the face of works of art one must not dream, but one must try hard to grasp their meaning.

II

'Music Appreciation' often gives a music student not much more than the perfume of a work, that narcotic emanation of music which affects the senses without involving the mind. No one listening to popular music would be satisfied with such an impression. There is no doubt about the moment when a man starts to like a song or dance. It is when he begins to sing or whistle it—in other words when he is able to remember it. If this criterion is applied to serious music, it becomes clear that one does not like more than its perfume unless one can keep it in mind.

Remembering is the first step toward understanding. To understand as simple a sentence as 'The table is round' requires keeping the *table* in mind. Forget the table and only the perfume of the sentence remains. Historical facts, biographies of authors and performers, anecdotes of their lives, pathetic, humorous, interesting or instructive, may be of some value to people who are otherwise deaf to the effects of music. But all this cannot help anyone to absorb and remember the content.

378

Of course the best way to train a musical ear is to expose it to as much serious music as possible. Musical culture would spread faster if people would read music, play music or even listen to music much more than they do today. Extensive familiarity with serious music is the foremost requirement of musical culture. But even this is not enough without thorough ear-training.

Ear-training, in the narrow sense, is practised in high schools and colleges with excellent results. Good methods have been developed, but, like teaching techniques in other musical subjects, they have become too abstract, to some extent have lost contact with the original purpose. A trained ear is valuable, but not especially so if the ear is the gateway to the auditory sense rather than the musical mind. Like harmony, counterpoint and other theoretical studies, ear-training is not an end in itself, but only a step towards musicianship.

One often hears the question, 'Why teach composition to people who will never try it again after their student days are over, people who have neither creative ability nor the creative impulse, for whom it is a nightmare to have to express something in an idiom quite foreign to their minds?'

The answer is this: just as almost anyone can be trained to draw, paint, write an essay or deliver a lecture, it must also be possible to make people with even less than mediocre gifts use the means of musical composition in a sensitive manner. The prospect of having to listen to their musical products makes such a possibility seem rather dubiously desirable, and it is certainly not the purpose of theory teaching to produce a surplus of unwanted composers. Still, every good musician should submit to such training. How can one enjoy a game without understanding its fine points, without knowing when the ball is sliced or curved, without an idea of strategy or tactics? And yet there are performers who simply do not know the bare construction, not to mention the subtleties of musical pieces!

Understanding the fine points—that is, understanding the game at all— demands a thorough preparation. Harmony, counterpoint and form need not be taught as branches of aesthetics or history. A few illustrations will show how this training can be used to better purpose.

If a student of harmony not only writes his examples, but also plays them afterwards, his ear will become acquainted with a number of facts. He will realize that chords are used in root positions and inversions and that there is a difference in structural weight between them. And when he hears a classical fermata on a six-four chord, he will not applaud, knowing that this cannot be the end of the piece. Even someone with absolute pitch might mistake the end of the first section of a symphony for the end of the movement if he knew nothing of the structural functions of tonality. Sometimes a deceptive cadence is similarly misunderstood.

Knowledge of harmony alone will not suffice to correct such errors. Further studies are necessary to fortify that knowledge and to anchor it firmly in instinct. Even people without absolute pitch can learn to recognize modulatory sections. Why should a composer write such sections at all if they have no effect upon the layman? A well-trained student of harmony will also have at least some acquaintance with the effects of centrifugal harmonies.

The study of counterpoint develops the capacity for listening to more than one voice. A listener who hears in a fugue only the repetitions of the theme may well complain of monotony. But if he also perceives the accompanying voices, which are often second and third subjects, he will come closer to understanding the true nature of contrapuntal composition. Even in homophonic compositions there are cases where one must hear more than the principal voice. Many extensions in the music of Mozart and Brahms are produced by a movement of the harmony contradictory to the melody, an effect which is lost on anyone who listens to the melody alone. Every note a master has written should be perceived. How much pleasure it gives the connoisseur to watch the second violin in a Mozart quartet, as it accommodates itself to the first, assists or contradicts, expresses sympathy or antipathy by characteristic interjections!

III

These examples may already have given a clue to how much more might be achieved through the study of form and orchestration.

It is a great mistake to believe that the object of form is beauty. There is no beauty in eight measures because they are eight, no lack of beauty in ten. Mozart's asymmetry is not less beautiful than Beethoven's symmetry. The principal function of form is to advance our understanding. Music should be enjoyed. Undeniably, understanding offers man one of the most enjoyable pleasures. And though the object of form is not beauty, by providing comprehensibility, form produces beauty. An apple tree does not exist in order to give us apples, but it produces them nevertheless.

Forms are primarily organizations to express ideas in a comprehensible manner. An attempt at self-expression is a useful approach to understanding the methods of the great composers. A student knows by experience that the repetition of a section may on one occasion be good, useful or inevitable, on another poor, unnecessary or monotonous, and he will recognize the meaning of repetition in the works of others. Repetition, if not monotonous, helps to convey a musical idea. Anyone trained to vary the basic motive of his own composition will probably be able to follow a complicated melody without involuntarily dreaming of irrelevant images.

It is the organization of a piece which helps the listener to keep the idea in mind, to follow its development, its growth, its elaboration, its fate. If you have been taught to provide your themes with limits, to distinguish principal and subordinate ideas, to combine fluency with lucidity, to divide distinctly into parts what cannot be conceived undivided, you will know how to make use of these earmarks in masterpieces as symbols to remember. The theme of the fourth movement of Beethoven's Quartet in A Minor, Op. 132, consists amazingly of ten measures and, more amazingly still, in its tenth measure reaches a provisional ending on the seventh degree of A minor: G major. Scarcely a musician would recognize the singularity of such a procedure if he had not been taught that themes like this ought to consist of eight measures only, and to end on the first, third or fifth degree. But anyone who knows this will easily recognize the theme whenever it appears in the development.

Without remembering, how could we understand variations? When a composer calls his piece *Variations on X*, he obviously wants us to understand every variation as a derivative of his chosen theme. The Haydn theme of Brahms' *Variations* has an 'A' section which consists of a ten-measure period characteristically subdivided at the fifth measure. It is difficult not to recognize this in the variations. Furthermore, the third section is unusual in that it is prolonged by means of an extension. No one, at first hearing, can grasp all the fine points of Brahms' variation technique, the harmonic and contrapuntal combinations, the many ways in which he treats the unevenness of his five-measure sections. Perhaps all this is not absolutely necessary for an adequate response to the music. But it is certainly a good approach to what the composer himself wants to tell us.

Composing trains the ear to recognize what should be kept in mind, and thus helps the understanding of musical ideas. Characteristic deviations from the norm, irregularities, will be guides in the no-man's-land of great ideas.

Now to speak of orchestration. My concept of colour is not the usual one. Colour, like light and shadow in the physical world, expresses and limits the forms and sizes of objects. Sometimes these elements serve as a camouflage. A musician likewise might wish to hide something. For instance, like a good tailor, he might wish to hide the seams where sections are sewn together. In general, however, lucidity is the first purpose of colour in music, the aim of the orchestration of every true artist. I do not wish to be a killjoy, but I must confess that I find the delight in colours somewhat overrated. Perhaps the art of orchestration has become too popular, and interesting-sounding pieces are often produced for no better reason than that which dictates the making of typewriters and fountain pens in different colours.

IV

It is obvious that not even a small percentage of music students will become composers. They cannot and they should not. It is also evident that many would-be composers and musicians who, through some study, have acquired a superficial knowledge of music, may presume to judge the activities of good artists and real creators. This is where a correct attitude on the part of the teacher becomes important. He must convince his students that the study of composition will not make them experts or acknowledged judges, that its only purpose is to help them understand music better, to obtain that pleasure which is inherent in the art. The possession of an ear trained through composing should not entitle a man to humiliate his innocent and less fortunate neighbour. It should give him only one pleasure: the pleasure of balance between the joy he expects from music and the joy he actually receives.

6

THE BLESSING OF THE DRESSING
1948

Professionalism in music had made great progress in the nineteenth century. But in the last quarter of this century there were great numbers of amateurs still alive—amateurs of all grades, ranging from violin players who could only play in the first position to those who could compete with excellent concert virtuosi. Many people had their weekly chamber music in their homes. They played all kinds of combinations: piano duets, violin and cello sonatas, piano trios and even string quartets. And also professional musicians played in string quartets or other combinations solely for their love of music, without aiming at another profit than this pleasure. I myself have participated very frequently in such groups and my profit from this work was a rather comprehensive acquaintance with classical chamber music.

The abolition of amateurism stems from the ambition of amateurs who wanted to compete with the professionals. The result was extremely destructive to the art of music. The necessities of competition now forced rivals to use improper means in order to make a success, and what is even worse is that those who as amateurs had formerly been impartial and unselfish, and ready to support needy or unfortunate artists, promoters of the arts, were now in the market themselves. Instead of buying music, instead of attending concerts, instead of enjoying music, they themselves demanded support.

While the rank of an artist, of a performer, of a virtuoso could still easily and speedily be determined, it became more difficult and demanded more time to do the same when a multitude of composers, of newly made-up geniuses began to appear on the horizon. Some of them had learned the craft thoroughly and at least knew something; others had been instructed superficially and used their commonplace talents to compete successfully with hard-working, serious composers.

To this increase in the number of musicians who composed corresponded proportionally an increase of those who taught composing. And to the lowering of the standard of the composers corresponded that of the standard of their teachers. However, one must state that there were many who had themselves been instructed competently and who were able to communicate their own knowledge; there were also composers of talent and experience, some of whom might have engaged themselves in research of the past or even the present, finding solutions to problems, describing compositorial techniques and improving teaching methods; there were also specialists who could not or did not want to teach more than a limited field of theory—for instance, harmony only, or counterpoint, or both, but not compositorial techniques. Unfortunately the great majority helped through their own incompetence to increase the number of ignoramuses who knew only a few tricks.

On the average, teaching was not bad. Really harmful was the condition that these teachers were professionals and had to make their living teaching. Accordingly, they had to accommodate to the pressure of competition and this meant 'teaching individually'—that is, making it easier for those who had less talent, without making it difficult enough for the talented.

It was not true, as it is in sports, that you had to accomplish something surpassing the average. A teacher who wanted to have a sufficient number of well-paying pupils had to reduce his demands on talent, skill and industry. Did the talent not suffice for symphonies or operas, a pupil could write songs or short piano pieces and finally even only popular music. Always a private teacher had to lead his pupils to a certain success.

I must admit that I never made such accommodations. When I said in my *Harmonielehre* that I taught individually, it was not to spare my pupils the effort to do the best. I would change nothing else but the order of the course, but did not omit matters a musician must know. You could postpone some problems which were too difficult in the beginning for later. You could give exercises preliminary to the harder task. But I had never given in with my main demands.

There existed also students who did not intend writing serious music. They only planned to write popular music—operettas and the like. Many of them were sincere enough to admit their own limitations and conceded their restricted aims.

I once had a pupil who had started harmony with me. About two months later he stopped taking lessons. He had been offered a position as second music critic on a great newspaper and was afraid too much knowledge might have unfavourable influence upon the spontaneity of his judgement. He made a career as a critic and even as a pedagogue.

As a teacher I never taught only what I knew, but rather what the pupil needed. Thus I have never taught a student 'a style', that is, the technical peculiarities of a specific composer, degraded to tricks, which to the master in question might have been the solution of a torturing problem. And if I say in the preface to my *Harmonielehre* that I tried to invent something for every student to serve his personal necessities, that does not mean that I made it easier for one of them.

Especially not, because I was insisting on one main demand: that a composer must not compose two or eight or sixteen measures today and again tomorrow and so on until the work seemed to be finished, but should conceive a composition as a totality, in one single act of inspiration. Intoxicated by his idea, he should write down as much as he could, not caring for little details. They could be added, or carried out later.

I used to say that the composer must be able to look very far ahead in the future of his music. It seems to me this is the masculine way of thinking: thinking at once of the whole future, of the whole destiny of the idea, and preparing beforehand for every possible detail. This is the manner in which a man builds his house, organizes his affairs, and prepares for his wars. The other manner is the feminine manner, which takes into account with good understanding the nearest consequences of a problem, but misses preparing for the more remote events. This is the way of the dressmaker, who might use the most valuable material without thinking whether it will last long, if only it makes the desired effect now—right now. It need not last longer than the fashion will last. It is the manner of some cooks who prepare a salad without questioning whether every ingredient is the right thing and fits well with every other, whether they will mix satisfactorily. There will be a French dressing—or perhaps a French-Russian dressing[1]—put on top of it, and this will connect everything. Composing then, in harmony with such advice, is a matter of producing a certain style.

I consider it as one of my merits that I did not encourage composing. I rather treated most of the hundreds of pupils in a manner that showed them I did not think too much of their creative ability.

I do not mean to say that I made it intentionally difficult for my pupils—rather, that I had no control over it. This can be proved by the following fact.

For many years I had tried in vain to teach my pupils some discoveries I had made in the field of multiple counterpoint. I worked hard to formulate this advice in a manner conceivable for a pupil, but I did not succeed. Only once, in one of the best classes I ever had, I considered the presentation of this problem and its solution as final, and I asked the class to compose for the next lesson something applying the methods emerging from my solution.

It was one of my greatest disappointments. Only one of my students had tried to use my advice, and he had misunderstood me as much as the rest of the class.

This experience taught me a lesson: secret science is not what an alchemist would have refused to teach you; it is a science which cannot be taught at all. It is inborn or it is not there.

This is also the reason why Thomas Mann's Adrian Leverkühn does not know the essentials of composing with twelve tones.[2] All he knows has been told him by Mr. Adorno, who knows only the little I was able to tell my pupils. The real fact will probably remain secret science until there is one who inherits it by virtue of an unsolicited gift.

The harshness of my requirements is also the reason why, of the hundreds of my pupils, only a few have become composers: Anton Webern, Alban Berg, Hanns Eisler, Karl Rankl, Winfried Zillig, Roberto Gerhard, Nikos Skalkottas, Norbert von Hannenheim, Gerald Strang, Adolph Weiss. At least I have heard only of these.

One more effect derived from it: all my pupils differ from one another extremely and though perhaps the majority compose twelve-tone music, one could not speak of a school. They all had to find their way alone, for themselves. And this is exactly what they did; everyone has his own manner of obeying rules derived from the treatment of twelve tones.

While I was not able to teach my students a style—I admit I was not able to do it, even if I would have overcome my dislike of so doing—there are other teachers who can do this and only this.

Thus we see a great number of composers of various countries and nationalities who compose about the same kind of music—music, at least, of such a similarity that it would be difficult to distinguish them from one another, quite aside from the question of their nationality. Advice for composing is delivered in the manner in which a cook would deliver recipes. You cannot fail; the recipe is perfectly dependable. The result is: nobody fails. One makes it as well as all the others.

Astonishingly, each considers it his national style, though different nationalities write the same.

It is the true internationalism of music in our time.

7

AGAINST THE SPECIALIST
c. 1940

I am opposed to the specialist.

I admit that a great specific technique cannot be acquired without intense practice, even at the expense of being as skilful in other, and even in related, matters.

But just as a doctor must know the whole body, so should a musician not only know harmony, or how to play the piano, or the flute, or how to conduct, and should not be called only a harmony teacher, or a pianist, or a flutist, or a conductor. In order to deserve the name of musician, he should not only possess a specific knowledge in one field, but he has to have an all-round knowledge of all the fields of his art.

Otherwise incidents will happen such as those mentioned here:

A band leader, chairman of a department of music, who is a tolerable teacher of some band instruments, has to make arrangements for a string quartet which is going to play Beethoven's 'Harp' Quartet—so-called because of a long broken-chord pizzicato section. 'Who will play the harp?', he asks one of his students.

Or that of a piano teacher. She takes up in two weekly lessons two measures of a piano concerto whose difficulties surpass by far the technique of the pupil. But in three or four years he will have mastered technically the whole 400 measures, without ever having realized the contents of the piece!

In addition to that, such a student will behave like a singer who knew only his part, but had no idea of the other singers' parts nor of the whole action. Thus, when he once had to die in the second act and left the stage, he never learned that his death had been avenged in the third act by the death of his murderer.

Similarly, pianists, violinists, and other concert soloists, when they have a long section of rests—say forty or more measures—might not care for what the orchestra has to say at this time. They merely wait, more or less patiently, for their catchwords.

Why should they make a greater effort to become acquainted with the spirit of a work of art if one can satisfy or even enthuse audiences, musicians and critics—if this can be achieved with more ease?

I used to ask my pupils, when they started to study a new work, not to play their instruments before they had studied the work thoroughly by reading it silently, building up in their minds an image of the piece. This image then served as a model to which the live sound had to be realized.

Compare that to the procedure of many conductors who do not care to become acquainted with a piece unless they know they will keep it in their repertory. They would learn how to 'beat' for the players: seven measures of Allegro 4/4, then eight measures ritardando, followed by three measures Allegro—again 4/4, after which three measures of 3/4—beating three Allegro, then four measures 5/8, and two measures 7/8. . . .

Such are the crimes of the specialist.

8

THE TASK OF THE TEACHER
1950

In my fifty years of teaching I have taught certainly more than a thousand pupils. Though I had to do it in order to make a living, I must confess that I was a passionate teacher, and the satisfaction of giving to beginners as much as possible of my own knowledge was probably a greater reward than the actual fee I received. This was also the reason why I accepted so many pupils who could not pay, even if they had not the background to study with me. Thus I said in such a case once: 'After all, if they cannot digest what I give them, it will damage them less to study with me than with a poorer teacher.'

All this time, in teaching compositorial subjects, I aimed for matters foreign to many composers: clear and distinctly phrased formulations, logical continuations, fluency, variety, characteristic contrasts and constructions, accommodated and changed in response to various purposes.

A teacher cannot help a student to invent many and beautiful themes, nor can he produce expressiveness or profundity. Instead, he can teach structural correctness and the requirements of continuity; he also may train a sense for the expansion and broadness, or, on the contrary, for brevity and limitation of the presentation, and a judgement of the productivity of an idea. He furthermore can influence the taste, thereby excluding triviality, talkativeness, superficiality, bombast, complacency, and other poor habits. It is, of course, not enough to lecture about these evils, or simply to refute them.

A true teacher must be a model of his pupils; he must possess the ability to achieve several times what he demands of a pupil once. It does not even suffice here to give direct advice for better procedures; he must work it out in the presence of the student, improvising several solutions to a problem, showing what is necessary.

All that takes much time. Therefore, there were not too many pupils to whom I could transmit all or part of such knowledge. Still, this was the reason why many of them, like Horwitz, Krüger, Jalowetz, Erwin Stein, Steuermann, Polnauer, Kort van der Linden, Rufer, Novakovic, Toldi, Rankl, Deutsch, Ratz, Herbert, Eisler, Trauneck, Kolisch, Zillig, Schacht, Hannenheim, Weiss, Gerhard, Erich Schmidt, Strang, Leonard Stein, Newlin, Hoffmann, Estep and others, studied more than two, even three or four years with me. But Anton von Webern and Alban Berg studied about five years with me.

Here, at the University of California at Los Angeles, I had not too often the opportunity of teaching the fine points of our art. Most of my students took only the one year of composition which the curriculum prescribed and only few remained for advanced studies.

In spite of the short teaching period, and though most of the students did not possess creative talent nor an adequate knowledge of the master works, I succeeded in having every one of them compose a Rondo.

My demands aggravated this task considerably. I urged them to include in this form at least six to seven different themes, different in character and expression, in construction, in harmony, in length and intrinsic procedure. There was to be: a main theme (if possible a ternary form with a contrasting middle section); a transition, including a liquidation and bridge; one or two subordinate themes, and a codetta; and the C-section of this A-B-A-C-A-B-A form was to contain another subordinate theme plus a *Durchführung*—that is, a modulatory elaboration. They all did not receive negative 'don't', 'avoid' and 'you must not', but positive advice. Almost all of the class could fulfill the demands in some way; the best two or three were able to write quite usable music, though, of course, with complete absence of originality.

In consideration of all this, one might perhaps understand that I, who always had tried to provide young people with the tools of our art, with the technical, aesthetic and moral basis of true artistry, must complain about teachers who teach their students nothing but the peculiarities of a certain style. Much harm has been done to an entire generation of high-talented American composers. It will probably require another generation of honest and profound instruction to repair this damage.

PART IX

COMPOSERS

BACH
1950

I

I used to say, 'Bach is the first composer with twelve tones.' This was a joke, of course. I did not even know whether somebody before him might not have deserved this title. But the truth on which this statement is based is that the Fugue No. 24 of the first volume of the Well-Tempered Clavier, in B minor, begins with a *Dux* in which all twelve tones appear. I have tried to find another example of this kind, but have not succeeded. I could, however, check only a part of his whole work.

It is an exceptional case; even in this fugue the *Comes* consists of only eleven different tones, and of the twelve repetitions and transpositions, only seven are complete, while five omit one or two of the twelve tones. Maybe an examination of the countersubjects and the episodes might exhibit more interesting facts. But what is more important here is that this fugue deserves the title of 'chromatic fugue' more rightfully than the one which is usually called so. It approaches a style of chromaticism in a manner different from Bach's ordinary procedure. In general, chromatic alterations appear as ascending or descending substitute leading-tones as in measures 1–2 of Fugue 14, vol. 1; or in half-tone progressions, as in measures 6, 12 (and others) of Fugue 22, vol. 2, or in Fugue 10, vol. 1. There are in vol. 1 two somewhat similar cases: Fugue No. 18 in G-sharp minor and, especially, Fugue No. 12 in F minor. But measures 33–34 of Fugue No. 19 are less chromatic than they look; they are in B minor, mixing features of the ascending scale with ordinary descending scales and with Bach's peculiar form of a descending minor scale.

In Fugue 24 the chromatically altered tones are neither substitutes nor parts of scales. They possess distinctly an independence resembling the unrelated tones of the chromatic scale in a basic set of a twelve-tone composition. The only essential difference between their nature and modern chromaticism is that they do not yet take advantage of their multiple meaning as a means of changing direction in a modulatory fashion.

II

I have always thought highly of the teacher Bach. Doubtless he possessed a profound insight into the hidden mysteries of tone-relations. He was certainly able to present his ideas clearly and understandably. But I am also convinced that he was not so sentimental as to renounce his contemporaries' application of *Schopfbeutler, Kopfstückeln und Ohrenreissen*,[1] if it helped to make his pupils work, practise and even only understand. And he was successful in that. One need only remember the unsurpassed excellence of so many of his sons and especially of Philipp Emanuel, who, I believe, must have possessed a tremendous knowledge of counterpoint. Probably Johann Sebastian had invested in him all his secrets of finding one's way with the hidden peculiarities of the tones. I am sure that had he not considered his father's style as obsolete, and had he possessed his inventive and expressive power and his personality, he might have become as great as his father.

Technically, I assume, he must have known the secrets that enabled the Old-One to build, in contradiction to the advice of theorists, on a broken chord, all the different themes of the *Art of the Fugue*, which admit all the canonic imitations, direct, in inversion, in augmentation and diminution.

He must have known this—and more; he also knew the contrary. He knew what to do and what not to do in order to produce a theme which would not lend itself to any treatment of this kind. For this reason I believe that he, Philipp Emanuel, was the originator of the *Royal Theme*.

Whether malice of his own induced him, or whether the 'joke' was ordered by the king, can probably be proved only psychologically; the great king knew how one feels after winning a battle and he wanted to see how another person behaves after losing a battle. He wanted to see the embarrassment of one who had experienced only battles which he won; he wanted to enjoy the helplessness of the victim of his joke, when the highly praised art of improvisation could not master the difficulties of a well-prepared trap. A trap it was; Philipp Emanuel had constructed a theme that resisted Johann Sebastian's versatility. In the *Art of the Fugue* a minor triad offered many contrapuntal openings; the Royal Theme, also a minor triad, did not admit one single canonic imitation. All the miracles that the *Musical Offering* presents are achieved by countersubjects, counter-melodies and other external additions.

The Royal joke, through Philipp Emanuel's skill, had been successful. But Johann Sebastian must have recognized the bad trick. That he calls his 'Offering', a *Musikalische Opfer* is very peculiar, because the German word *Opfer* has a double meaning: 'offering', or rather 'sacrifice' and 'victim' — Johann Sebastian knew that he had become the victim of a 'grand seigneur's' joke.

III

Many musicians today are inclined to overestimate merits which are obvious even to the lesser minds of average men, at the expense of merits which shine less brilliantly. I am not in opposition to overestimation of the art of counter-point, nor do I overestimate other techniques. In considering such differences of style not as techniques, but as manners of expression, one will do justice also to the particularities of other ways of presentation. Wagner's balance of harmony, in a style at his time still catalogued as modulatory, the illustrative power of his orchestration, the emotional quality of his melodies; Brahms' structural finesses, the richness of his fundamental harmony, the beauty of his melodies; Beethoven's logic, the originality of his invention, his impulsive personality, the variety of his directions; Schubert's ability to use rather simple structural devices, in spite of which he could ennoble a popular touch in his melodies; Mozart's unique capacity of combining heterogeneous elements in the smallest space—all these are merits which deserve just as much praise as do contrapuntal achievements. And though one may believe me when I say that I am the last one to degrade the merits of contrapuntal writing, one must take into consideration that no real master's merits were hindered by a difficulty he had to overcome. To the real master there is no difficulty, and what a layman or a musician will call one is none to him; he speaks his native language. To the one it is counterpoint, to the other, orchestra colour and rich harmony, or logic or beauty, and so forth.

I am fortunate to have learned a few facts, reported to me by a friend. He was a composer who believed in his inspiration, whether it dictated to him music in agreement with theory and aesthetics or not. He told me that, in several cases, he had written at first only the melody of quite a long section. Thereafter he would add a second line, an accompanying voice, without even looking at the first line; gradually he added, by the same procedure, a sufficient number of voices to complete the setting. The result was astonishing; nobody would discover that this had been produced in such an unusual manner, under such extraordinary conditions.

He was afraid that people would believe it was mere nonsense he had written, or that the whole story was untrue. He assured me that some such passages were at least as good as others, if not better, and that he must have been in a kind of trance. He had had the feeling that he was merely copying from a model he saw —or heard—in front of him.

It seems to me that only this can explain miracles like that of the *Art of the Fugue* and all similar miracles performed by great masters. These are miracles which no human brain can produce. The artist is only the mouthpiece of a power which dictates what to do.

Born to this language, Bach translated the will of this power into terms of human counterpoint.

IV

I have speculated much about the fact that Bach writes, on the one hand, so many fugues which deal with the most complicated contrapuntal combinations of canons of all forms and of multiple counterpoint of counter-subjects, and, on the other hand, composes a great number in which nothing of this kind can be observed, and which seem to correspond to the most superficial concept of the several entrances of themes 'fleeing from one another'. Such examples are, among others, in vol. 1, Nos. 1, 3, 6, 9, 10, and 17 (*Well-Tempered Klavier*).

It is difficult to believe that there should not be present here the same high art which we observed in those pieces where it is quite obvious. I rather believe there is a hidden mystery which has not yet been discovered. I have frequently tried to discover such a principle therein, but in vain. Nevertheless, I always feel that something is going on that catches my attention in a peculiar way. What is it?

I want to suggest that gifted and experienced musicians should try to solve this problem. I myself have assumed that one such principle could be detected as deriving from multiple counterpoint of the second, third, fourth, sixth and seventh. Whether such treatment is applied to a whole theme or only to parts of it, or even only to main notes, or to a counter-subject, or to the material of episodes, it may produce the themes, configurations, combinations and variants needed to produce all the contrasts, the variety and the fluency of a piece.

Research into these problems should be conducted according to viewpoints of compositorial technique, rather than according to aesthetics. Accordingly it might be of some assistance if I offer herewith my own theory of the nature of contrapuntal compositions.[2]

Music of the homophonic-melodic style of composition, that is, music with a main theme, accompanied by and based on harmony, produces its material by, as I call it, *developing variation*. This means that variation of the features of a basic unit produces all the thematic formulations which provide for fluency, contrasts, variety, logic and unity, on the one hand, and character, mood, expression, and every needed differentiation, on the other hand—thus elaborating the *idea* of the piece.

In contrast, contrapuntal composition does not produce its material by development, but by a procedure rather to be called *unravelling*. That is, a basic configuration or combination taken asunder and reassembled in a different order contains everything which will later produce a different sound than that of the original formulation. Thus, a canon of two or more voices can be written in one single line, yet furnishes various sounds. If multiple counterpoints are applied, a combination of three voices, invertible in the octave, tenth and twelfth, offers so many combinations that even longer pieces can be derived from it.[3]

According to this theory, one should not expect that new themes occur in such fugues, but that there is a basic combination which is the source of all combinations.

I cannot believe that the author of the *Art of the Fugue* here composed only what most musicians perceive: piano pieces, based merely on the external and superficial characteristics of succeeding entrances of a theme. At least, if such were the case, he would not have called them fugues, but perhaps suites, inventions, partitas, etc.

March 10, 1950

2

BRAHMS THE PROGRESSIVE
1947

I

It has been said that Brahms' social manners were often characterized by a certain dryness. This was not the 'Unknown' Brahms.[1] Vienna knew his method of surrounding himself with a protective wall of stiffness as a defence against certain types of people, against the obtrusiveness of oily bombast, moist flattery, or honeyed impertinence. It is not unknown that those annoying bores, those sensationalists who were out for a good anecdote and those tactless intruders into private lives got little better than dryness. When the sluices of their eloquence were open and the flood threatened to engulf him, dryness was no protection. This is why he was often forced to resort to rudeness. Even so, his victims may have tacitly agreed to nickname what had befallen them 'Brahmsian dryness'; and it may be assumed that each one rejoiced at the other's misfortune, but thought that he himself had been done wrong.

Dryness or rudeness, one thing is certain: Brahms did not want to express high esteem in this manner.

Contemporaries found various ways to annoy him. A musician or a music lover might intend to display his own great understanding, good judgement of music, and acquaintance with 'some' of Brahms' music. Hence he dared say he had observed that Brahms' *First Piano Sonata* was very similar to Beethoven's *Hammerklavier* Sonata. No wonder that Brahms, in his straightforward manner, spoke out: 'Das bemerkt ja schon jeder Esel.' ('Every jackass notices that!')

A visitor meant to be complimentary when he said: 'You are one of the greatest living composers.' How Brahms hated this 'one of'. Who does not see that it means, 'There are a few greater than you, and several of equivalent rank?'

But doubtless the most annoying were those visitors (like one composer from Berlin) who told him: 'I am an admirer of Wagner, the progressive, the innovator, *and* of Brahms, the academician, the classicist.' I do not remember what kind of dryness or rudeness he applied in this case, but I know there was a great

398

story in Vienna about the manner in which Brahms presented his esteem for this flattery.

But after all, it was the attitude of the time; those who disliked Wagner clung to Brahms, and vice versa. There were many who disliked both. They were, perhaps, the only non-partisans. Only a small number were able to disregard the polarity of these two contrasting figures while enjoying the beauties of both of them.

What in 1883 seemed an impassable gulf was in 1897 no longer a problem. The greatest musicians of that time, Mahler, Strauss, Reger, and many others had grown up under the influence of both these masters. They all reflected the spiritual, emotional, stylistic and technical achievements of the preceding period. What then had been an object of dispute had been reduced into the difference between two personalities, between two styles of expression, not contradictory enough to prevent the inclusion of qualities of both in one work.

II

Form in Music serves to bring about comprehensibility through memorability. Evenness, regularity, symmetry, subdivision, repetition, unity, relationship in rhythm and harmony and even logic—none of these elements produces or even contributes to beauty. But all of them contribute to an organization which makes the presentation of the musical idea intelligible. The language in which musical ideas are expressed in tones parallels the language which expresses feelings or thoughts in words, in that its vocabulary must be proportionate to the intellect which it addresses, and in that the aforementioned elements of its organization function like the rhyme, the rhythm, the metre, and the subdivision into strophes, sentences, paragraphs, chapters, etc. in poetry or prose.

The more or less complete exploitation of the potency of these components determines the aesthetic value and the classification of the style in respect to its popularity or profundity. Science must explore and examine all facts; art is only concerned with the presentation of characteristic facts. Even Antony, when addressing the Roman people, realizes that he must repeat his '. . . and Brutus is an honourable man' over and over, if this contrast is to penetrate into the minds of simple citizens. Repetitions in Mother Goose songs are of course on a different level and so is the organization of popular music. Here one finds numerous slightly varied repetitions, as in the otherwise very beautiful *Blue Danube Waltz*.

Ex. 1

Here are six repetitions, and almost all are based on the alternation of tonic and dominant.

Though richer in harmony, the example from Verdi's *Il Trovatore* is of no higher order:

Ex. 2

An artist or an author need not be aware that he accommodates his style to the listener's capacity of comprehension. An artist need not think very much, if only he thinks correctly and straightforwardly. He feels that he obeys the urge of a spring within himself, the urge to express himself, just like a clock, which indicates twenty-four hours every day, without questioning whether it means 'this' day, this month, this year, or this century. Everyone knows this, except the clock. The artist's response to the urge of his motor occurs automatically without delay, like that of every well-lubricated mechanism.

It is obvious that one would not discuss the splitting of atoms with a person who does not know what an atom is. On the other hand, one cannot talk to a trained mind in Mother Goose fashion or in the style of what Hollywoodians call 'lyrics'. In the sphere of art-music, the author respects his audience. He is afraid to offend it by repeating over and over what can be understood at one single hearing, even if it is new, and let alone if it is stale old trash. A diagram may tell the whole story of a game to a chess expert; a chemist recognizes all he wants to know by glancing at a few symbols; but in a mathematical formula are combined the distant past, the actual present, and the most remote future.

Repeatedly hearing things which one likes is pleasant and need not be ridiculed. There is a subconscious desire to understand better and realize more details of the beauty. But an alert and well-trained mind will demand to be told the more remote matters, the more remote consequences of the simple matters that he has already comprehended. An alert and well-trained mind refuses to listen to baby-talk and requests strongly to be spoken to in a brief and straight-forward language.

III

Progress in music consists in the development of methods of presentation which correspond to the conditions just discussed. It is the purpose of this essay to prove that Brahms, the classicist, the academician, was a great innovator in the realm of musical language, that, in fact, he was a great progressive.

This may seem contestable to an incarnate 'old-Wagnerian,' who has grown old, or simply an 'old-Wagnerian' by birth. There were still fireproof 'old-Wagnerians' born at the time of my own generation and even ten years later. Pioneers of musical progress on the one hand, and keepers of the Holy Grail of true art on the other, they considered themselves entitled to look with contempt at Brahms the classicist, the academician.

Gustav Mahler and Richard Strauss had been the first to clarify these concepts. They had both been educated in the traditional as well as in the progressive, in the Brahmsian as well as in the Wagnerian philosophy of art (*Weltanschauung*). Their example helped us to realize that there was as much organizational order, if not pedantry in Wagner as there was daring courage, if not even bizarre fantasy in Brahms. Does not the mystic correspondence of the numbers of their dates suggest some mysterious relationship between them? Brahms' one-hundredth birthday anniversary in 1933 was the fiftieth anniversary of the death of Wagner. And now, as this essay is being rewritten, we commemorate the fiftieth anniversary of Brahms' death.

Mysteries conceal a truth, but direct curiosity to unveil it.

401

IV

How great an innovator Brahms was in respect to harmony can be seen in this example from his String Quartet in C minor, Op. 51, No. 1. (ms. 11–23).

Ex. 3

This is the contrasting middle section of a ternary form whose a-section is already rich enough harmonically in comparison with the I–V or I–IV–V harmony, intermixed occasionally with a VI or III and sometimes a Neapolitan triad, of Brahms' predecessors. To base a main theme on such a rich harmony seemed a daring enterprise to the ears of the time.

But the harmony of this middle section competes successfully with that of many a Wagnerian passage. Even the most progressive composers after Brahms were carefully avoiding remote deviation from the tonic region in the beginning of a piece. But this modulation to the dominant of a minor region on B (at *), and the sudden, unceremonious and precipitate return to the tonic, is a rare case. The succession of three major triads on E flat, D flat and C respectively in the coda of the first movement of the *Eroica* (ms. 551–561) and the juxtaposition of two unrelated triads (on B and B♭) in the following example from Schubert are cases of a similar procedure.

Ex. 4

Schubert, *In der Ferne*
Mut - ter- haus   has - sen-den

Examples from Wagner in which similar progressions occur are often not easily analysed, but they prove less complicated than one might have expected. For instance, the motive of the *Todestrank*, from *Tristan und Isolde*,

Ex. 5

t: VI
SM: I   ♯ (Neap.)   IV   ♯   V
                       VI

unmasks itself as remaining within the closer relations of the tonality. Also not very distant is the harmonic deviation in Isolde's order to Tristan: 'Befehlen liess dem Eigenholde . . .'

Ex. 6

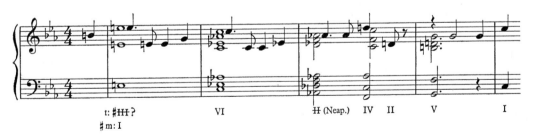

t: ♯♯♯?   VI   ♯ (Neap.) IV II   V   I
♯m: I

But the 'Traurige Weise', the English Horn solo of Act III,

Ex. 7

shows in its modulatory section no more remote modulation than the end of the a-section of the aforementioned C minor string quartet of Brahms:

Ex. 8

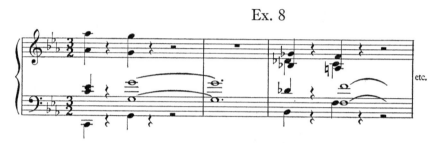

These are in essence chromatically descending triads, most of them inversions; their treatment is similar to that of Neapolitan triads. Some examples of their appearance in classic music are illustrated in Example 9 a, b, c.

Ex. 9

If there is no decisive difference between Brahms and Wagner as regards extension of the relationship within a tonality, it must not be overlooked that Wagner's harmony is richer in substitute harmonies and vagrants, and in a freer use of dissonances, especially of unprepared ones. On the other hand, in strophic, songlike forms and other structures, such as represent the Wagnerian version of arias, the harmony moves rather less expansively and more slowly than in similar forms of Brahms. Compare, for instance, the 'Winterstürme wichen dem Wonnemond', the 'Als zullendes Kind, zog ich dich auf' or the song of the Rhine Daughters to Brahms' song 'Meine Liebe ist grün,' or the main theme of the String Quintet in G, Op. 111, which starts roving in its third measure, or the Rhapsody, Op. 79, No. 2, which almost avoids establishing a tonality.

V

Ternary, rondo, and other rounded forms appear in dramatic music only occasionally, as episodes, mostly at lyrical resting-points where the action stops or at least slows down—in places where a composer can proceed along formal concepts and can repeat and develop without the pressure of the progress of an action, without being forced to mirror moods or events not included in the character of his material.

Dramatic music resembles in its modulatory character the modulatory elaboration (*Durchführung*) of a symphony, sonata, or other rounded form. Wagner's *Leitmotiven* usually contain some germinating harmonies in which the urge for modulatory changes is inherent. But simultaneously they fulfil another task, an organizational task, which shows the formalistic side of Wagner's genius.

The recitative in pre-Wagnerian operas was also modulatory. But it was unorganized, if not incoherent, with respect to thematic and even motivic requirements. The 'Leitmotiv' technique represents the grandiose intention of unification of the thematic material of an entire opera, and even of an entire tetralogy. An organization as far-reaching as this deserves an aesthetic rating of the highest order. But if foresight in organization is called formalistic in the case of Brahms, then this organization is also formalistic, because it stems from the same state of mind, from one which conceives an entire work in one single creative moment and acts correspondingly.

When Brahms, towards the end of the last movement of his Fourth Symphony, carries out some of the variations by a succession of thirds,

405

Ex. 10

he unveils the relationship of the theme of the Passacaglia to the first movement. Transposed a fifth up,

Ex. 11

it is identical with the first eight notes of the main theme,

Ex. 12

and the theme of the passacaglia in its first half admits the contrapuntal combination with the descending thirds.

Ex. 13

People generally do not know that luck is a heavenly gift, equivalent to, and of the same kind as, talent, beauty, strength, etc. It is not given for nothing—on the contrary, one must deserve it. Sceptics might attempt belittling this as a mere 'lucky chance'. Such people have a wrong evaluation of both luck and inspiration and are not capable of imagining what both can achieve.

It would look like a high accomplishment of intellectual gymnastics if all this had been 'constructed' prior to inspired composing. But men who know the power of inspiration, and how it can produce combinations no one can fore-see, also know that Wagner's application of the Leitmotiv was, in the great majority of cases, of an inspired spontaneity. As often as Siegfried came to his mind, his mind's eye and ear saw and heard him just as his motive depicts him:

Ex. 14

VI

I assume that I have been the first to lay down a principle which, about four decades ago, began directing and regulating my musical thinking and the formu-lation of my ideas, and which played a decisive role in my self-criticism.

I wish to join ideas with ideas. No matter what the purpose or meaning of an idea in the aggregate may be, no matter whether its function be introductory, establishing, varying, preparing, elaborating, deviating, developing, concluding, subdividing, subordinate, or basic, it must be an idea which had to take this place even if it were not to serve for this purpose or meaning or function; and this idea must look in construction and in thematic content as if it were not there to fulfil a structural task. In other words, a transition, a codetta, an elaboration, etc., should not be considered as a thing in its own end. It should not appear at all if it does not develop, modify, intensify, clarify, or throw light or colour on the idea of the piece.

This does not mean that functions of these types can be absent in a composition. But it means that no space should be devoted to mere formal purposes. And it means that those segments or sections which fulfil structural requirements should do so without being mere trash.

This is no critique of classic music—it merely presents my personal artistic code of honour which everybody else may disregard. But it seems to me that the progress in which Brahms was operative should have stimulated composers to write music for adults. Mature people think in complexes, and the higher their intelligence the greater is the number of units with which they are familiar. It is inconceivable that composers should call 'serious music' what they write in an obsolete style, with a prolixity not conforming to the contents—repeating three to seven times what is understandable at once. Why should it not be possible in music to say in whole complexes in a condensed form what, in the preceding epochs, had at first to be said several times with slight variations before it could be elaborated? Is it not as if a writer who wanted to tell of 'somebody who lives in a house near the river' should have to explain what a house is, what it is made for, and of what material, and, after that, explain the river in the same way?

Some people speak of the 'dying romanticism' of music. Do they really believe that making music, playing with tones, is something realistic, or what? Or is it that romanticism has to resign in favour of senseless prolixity?

VII

In order to grasp thoroughly the development of musical construction during the epoch from Bach to Brahms it is necessary to go back to the period when the style of contrapuntal construction was abandoned and the aesthetic of the homophonic-melodic style was formulated. Comparing the compositions manufactured in response to this aesthetic with those of J. S. Bach on the one hand and of Haydn, Mozart, Beethoven and Schubert on the other, one understands why such ruthless propaganda had to be applied to eliminate J. S. Bach, but one is astonished that such fruits can be derived from so scanty a soil.

Under the leadership of Keiser, Telemann and Mattheson, composers were asked to let alone 'great art'; to strive with effort to write light (that is effortless) music; to see that a theme is provided with 'a certain something' (*ein gewisses Etwas*) which seems to be familiar to everybody; to write in the light manner of the French. To Mattheson, counterpoint was a mere mental exercise without emotional power. As it has happened frequently, these men were highly esteemed in their lifetime, while Bach was little known. But one must doubt that men were inspired geniuses who composed according to such advice, like cooks obeying a cookbook, or some of their music would have survived. This was not a natural development; it was not evolution, but man-made revolution. One can only express what one possesses inwardly. A style cannot make one richer. Thus these musicians live only because of the musicologists' interest in dead, decayed matter.

It is known that Mozart and Beethoven looked on some of their predecessors with great admiration. Fortunately, however, the versatility, inventiveness and power of emotion kept these masters free from the shackles of an aesthetic of popular complaisance.

VIII

True, much of the organization of classic music reveals, by its regularity, symmetry and simple harmony, its relation with, if not derivation from, popular and dance music. Construction by phrases of the same length, especially if their number of measures is two, four or eight times two, and if subdivision into two equally long segments adds a certain kind of symmetry, contributes much to memorability; knowing the first half, it is almost possible to conjecture the second half. Deviation from regularity and symmetry does not necessarily endanger comprehensibility. One might accordingly wonder why in Haydn's and Mozart's forms irregularity is more frequently present than in Beethoven's. Is it perhaps that formal finesses have diverted a listener's attention, which should concentrate upon the tremendous power of emotional expression? There are not too many cases like that of the String Quartet Op. 95 in F minor (see Example 9b).

Construction by phrases of unequal length accounts for many of the irregularities in Haydn's and Mozart's music. These differences are produced by extension of a segment, by internal repetitions or by reductions and condensations. Such is the case in many of Haydn's and Mozart's Menuets, according to which one might be inclined to consider menuets as a song-like form, rather than as a derivative of dance music.

Example 15, from a piano Sonata by Haydn, consists of two segments of two measures and two of three measures: $2+3$ and $2+3$.

Ex. 15

Example 16 from the String Quartet in B♭ major by Mozart is richer in organization: $3+1+1+3$ (the latter is perhaps a unit of $2+1$).

Ex. 16

The whole theme comprises eight measures; thus the irregularity is, so to speak, subcutaneous (i.e. it does not show up on the surface).

While Haydn's example is still symmetrical, this is entirely unsymmetrical and thereby renounces one of the most efficient aids to comprehension. But it is not yet what deserves to be called 'musical prose'. One might rather be inclined to ascribe such irregularity to a baroque sense of form, that is, to a desire to combine unequal, if not heterogeneous, elements into a formal unit. Though such a hypothesis is not without foundation, it seems that there is another, more artistic and psychological explanation.

Mozart has to be considered above all as a dramatic composer.

Accommodation of the music to every change of mood and action, materially or psychologically, is the most essential problem an opera composer has to master. Inability in this respect might produce incoherence—or worse, boredom. The technique of the recitative escapes this danger by avoiding motival and harmonic obligations and their consequences. The 'Arioso' liquidates rapidly and ruthlessly that minimum of obligations in which it might have engaged. But the 'Finales' and many 'Ensembles' and even 'Arias' contain heterogeneous elements to which the technique of lyric condensation is not applicable. In pieces of this type a composer must be capable of turning within the smallest space. Mozart, anticipating this necessity, begins such a piece with a melody consisting of a number of phrases of various lengths and characters, each of them pertaining to a different phase of the action and the mood. They are, in their first formulation, loosely joined together, and after simply juxtaposed, thus admitting to be broken asunder and used independently as motival material for small formal segments.

A striking example of this procedure can be seen in the Finale (No. 15) of Act 2 of *The Marriage of Figaro*. The third section of this Finale, an Allegro, starts after Susanna's line 'Guardate, guardate qui ascoso sarà' with a theme in B flat, consisting of the three phrases *a, b, c*, in Example 17.

Ex. 17

411

To this are added later *d* in ms. 22–23 and *e* in ms. 25–29.

Ex. 18

This Allegro-section comprises 160 measures and contains an astonishingly great number of segments, all of which are built, almost exclusively, out of variations of these five little phrases in a constantly changing order.

Similar construction can be found in many of the ensembles, of which the Terzet (No. 7) and the Sextet (No. 18) are outstanding specimens. But even duets, though one might expect here not so loose a formulation, derive all of it from illustrating segments, whose features show little external relationship. It is admirable how closely the action and the mood of the actors is portrayed in the opening Duet (No. 1). Both Figaro and Susanna are deeply concerned about affairs of their own. Figaro is measuring the walls of their future apartment, Susanna trying on a new hat, admiring her looks—neither of them has an ear or an eye for the other person. Thus, while Figaro lays out his measuring tape (Ex. 19, phrase *a*), extends it (phrase *b*, the syncopation in the bass), and counts the number of lengths ('cinque', phrase *c*),

Ex. 19

Susanna tries in vain to attract his interest to her attire.

Ex. 20

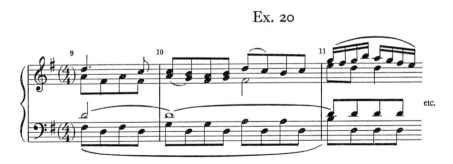

Wagner or Strauss could not do this better.

Organization based on different and differently shaped elements proves to be a vision of the future. A composer of operas, of oratorios (as Schweitzer shows in analysing Bach's music to words) or even of songs, who does not prepare for far remote necessities acts as silly and brainless as a pedantic performer who insists on playing classic music with metronomically measured equal beats—as if it were dance music. Of course, in the stiff confinement of a Procrustean bed, no modification can fit, and even those ritardandi and accelerandi (Schumann's 'immer schneller werdend') which the composer himself demands will never turn out satisfactorily.

A wise performer, one who is indeed a 'servant to the work', one who possesses the mental elasticity of a rank equal to that of a musical thinker—such a man will proceed like Mozart or Schubert or others. He will systematize irregularity, making it a component principle of the organization.

IX

Analysts of my music will have to realize how much I personally owe to Mozart. People who looked unbelievingly at me, thinking I made a poor joke will now understand why I called myself a 'pupil of Mozart', must now understand my reasons. This will not help them to appreciate my music, but to understand Mozart. And it will teach young composers what are the essentials that one has to learn from masters and the way one can apply these lessons without loss of personality.

Mozart himself had learned from Italian and French composers. He had probably learned also from Ph. E. Bach. But certainly it was his own musical thinking that enabled him to produce constructions like the above-mentioned ones.

The preceding analysis may have suggested the idea that irregular and unsymmetrical construction is an absolute and inescapable result of dramatic composing. If this were true one ought to find more of it in Wagner's music. However, Wagner, who in his first period was strongly influenced by contemporary Italians, has seldom abandoned a two-by-two-measure construction, but has made great progress in the direction of musical prose—that is, toward the goal which Brahms also strove for, but on a different road. The difference between these two men is not what their contemporaries thought; it is not the difference between Dionysian and Apollonian art, as Nietzsche might have called it. Besides, it is not as simple as that between Dionysus and Apollo: that the one, in intoxication, smashes the glasses which the other has produced in an intoxication of imagination. Things happen thus only (if this is not too pompous a word for what is so little and so late) in the imagination of a biographer or a musicologist. Intoxication, whether Dionysian or Apollonian, of an artist's fantasy increases the clarity of his vision.

Great art must proceed to precision and brevity. It presupposes the alert mind of an educated listener who, in a single act of thinking, includes with every concept all associations pertaining to the complex. This enables a musician to write for upper-class minds, not only doing what grammar and idiom require, but, in other respects lending to every sentence the full pregnancy of meaning of a maxim, of a proverb, of an aphorism. This is what musical prose should be—a direct and straightforward presentation of ideas, without any patchwork, without mere padding and empty repetitions.

Density of texture is certainly an obstacle to popularity; but prolixity alone cannot guarantee general favour. Real popularity, lasting popularity, is only attained in those rare cases where power of expression is granted to men who dwell intensely in the sphere of basic human sentiments. There are a few cases in Schubert and Verdi, but many in Johann Strauss. Even Mozart, when, in *The Magic Flute*, he temporarily abandoned his own highly refined and artistic style of presentation in favour of the semi-popular characters he had to portray musically, did not fully succeed; the popular parts of this opera never attained the success of the serious parts. His stand was on the side of Sarastro and his priests.

In the epoch between Mozart and Wagner one does not find many themes of an irregular construction. But the following example, a transition from the end of the main theme to the subordinate theme in the first movement of Mozart's String Quartet in D minor, certainly deserves the qualification of musical prose.

Even if one ignores the first four little phrases which conclude the main theme, and also the imitations (marked 14th and 17th) by which the modulation is finished, there remain nine little phrases varying in size and character within no more than eight measures. The smallest (the 5th, 6th and 7th) are only three

Ex. 21

415

eighth notes long—in spite of which they are so expressive that one is almost tempted to put words underneath. One regrets not possessing the power of a poet to render in words what these phrases tell. However, poetry and lyrics would not deprive it of the quality of being prose-like in the unexcelled freedom of its rhythm and the perfect independence from formal symmetry.

X

Asymmetry, combinations of phrases of differing lengths, numbers of measures not divisible by eight, four or even two, i.e. imparity of the number of measures, and other irregularities already appear in the earliest works of Brahms. The main theme of the first Sextet in B flat, Op. 18, consists of nine measures (or, rather, 10, because of the upbeat-like measure which introduces the repetition of this theme in the first violin at *).

Ex. 22

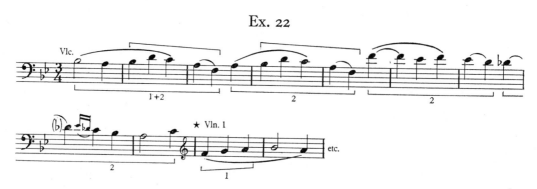

The construction then appears as 3 (or $1+2)+2+2+2+1 = 10$.

The subordinate theme of the same movement connects its two motive forms a and b, first to build two two-measure phrases followed by a three-measure and a two-measure phrase, totalling nine measures.

Ex. 23

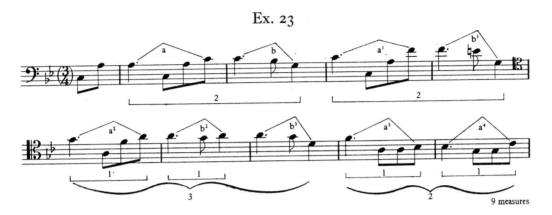

The Scherzo from the second Sextet, Op. 36, starts with a theme which comprises seventeen measures, though in the seventeenth measure another phrase begins overlappingly.

Ex. 24

There are two rhythmical shifts (at *), but the most interesting feature is presented by the ambiguity of the ending of the second phrase. One wonders whether measures 9ff. do not belong to this phrase.

Though these irregularities do not measure up to the artfulness of the Mozart examples, they still present a more advanced phase of the development toward liberation from formal restrictions of musical thoughts, because they do not derive from a baroque feeling, or from necessities of illustration, as is the case in dramatic music.

Other asymmetrical structures occur in songs of Brahms. They derive probably in part from the rhythmic peculiarities of the poems upon which they are based. It is well known that Brahms' aesthetic canon demanded that the melody of a song must reflect, in one way or another, the number of metrical feet in the poem. Accordingly, if there were three, four, or five metrical feet, the melody should consist of the same number of measures or half-measures. For instance, the first-half of 'Meerfahrt' (H. Heine) consists exclusively of three-measure phrases, on account of the poem's metre of three metrical feet.

Mein Líebchen wir sássen beisámmen
tréulich im léichten Káhn

Ex. 25

The *Lied* 'Feldeinsamkeit' is based on verses of five metrical feet; accordingly, one might expect that the corresponding first two phrases would be five measures of five half-measures long. But the first phrase is condensed to two measures, to which the second phrase adds three measures, thus reflecting the metre of the verses.

Ex. 26

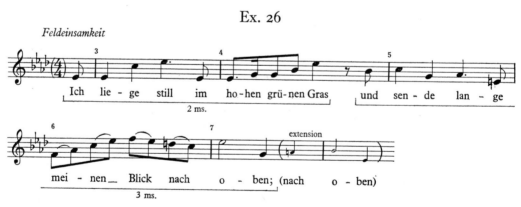

The poem 'Am Sonntag Morgen zierlich angetan' has *five* metrical feet, but the melody consists of phrases three measures long, that is, six half-measures —the result of the prolongation of the pause between the phrases, which could be a sixteenth-rest only.

Ex. 27

Geuss nícht so láut der líebentflámmten Líeder
Tónréichen Scháll
Vom Blútenást des Ápfelbáums herníeder
Ó Náchtigáll

This poem has an interesting metre: 5 + 3 + 5 + 3 metrical feet. Note also the spondaic metre of every second line. The dotted half note in measure 2 causes the extension of the first phrase to six, or rather seven half-measures. The second line, if treated proportionally, should comprise about four half-measures, but occupies, inclusive of the half-rest, five half-measures.

Ex. 28

These irregularities are more than the metre of the poem demands. In many other examples the length of the phrase differs from the number of metrical feet; for instance, in Example 29, the two times three metrical feet of the first two lines could fit well in the space of seven or eight half-measures, instead of the seventeen half-measures apportioned to them.

Ex. 29

Wie Me - lo - di - en___ zieht es mir lei - se durch den Sinn, wie Früh - lings-blu - men blüht es, und schwebt wie Duft da - hin und schwebt wie Duft da - hin.

Similarly, the poem 'An den Mond', with its regular rhythm of four metrical feet, does not require the three-measure construction.

Ex. 30

An den Mond

Sil - ber-mond mit blei-chen Strah-len pflegst___ du Wald und Feld zu ma-len

'Beim Abschied' has lines of four rhythmical feet, but the phrases are stretched to occupy five measures.

Ex. 31

Beim Abschied

Ich müh' mich ab und kann's nicht ver - schmer - zen und kann's nicht ver - win - den in mei - nem Her - zen.

The irregularity is also not required by the metre (four metrical feet) of the poem in 'Mädchenlied'. It is the inserted fifth measure, the stretching in measures 8 and 9 and the addition of two one-measure phrases that bring up to ten and twelve measures respectively what could be put into eight measures.

Ex. 32

The irregularities of 'Immer leiser wird mein Schlummer' are partly caused by the changing metre of the poem.

Ex. 33

But an attempt to condense these phrases

Ex. 34

illustrates at once that the little piano interludes which separate and prolong the phrases are suggested by the mood of the poem. This looser construction prepares for an even richer freedom of phrasing which occurs in this continuation.

The same foresight may be the cause of the extensions in 'Verrat' (Example 35). There is no metrical feature demanding the fifth and the tenth measures, both of which are again piano interludes. In later parts of the poem deviations from this metre occur, and this is the place where deviations from even-numbered structures increase. The length of the phrases is different, and the upbeats with which they begin (marked Λ) fluctuate between one, three, and five eighths.

Ex. 35

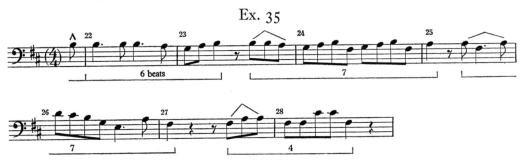

The most important capacity of a composer is to cast a glance into the most remote future of his themes or motives. He has to be able to know beforehand the consequences which derive from the problems existing in his material, and to organize everything accordingly. Whether he does this consciously or subconsciously is a subordinate matter. It suffices if the result proves it.

Thus one must not be astonished by an act of genius when a composer, feeling that irregularity will occur later, already deviates in the beginning from simple regularity. An unprepared and sudden change of structural principles would endanger balance.

XI

I cannot renounce the opportunity to illustrate the remoteness of a genius's fore-sight. In Example 36a (Beethoven's String Quartet Op. 95) there appear in the first measure the three notes D♭, C♮ and D♮ (36a and b).

Ex. 36

In Example 36c this succession is retrograded to D♮, C♮, D♭ and transposed a seventh up.

A comparison of Example 37a, b, and c with Example 36d, e, f, and g unveils the origin of the enigmatic procedures in the upper and lower voices of measures 7–9 and simultaneously shows how the strange figure in measure 36 (example 37b) is related to the basic idea.

Moreover, the relation of the still more enigmatic segment in measures 38–43 (and later in 49–54) with the main theme is thus revealed. The same succession of tones, direct and reversed, appears also several times in the following movements. It would be presumptuous to say that it is 'the' basic feature of the structure, or that it had a great influence on the organization of this string quartet; perhaps its function is only that of a 'connective'. I believe its reappearances, its reincarnation in other themes can just as well be caused subconsciously; the

Ex. 37

mind of a composer is dominated by every detail of his idea, the consequences of which accordingly will show up involuntarily and unexpectedly. Of course, only a master who is sure of himself, of his sense of form and balance, can renounce conscious control in favour of the dictates of his imagination.

XII

Illustrations of the tendency toward asymmetrical construction among post-Wagnerian composers are very numerous. Though the natural inclination to build two- or four-measure phrases is still present, deviation from multiples of two is achieved in many fashions.

The main theme of Anton Bruckner's Seventh Symphony, for instance, contains one segment of five (3 + 2) measures and another of three measures. Neither three-measure unit can be classified as an extension of two measures or a condensation of four measures. They are both 'natural'.

Ex. 38

The asymmetry in the main theme of Gustav Mahler's Second Symphony is due to the irregular appearance of one-measure units.

Ex. 39

425

The irregularities in the subordinate theme of the Scherzo in Mahler's Sixth Symphony are only partly caused by its composition of 3/8, 4/8, and 3/4 metre. The units are also different in length. The first two comprise seven eighth-notes, the third comprises ten eighth-notes and in the continuation even greater differences appear. Also these irregularities could scarcely be traced back to even numbers.

Ex. 40

An extraordinary case, even among contemporary composers, is the melody from 'Abschied', the last movement of Mahler's *Lied von der Erde*. All the units vary greatly in shape, size and content, as if they were not motival parts of a melodic unit, but words, each of which has a purpose of its own in the sentence.

Ex. 41

The main theme from Richard Strauss' *Symphonia Domestica* is distinctly an indivisible unit of five measures. It ends overlapping the entrance of the oboe.

426

Ex. 42

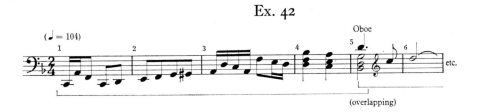

Another theme of the same work consists of two- and one-measure units.

Ex. 43

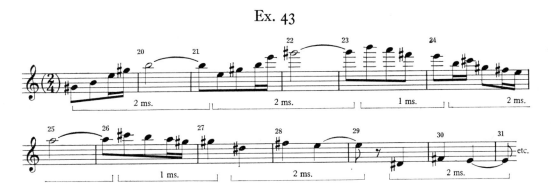

Also, an indivisible five-measure unit is the first phrase of Max Reger's Violin Concerto. A three-measure phrase completes this part of the sentence.

Ex. 44

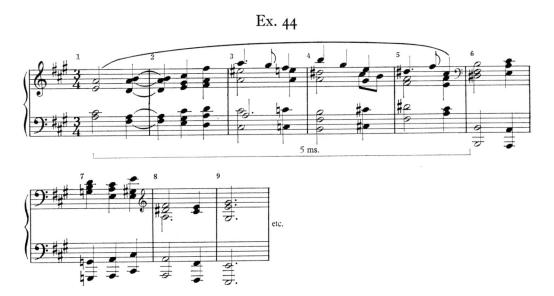

The 'cello solo from 'Serenade' (Schoenberg, *Pierrot Lunaire*, Op. 21) consists of an irregular change of one- and two-measure units.

Ex. 45

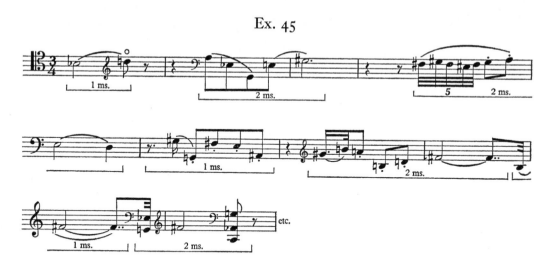

XIII

One might interpret some of the irregularities in the examples from Haydn, Mozart and Brahms as caused by special purposes, as, for instance, the desire to satisfy a baroque sense of form; or to accomplish a more definite separation of the phrases by 'punctuation'; or to assist in the dramatic characterization of various actors in an opera; or to comply with the metrical peculiarities of the poem of a song—as has been shown in previous discussions.

But none of these reasons will explain irregularities such as have been mentioned in the music of post-Wagnerian composers. Evidently their deviations from simple construction no longer derive from exclusively technical conditions, nor do they serve to provide a stylistic appearance. They have become incorporated into the syntax and grammar of perhaps all subsequent musical structures. Accordingly, they have ceased to be recorded as merits of a composition— though unfortunately many illiterate composers still write two plus two, four plus four, eight plus eight unchangingly.

XIV

Again: it does not matter whether an artist attains his highest achievements consciously, according to a preconceived plan, or subconsciously, by stepping blind-folded from one feature to the next. Has the Lord granted to a thinker a brain of unusual power? Or did the Lord silently assist him now and then with a bit of His own thinking? Our Lord is an extremely good chess player. He usually plans billions of moves ahead, and that is why it is not easy to understand Him. It seems, however, that He likes helping in their spiritual problems those He has selected—though not enough in their more material ones.

Again: asymmetry and imparity of structural elements are no miracle in contemporary music, nor do they constitute a merit. A contemporary composer connects phrases irrespective of their size and shape, only vigilant of harmonic progression, of rhythmic and motival contents, fluency and logic. But otherwise he chooses his way like a tourist, freely and nonchalantly if he feels he has time, strictly and carefully if he feels he is under pressure. If only he never loses sight of his goal!

Merits of contemporary compositions may consist of formal finesses of a different kind. It may be the variety and the multitude of the ideas, the manner in which they develop and grow out of germinating units, how they are con-trasted and how they complement one another; it may also be their emotional quality, romantic or unromantic, subjective or objective, their expression of moods and characters and illustration.

Contemporary compositorial technique has not yet arrived at a freedom of construction comparable to that of a language. Evidently, however, parity and symmetry play a lesser role today than they did in earlier techniques; and the aspiration for a strictness resembling that of the hexameter or pentameter, or that of the structures of the sonnet or the stanza in poetry is rare. There are even composers who preserve little of the features of the theme in their variations—a queer case: why should one use a form of such strictness, if one aims for the contrary? Is it not as if one would string a violin E-string on a double bass? One is ready to ignore discrepancies of this kind and degree in favour of overwhelm-ing merits in other respects. But the aesthetic background for a just and general judgement has become very questionable at present.

XV

This discussion will be concluded by two illustrations of Brahms' contribution toward the development of the musical language: the main theme of the Andante from the A minor String Quartet, Op. 51, No. 2, and the third of the 'Vier Ernste Gesänge', Op. 121, 'O Tod, O Tod, wie bitter bist du!'.

Both these themes are specimens of a perhaps unique artistic quality, as regards their motival elaboration and internal organization.

Ex. 46

As the analysis unveils, the A major Andante contains exclusively motive forms which can be explained as derivatives of the interval of a second, marked by brackets *a*:

b then is the inversion upward of *a*;

c is *a* + *b*;

d is part of *c*;

e is *b* + *b*, descending seconds, comprising a fourth;

f is the interval of a fourth, abstracted from *e*, in inversion.

The first phrase—*c*—thus consists of *a* plus *b*. It also contains *d* (see bracket below), which also functions as a connective between the first and the second phrase (at *).

The second phrase consists of *e* and *d*; with the exception of its upbeat (the eighth note *e*) and the two notes c♯ and b, it presents itself as a transposition of the first phrase (see above at §), one step higher. It also furnishes the interval of a fourth, *f*.

The third phrase contains *e* twice, the second time transposed one step higher.

The fourth phrase is distinctly a transformed transposition of *c*.

The fifth phrase, though it looks like a variant of the preceding phrase, merely contains *c*, connected with the preceding by *f*.

The sixth phrase, consisting of *e*, *d*, and *b*, contains a chromatic connective b♯, which could be considered as the second note of a form of *a*. This b♯ is the only note in the whole theme whose derivation can be contested.

Sceptics, however, might reason that steps of a second or even fractions of a scale are present in every theme without constituting the thematic material. There exists an enormous multitude of methods and principles of construction, few of which have yet been explored. I deem it probable that many musicians are acquainted with these two analyses which I broadcast in 1933 on celebrating Brahms' 100th birthday anniversary. But one who objects to my conclusions must not forget that the second example exhibits a similar secret, this time dealing with thirds (see Ex. 47, pages 432 and 433).

This example has a certain resemblance to the main theme of Brahms' Fourth Symphony—in both the structural unit is the interval of a third. The first phrase in the voice part consists of a succession of three thirds b–g, g–e and e–c, marked *a*.

Ex. 47

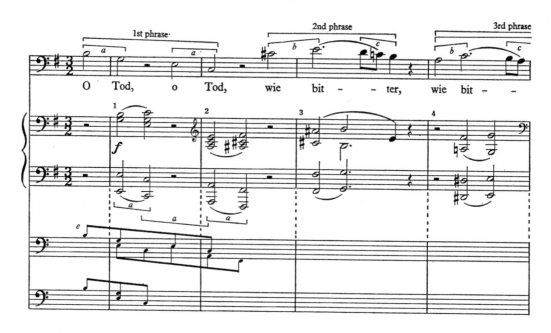

The second phrase is built from the inversion of *a*, c♯–e, marked *b*, and *c*, which is *a* with an inserted passing note c.

The third phrase is a sequence of the second phrase and is (characteristically!) a third lower.

The fourth phrase, in which the voice follows the piano with a small canonic imitation, inverts the interval of a third (b–g and e–c respectively) into a sixth *d*. Observe also the relation of a third between the two points ⊕–⊕ in measures 6–7 in voice and piano.

The fifth and sixth phrases, with part of the seventh, are founded upon the notes marked *f*, g–b–d–f♯, which are an inversion of the descending thirds of the first phrase. Besides, the left hand in measures 8 and 9 contains the succession of thirds, though the first two notes have changed their places (see **). Furthermore, the left hand in measure 10 contains six tones building a chain of thirds *e* (⊠). The voice part consists mainly of thirds, some of them including passing notes. Besides, here where the climactic concentration approaches a cadence, the interval of a third appears abundantly, and *e* also occurs in successions.

Ex. 48

See also Example 48a and b. Here again the third is reversed as a sixth (48a) in the voice and imitated in the bass (48b).

The sense of logic and economy and the power of inventiveness which build melodies of so much natural fluency deserve the admiration of every music lover who expects more than sweetness and beauty from music. But though I know offhand only one example of such complexity of construction by a pre-Brahmsian composer—by Mozart, of course (see Example 51 from the Piano Quartet in G minor)—I must state that structural analysis reveals even greater merits.

The Andante from the A minor String Quartet (Example 46) contains six phrases in eight measures. The length of these phrases is $6+6+6+4+4+6$ quarter notes. The first three phrases occupy five and three-eighths (or five and one-half) measures. The first phrase ends practically on the first beat of measure 2. In order to appreciate fully the artistic value of the second phrase's metrical shift, one must realize that even some of the great composers, Brahms' predecessors, might have continued as in Example 49, placing the second phrase in the third measure.

Ex. 49

Brahms might have tried to place the first three phrases into three 6/4 measures.

Ex. 50

*actually $\frac{3}{2}$

If, then, the next two phrases would fit into two 4/4 measures, it might be doubtful whether the accentuation of the last phrase (at *) is adequate, if all the preceding phrases had their main accents placed on first beats. But, besides, this notation would reveal the imparity of the construction even more, because the theme then becomes seven measures.

In Brahms' notation these subcutaneous beauties are accommodated within eight measures; and if eight measures constitute an aesthetic principle, it is preserved here in spite of the great freedom of construction.

The example from Mozart (Example 51) is an enigma—not to the performer, but to the analyst who is interested in the grammar, syntax, and linguistics of music.

Ex. 51

It consists of three little segments, or phrases, whose metrical position is intricate. The beginning of the first phrase on a third beat is marked *sf*, demanding a stronger accent than the third beat usually carries. The following first beat is marked *p* and if this means 'cancellation of the accent',[2] one might assume that it means a change of time, as indicated in Example 51d and 51e, where the changes of the metre are carried out. But in measure 2, the fourth beat is also marked *sf* and accentuation of the following beat is also cancelled, or at least reduced. For this reason one might suppose that the second phrase does not begin, as the brackets above indicate, at the second beat of measure 3, but at the fourth beat of measure 2, with the *sf*, as indicated below the left hand. It is also possible that the note on the third beat (the f♯) should retain its accent, thus producing a spondee.

In addition to all these problems, the 'cello, when this little segment is repeated, contributes a problem of its own, by *sf*-accents which partly contradict those of the main voice (Example 51b). The structural intricacy of this example is paralleled by the polyrhythmic construction of the second variation in the Finale of the String Quartet in D minor (Example 52a). Today one will write this as in Example 52b. An example from the Menuet of the C major String Quartet (52c) may serve as a further justification for entering into an examination of such subtle problems. This example is one which suggests a phrasing contrary to the metre. Here a unit of five quarter-notes is repeated on different beats, while the accompaniment remains unchanged.

Ex. 52

437

Beethoven is a great innovator as regards rhythm. Remember, for instance, the last movement of the Piano Concerto in E♭, or the Menuet of the String Quartet, Op. 18, No. 6, etc. But structurally, as previously stated, he is generally rather simple. Though, however, the lucidity of presentation balances satisfactorily the heavy load of emotions his ideas carry with them, it is needless to say that abandonment of Mozart's unequal and unsymmetric foundations would have been an extremely regrettable loss. The idea cannot be rejected that the mental pleasure caused by structural beauty can be tantamount to the pleasure deriving from emotional qualities. In this sense Brahms' merit would be immense, even if he had preserved this way of thinking only in the manner of a technical device. But—and this characterizes his high rank—he has surpassed it.

If a man who knows that he will die soon makes his account with earth and with heaven, prepares his soul for the departure, and balances what he leaves with what he will receive, he might desire to incorporate a word—a part of the wisdom he has acquired—into the knowledge of mankind, if he is one of the Great. One might doubt about the sense of life if it then would be a mere accident that such a work, a life-terminating work, would not represent more than just another opus. Or is one entitled to assume that a message from a man who is already half on the other side progresses to the uttermost limit of the still-expressible? Is one not entitled to expect therefrom perfection of an extra-ordinary degree, because mastership, a heavenly gift, which cannot be acquired by the most painstaking assiduity and exercise, manifests itself only once, only one single time in its full entirety, when a message of such importance has to be formulated?

I imagine that at this point Brahms' protective wall of dryness might enter the picture, and that he might stop me: 'Now it's enough poetry. If you have to say something, say it briefly and technically without so much sentimental fuss.'

Before obeying this order, I am pressed to say that this third of the *Vier Ernste Gesänge*, 'O Tod, O Tod, wie bitter bist du', seems to me the most touching of the whole cycle—in spite of its perfection, if not *because* of it. Intuition, inspiration and spontaneity in creation are generally characteristically combined with speed. But 'was glaubt er, dass ich an seine elende Geige denke, wenn der Geist mich packt?' (Do you really suppose I think of your miserable violin, if the spirit gets hold of me?)—this is how the artist himself feels whether he creates in hard labour or only by a kind of toying.

There is no doubt that Brahms believed in working out the ideas which he called 'gifts of grace'. Hard labour is, to a trained mind, no torture, but rather a pleasure. As I have stated on another occasion: if a mathematician's or a chess player's mind can perform such miracles of the brain, why should a musician's mind not be able to do it? After all, an improviser must anticipate before playing, and composing is a slowed-down improvisation; often one cannot write fast enough to keep up with the stream of ideas. But a craftsman likes to be conscious of what he produces; he is proud of the ability of his hands, of the flexibility of his mind, of his subtle sense of balance, of his never-failing logic, of the multitude of variations, and last but not least of the profundity of his idea and his capacity of penetrating to the most remote consequences of an idea. One cannot do this with a shallow idea, but one can, and one can *only*, with a profound idea —and there one *must*.

It is important to realize that at a time when all believed in 'expression', Brahms, without renouncing beauty and emotion, proved to be a progressive in a field which had not been cultivated for half a century. He would have been a pioneer if he had simply returned to Mozart. But he did not live on inherited fortune; he made one of his own. True, Wagner has contributed to the development of structural formulations through his technique of repetitions, varied or unvaried, because they freed him from the obligation of elaborating longer than necessary upon subjects which he had already clearly determined. Thus this language admitted turning to other subjects, when the action on the stage demanded it.

Brahms never wrote dramatic music—and it was rumoured in Vienna that he had said he would rather write in the style of Mozart than in the 'Neudeutsche Stil'. One can be sure it would not have been Mozart's style, but pure Brahms, and though he might have repeated whole sentences, and even single words in the text, in the manner of pre-Wagnerian opera, he could not have entirely disregarded the contemporary feeling for dramatic presentation; he would not let an actor die during a da capo aria, and repeat the beginning after death. On the other hand, it would be highly enlightening to see all the dramatico-musical requirements carried out over Brahms' immensely advanced harmony.

It might be doubtful whether Brahms could have found a libretto fitting to what he liked and to the emotion he was capable of expressing. Would it have been a comic opera, a comedy, a lyric drama or a tragedy? He is many-sided, and one can easily find in his music expressions of all sorts, with the possible exception of violent dramatic outbursts such as one finds in Wagner and Verdi. Who knows? If one considers Beethoven's *Fidelio*, which is distinctly symphonic in its organization, remembers the tremendous outburst at the end of the second act, 'O namenlose Freude!' (Oh inexpressible joy!) and compares that with the strictly symphonic style of the greater part of the third act, one may get an impression of what a genius is capable 'wenn der Geist ihn packt'.

'O Tod, O Tod, wie bitter bist du' has been analysed as regards its eminent motival logic. In Example 47 are also marked the beauties of its phrasing. It seems superfluous to discuss these features here in detail; a few remarks should suffice to illustrate what has been contended in the course of this research.

The whole first part of this song contains in twelve measures thirty-six half notes. The phrasing (in the voice) apportions six half notes to the first phrase, four to the second, five to the third, five and a half to the fourth, three and a half to the fifth (counting only one upbeat eighth-note), three to the sixth, four and a half to the seventh, and five and a half to the ending phrase. One may appreciate the rhythmic shift of the third phrase to another beat and a further shift produced through the beginning of the little canon in measures 6 and 7.

Brahms' domain as a composer of songs, chamber music and symphonies has to be qualified as epic-lyric. The freedom of his language would be less surprising were he a dramatist. His influence has already produced a further development of the musical language toward an unrestricted, though well-balanced presentation of musical ideas. But, curiously, the merits of his achievements will shine brighter when more and more are incorporated into the dramatic technique. The opera composer will then become able to renounce a makeshift technique which is a shortcoming not only in the operas of the great pre-Wagnerians. As the contribution of the singer-actor to the dramatic expression is only a part of the drama, the orchestra, at first only an accompanying factor, has developed into a dominant one. It not only illustrates mood, character and action, but also determines the tempo of the action, and, through its own formal conditions, extends or limits all that happens. In order to realize the consequences of the orchestra's predominance, one must remember the frequent repetitions of text in pre-Wagnerian operas. They serve to correspond to the trend towards expansion of the form originated in the orchestra. Then there are those occasions when a melody does not accommodate to the text. These are the places where the singer dwells on the dominant of the chord while the orchestra continues to build up the formal and thematic elaborations of his part. These are the places in more recent works where the orchestra plays like a symphony, showing little regard for the requirements of the singer, and—an ultramodern pseudo-progressive accomplishment—complete disregard for what is to be expressed by the stage, word and voice, sometimes even counteracting them.

Applying here Brahms' contributions to an unrestricted musical language will enable the opera composer to overcome the metrical handicaps of his libretto's prose; the production of melodies and other structural elements will not depend on the versification, on the metre, or on the absence of possibilities for repetitions. There will be no expansion necessary for mere formal reasons and changes of mood or character will not endanger the organization. The singer will be granted the opportunity to sing and to be heard; he will not be forced to recite on a single note, but will be offered melodic lines of interest; in a word, he will not be merely the one who pronounces the words in order to make the action understandable. He will be a singing instrument of the performance.

It seems—if this is not wishful thinking—that some progress has already been made in this direction, some progress in the direction toward an unrestricted musical language which was inaugurated by Brahms the Progressive.

3

FRANZ LISZT'S WORK AND BEING
1911

Liszt's importance lies in the one place where great men's importance can lie: in faith. Fanatical faith, of the kind that creates a radical distinction between normal men and those it impels. Normal men *possess* a conviction; the great man is *possessed* by a faith. In a certain sense actions are more characteristic for the normal man than for the man of faith, since they manifest in the former a rational connection with the conviction underlying them. Whereas the acts of those who live by obscure but loftily aspiring instincts must remain incomprehensible to anyone incapable of tracing back an effect beyond the nearest cause. It is easier to find such causes in a conviction that merely gives a more intense colour to the surface, than to trace them right back to the instincts. If one compares the actions of the normal man with his convictions, one usually finds they coincide; but if one compares them with his instincts, one finds the crassest incongruence. But the work, the perfected work of the great artist, is produced, above all, by his instincts; and the sharper ear he has for what they say, the more immediate the expression he can give them, the greater his work is. That is exactly the relationship, or perhaps it is even more direct, between faith—faith independent of reason—and instinctive life. So if convictions and their resultant actions get farthest away from the primal source, while faith remains closest to it, then the work stands roughly in the middle. This explains, on the one hand, what every artist knows as the 'undissolved residue', the difference between his expressive urge and his powers of depiction—and, on the other hand, the formal urge, which uses unification of the outward phenomenon to disguise the gaps and deficiencies of the inner. And it also explains why the personality of an artist can hardly be typified by the single work, but by the sum total of all of his works—for it is only from the total that there clearly emerges the faith of his instinctive life.

This faith, this fanatical faith, is just as characteristic of Liszt as of any great man. He was in contact with his instinctive life, was in touch with the primal source of his personality, and so he possessed the capacity to believe. He believed in himself, he believed in One Who was greater than himself, he believed in progress, in culture, in beauty, in morality, in humanity. And he believed in God! And all this faith arises from no other cause than the powerful instinct of a man who wishes to raise others, too, to the heights of goodness that he feels in himself. Such a man is no longer an artist, but has become something greater: a prophet.

Beside this faith, how little works mean to those who feel sweetness even when they are not licking honey, who see beauty even when it is invisible, who grasp infinity even without having measured it. How little they care about the genius' errors, since they know that only he who *seeks* can err—that the others do wrong and bad things when they are not forced to do what is right, whereas error belongs among the prerogatives of genius.

Liszt created an art form which our time necessarily regards as a mistake, while a later time will perhaps again see exclusively the genius' insight on which it is based. Both are right, and perhaps it is only because we are continuing the insight along another path that we see rather the mistake. Liszt replaced an old visionary form by a new. A new expressive form had to arise from this. But he *consciously* replaced the old form by a new, and the old visionary form by a third party's vision, instead of his own. These two acts of his consciousness prevented the discovery made by his intuition from being transformed directly and purely into an artistic deed. That was his error—he let his conscious intellect perfect a work which would have succeeded more completely without it. He had a true insight: that although the musician is a personality expressing himself in music, he is also (to say it for the moment in Liszt's sense) a personality with poetic feelings. For this reason, craftsmanly deftness, technique and play with material are less remarkable in the work of art than are the things behind them—the personality, the true artist-being, that draws from direct vision.

But in transferring this idea into the language of music, a few mistranslations occurred: he translated the directly visionary personality into the poetically feeling one, the latter into the poet and finally the poet into the poem. Thus he produced second-hand poetry instead of exclusively allowing his own visionary form, the poet in himself, direct musical expression. It was not such a great mistake as it seems; the real artist has a fortunate way of making an unconscious correction, since, after all, he finally brings to the surface only what was in him. So that perhaps Liszt was not expressing his poets and poems, but probably himself after all. Only it is certain that such a process narrows the pipe from which one's own being streams, reduces the generosity of the primal source, and obliges the intellect to make completions which can not be homogeneous with the primal material.

That leads him to his second error, to his form. This, too, was inspired by a deep insight, but unfortunately only inspired, not also carried through to the end in the fructifying warmth of the centre of spiritual movement and birth. So it came imperfect into the world and went ailing. One must realize, or better still *feel*, that a form does not satisfy an expressive need, or does not even correspond to one. But one must then have no qualms about letting oneself be guided by this expressive need, and one must not hamper it in creating its own form; one must avoid the disturbing intervention of the constantly worried, frightened intellect. If, in criticizing form, one trusted one's expressive need when it rejected an old form, then one must also trust it in creating, when it attempts to produce a new, individual form appropriate to itself. Otherwise it would criticize the new form the intellect forces on it, just as it criticized the old into which unreason, convention, tried to force it. But Liszt's form is a broadening, a combination, a re-welding, a mathematical and mechanical further development of the old formal components. Mathematics and mechanics cannot produce a living being. Inspired by a true feeling, a rightly-functioning intellect brought this form to completion. But a rightly-functioning intellect almost always does the opposite of what is appropriate to a true feeling. A true feeling must not let itself be prevented from going constantly down, ever and anew, into the dark region of the unconscious, in order to bring up content and form as a unity.

Liszt replaced an old form by a new. What he thus did is certainly a worse formalism than that of the masters who had lived in the old forms. For they really had lived in them! They truly thought in that space, it was their home, they were almost born there, and therefore they moved in it with the most complete freedom. There, form is not felt as a boundary that hems them in, but as a framework, a brace, the support for the construction.

Those seem to me to be the two errors that show Liszt's actions to have differed from what should have come of his faith. He, for whom the poet stood foremost, suppressed the poet in himself by letting other poets talk him into too much. He, who felt form as a formalism, created a far worse formalism—one which is uninhabitable, because in his forms invented by the intellect no living being has ever dwelt. His real, inner personality, therefore, pervades his work to a smaller degree, shows itself in far less suitable forms, than ought to be the case with the artist, with this artist who possessed intuition. And perhaps the sound of his voice often gives little warmth, merely because it echoes so loudly in his bare, cold, uninhabitably arranged form.

Although his work thus seems to fall a little short of certain demands, one must not overlook how much there is in it that is truly new musically, discovered by genuine intuition. Was he not after all one of those who started the battle against tonality, both through themes which point to no absolutely definite tonal centre, and through many harmonic details whose musical exploitation has been looked after by his successors? Altogether his effect has perhaps been greater, through the many stimuli he left behind for his successors, than Wagner's has been—Wagner, who provided a work too perfect for anyone coming later to be able to add anything to it. But there is certainly no need to think of him only in this way. One need think merely of his *Christus* to know a work whose effect has still to dawn. Perhaps the day has almost come when contact will be re-established with its tone, its intentions, for our time is again seeking its God; this search characterizes it better than do the most outstanding technical achievements.

If I am now to sum up Liszt's importance for the development of our musical life, I must first establish that this error is not the reason why he is less important than one would like to believe. For this error is no such great misfortune, when one considers that an old error is always replaced by a new one; that in relation to every new insight, the earlier one shows up as error; and that the resulting series is infinite. Infinite as our aspiration, infinite as the distance from the goal. And even were the misfortune greater, there would still remain the one effect which arose directly from his vision, and to which we owe the fact that nowadays one notices not only technical skill (something few people have ever understood anyway), but also the artist's personality to some degree. And the other effect, that we have learned to think about the relationship between form and content in a different way from before. It may well be assumed that Liszt's works will not achieve the kind of popularity ascribed to the works of the classics. It is not impossible, even, that his work will be quite forgotten: the works of great men, too, can be forgotten. *But their name remains!* It becomes a *household word* that awakens lofty ethical imaginings. It becomes part of the language, so to speak, becomes a *means of expression*, a possible way of creating understanding for the times when we wish to speak of humanity's highest aims.

And there, too, Liszt's importance may well lie, like that of any great man. One may provide a model through his work, another through his personality. The more intimately work and personality coincide, the longer this model may hold good. But whether it is effective, whether it has influence on life—that I must doubt. For musical life, for example, is certainly much the same in its essentials as it was before Liszt. It has a different colour, partly different forms, and above all many new names. But the essence, the routine, the fashion, the ignorance and pettiness, the envy and the intrigue, the success of the incompetent and mediocre, the failure of the truly important, the money-making of the adaptable and the poverty of the independent-willed—that has all stayed the same as it was before. Not only Liszt but every great man has provided a model which should have taught his age that things needed changing, and why, and how. But the age takes no notice; musical life merely gives itself a few new names, turns over on to the other ear, and hears only what can never seriously be the main point: the middle parts. 'Middle parts to the fore!' is its motto. Musical life has its great ones on whom to model itself, and it honours them—but from a distance! For it is dominated by the small ones. And those who lead a musically active life have, in their contact with the others, so wholly extinguished the last sparks of musical *joie de vivre* that one can not think of them without bitterness, when they get together to celebrate festivals in the name of those against whose spirit they are sinning.

Great men's effect, if any, on life is infinitely slight. If one observes what Plato, Christ, Kant, Swedenborg, Schopenhauer, Balzac and others thought, and compares it with what people now believe and the way people now conduct their lives; when one sees that only a very small number of people think that way, whereas the others behave as if those ideas had never existed—then one doubts whether progress exists. And the works of the great climb higher, into the very sphere of pointlessness. One realizes that their importance lies, at most, in the model they provide for those who would have come to the truth even without any model. In this sense evolution does perhaps take place after all; progress can never prevent the emergence of new men who think upon the truth. So we are approaching the goal!

In life, deeds alone can prove effective; even works are too far removed. But faith, fanaticism, which is hardly a work and certainly not a deed, keeps its distance—a distance spanned by no bridge to a real world which frames its models and hangs them in ceremonial halls, so that they look on when the hale and hearty honour the names of those whose spirit they would rather not comprehend.

4

GUSTAV MAHLER: IN MEMORIAM
1912

Gustav Mahler was a saint.

Anyone who knew him even slightly must have had that feeling. Perhaps only a few understood it. And among even those few the only ones who honoured him were the men of good will. The others reacted to the saint as the wholly evil have always reacted to complete goodness and greatness: they martyred him. They carried things so far that this great man doubted his own work. Not once was the cup allowed to pass away from him.[1] He had to swallow even this most bitter one: the loss, if only temporarily, of his faith in his work.

How will they seek to answer for this, that Mahler had to say, 'It seems that I have been in error.' How will they seek to justify themselves when they are accused of having brought one of the greatest composers of all time to the point where he was deprived of the sole, the highest recompense for a creative mind, the recompense found when the artist's faith in himself allows him to say, 'I have not been in error.' Let it be remembered that the creative urge continues, the greatest works are conceived, carried through and born, but the creator, who brings them forth, does not feel the bliss of generation; he feels himself merely the slave of a higher ordinance, under whose compulsion he ceaselessly does his work. 'As if it had been dictated to me,' Mahler once said, to describe how rapidly and half-unconsciously he created, in two months, his Eighth Symphony.

What the whole world would some day believe in, he no longer believed in. He had become resigned.

Rarely has anyone been so badly treated by the world; nobody, perhaps,

447

worse. He stood so high that even the best men often let him down, because even the best did not reach his height. Because in even the best there is yet so much impurity that they could not breathe in that uttermost region of purity that was already Mahler's abode on earth. What, then, can one expect of the less good and the wholly impure? Obituaries! They pollute the air with their obituaries, hoping to enjoy at least one more moment of self-importance; for those are the moments when dirt is in its element.

And the more exactly such a man knows how much he himself will come to be despised, and how just it will be, the more 'respected' the writers he quotes for their mistaken judgements of Mahler. As if it had not always been so: lack of respect for the work of the great has won people their contemporaries' respect. But what did posterity have to say?

Admittedly such people are not worried about posterity, otherwise they would have to do away with themselves. I do not believe there is one man who would want to go on living if he realized the shame he has piled on himself by offending against the highest there is among men. It must be terrible for such a man, thoughtlessly living from one day to the next, to become suddenly conscious of the full extent of his guilt.

Enough of him!

To Gustav Mahler's work!

Into its pure air!

Here is the faith that raises us on high. Here is someone believing, in his immortal works, in an eternal soul. I do not know whether our soul is immortal, but I believe it. What I do know, though, is that men, the highest men, such as Beethoven and Mahler, will believe in an immortal soul until the power of this belief has endowed humanity with one.

Meanwhile, we have immortal works. And we shall know how to guard them.

5

GUSTAV MAHLER
(*1912, 1948*)

Instead of using many words, perhaps I should do best simply to say: I believe firmly and steadfastly that Gustav Mahler was one of the greatest men and artists. For there are only two possibilities of convincing someone of an artist's greatness: the first and better way is to perform his work; the second, which I am forced to use, is to transmit my belief in this work to others.

Man is petty! Truly, we should have faith that our belief will transmit itself directly. Our passion for the object of our veneration must so inflame us that everyone who comes near us must burn with us, must be consumed by the same ardour and worship the same fire which is also sacred to us. This fire should burn brightly in us that we become transparent, so that its light shines forth and so illuminates even the one who, until now, walked in darkness. An apostle who does not glow preaches heresy. He to whom the halo of sanctity is denied does not carry the image of a god within himself. For the apostle does not shine by himself, but by a light which uses his body merely as a shell; the light pierces the shell, but it graciously grants the glowing one the appearance of shining by himself. We, who are inspired, must have faith; men will sympathize with this ardour, men will see our light shining. Men will honour the one who we worship —even without our doing anything about it.

Man is petty. We do not believe enough in the whole thing, in the great thing, but demand irrefutable details. We depend too little upon that capacity which gives us an impression of the object as a totality containing within itself all details in their corresponding relationships. We believe that we understand what is natural; but the miracle is extremely natural, and the natural is extremely miraculous.

The more exactly we observe, the more enigmatic does the simplest matter become to us. We analyse because we are not satisfied with comprehending nature, effect and function of a totality as a totality and, when we are not able to put together again exactly what we have taken apart, we begin to do injustice to that capacity which gave us the whole together with its spirit, and we lose faith in our finest ability—the ability to receive a total impression.

I shall give an example which will seem familiar to anyone who observes himself carefully enough. I remember distinctly that the first time I heard Mahler's Second Symphony I was seized, especially in certain passages, with an excitement which expressed itself even physically, in the violent throbbing of my heart. Nevertheless, when I left the concert I did not fail to test what I had heard according to those requirements which were known to me as a musician, and with which, as is generally believed, a work of art must unconditionally comply. Thus I forgot the most important circumstance—that the work had, after all, made an unheard-of impression on me, inasmuch as it had enchanted me into an involuntary sympathy. Indeed, a work of art can produce no greater effect than when it transmits the emotions which raged in the creator to the listener, in such a way that they also rage and storm in him. And I was overwhelmed; completely overwhelmed.

The intellect is sceptical; it does not trust the sensual, and it trusts the supersensual even less. If one is overwhelmed, the intellect maintains that there are many means which might bring forth such an overwhelming emotion. It reminds us that no one can view a tragic event in life without being most deeply moved; it reminds us of the melodramatic horror-play, whose effect none can escape; it reminds us that there are higher and lower means, artistic and inartistic. It tells us that realistic, violent incidents—as, for example, the torture scene in *Tosca* —which are unfailingly effective should not be used by an artist, because they are too cheap, too accessible to everyone. And it forgets that such realistic means will never be employed in music, and especially not in the symphony, because music is always unreal. In music, no one is every really killed or tortured unjustly; here, there is never any event which could awaken sympathy *in itself*, for only musical matters appear. And only when these events have power to speak for themselves—only when this alternation of high and low tones, fast and slow rhythms, loud and soft sounds, tells of the most unreal things that exist—only then are we moved to utmost sympathy. He who has once felt the impact of this purity remains immune to all other impressions! It is entirely out of the question that musical sentiment can be traced to impure sources, for the means of music are unreal, and only reality is impure!

A man who has been overwhelmed and knows that his artistic and ethical culture is on a high level, and thus has confidence in himself and believes in his culture, need not concern himself with the question of whether the means were artistic. And he who is not overwhelmed is concerned even less. It is enough for him that he was neither overwhelmed—nor repelled! Why, then all the bombastic words? For this reason: we like to make our judgements agree with those of others at any price, and when this does not work, we strive to achieve the advantage of a well-informed and well-fortified position of our own. Differences of understanding are only partly causes of splitting into parties; far more is due to the justifications. They make the disagreement endless. It is not certain that what I call red is really the same in the eye of another as it is in mine. And nevertheless agreement is easily reached here, so that there is no doubt what is red and what is green. But the moment one tried to explain *why* this is red, that green, dissension would certainly set in. The simple experience of the senses: 'I see what is called red' or 'I feel that I am overwhelmed' can be easily stated by anyone who is intelligent enough. And he should have the courage to consider the fact that he is not overwhelmed as something self-evident but completely unimportant to the object, just as one who is deaf may not disown sounds, or one who is colour-blind, colours.

The work of art exists even if no one is overwhelmed by it, and the attempt to rationalize one's feelings about it is superfluous, because this attempt always exhibits the characteristics of the subject and never those of the object: the onlooker is colour-blind, the listener deaf; the art-lover was in the wrong mood, was unfitted (perhaps only at the moment, perhaps permanently) to receive an artistic impression.

But how does it come about that someone who has tried with the best will in the world to understand arrives at such perverted judgements, in spite of having received an impression? Here and there one has come across a passage which one does not like; a melody which one finds banal, which seems to be unoriginal; a continuation which ones does not understand, for which one thinks to find a better substitute; a voice-leading which seems to scorn all the requirements heretofore set up for good voice-leading. One is a musician, belongs to the guild, is capable of doing something oneself (or perhaps not!) and always knows exactly how the thing should be done, if indeed it should be done at all. It is pardonable that such a one feels justified in cavilling at details. For we all cavil over the works of the greatest masters. There is scarcely anyone who, if he received an order to create the world better than the Lord God Almighty had done it, would not undertake the task without further ado. Everything which we do not understand we take for an error; everything which makes us uncomfortable we take for a

451

mistake of its creator. And we do not stop to think that, since we do not understand the meaning, silence, respectful silence, would be the only fitting response. And admiration, boundless admiration.

But, as has been said, we are petty; simply because we cannot survey the great thing in its entirety, we concern ourselves with its details—and, as punishment for our presumptuous behaviour, we fail even there. We are wrong all the way down the line. In every case where human understanding tries to abstract from divine works the laws according to which they are constructed, it turns out that we find only laws which characterize our cognition through thinking and our power of imagination. We are moving in a circle. We always see and recognize only ourselves, only, at most, our own being, as often as we think we are describing the essence of a thing outside ourselves. And these laws, which are, at best, those of our intellectual capacity, we apply as a yardstick to the work of the creator! On the basis of such laws, we judge the work of the great artist!

Perhaps it has never been harder to give an artist his proper due than today. Overvaluation and undervaluation have probably hardly ever before been such inevitable results of the business of art. And it has never been more difficult for the public to tell who is really great and who is just a big name of the day. Countless men are producing. They cannot all be geniuses. A few set the pace, the others merely imitate. But if the many imitators want to stay in the race, they must quickly find out what is the latest brand good in the market. The publishers, the press and publicity take care of this, and achieve the result that one who is creating something new is not left alone for long. Bee-like industry, which today in all fields achieves the success which only talent should have, asserts itself here too, and brings it about that the epoch is expressed not by the solitary great man, but by a throng of little men. The truly great have always had to flee from the present into the future, but the present has never belonged so completely to the mediocre as it does today. And no matter how great the gap, they will try to bridge it—they even stake out their claims on the future. No one wants to write just for today, even if he can hardly be believed in for as long as one day. There are only geniuses, and to them belongs even the future. How can we find the right way here? How can we tell who is really great, when the high average is so widely distributed that we forget height in favour of breadth? We really talk far too much about the Alps and too little about Mont Blanc.

It is almost excusable that the public fails here, for there are always many who provide what is suitable to the needs of our time in a much more accessible form than can be offered by someone who already belongs to the future. One can be modern today without aiming for the best. One has so wide a selection among the moderns that the spirit of the time is accessible 'to the most refined taste and also to the less well-to-do, in all shades and in all price-brackets.' Who will strain himself under these circumstances? One is modern—that is enough. Eventually, one is even ultramodern—that makes one interesting. One has a programme, principles, taste. One knows what it is all about. One knows all the critical clichés. One knows exactly what are the current trends in art. Yes, one could almost establish in advance the very problems and methods with which the art of the immediate future will have to concern itself, and I am only surprised that no one has yet hit upon the idea of combining all these possibilities and concocting a guide-book to the future.

This is the unexpected result which Wagner attained when he created Beck-messer as a warning for too-hasty critics. Everyone considers himself a con-noisseur of new art, and the Beckmessers of today affirm that they have become more 'broad-minded'. But this is obviously false, for the good is and remains good and must therefore be persecuted, and the bad is and remains bad and must therefore be promoted. Thus the praised broadening of the mind appears to be rather softening of the brain. For these men have lost every standpoint and all limitations, since they do not notice that they are even more narrow-minded than those who at least praised what 'ran according to their rules'.

Otherwise, the same old catchwords could not always be dragged in every time that a really great man was under consideration. For example: Mahler has written unusually extensive works. Everyone feels, or thinks he knows, that in them something exceptionally high and great strives for expression. What worn-out commonplace would come more readily to a broad-minded man than this: he strives for the highest but does not possess the strength to perform what he desires? And who says it? Those critics who have accommodated their very broad-mindedness to the common interest. Those who are less good, as well as the very bad ones—for it is a point of honour with them to agree on basic things. This sentence is, therefore, one of those thoughtless clichés which must be hated above all because they are almost without exception applied to those men to whom they are least appropriate. Little men come out of it very well. But as soon as it is said of someone that he strives for the highest, etc., I know at once that he has either not striven for it or has not reached it! That is, after all, something to be depended upon. But which measurement is that greatness established for which Mahler is supposed to have striven in vain? In the dimensions of the works, and in a circumstance which seems to me immaterial in relation to the real aspirations of the artist: in the subject-matter and texts on which several movements of his symphonies are based. Mahler has spoken of death, of resurrection, of fate; he has composed *Faust*. And these are supposed to be the greatest things. But nearly every musician in earlier times composed church music and concerned himself with God—that is, with something still higher; and he could strive unconcernedly for the highest, without anyone's measuring his work with that yardstick. On the contrary, if it is really great to stand in the shadow of the great themes, one ought actually to require this of an artist. In reality, there is only one greatest goal towards which the artist strives: *to express himself*. If that succeeds, then the artist has achieved the greatest possible success; next to that, everything else is unimportant, for everything else is included in it: death, resurrection, Faust, fate—but also the lesser and yet not less important moments, the emotions of the soul and spirit which make a man creative. Mahler, too, tried only to express himself. And that he succeeded can be doubted by no one who is in the slightest degree capable of comprehending how isolated this music has remained, although the imitators are so busy trying to catch up with everything that has a chance of capturing the market. That there are no imitations of these symphonies which resemble their model in the slightest degree, that this music seems inimitable (like everything that one man alone can achieve)—all this proves that Mahler was capable of the greatest possible achievement of an artist: self-expression! He expressed only himself, and not death, fate and Faust. For that could also be composed by others. He expressed only that which, independent of style and flourish, portrays himself and himself alone, and which therefore would remain inaccessible to anyone else who tried to achieve it merely by imitating the style. But this style itself seems, in an enigmatic and heretofore unfamiliar way, to exclude imitation. Perhaps this is because here, for the first time, a mode of expression is so inseparably bound up with the subject to which it applies that what usually appears merely as a symptom of the outward form is here, simultaneously, material and construction as well.

I wish to concern myself with several things which were said against Mahler's work. Next come two accusations: against his sentimentality and against the banality of his themes. Mahler suffered much from these accusations. Against the latter, one is almost defenceless; against the former, completely so. Think of it: an artist, in all good faith, writes down a theme just as his need for expression and his feelings dictate it to him, without changing a note. If he wanted to escape banality, it would be easy for him. The meanest tunesmith, who looks harder at his notes than into himself, is capable of 'making' a banal theme interesting with a few strokes of his pen. And most interesting themes originate in this way —just as every painter can avoid trashy detailed painting by painting just as trashily with broad strokes. And now imagine this: this most sensitive, spiritually most elevated man, from whom we have heard the most profound words—precisely this man was supposed to be unable to write unbanal themes, or at least to alter them until they no longer appeared banal!

I think he simply did not notice it, and for one reason alone: *his themes are actually not banal.*

Here I must confess that I, too, at first considered Mahler's themes banal. I consider it important to admit that I was Saul before I became Paul, since it may thence be deduced that those 'fine discriminations' of which certain opponents are so proud were not foreign to me. *But they are foreign to me now*, ever since my increasingly intense perception of the beauty and magnificence of Mahler's work has brought me to the point of admitting that it is not fine discrimination, but, on the contrary, the most blatant lack of the power of discrimination, which produces such judgements. I had found Mahler's themes banal, although the whole work had always made a profound impression on me. Today, with the worst will in the world, I could not react this way. Consider this: if they were really banal I should find them far more banal today than formerly. For banal means rustic, and describes something which belongs to a low grade of culture, to no culture at all. In lower grades of culture there is found, not what is absolutely false or bad, but what used to be right, what is obsolete, what has been outlived, what is no longer true. The peasant does not behave badly, but archaically, just as those of higher rank behaved before they knew better. Therefore, the banal represents a backward state of ethics and state of mind, which was once the state of mind of the higher ranks; it was not banal from the beginning, but became banal only when it was pushed aside by new and better customs. But it cannot rise up again—once it is banal, it must stay banal. And if I now maintain that I can no longer find these themes banal, they can never have been so; for a banal idea, an idea which appears obsolete and worn-out to me, can only appear more banal on closer acquaintance—but in no case noble. But if now I discover that the oftener I look at these ideas the more new beauties and noble traits are added to them, doubt is no longer possible: the idea is the opposite of banal. It is not something which we were long ago done with and cannot mis-understand, but something the deepest meaning of which is as yet far from com-pletely revealed, something so profound that we have not become aware of more than its superficial appearance. And, in fact, this has happened not only to Mahler, but also to nearly all other great composers, who had to submit to the accusation of banality. I call to mind only Wagner and Brahms. I think that the change in my feeling provides a better yardstick than the judgement on first hearing which everyone is very quick to come out with as soon as he runs into a situation which he really does not understand.

   The artist is even more defenceless against the accusation of sentimentality than against that of banality. Mahler, halfway giving in to the latter because his self-confidence had been undermined, could defend himself by saying that one ought not to look at the theme, but at what comes out of it. He need not have done this. But the criticism was so general that he was forced to believe himself in the wrong—after all, the best musicians and all the other worst people were saying so! But there is no defence against the other accusation, that of senti-mentality. That hits home as hard as calling something trash. Everyone who really likes nothing but trash is in a position to give a stab in the back to the most honourable and important man, to the one who turns most violently away from the merely pleasing (which after all, is really what trash amounts to), and thus to degrade him and also to rob him of inner security. The way of attacking signifi-cant works of art is different now from what it used to be. Formerly, an artist was reproached if he did not know enough; now it is a cause for criticism if he knows too much. Smoothness, which was formerly a quality to be sought, is today an error, for it is trashy. Yes, one paints with broad strokes today! Everyone paints with broad strokes, and he who does not paint with broad strokes is trashy. And he who does not possess humour or superficiality, heroic greatness and Greek serenity, is sentimental. It is very fortunate that the ethics of Red Indian stories have not yet become the model for our attitudes towards art. Otherwise, aestheticians would consider only Indian lack of sensitivity to pain, in addition to Greek serenity, as unsentimental.

456

What is true feeling? But that is a question of feeling! That can only be answered by feeling! Whose feelings are right? Those of the man who disputes the true feelings of another, or those of the man who gladly grants another his true feelings, so long as he says just what he has to say? Schopenhauer explains the difference between sentimentality and true sorrow. He chooses as an example Petrarch, whom the painters of broad strokes would surely call sentimental, and shows that the difference consists in this: true sorrow elevates itself to resignation, while sentimentality is incapable of that, but always grieves and mourns, so that one has finally lost 'earth and heaven together'. To elevate oneself to resignation: how can one speak of a sentimental theme, when this complaining, sorrowing theme may, in the course of events, elevate itself to resignation? That is as wrong as when one speaks of a 'witty phrase'. The whole man is witty—full of wit—but not the single phrase. The whole work can be sentimental, but not the single passage. For its relationship to the whole is decisive: what it becomes, what importance it is granted in the whole. And how Mahler's music elevates itself to resignation! Are 'heaven and earth together' lost here, or is there not rather portrayed here, for the first time, an earth on which life is worth living, and is there not then praised a heaven which is more than worth living for? Think of the Sixth Symphony—of the frightful struggle in the first movement. But then, its sorrow-torn upheaval automatically generates its opposite, the unearthly passage with the cowbells, whose cool, icy comfort from a height which is reached only by one who soars to resignation; only he can hear it who understands what heavenly voices whisper without animal warmth.

Then, the Andante movement. How pure is its tone to one who knows today that it was not banality which kept it from pleasing, but the strangeness of the emotions of a thoroughly unusual personality which kept it from being understood! Or the post-horn solo in the Third Symphony, at first with the divided high violins, then, even more beautiful if possible, with the horns. This is a mood of nature, of 'Greek serenity', if it must be so—or, more simply, of the most marvellous beauty, for one who does not need such slogans! Or the last movement of the Third! The entire Fourth, but especially its fourth movement! And its third! And its second and first movements too! Yes, all of them! Naturally; all of them; for there are no beautiful passages by great masters, but only entire beautiful works.

Incredibly irresponsible is another accusation made against Mahler: that his themes are unoriginal. In the first place, art does not depend upon the single component part alone; therefore, music does not depend upon the theme. For the work of art, like every living thing, is conceived as a whole—just like a child, whose arm or leg is not conceived separately. The inspiration is not the theme, but the whole work. And it is not the one who writes a good theme who is inventive, but the one to whom a whole symphony occurs at once. But in the second place, these themes are original. Naturally, he who looks at only the first four notes will find reminiscences. But he behaves as foolishly as one who looks for original words in an original poem; for the theme consists not of a few notes, but of the musical destinies of these notes. The small form which we call a theme ought never to be the only yardstick for the large form, of which it is relatively the smallest component part. But the observation of nothing but the smallest parts of the theme must lead to those abuses against which Schopenhauer turned when he demanded that one must use the most ordinary words to say the most extraordinary things.

And this must also be possible in music; with the most ordinary successions of tones one ought to be able to say the most extraordinary things. Mahler does not need that as an excuse. Although he strove for the most far-reaching simplicity and naturalness, his themes have a structure all their own—true, not in the sense in which many writers play around with words. For an example, I wish to cite one writer who always left out the reflexive pronoun in order to achieve a personal note. But Mahler's themes are original in the highest sense, when one observes with what fantasy and art, with what wealth of variation there comes out of a few such tones an endless melody, which is often difficult to analyse even for someone skilled in that process—when one takes note of the thoroughly original musical phenomena arrived at by each of his themes in the most natural way possible. From the fact that this way is so completely original one can recognize which elements are to be ascribed to the brain and which to the heart. That is: the way, the goal, the whole development of everything at once, the whole movement; naturally, the theme as well—but not the first few relatively unimportant notes!

One must go even further: it is not at all necessary for a piece of music to have an original theme. Otherwise, Bach's chorale preludes would not be works of art. But they certainly are works of art!

So it always goes with very great men. At each are fired all those accusations of which the opposite is true. Yes, *all*, and with such accuracy that one must be taken aback by it. For this shows, contrary to one's expectations, that the qualities of an author are really noticed already at the first hearing, but are merely wrongly interpreted. Whenever the most personal of the composer's peculiarities appear, the listener is struck. But instead of recognizing immediately that this is a special feature, he interprets the blow as a blow of offence. He believes that there is a mistake, a fault here, and fails to see that it is a merit.

One should really have been able to recognize Mahler's high artistry on one's first glance at his scores. Today I cannot understand at all how this escaped me. The unheard-of simplicity, clarity, and beauty of arrangement immediately struck me in these scores. It reminded me of the aspect of the greatest masterworks. But I did not yet know then what I know today: that it is entirely out of the question for someone to accomplish something masterly in any respect who is not a master in every respect. Therefore, anyone who can write such scores has one of those minds in which perfection automatically originates. And the concept of perfection completely excludes the concept of imperfection; therefore, it is not possible to give a representation of an imperfect thing which produces the impression of perfection. From the aspect of the score alone a musician who has a feeling for form must recognize that this music can only be by a master.

And Gustav Mahler had to endure being told that he knew nothing. As a matter of fact, opinion was divided. Some asserted that he could do everything in a very refined manner, and, in particular, orchestrated very effectively, but that he had no inventiveness and that his music was empty. These were the more complicated blockheads. The simpler ones were good at part-leading, and therefore scorned instrumentation and everything else which could be accomplished by another and not by them. They knew very well that one ought not to compose in this manner. These are the same people who have always known how masters ought not to compose, if they want to remain such bunglers as these amateurs. They have always set up the standards for Beethoven, Wagner, Hugo Wolf, and Bruckner, and in every period would have known exactly what the only right thing is. Nothing has survived of this omniscience but its ridicule—but that permeates the entire history of music.

The artistry of melodic construction is especially striking in Mahler, who wrote entirely tonally, and to whom, therefore, many harmonic means of contrast were not as yet available for his purposes. It is incredible how long these melodies can become, although certain chords have to be repeated in the process. And in spite of this no monotony sets in. On the contrary, the longer the theme lasts, the greater is its final impetus; the force which drives its development increases with uniformly accelerating motion. No matter how hot the theme may have been *in statu nascendi,* after a while it is not burnt out, but burns even brighter, and whereas in someone else's music it would long since have exhausted itself and vanished, here it only now rises to the highest pitch of excitement. If that is not capability, it is at least potency. Something similar appears in the first movement of the Eighth Symphony. How often does this movement come to E flat, for instance on a four-six chord! I would cut that out in any student's work, and advise him to seek out another tonality. And, incredibly, here it is right! Here it fits! Here it could not even be otherwise. What do the rules say about it? Then the rules must be changed.

One should observe the curious structure of many themes, even of shorter ones. The first theme of the Andante of the Sixth Symphony, for example, is ten measures long. In constitution it is a period, which would normally be eight measures long. But in the fourth measure,

Ex. 1

where the caesura would come in a period, the note G♭, which can be a dotted quarter-note, as in Example 2,

Ex. 2

is extended to three quarters; this shifts the eighth-note figure $\boxed{c}$ into the fifth measure. Thus the antecedent of the period becomes four and a half measures long. In a symmetrical period the consequent is equally long; this would produce nine measures in all. The consequent begins in the fifth measure, and if a new extension, corresponding to the previous one, did not take place in the seventh measure, the period would end, as in Example 3, in the ninth measure.

Ex. 3

Ex. 4

But it is not absolutely necessary for this melody to become ten measures long. Example 3 shows that in spite of the extension in the seventh measure an ending on the first beat of the ninth measure is possible. This indicates that in measures 8 and 9 there follows a further artificial extension, although cadential contraction already set in here.

It is amazing how these deviations from the conventional balance each other, even postulate each other. This demonstrates a highly developed feeling for form, such as one finds only in great masterpieces. This is not the *tour de force* of a 'technician'—a master would not bring it off, if he made up his mind to it in advance. These are inspirations which escape the control of consciousness, inspirations which come only to the genius, who receives them unconsciously and formulates solutions without noticing that a problem has confronted him.

A well-known writer on music called Mahler's symphonies 'gigantic symphonic potpourris'. The term 'potpourris' naturally applies to the banality of invention and not to the form, for 'gigantically conceived' is supposed to apply to the form. Now, in the first place, there are also potpourris of classical music, from operas of Mozart, Wagner, etc. I do not know whether such a thing exists, but in any case it is easily conceivable that a potpourri could also consist of nothing but the most beautiful themes of Bach or Beethoven, without being anything but potpourri for all that. Therefore, the banality of the themes is not a significant feature of the potpourri. But in the second place, the characteristic of the potpourri is the unpretentiousness of the formal connectives. The individual sections are simply juxtaposed, without always being connected and without their relationships (which may also be entirely absent) being more than mere accidents in the form. But this is contradicted by the term 'symphonic', which means the opposite. It means that the individual sections are organic components of a living being, born of a creative impulse and conceived as a whole. But this phrase, which really has no meaning in itself, which falls apart because it is thrice contradictory—this phrase became all the rage in Germany. In Vienna, where the worst evils are always possible in the press, someone even found it necessary to cite it in Mahler's obituary.

I find that quite fair. For the great artist must somehow be punished in his lifetime for the honour which he will enjoy later.

And the esteemed music critic must somehow be compensated in his lifetime for the contempt with which later times will treat him.

The only thing which everyone admitted to be valid in Mahler was his orchestration. That sounds suspicious, and one might almost believe that this praise, because it is so unanimous, is just as unfair as the above-mentioned unanimities. And, in fact, Mahler never altered anything in the form of his compositions, but he was always changing the instrumentation. He seems to have felt that this was imperfect. It is certainly not, it is certainly of the highest perfection, and only the anxiety of the man who, as a conductor, had to strive for a clarity which he, as a composer, certainly did not find so necessary—since music assures the divine prerogative of anonymity of feelings, of obscurity for the uninitiated—only this anxiety drove him ever to seek, as a substitute for the perfect, the more perfect. But that does not exist. In any case, it is indicative that he was rather mistrustful of this universal praise. And it is a wonderful characteristic of great men that they view praise as fitting to them, but endure it even less patiently than they endure blame. But there is something more. I am firmly convinced that if one asks those who praise Mahler's orchestration just what they mean, they will name something that he would have disliked. There is even proof of this; nearly everyone who orchestrates today orchestrates well— if you read the critics. And there is certainly a difference between this good orchestration and Mahler's thinking for orchestra!

What first strikes one about Mahler's instrumentation is the almost unexampled objectivity with which he writes down only what is absolutely necessary. His sound never comes from ornamental additions, from accessories that are related not at all or only distantly to the important material, and that are put down only as decorations. But where it soughs, it is the theme which soughs; the themes have such a form and so many notes that it immediately becomes clear that the soughing is not the *aim* of this passage, but its *form* and its *content*. Where it grunts and groans, the themes and harmonies grunt and groan; but where it crashes, gigantic structures clash against one another; the architecture crumbles; the architectonic relationships of tension and pressure are in revolt. But among the most beautiful sounds are the delicate, fragrant ones. Here, too, he brings unheard-of novelty, as, for example, in the middle movements of the Seventh Symphony, with their sonorities of guitar, harp, and solo instruments. This guitar in the Seventh is not introduced for a single effect, but the whole movement is based on this sonority. It belongs to it from the very beginning, it is a living organ of the composition: not the heart, but perhaps the eyes, whose glance is so characteristic of its aspect. This instance is very close—in a more modern way, naturally—to the method of the classical composers, who built whole movements or pieces on the sonority of a specific instrumental group.

Probably we shall soon find out in detail that (and how) Mahler, in such ways, is much closer to classical music than he appears to be. Today it is not always easy to recognize this, and naturally it is not always true. On the contrary, up to a certain degree he must depart from it, because he progresses beyond it. But he goes beyond it not so much in forms, proportions, and extent, which are only the outer consequences of the inner happenings, as in content. This does not mean that the content is greater, more significant or more earth-shaking than in the works of other great masters, for there is only one content, which all great men wish to express: the longing of mankind for its future form, for an immortal soul, for dissolution into the universe—the longing of this soul for its God. This alone, though reached by many different roads and detours and expressed by many different means, is the content of the works of the great; and with all their will they yearn for it so long and desire it so intensely until it is accomplished. And this longing is transmitted with its full intensity from the predecessor to the successor, and the successor continues not only the content but also the intensity, adding proportionally to his heritage. This heritage carries responsibility, but it is imposed only upon one who can assume this responsibility.

It seems to me almost petty that I should speak of the conductor Mahler in the same breath as the composer. Not only was he always appreciated as a conductor even by the most stupid opponents, but one might also consider that the purely reproductive activity would be of merely secondary importance in comparison with the creative activity. But there are two reasons which induce me to take up this discussion. In the first place, nothing about a great man is secondary. Actually, every one of his acts is somehow productive. In this sense, I should have found that more interesting and instructive than learning how one of our musical bigwigs composes on a 'sacred subject'. But, in the second place, it seems to me as if even this activity has not yet been completely comprehended in its most important aspect. Certainly, many have extolled his demonic personality, his unheard-of sense of style, the precision of his performances as well as their tonal beauty and clarity. But, for example, among other things I heard one of his 'colleagues' say that there is no special trick to bringing off good performances when one has so many rehearsals. Certainly there is no trick to it, for the oftener one plays a thing through, the better it goes, and even the poorest conductors profit from this. But there is a trick to feeling the need for a tenth rehearsal during the ninth rehearsal because one still hears many things that can become better, *because one still knows something to say in the tenth rehearsal.* This is exactly the difference: a poor conductor often does not know what to do after the third rehearsal, he has nothing more to say, he is more easily satisfied, because he does not have the capacity for further discrimination, and because nothing in him imposes higher requirements. And this is the cause: the productive man conceives within himself a complete image of what he wishes to reproduce; the performance, like everything else that he brings forth, must not be less perfect than the image. Such re-creation is only slightly different from creation; virtually, only the approach is different. Only when one has clarified this point to oneself does one comprehend how much is meant by the modest words with which Mahler himself characterized his highest aim as a conductor: 'I consider it my greatest service that I force the musicians to play exactly what is in the notes.' That sounds almost too simple, too slight, to us; and in fact it is so, for we might ascribe the effects which we knew to far more profound causes. But if one imagines how precise must be the image engendered by the notes in one who is creative, and what sensitivity is necessary in order to distinguish whether the reality and the image correspond to one another; if one thinks of what is necessary in order to express these fine distinctions so understandably that the performing musician, while merely playing the right notes, now suddenly participates in the spirit of the music as well—then one understands that with these modest words everything has been said.

This modesty was so characteristic of Mahler. Never a movement which was not exactly consistent with its cause! It was just as large as it had to be; it was executed with temperament, with life, energetically, powerfully, for temperament is the executive of conviction, and it will never be inactive. But there were no outbreaks without cause—none of that false temperament which today brings such great success to those who imitate Mahler's earlier manner of conducting. When he conducted thus, turning with violent movements to individual instrumental groups, really acting out for them the power and force which they were to express, he had arrived at the boundary of manly maturity which still permits that sort of thing. When he had crossed the boundary, the change set in, and he conducted the orchestra with unexampled composure. All exertion took place in the rehearsals, the violent gestures disappeared, even greater clarity of the power of verbal expression replaced them. Here a young man had passed into maturity, and did not strive to retain the gestures of youth, because he never deceived, but always did what was fitting to his situation. But he would never have conducted quietly while he was young; the rubato corresponded to his youth, the steadiness to his maturity. And let it be said to those younger conductors who today imitate Mahlerian composure that this is not in his spirit. His was a different concept. To emulate him means always to be as one's own feelings dictate. The other thing is mere aping. For him there were no other rules than these, and no models for him to imitate. One has to live up to one's models. But that takes courage. This Mahler possessed in the highest degree. Nothing could keep him from taking the utmost risks for what he deemed to be necessary. This was shown by his direction of the Vienna Opera, and by the enemies whom he won for himself because of it. He unified all the worst people in Vienna; the most unreliable ones were tied down, became fighters against him for a dead certainty. But he also had the courage to endure, to be patient. He was innocently involved in an affair, in spite of which he took the assaults of the press without batting an eyelash, because in order to answer them he would have had to sacrifice a younger friend, and he did not want to do that. Smiling, he took the whole thing as a matter of course, and never breathed a word of it later.

In Vienna, as director of the Imperial Opera, he did not serve as a musician alone. He not only demanded from musicians and singers an approach to perfection and selfless devotion to the will of the masterworks, but he was also their interpreter in the explanation of the poetic content. How deeply his thinking penetrated into the intent of the masters may be illustrated by the following example.

In a conversation about Wagner's poems I observed that I was unable to decipher the deeper meaning of the text of *Lohengrin*. The mere tale, with its romantic wonders, curses, bewitchments, magic potions, and metamorphoses, did not seem to correspond to deeper human feelings. In spite of the great impression made by the summons to patriotism and by the consecration of the Grail, it was hard to blame Elsa for wanting to know Lohengrin's origin, even if Ortrud had not aroused her suspicion.

'It is the difference between man and woman,' explained Mahler. 'Elsa is the sceptical woman. She is incapable of having the same degree of confidence in the man that he showed when he fought for her, believing in her without questioning her guilt or innocence. The capacity for trust is masculine, suspicion is feminine.' Certainly, suspicion originates in the fear of the one who needs protection, while trust results from the sense of power of her protector, the protector of Brabant. This interpretation reveals the deeply human background of the rather theatrical 'Nie sollst du mich befragen.'

Mahler, a man racked with passion, who had gone through all the storms of life, who had been hounded by friends, who had himself exalted and overthrown gods, at the climax of his life possessed that composure, that moderation, that perspective, which he obtained by purification of the mind from dross. This enabled him always to see the most profound aspect of the works of the great; upon this was based an unswerving respect, which we younger men were on the way to losing.

Mahler was no friend of programme music. Though he—an autocrat—did not like to discuss such things, he did not like it any better when people, flattering, would say what they assumed he would like. A younger conductor had to experience this when, in addition, he made one more mistake in attacking Wagner. 'The words of Wagner that you quote are entirely clear to me,' he wrote; 'that our music reflects the purely human (and everything that goes with it, including the intellectual) in one way or another cannot be denied. As in all art, it is matter of appropriate means of expression! But what one puts into music is always the *whole*, feeling, thinking, breathing, suffering man.' Against this, he continued, there need be no objection if a musician expresses himself therein— but not a poet, a philosopher, a painter!

Such wisdom protected him from exaggeration. Apostles are often more papistical than the Pope, because they lack the proper moderation. He knew that one thing is not absolutely false in itself any more than its opposite is absolutely true in itself. Therefore, his deeply rooted cognition of real values would not permit fitting respect to be denied to one of the truly great. Perhaps this reaction originated in his code of honour, just as every officer will immediately, under all circumstances, revenge an insult to another officer.

This happened to me. In my development there was a phase during which I took a negative, even an inimical stand against Wagner, whom I had previously honoured with the highest. It seems that I expressed myself about it to Mahler with violent and arrogant words. Although visibly shocked, he replied with impressive calm that he knew such states of mind, he too had passed through such stages of development. This would be nothing lasting; for one always comes back again and again to the truly great ones. They stand unshakeably in their places and it is commendable never to lose our respect for them.

This reprimand was of great consequence to me ever afterwards, for it became clear to me that only he is capable of respect who deserves respect himself, and that this sentence could even be inverted: he who cannot respect another is himself unworthy of respect. And this realization is especially important today, when social climbers belittle a great man in order to seem greater themselves.

I have tried to define the difference between genius and talent as follows:

Talent is the capacity to learn, genius the capacity to develop oneself. Talent grows by acquiring capacities which already existed outside of itself; it assimilates these, and finally even possesses them. Genius already possesses all its future faculties from the very beginning. It only develops them; it merely unwinds, unrolls, unfolds them. While talent, which has to master a limited material (namely, what is already given) very soon reaches its apex and then usually subsides, the development of the genius, which seeks new pathways into the boundless, extends throughout a lifetime. And therefore it comes about that no one single moment in this development is like another. Each stage is simultaneously a preparation for the next stage. It is an eternal metamorphosis, an uninterrupted growth of new shoots from a single kernel. It is then clear why two widely separated points in this development are so strangely different from each other that at first one does not recognize how much they belong together. Only on closer study does one perceive in the potentialities of the earlier period the certainties of the later one.

The pictures of Mahler furnish me with remarkable proof of this statement.

Here is one which shows him at the age of about eighteen. Everything is still unrevealed. This is a youth who still does not foresee what will take place within him. He does not look like those young artists to whom it is more important to look great than to be great. He looks like one who is waiting for something which is about to happen, but which he does not yet know about. A second picture shows him about twenty-five years old. Here something has already taken place. Curiously, the forehead has become higher; the brain obviously takes up more room. And the features! Formerly, in spite of all their striking seriousness, they were almost those of one who wants to gather a little more strength before he sets to work; now they are tense. They betray that he already knows the good and evil of the world, but they are almost arrogant; he will soon make all of them look small. But now we skip to the head of the fifty-year-old man. This development seems miraculous. It shows almost no resemblance to the youthful pictures. The development from within has given it a form which, I might say, has swallowed up all the previous phases. Certainly they too are contained in the final form. Certainly anyone who can see has already detected the whole man in the youthful pictures. But, when one looks backwards at the earlier stages— though they themselves are certainly expressive, it is as difficult to discover the expression of the mature man in them as it is to see the beams of a lesser light next to a very bright one. One must avert one's eyes from the certainties of the older face for a long time before one can again see the potentialities in the younger one. Here the thoughts and feelings that moved this man have created a form. This is not what happens to the young geniuses who look their best when they are young, and who turn into Philistines, even outwardly and visibly, when they grow older. One cannot learn one's appearance. And what one has learned does not remain, but goes away. But what is inborn goes from one climax to the next, develops itself to ever higher forms of expression. It makes leaps which become more enigmatic to the observer the more urgently he desires to understand them. Mahler's development is one of the most overwhelming ones. Actually, everything which will characterize him is already present in the First Symphony; here already his life-melody begins, and he merely develops it, unfolds it to the utmost extent. Here are his devotion to nature and his thoughts of death. He is still struggling with fate here, but in the Sixth he acknowledges it, and this acknowledgement is resignation. But even resignation becomes productive, and rises, in the Eighth, to the glorification of the highest joys, to a glorification only possible to one who already knows that these joys are no longer for him; who has already resigned himself; who already feels that they are merely an allegory for even higher joys, a glorification of the most supreme bliss, as he also expresses it verbally in the letter to his wife where he explains the final scenes of *Faust*:

'*All that is passing* (what I performed for you on those two evenings) is but a *likeness*; naturally, inadequate in its earthly appearance—*but there*, freed from the corporeality of earthly insufficiency, it will become *real*, and then we need no more paraphrases, no more comparisons—likenesses—*there has already been done* what I tried to describe here, which is *simply indescribable*. And what is it? Again, I can tell you only through a comparison:

The Eternal Feminine has drawn us upward—we are there—we are at rest —we possess what we on earth could only long for, strive for . . .'

That is one way to reach the goal! Not just with the understanding, but with the feeling that one already lives there *oneself*. He who looks on the earth thus no longer lives upon it. He has already been drawn upwards.

In musical matters, Mahler's development exhibits an uninterrupted ascent. Certainly, the first symphonies already display great formal perfection. But when one thinks of the tautness and compactness of the form of the Sixth, where there is no superfluous note, where even the most far-reaching extension is an essential part of the whole and is fitted in organically; when one tries to comprehend that the two movements of the Eighth are nothing else than a single idea of unheard-of length and breadth, a single idea conceived, surveyed and mastered in the same moment—then one wonders at the power of a mind which could already trust itself for unbelievable feats in its young years but which has made real the most improbable.

And then in *Das Lied von der Erde* he is suddenly capable of producing the briefest and most delicate forms. This is most extraordinary, but understandable: infinity in the Eighth, the finite nature of earthly things in this work.

His Ninth is most strange. In it, the author hardly speaks as an individual any longer. It almost seems as though this work must have a concealed author who used Mahler merely as his spokesman, as his mouthpiece. This symphony is no longer couched in the personal tone. It consists, so to speak, of objective, almost passionless statements of a beauty which becomes perceptible only to one who can dispense with animal warmth and feels at home in spiritual coolness. We shall know as little about what his Tenth (for which, as also in the case of Beethoven, sketches exist) would have said as we know about Beethoven's or Bruckner's. It seems that the Ninth is a limit. He who wants to go beyond it must pass away. It seems as if something might be imparted to us in the Tenth which we ought not yet to know, for which we are not yet ready. Those who have written a Ninth stood too near to the hereafter. Perhaps the riddles of this world would be solved, if one of those who knew them were to write a Tenth. And that probably is not to take place.

We are still to remain in a darkness which will be illuminated only fitfully by the light of genius. We are to continue to battle and struggle, to yearn and desire. And it is to be denied us to see this light as long as it remains with us. We are to remain blind until we have acquired eyes. Eyes that see the future. Eyes that penetrate more than the sensual, which is only a likeness; that penetrate the super-sensual. Our soul shall be the eye. We have a duty: to win for ourselves an immortal soul. It is promised to us. We already possess it in the future; we must bring it about that this future becomes our present. That we live in this future alone, and not in a present which is only a likeness, and which, as every likeness, is inadequate.

And this is the essence of genius—that it is the future. This is why the genius is nothing to the present. Because present and genius have nothing to do with one another. The genius is our future. So shall we too be one day, when we have fought our way through. The genius lights the way, and we strive to follow. Where he is, the light is already bright; but we cannot endure this brightness. We are blinded, and see only a reality which is as yet no reality, which is only the present. But a higher reality is lasting, and the present passes away. The future is eternal, and therefore the higher reality, the reality of our immortal soul, exists only in the future.

The genius lights the way, and we strive to follow. Do we really strive enough? Are we not bound too much to the present?

We shall follow, for we must. Whether we want to or not. It draws us upward.

We must follow.

This, it seems to me, is what Gustav Mahler's work, like the work of every great man, was allowed to tell us. It has been told us often, and will have to be told us much oftener still before we grasp it completely. It always becomes very quiet after one of these great men has spoken. We listen. But soon life overwhelms us again with its noise.

Mahler was allowed to reveal just so much of this future; when he wanted to say more, he was called away. For it is not to become entirely quiet yet; there is to be still more battle and noise.

And we are still to glow with the reflection of a light which would blind us if we saw it.

I have fought here for Mahler and his work. But I have indulged in polemics, I have spoken hard and sharp words against his opponents. I know that if he were listening he would smile and wave it away. For he is where retaliation is no longer practised.

But we must fight on, since the Tenth has not yet been revealed to us.

6

'ROBERT SCHUMANN AS CRITIC'
Commentary on an Article by Otto Reiner in *Vossische Zeitung*,
November 6, 1931

REINER: (In Schumann's writing) there is a wealth of the most subtle artistic observations thrown away in marginalia, like small change. . . . For example: 'On their own, the ideas of Kalkbrenner and of Beethoven resemble each other. Their context makes all the difference. . . . Dissect a Beethoven symphony. Tear out even the most beautiful of ideas, and then see whether, in itself, it is significant!'. Is not the entire protest against the over-valuing of 'inspiration' here expressed in a couple of sentences—the appeal to the total musical impression, the very thing on which Paul Bekker has recently based an aesthetic of symphonic form?

SCHOENBERG: Naturally, neither the one nor the other is true. Beethoven's themes doubtless differ from Kalkbrenner's—I do not know him. The second hand always ensures that, and the first need do nothing to oppose it. And Beethoven's themes are in themselves obviously very beautiful and apt to arouse the deepest interest. Even were there no other reason, they must be so because no single moment in a work of art may neglect to be so. Why should the themes be any exception? A homogeneous structure is never built from uneven material!

But—and this also straightens out the kinks in the theory of inspiration—what occurs to one as 'inspiration' is not the theme but *the work*, just as (I am always saying this!) an apple-tree thinks up a complete apple, and a man produces a complete child, not merely parts of them. But the theme is a special formation, an accessibly plastic one, required by certain forms in order to provide a fitting point of departure for the later development. Since in its course this may wander far afield (subsidiary idea, variation, modulation(!)), the principal theme must be moulded so as to be very easy to grasp and liable to stick in the mind.

REINER: Browsing among Schumann's writings, one indeed meets with still more surprises. Schumann was quite right when he sometimes called his periodical[1] a paper 'for the music of the future'. There is a whole series of passages in which he anticipates much later insights and views. Long before Albert Schweitzer he recognized in Bach's fugues 'character-pieces of the loftiest kind—at times, truly poetic formations.'

SCHOENBERG: In its day, that was certainly a profitable thing to do. For the only way to make great ideas accessible to one's contemporaries was—and is: it goes on!—to make them tasty, to have them awaken 'moods' which should rather be left sleeping, to use sleight-of-hand so that every disturbing feature of the idea disappears. Nothing is more unpopular than brain. One man's brain arouses many others' feelings—to put it generously: for one may well have one's doubts about such feelings. They are certainly there merely to gainsay the original brain. No more than that. 'No feeling without brain!'—that is what I believe.

In its time, this way of establishing contact, at least, between musicians and Bach may indeed have been of service. But it did a lot of harm. Bach's music does undoubtedly contain images born of a fantasy in which a man's world-feeling (*Weltgefühl*), world plus feeling, is expressed—expressed in the pictorial language of music, in a language, via a mode of expression, a handling of this language and a complex consistency of presentation, all of which—at least for the musician—should take no second place (that is to say, should not merely come after whatever fascinates him in a human way, i.e. the vision of the world). So the musician, just because he is a musician, should be intensely interested to discover (and delight in), the *way* this mode of expression works, and what kind of brain, stretched to its limits, could succeed in presenting such images, such feelings. After all, they are not everyday images and feelings ('at times, truly poetic formations'), so they require for their presentation a brain that is no everyday one either.

And that is where Schumann made his mistake; he underlaid Bach with everyday images and feelings in order to distract attention when it was time to grasp

473

his unusual ones. *They* would have put people off: too much brain was needed to produce them.

Barcelona. November 11, 1931

7

ALBAN BERG (1)
1949

When Alban Berg came to me in 1904, he was a very tall youngster and extremely timid. But when I saw the compositions he showed me—songs in a style between Hugo Wolf and Brahms—I recognized at once that he was a real talent. Consequently I accepted him as pupil, though at this time he was unable to pay my fee. Later his mother inherited a great fortune and told Alban, as they now had money, he could enter the conservatory. I was told that Alban was so upset by this assumption that he started to weep and could not stop weeping until his mother allowed him to continue with me.

He was always faithful to me and remained so during all of his short life. Why did I tell this story? Because I was greatly surprised when this soft-hearted, timid young man had the courage to engage in a venture which seemed to invite misfortune: to compose *Wozzeck*, a drama of such extraordinary tragedy that it seemed forbidding to music. And even more: it contained scenes of everyday life which were contrary to the concept of opera which still lived on stylized costumes and conventionalized characters.

He succeeded. *Wozzeck* was one of the greatest successes of opera.

And why? Because Berg, this timid man, was a strong character who was faithful to his ideas, just as he was faithful to me when he was almost forced to discontinue studying with me.

He succeeded with his opera as he had succeeded in his insistence on studying with me. Making the belief in ideas one's own destiny is the quality which makes the great man.

ALBAN BERG (2)
1930

I gladly take the chance of paying my tribute to the work and creation of my pupil and friend Alban Berg. For he and our mutual friend, his fellow-pupil Anton von Webern, were after all the most powerful confirmation of my effect as a teacher, and these are after all the two who in times of the severest artistic distress gave me support so firm, so reliable, so full of affection, that nothing better is to be found in this world.

But anyone who would like to believe that I am here only repaying gratitude and friendship by these words of recognition must not forget that I can read a score; that from certain scores which at that time struck all other musicians as hieroglyphics I could gain a living image of the ideas there, and arrive at an impression of this talent. And it is my pride that the certainty of this impression, and its correctness, put me in a position to guide these high gifts whither they had to go: to the most wonderful flowering of their individuality, to complete independence. But the necessary character—that, he himself provided; it was there from the very first lesson. And he will retain it to his last hour.

I would most like to say: 'Friendship above all!'

But I have to say: 'Art above all!'

Here again I need not hesitate; here the demands of friendship and of art are one; here the friend can exuberantly praise the artist, and the artist the friend. Indeed, both have to, if they are to be just.

And I want to be just: hail, Alban Berg!

April 10, 1930

GEORGE GERSHWIN
1938

Many musicians do not consider George Gershwin a serious composer. But they should understand that, serious or not, he is a composer—that is, a man who lives in music and expresses everything, serious or not, sound or superficial, by means of music, because it is his native language. There are a number of composers, serious (as they believe) or not (as I know), who learned to add notes together. But they are only serious on account of a perfect lack of humour and soul.

It seems to me that this difference alone is sufficient to justify calling the one a composer, but the other none. An artist is to me like an apple tree: When his times comes, whether he wants it or not, he bursts into bloom and starts to produce apples. And as an apple tree neither knows nor asks about the value experts of the market will attribute to its product, so a real composer does not ask whether his products will please the experts of serious arts. He only feels he has to say something; and says it.

It seems to me beyond doubt that Gershwin was an innovator. What he has done with rhythm, harmony and melody is not merely style. It is fundamentally different from the mannerism of many a serious composer. Such mannerism is based on artificial presumptions, which are gained by speculation and are conclusions drawn from the fashions and aims current among contemporary composers at certain times. Such a style is a superficial union of devices applied to a minimum of idea, without any inner reason or cause. Such music could be taken to pieces and put together in a different way, and the result would be the same nothingness expressed by another mannerism. One could not do this with Gershwin's music. His melodies are not products of a combination, nor of a mechanical union, but they are units and could therefore not be taken to pieces. Melody, harmony and rhythm are not welded together, but cast. I do not know it, but I imagine, he improvised them on the piano. Perhaps he gave them later the finishing touch; perhaps he spent much time to go over them again and again— I do not know. But the impression is that of an improvisation with all the merits and shortcomings appertaining to this kind of production. Their effect in this regard might be compared to that of an oration which might disappoint you when you read and examine it as with a magnifying glass—you miss what touched you so much, when you were overwhelmed by the charm of the orator's personality. One has probably to add something of one's own to re-establish the first effect. But it is always that way with art—you get from a work about as much as you are able to give to it yourself.

I do not speak here as a musical theorist, nor am I a critic, and hence I am not forced to say whether history will consider Gershwin a kind of Johann Strauss or Debussy, Offenbach or Brahms, Lehár or Puccini.

But I know he is an artist and a composer; he expressed musical ideas; and they were new—as is the way in which he expressed them.

10

KRENEK'S *SPRUNG ÜBER DEN SCHATTEN*
1923

I have just read quickly through Krenek's opera 'Sprung über den Schatten'. A talented man, anyway. Almost everywhere, even in the text, and throughout the music, one could put one's finger on his sources; but all the same this is a genuine talent. The only disagreeable, or at least incomprehensible thing, is the wisdom of this young man of 23 or 24; how does he know it is the same for the whole of humanity? From books? From literature? But wisdom such as that needs a basis of experience. To accept it uncritically from Wedekind, Kraus, Altenberg, Kokoschka and one or two French writers is journalistic. For if it is something that can be accepted uncritically, any new illustration of it is *superfluous*, and counts as at most the expression of an attitude. Which, after all, comes (if from a very different direction) suspiciously near the very idealism that tendencies such as these experiences set out to oppose! A distinction has to be drawn: one may very well value the needs of youth above the experience of age. But a younger man cannot grasp the vices of age with pity and tolerance. That is literature, as surely as it believes itself life. Merely a different literary *direction*! I do not overlook the fact that little else is possible. If a young man wished to express the things he had seen for himself, they could only consist of a certain blur, the haze before the eyes that comes of too much fire in the blood; the only truth in it all would be that he was not yet seeing anything. Instead, all young people demonstrate without exception (I was the same, incidentally) that they have artistic gifts, that their views are in keeping with art, and that they know how to present them in a way resembling art. Somewhere along the line there will then be signs of the unusual thing personally felt, personally said. For all that, I have to say that precisely in the sexual sphere do I find such proverbial wisdom disagreeable. Here of all places is it impossible to learn from others; here of all places is it natural to work very gradually towards generalizations, and here of all places does one owe them, unless they are premature, to comparison with other people's experiences. Perhaps one should only write others off into an inky grave once one has made one's own bed and lain in it for a while—and only in so far as one is absolutely obliged to do either. Here I am amazed at a young man's really believing nobody can 'leap over his own shadow'. I think it would be more like him to believe 'nobody old can', or, best of all, 'nobody can but me'. This last piece of wisdom I find more suited to man, particularly a young man.

But I believe something else—that it is not even the artist's business to come to such enormously knowing, universal conclusions. As far as he is concerned, what other people report always has something untrue about it; it was not experienced by *him*, but perhaps by *someone else*. Only what *he* feels can be true for him, so he feels; furthermore, that when anything happens to him it is the first time it has happened since the dawn of human consciousness—hence the importance of pinning it down as rapidly as possible in art: it could be lost to the world. Naturally, when one knows a certain amount of literature one knows (and, if sober-minded enough, one draws the distinction every moment!) that others have felt the same already, and that one must say things which (at least in literature) no author has ever felt before—things, then, one has also not yet felt oneself. 'Il resto no l'dico—ognuno lo sa!' (*Figaro*).

Moreover, this particular wisdom is so cheap that there is far more credit in being a fool, every man's fool, and remaining ignorant of it, except perhaps by hearsay. Take any youngish commercial traveller, with a sweetheart in every city: he will soon enough get to know all about love and fidelity. From the outset, a man like that is shielded against disillusionment of the kind sought by those fools who don't want to be told, only to feel! Traveller's tales are full of things that people already know; in any case they are unfitted to believe anything different. Does not a man such as Kraus realize at any operetta that his former views about the relationship between men and women hardly need propaganda making for them, but that on the contrary they are common property in the worst sense of the word? Is not a Kraus certain to find a Liebstöckl[1] clinging to him in devotion, however destructive his attacks, when it is a case of improving the world in this respect? Let the do-gooders at least leave to their unhappiness all those who are none the wiser once they have had something explained to them (since to understand it they are fated to sacrifice—vainly—their lives!). For who wants them to be happy? Their own like!

Musically, too, I have similar reservations about this work. Here, too, I find a lack of real faith in what is uncertain, untested, problematic, dangerous: the essence of composition with twelve tones. It is accepted merely as a matter of taste, a fashionable commodity; and, on the other hand, superstitious belief in the need for tonality, in the eternal laws of art, handed down but quite un-felt. Nobody can doubt that I have a good ear for tonality. I have proved as much. But that means I also have it for twelve-tone composition, and that is why in my *Harmonielehre* of 1910/11 I was already able to state the basic principle governing repetition of notes in the vertical. But since that is no commercial traveller's wisdom, preached and believed by commercial travellers, there are very many young masters (we are living in the age of very young masters) who prefer not to believe it. It could be, of course, that this law applies only temporarily, like the law about parallels. But I do not believe its time is already past—rather that it is only just arriving. In any case it is necessary, as I have already said elsewhere, first to satisfy with these resources alone all the demands posed by form. Perhaps I am old-fashioned here, but it strikes me (begging everyone's pardon) as a matter of honour. But apart from that, I heard from the very first moment that these chords will not, for the time being, mix with those used earlier.

Not to believe this strikes me as a sign of extraordinary talent, and in my view the only possible criticism is—that success was never yet so rapid! Incidentally the work is certainly not lacking in boldness. It contains difficulties almost approaching those in my theatrical works, and he certainly deserves respect for refusing to make concessions to ease of performance such as might detract from presentation of the idea.

There will be many a cross word about the presence of foxtrots and jazz. I find that quite unjustified: certainly the themes Beethoven, Brahms, Wolf and others took from, gipsy, Russian, Polish, Irish, Spanish and other music are on no higher a level, in themselves, than Negro dances (which have often been composed by white city-dwellers anyway). The question is always, *who* does it. It is not a thing I shall do. I have never had much time for any of that, and am pleased that once in the conversations with Eckermann I found something very applicable here. Goethe comes out against the cult of 'old Germany', saying he can understand someone's occasionally disguising himself, but not that someone should go about in a mask his whole life long. I think that applies directly to this question of using foreign folk-music: is one not going about in a mask one's whole life long, if one has got involved with foreign folk-songs even once? Perhaps not! Anyway, I do not feel inclined to disguise myself, even once. I do not want to gain any advantage from looking like someone else; but I do not like being mistaken for anyone else, either.

Much here makes a disturbing and disagreeable impression. Often one thinks of satire, of copies of styles; I thought it possible, for instance, that he was trying in the music of this character Goldhaar (is that not meant to sound like 'Schoenberg'?), to parody my style. Very inadequately, very one-sidedly, and quite wrongly, for in any case he has not heard the main point. But I do not in fact believe it, for I remembered at once that I had been struck by similar melodic turns in his very first works, and convinced myself that here there is in fact no more than a very high degree of dependence.

In a certain way Krenek seems to be following principles. It looks to me as if one of them, for example, could be formulated as follows: nothing systematic, even in the smallest figures. That comes somewhere near my principle (that is to say, it really exaggerates it) of never repeating without varying. As a principle it is certainly not a bad one. The only questionable thing is how to reconcile with it the use of such forms as passacaglia and fugue. Also I find these two forms in part pedantically adhered to, in part used with a freedom born of defective understanding. In any case, he does not see the point of these forms. But alongside all this condemnation, I must say that he is quite certainly someone who expresses himself as a musician. This language is his native language. Whether he says good or bad things, shallow or profound ones, the fact that he has to say them, and his ability to say them, are not open to doubt for him or for his listeners. And the impression given by the whole is undeniably original. Even if in many details one knows one has already heard the same from my teaching, or at least similar things in Stravinsky, Szymanowski, Bartók and the like. His length and the way he achieves it can be traced back to the influence of Mahler, Schreker and Reger. New resources in keeping with art of this kind, such as occur in my works, are not to be expected here, so far as I can see up to now.

Mödling. December 21, 1923

11

IGOR STRAVINSKY: *DER RESTAURATEUR*
1926

Stravinsky pokes fun at musicians who are anxious (unlike himself—he wants simply to write the *music of today*) to write the *music of the future*. I could not say such a thing without at least giving an inkling of the reasons why any music that is fully and truly of the present must also belong to the future. But I am not sure that is what Stravinsky means. He seems rather to find it old-fashioned to regard any work of art as significant for any period beyond the present. And he apparently believes this even though elsewhere he actually admits such significance, constantly finding new points to 'take up': Bach, Scarlatti, Clementi, etc. It seems to me, furthermore, that this attitude is no more deeply based than a good many other phenomena of mass psychology.

One example (naturally I can not pursue every piece of rubbish): nowadays it is the fashion to find criminals sympathetic. Certain deficiencies of the law, certain lapses by guardians of the law, particularly the police, have fostered this sympathy.

Now surely it is impossible to have a serious discussion with someone unless he admits that the following proposition is true: however imperfect laws and their administration may be, it still remains the duty of the enlightened man, even while he actively opposes a law, not to infringe it. A thief from principle is no less in the wrong than an unprincipled thief. It may be humane to judge the former more leniently, but this has the bad result that the latter then also comes off better. Many present-day people, with their petty journalistic way of thinking, contrast the dull policeman with the interesting, sympathetic offender. But no serious mind will see in this more than a cheap piece of fashionable foolishness.

It is rather the same here. In all fields of thought there is an undeniable need to produce things to last longer than grease-proof paper and neckties. It may be appropriate to build exhibition buildings to be pulled down after three months; to invent machines for weaving fashionable material; even pyramids need not be planned for all eternity. But, on the other hand, the aim in seeking a cancer cure can only be a permanently effective one; we want to know something unchangingly valid about the course of the stars and the fate of the soul after death.

Maybe for Stravinsky art falls not into this last category but among the fashionable materials and neckties. In that case, he is right in trying merely to satisfy the customers.

I, however, never reckoned to fall among window-dressers. Nor, I think, did any of those who are my models. And I believe not even Muzio Clementi may be so assessed, since he is still good enough to serve as a model for Stravinsky.

July 24, 1926

12

STRAVINSKY'S *OEDIPUS*
1928

The orchestra sounds like a Stravinsky-imitation by Krenek.

I do not know what I am supposed to like in *Oedipus*. At least, it is all negative: unusual theatre, unusual setting, unusual resolution of the action, unusual vocal writing, unusual acting, unusual melody, unusual harmony, unusual counterpoint, unusual instrumentation—all this is 'un', without *being* anything in particular.

I could say that all Stravinsky has composed is the dislike his work is meant to inspire.

My remarks about Stravinsky now strike me not only as less witty than they did a few hours ago, but as something almost equally bad: rather philistine. Naturally I can do nothing about it, even though it is evidence against me and for the work. I know, after all, that the works which in every way arouse one's dislike are precisely those the next generation will in every way like. And the better the jokes one makes about them, the more seriously one will later have to take them. I can make jokes here but should not use it as a way of by-passing this problem. And yet I can only say what I really think. Moreover I have to set down on paper—for my own sake (it is something I often forget)—that I am always prepared to praise Stravinsky, when I like what he does; that I am always pleased when I can like something, and that I am not at all fond of being malicious, though naturally as stupid as the next man when I dislike something.

But what do I care? I still believe this work is nothing—even though I really liked *Petrushka*. Parts of it very much indeed.

February 24, 1928

13

ANTON WEBERN: FOREWORD TO HIS
SIX BAGATELLES FOR STRING QUARTET, OP. 9
1924

While the brevity of these pieces is their eloquent advocate, such brevity stands equally in need of advocacy. Think what self-denial it takes to cut a long story so short. A glance can always be spun out into a poem, a sigh into a novel. But to convey a novel through a single gesture, or felicity by a single catch of the breath: such concentration exists only when emotional self-indulgence is correspondingly absent.

These pieces will be understood only by someone who has faith in music as the expression of something that can be said only musically. They can no more withstand criticism than this faith can, or any other. If faith can move mountains, disbelief can refuse to admit they are there. Against such impotence, faith is impotent.

Does the performer now know how he is to play these pieces—the listener, how he is to take them? Can any barriers remain between performer and listener, when both are men of faith? But how is one to deal with the heathen? With a fiery sword, they can be kept in check, bound over: but to be kept spell-bound—that is only for the faithful. May they hear what this stillness offers!

Mödling. June 1924

14

ANTON WEBERN: *KLANGFARBENMELODIE*
1951

Dorian-Deutsch[1] studied with Webern, and recently, when he visited me, he told how Webern was the first to write *Klangfarbenmelodien*,[2] and that I then used this at the end of the *Harmonielehre*.

Anyone who knows me at all knows that this is not true. It is known that I should not have hesitated to name Webern, had his music stimulated me to invent this expression. One thing is certain: even had it been Webern's idea, he would not have told it to me. He kept secret everything 'new' he had tried in his compositions. I, on the other hand, immediately and exhaustively explained to him each of my new ideas (with the exception of the method of composition with twelve tones—that I long kept secret, because, as I said to Erwin Stein, Webern immediately uses everything I do, plan or say, so that—I remember my words—'By now I haven't the slightest idea who I am.'). On each of these occasions I then had the pleasure of finding him highly enthusiastic, but failed to realize that he would write music of this kind sooner than I would.

It was like that when I had just completed the first two of the Three Piano Pieces, Op. 11. I showed him them and told him that I was planning a cycle (which I never wrote), among which would be a very short piece, consisting of only a few chords. This he found most surprising, and it was obviously the cause of his extremely short compositions. I also discussed what would be essential if a short piece were not to be merely a 'shortened' one: concentration of the expression and of the phrases.

But as far as *Klangfarbenmelodien* are concerned it is above all untrue that I invented this expression after hearing Webern's *Klangfarben*-compositions. Particularly, anyone can see that I had thought of progressions of tone-colours equalling harmonic progressions in terms of inner logic. These I called melodies, because, like melodies, they would need to be given form, and to the same extent —but according to laws of their own, in keeping with their nature.

I remember that Webern several times showed me compositions and insisted that I should recognize them as 'ternary Lied-forms'. When he tried to apply that to *Klangfarbenmelodien*, that was highly naïve. For progressions of tone-colours would certainly demand constructions different from those required by progressions of tones, or of harmonies. For they were all that, and specific tone-colours as well.

Klangfarbenmelodien would demand a particular organization, which would perhaps show a certain similarity to other musical forms; but they would have to take into account the demands imposed by a new factor, tone-colours. Quite different forms had to be produced by homophony and by the art of counterpoint. The latter did not have the chance of linking contrasted phrases with each other; but since homophony freed harmony from the obligations imposed by the art of counterpoint, with its combinations of parts, it could find a different way of working out its material.

It is certainly most naïve to think that *Klangfarbenmelodien* will be like ternary songs. The two will be no more similar than a scherzo and a fugue.

And since I could make no prophecy, I was content to use the expression, not thinking that it could be taken so superficially.

May 3, 1951

15

ZEMLINSKY
1921

The worldly-wise, should they want to establish exactly how much my assessment of Zemlinsky can contribute to their stock of common knowledge, would
have to subtract as follows: he was my teacher, I became his friend, later his
brother-in-law, and in the years since then he has remained the man whose
attitude I try to imagine when I need advice. So my judgement is partial (out
of partiality for my good and lasting idea of him), and my hand very much
swayed (by a predilection for virtues which have grown since I first began to
appreciate them).

Considering the low value my judgement of this master can have after all
that, I find it best not to pronounce one but rather to consider why it is so hard
to assess him adequately.

Anyone who has been at a first performance of a Zemlinsky opera and wit-
nessed its great success, then expected the work in question to go on a triumphal
progress through all the opera houses. But after a few performances it was all
over. This is what happened: the first-night audience included many musicians
and music-lovers, among whom there are still a good proportion capable of
absorbing an opera through their ears. But the success attracted the public to
the remaining performances, and the public is no more willing to be disturbed
by music at the opera than at the cinema—just so long as there is something to
look at. In this it is exactly like its theatre directors and conductors, who ask
first, 'What about the libretto?' Although it is hard for a musician to speak to
the ears of those who have only eyes, Zemlinsky is too good a man of the theatre
not to bear all this in mind. But for him it is as it was for Verdi, who browsed
vainly through the whole of literature, seeking a possible libretto. For people
like myself—I am no man of the theatre—the power of his music can open up
vistas wider than those of the stage; but the public, who see better, look to the
author of the text, by refusing the author of the music their interest. I do indeed
think that the opera composer, like the symphonist, can wait till he is understood. Let him think of *Fidelio*, whose untheatrical libretto was finally forced by

the music to *help* in creating a work of art unprecedented throughout the literature of the theatre: a stage symphony. Let him realize that one need not blame oneself, like Beethoven, who remoulded his Fidelio symphony into a new Fidelio symphony (which the public again recognized straight away as a symphony). Nor, on the other hand, need one believe, as Mozart did, that *Don Giovanni* is not for Vienna, though probably for Prague—since both were for it in the end. All the same I can appreciate that an opera composer would like still to be alive when success comes, and to discover then whether he is already speaking that language in which one can express oneself so that everyone thinks they understand, even if they take nothing in. To say everything, and yet to keep it so secret that the theatre-goer never meets with anything that might disturb him. Perhaps Goethe meant something similar when he explained that he had written so little for the theatre because he was too little performed.

Zemlinsky will only begin to be valued as his masterly talent deserves, when his librettist pleases the public. Only then will they see how hard to understand it all is, when one has only good ears and mind. And certain people will then understand why even I, who am in good practice, must listen repeatedly in order to perceive this beauty and fullness, despite the friendship and loyalty already adduced and subtracted. And I shall be forgiven, for by then people will have begun to hear his operas often enough to notice the music too.

But, in the last event, there is time for that: Zemlinsky can wait.

July 1, 1921

PART X

SOCIAL AND POLITICAL MATTERS

1

PARSIFAL AND COPYRIGHT
1912

When some time ago there was discussion of the question whether a prolongation of the copyright protection period for *Parsifal* should be aimed at, there was not a sharp enough separation of the questions involved. People with an unjustified material interest in the matter tried to hide behind artistic sentimentalities, so that others with justified claims were deprived of the courage to protect their own skin. The present-day trader in the arts loves to be regarded as a kind of Maecenas, and the artist, even when he sees through his emotion, is glad to believe in it, since, after all, it does only too much honour to art. That is probably why no result was arrived at—because people did not tell themselves clearly that here three questions are involved which should not be allowed to blur one another: piety towards Wagner's wishes, the artistic and moral matter of the sacred festival drama, and, taking in both, the legal and financial side which has to do with an author's copyright. Whereas the public shares an interest in the first two questions (since it sees itself as a protector in matters that affect its ideals), the third one involves mainly the standing of authors and also, to a certain degree, of publishers, theatre-directors, etc. Only the latter stand to gain when genuinely artistic and moral questions become befogged, for then they can advance their business interests. Let the artist simply stand on his rights: one will see that the idealistic side (which indeed concerns him most closely) does not come off second-best; and that the material-legal claims of artists always offend against the traders' sentimentalities, but never against an ideal interest. One must, however, make a clear separation: artistic-moral and financial-legal.

First, the artistic aspect. For me, for my feelings and for my insight, one thing stands beyond all doubt: those in Bayreuth could not possibly have desired anything but the thing they in fact desired—prolongation of the copyright protection period for *Parsifal*. No son may ignore the last wish of his father, least of all the son of such a father. For me it is clear that the demands of Bayreuth really have no other end than to fulfil Wagner's will, which has to be held as sacred there; to see that it prevails without second thoughts, even in matters where such second thoughts may be a downright artistic necessity. Siegfried Wagner is trying simply to fulfil the legacy of Richard Wagner, according to strict principle, even at the expense of art. Such a father's son—who as an artist is incidentally the victim, beyond all doubt, of a pedantic theory; who is valued not at his own worth but according to a supposed natural law by which an important man may not have an important son, although Johann Sebastian Bach had two very important sons, and although Siegfried Wagner is a deeper and more original artist than many who are very famous at present—such a father's son can act in no other way, even though (and this has to be said) his father would have acted differently.

Thus Bayreuth has simply come down on the side of a moral principle, and solely a moral principle. Not, say, an artistic one. Wagner's idea did originate in moral intentions as well as artistic ones. But since evolution has taught us to think differently on both points; since, for example, Wagner's taste in scenic matters, in painting, is rightly no longer shared by us; since his moral intention has achieved not what he aimed at but the exact opposite—we feel ourselves bound to his wishes only by a feeling of piety. On that point there are two possible attitudes. One, the son's; the other, the father's—that of the great revolutionary who saw that the last word in piety toward the masters lies in ridding their works' true essence of whatever in it is merely mortal, in order to let their immortality register in all the greater purity; who found altering the composer's express wishes not only within the bounds of piety but in fact a commandment. He was certainly the first to propose changing Beethoven's scoring, and to make corrections at points where Beethoven was bound to fall down 'since our wisdom is simplicity'.

Had Wagner lived to see how his idea, for all its initial beauty and morality, had become out-dated, and to some extent carried to absurdity, then he would have recognized that it was one of a great man's great mistakes; he would have loved it as such, with all the tenderness with which the great love even the defects of the great—but he would have taken steps to eliminate its bad consequences!

This idea has been carried to absurdity. Its intention—to give people of a high spiritual level a few sacred hours once a year—is not realized today, because it is for the most part not this distinguished public that comes to Bayreuth, but almost exclusively the artistic snobs of all nations, plus the arrested developers, the old Wagnerians, who are inimical to the art of their own day. These two types, who are certainly not the audience Wagner had in mind, predominate at Bayreuth, as everywhere else; and of the distinguished, only those come who are rich and independent enough to be able to visit a fashionable resort. But the artists and the true art-lovers, who have no money, have to stay at home, and I know a musician of repute who is no longer young and who has still not heard *Parsifal*, because he is not rich enough. Not to mention the many artists, painters, poets, and students, who go to every Wagner performance but do not know *Parsifal*.

Wagner cannot possibly have wanted this! For even if there were more grants to visit Bayreuth, they would provide a solution only in odd cases, not in principle.

Artistically, things are still worse. First, from the technical point of view. World-wide co-operation and work are needed to overcome the musical, instrumental, vocal, scenic, painting and other problems contained in a work such as *Parsifal*. We know indeed what great progress there has been in orchestral technique since Wagner, the new possibilities created by the work of important musicians. Anyone who ever rehearsed works that make great demands on the performers knows why a composer's will cannot be fulfilled—in sound-quality, for instance: so long as it is technically difficult, no instrumentalist will arrive at a hair's-breadth appreciation of the role his own part plays in the total body of sound. Each one plays with insufficient or incorrect expression, materially speaking too loud, though in places too weakly. Only when every difficulty can be effortlessly overcome, *and with Wagner that means only now*, only then can there materialize a sound, an expression homogeneous with the other formal values. Only then does unity materialize. Two figures speak for themselves: in Bayreuth *Parsifal* is given five times a year, while in Berlin or Vienna it would be given ten times, so that the musicians would have twice as much opportunity to become more fluent. I am certainly not overrating technique. But 'the material is a devil', which one must first drive out through technique, if one is to enter into the higher sphere of the spiritual. So it is indispensable for serious artists to compete in all seriousness at setting standards and then surpassing them.

In many respects Bayreuth is probably at the high level desired for Wagner's works. But its principle of keeping *Parsifal* for the leading conductors meant, for example, that the greatest musician of our time, Gustav Mahler, who in Vienna gave Wagner performances of unparalleled beauty—Mahler, who understood how to subordinate to the single, purely spiritual end everything that present-day musicians and singers can do, so that one could forget the existence of material and matter—that this musician never came to conduct *Parsifal*! Again, Wagner could not have wanted that.

But, it seems to me, the weightiest point of principle against the Bayreuth monopoly of performances is that a style cannot arise when the object around which it is supposed to develop is kept away from living influences. For style is not what people usually imagine. It is not something faithfully guarded, expanding only inwards with no further outward development; it is the opposite—something constantly changing, inwards and outwards. That pleasurable feeling of equilibrium, of poise, which we call style—how is it to develop, if one of its hosts remains the same while the other alters? How is it to exist, if the work of art behaves as people behaved in 1890, whereas the listener's sensations are the sensations of people in 1912? Nobody can deny that times have changed—not even the people who regret the change.

The Bayreuth monopoly is hardly calculated to produce a style, because it cherishes tradition. And tradition is the opposite of style, although the two are often confused.

For these reasons I have to decide against the Bayreuth monopoly of performances. But I feel that Wagner's will could be fulfilled according to his spirit, if performances of *Parsifal* were allowed only on holy days, as happens with Liszt's *St. Elisabeth*, for example. However, at least every other performance should be given exclusively for young artists, who would be admitted free. That could well be demanded of the many theatre-directors who are now growing rich on Wagner. And I herewith put forth this idea to the public for discussion.

Now for the financial and legal side.

First of all, there is no precedent, in a society based on private property, for anyone's entertaining even the slightest doubt whether an author has a claim to the proceeds of his works. The legal position before the existence of the current copyright law—a position in which artists went hungry when their works had long been bringing the traders very high returns—was something so monstrous that one can understand how those profiting by it tried to hide their shame by giving to artists, as a special favour, as 'protection' (expressed in the words 'copyright protection') something that is a natural right. It is incredible; no single one of our possessions (our property extrinsic to our own bodies) is so wholly our personal property as is everything of the mind. And that, of all things, was free to all. More: there is no property that the owner may not bequeath to his most distant descendants, without any possible legal objection. But the property rights in things of artistic value are limited to thirty years.

Here again we find that fog of sentiment at work, trying to make us believe the spiritual and artistic interests of the general public demand that editions of works should become cheaper. But if one takes a closer look, it is rather a different matter. Let us assume that the heirs of an author would, after the present copyright period, go on drawing a share of, say, ten per cent. A work now costing one mark would have to cost one mark ten pfennigs, and a ten-mark work, eleven. Such contributions are not so high as to prevent the broad masses from procuring books and music. For the broad masses always seem to have money to spare for trashy operettas and fashionable rubbish which are sold at much higher prices. And apart from that, it is entirely right that an artist should provide for his descendants, his great-grandchildren, and not for the artistic mob that buys trashy operettas. Any sacrifice on his part would be too great if it allowed such people to buy a cheap complete edition which the artist would not live to see. An author can learn a lot from seeing Lortzing's daughter or grand-daughter, who live in needy circumstances, at a performance of *Waffenschmied*, put on by a theatre-director because it is good box-office. I personally love Wagner so much that I include even his descendants, his most distant heirs, in this love—so much so that their well-being is more important to me than the libraries of so-called art-lovers. For true art-lovers, even if they are poor, do not shrink from sacrifices for the sake of a book they want to own.

So clear away the fog and let us see the facts it tries to obscure: *copyright expires after thirty years, not so that needy art-lovers can be given access to works at low cost, but because the other publishers are unwilling to stand by and see just one of them profiting by an author who sells well*—because those other publishers want to reprint that author. The reprint piracy, which copyright law makes impossible at least during the period of protection, will not let itself be entirely suppressed, and this is concealed under all the idealistic talk of 'free access'.

495

Anyone who has recognized this as the real reason for the expiry of copyright protection will now find it easy to agree with my demands:

1. The right of an author to the proceeds of his works should be made in every way compatible with all other property rights. The author or his heirs can do as they please with it, as with all other property. Let the right to inherit it exist as long as a right of heritability exists for other property.

2. On the other hand, thirty years after the death of the author it is in order for anyone to reprint and perform, provided he delivers to the heirs or their representatives a share of the proceeds, perhaps to be determined by law.

It is necessary to give the first publisher a monopoly of the work for a certain time, since he has to recover his costs. But it is just as necessary for it then to be taken from him again, so that editions remain dear no longer than is strictly necessary. The resulting competition would see to that. But it could harm neither the competitors nor the buying public to have to pay the author's heirs a share of the profits.

A copyright law of this kind would do justice to all who deserve it, and to others too. I know and am convinced that it was not for the sake of money that Bayreuth tried to have the copyright protection period prolonged. The continuing flow of income would have enabled Wagner's heirs to keep their performances of *Parsifal* at such a level that they would have been the only ones, even though there are others: the only ones wholly on a level in keeping with Wagner's demand that the work be a sacred festival-drama.

This copyright law should be made retroactive, so that a share would have to be paid on the works even of authors long dead. If there are no longer any living heirs of the author, the contributions would go to an account devoted to the following purposes: sickness- and old-age insurance for artists and their surviving relatives, scholarships for young artists, and printing and performance of their works.

Once rid of the fog of sentiment so dear to the traders, there is an open view into possibilities no serious sensibility may ignore. It seems to me more just to bear these in mind than to consider the traders—and more productive. And so I hope that artists will be found to take up my idea, and to help in realizing it.

Berlin-Zehlendorf. February 1912

2

COPYRIGHT
1949

The copyright law was considered up to now as forbidding pirates to steal an author's property before a maximum of fifty-six years after its registration. After this time every pirate could use it freely, making great profits without letting the real owner 'participate' in the profits of his property.

The moral which had created a law of this kind seemed so low and unintelligible that one always wondered in whose interest it was created, and why an author should be deprived of his property only for the advantage of shameless pirates, while every other property could be inherited by the most distant relatives for centuries. Nobody can prove that the 10 per cent which the author —the creator, the real owner of this property—would receive after the fifty-six years would have caused any damage to the public. Because, if a work is still sellable after fifty-six years, the editions which a publisher prints can be so large that the cost of products decreases to 25 per cent of the cost of the smaller editions. Accordingly, the prices after the expiration of the 'protection period' go down 60 per cent and more (as, for instance, the cases of Wagner and Brahms indicate). Accordingly, even at 60 per cent plus 10 per cent for the author, the public would buy the work for much less than during the 'protection period'.

All this seems to be perfectly senseless and one can only think that it is maliciousness against the heirs of an author—while other heirs remain unmolested!

Now I have discovered the true solution to this problem:

At the time when this law was made there did not yet exist the so-called 'small rights'; there was not yet the radio, the movies, recordings, there was no payment for performance. At this time most authors sold their works to a publisher entirely, with all rights included. The participation of the authors in royalties of sales, of rentals, of performances, recordings, radio, and movie transcriptions was not foreseen by the author nor by the publisher. I conclude that the law was not made to deprive the author of his property.

It was made in analogy to the patent laws, admitting exclusive rights only for a limited time. A publisher, a manufacturer was not considered as the only one who should profit from other people's creation. And especially in respect to the patent laws there are many interests which require protection. Never could it have become possible that everybody could travel by railroad or steamship or possess an automobile, if one manufacturer had the production monopolized. One should also here regret the poor inventor who seems to be damaged. But generally an inventor is forced to sell his patent to a powerful man, because he is unable to produce himself. If there were such a thing as 'Human Rights', he should be protected—though the risk of marketing a new invention is a great one, and seldom is an invention from the very beginning perfect enough to become a success. Think of all the improvements which were required to make an automobile as perfect as it must be.

Such is not the case in the realm of copyright. A publisher's risk is not as large and he usually gambles on several numbers, one of which might cover all possible losses. The publisher is seldom forced to make improvements. Generally the works are finished and ready to be sold. Still, if one had the monopoly, he would not reduce the prices, as Schott's and Simrock's attitude proved, and therefore his rights must be limited. He is still thereafter in the position to compete successfully with the pirates, especially if he improves his editions.

It seems to me that this was the intention of the lawmakers. It is regrettable that they had no imagination to foresee at least some of the values which might be added to a work, and that they worded this law so poorly that the wrong interpretation was possible—that the law wanted to deprive the creator and serve the pirates.

How it was possible to extend this misinterpretation to royalties, performance fees, recording fees, etc., is entirely unintelligible. Admitting that the lawmakers in whose hands our destiny was delivered were unthinking and possessed no imagination, one is still surprised that nobody tried to find out for which purposes such a law should serve. In whose interest was it? Is the interest of those people to whom it is advantageous worthy of protection? Or is this law based on the same consideration as the law which protects the criminal instead of the victim?

3

SUCCESS—THE END OF BOHEMIANISM
1928

Although any generation seems to think its own Bohemianism was the last, one really doubts whether our kind still exists—that is to say, the romantic Bohemianism based principally on being good at earning nothing and bad at managing just the same; being regularly and happily on one's last legs, and laughing at precisely that, rather than losing one's sense of humour; and, most of all, on having a self-confidence which only put up with being passive because one's every-ready fantasy, working independently, immediately created a world of activity. Did not this Bohemianism live on odds and ends of non-possessions, feed itself on anecdotes of debts acquired though not paid, keep itself warm by running away from creditors, and find material for its clothes in the material advantages it arrogantly rejected?

Was it really so asocial, though? Certainly it did all that merely for honour's sake (something uncharacteristic of people in general)—'disinterestedly', merely out of the conviction that certain renunciations are necessary and certain comforts dispensable. An artist who is no Bohemian: what an impossibility! But in the end practically every one of the many I have known lost his only possession, which was just this Bohemian's honour; lost it through the worst offence a true Bohemian can commit—through a success for which he was at least unconsciously to blame.

In this shameful way nearly all those I have known sank to the heights of the top civic positions.

They were no true Bohemians, then! Joking apart, the thoroughgoingness of that way of life, the deliberate nature of its morality, the exaggeration it shows at every point—all that spells imitation, and even here we find the calm self-evident quality of the born Bohemian replaced by extremism, heatedness and complacency. Certainly Bohemians 'for the duration', such as we all were, have to get through it quicker, since they stay only a short while. True Bohemians never stop being Bohemian. They certainly have laws less strict than do those 'more Popish than the Pope'. Their law is within themselves and differs in some way from that

499

of other men, so that they seem never to be rightly placed to make contact with the rest of mankind. Their condition reminds me of one that often happens with me on waking up. I seem temporarily to have lost my sense of direction, cannot find my way into the mutual relationship of position between my body and the window or the bed or the door, and I have a feeling roughly as if my right side were on the left. I explain it to myself by saying that my soul has been outside my body, and on its return it has got in the wrong way round.

I think that true Bohemians must feel rather like that! Much, or indeed all, that we and they see as right, they feel as left.

They, and only they, are the ones who will never find the calm of the good citizen!

4

DOES THE WORLD LACK A PEACE-HYMN?
1928

The question of peace and war is not a human one but, on the contrary, a political one—that is a fact I cannot overlook. But I have nothing to do with politics—in whose utterances, at even their most nonsensical, human, artistic or any other similar feelings still have no influence—and I would rather be allowed to keep my irrelevant private opinions to myself.

There are further reasons why one cannot seriously believe that the arts influence political happenings. Artistically speaking, it is all the same whether someone paints, writes or composes; his style is anchored in his time. But by what chord would one diagnose the Marxist confession in a piece of music, and by what colour the Fascist one in a picture?

Perhaps the outermost surface of a peace hymn, the words' bright, simple, direct message, which does indeed often serve in works of art to divert one's attention from the ideas that lie far below—perhaps such naked and open poverty could have some sort of effect in reconciling the peoples. Through its pitiful quality. Similarly, music at a comparably unorganized level can be a world-wide platform for banality and lack of ideas, and so serve to 'put the peoples in touch'. But that a *work of art* should exert any such influence is neither to be hoped nor to be wished.

So it can not be an artist's business to write such hymns, either. The truly popular ones show no signs of art; neither the *Marseillaise* nor the *Internationale*. And surely *God Save the King*, when originally composed, had a different tempo and character from those it has as now sung.

I have no exact information as to when war-songs such as the *Marseillaise*, the *Internationale* or the Fascist hymn saw the light, but I believe Beethoven's 'Battle of Vittoria' was written only after Wellington's victory. And in all political matters that seems to me the only form of behaviour worth recommending to musicians as in keeping with the times—*post festum*. Music then arrives just in time for the feast.

5

TWO SPEECHES ON THE JEWISH SITUATION
1934 and 1935

I

Ladies and Gentlemen:

There are among you certainly many who know about my person only the fact of my so-called expatriation and probably some who know this fact for not much longer than a few minutes.

They fear—I can understand it—to hear now some of those nightmare-tales which cause an agreeable kind of shuddering and give the speaker the feeling of having deeply affected his hearers, and, in that regard, are very satisfactory. But unfortunately they are not in the slightest degree as satisfactory if you regard their influence on the state of German Jewry or on World Jewry.

I must disappoint this part of my hearers, for from the very beginning it was my opinion that the state of Jewry cannot be bettered by such nightmare-tales or by fighting against Germany. But I want to abstain from politics and, preferring other subjects, I must disappoint also another group of my hearers. Namely, those who know a little more about me: who have learned from all the musical misdeeds attributed to my person—that I am the so-called 'father of modern music', that I have broken the eternal rules of musical art and aesthetics, that I have spoiled not only my own music, but also that of the classics and of the past, present and future times, that I am a sort of musical gangster who has forced men who know how to distinguish between Beethoven and Gershwin to protect themselves only by being conservatives, opposed to the terror of atonality —this terrible atonality!

I must disappoint them.

It is not at all my intention to speak about terrors—neither about the one which made me suffer myself, nor about the one by which, as I have stated, I made others suffer. I did not come into this marvellous country to speak about terrors—but to forget them.

Let us leave them!

As the snake was expatriated, as it was driven out of paradise, as it was sentenced to go on its belly and to eat dust all the days of its life—this was another kind of expatriation. For the snake came out of paradise and, going on its belly, symbolized, I fear, a certain lack of freedom. And, I fear further, the dust it had to eat, this poor food, was rationed out as in war-time so that the animal could not get enough to appease its hunger and was forced to eat ersatz-dust, surrogate-dust.

I, on the contrary, came from one country into another, where neither dust nor better food is rationed and where I am allowed to go on my feet, where my head can be erect, where kindness and cheerfulness is dominating, and where to live is a joy and to be an expatriate of another country is the grace of God. I was driven into paradise!

Hollywood. October 9, 1934

II

Ladies and Gentlemen:

When we young Austrian-Jewish artists grew up, our self-esteem suffered very much from the pressure of certain circumstances. It was the time when

Richard Wagner's work started its victorious career, and the success of his music and poems was followed by an infiltration of his *Weltanschauung*, of his philosophy. You were no true Wagnerian if you did not believe in his philosophy, in the ideas of *Erlösung durch Liebe*, salvation by love; you were not a true Wagnerian if you did not believe in *Deutschtum*, in Teutonism; and you could not be a true Wagnerian without being a follower of his anti-Semitic essay, *Das Judentum in der Musik*, 'Judaism in Music'.

Wagner, perhaps not sure of his own pure Aryan blood, gave Jewry a chance: 'Out of the ghetto!' he proclaimed, and asked Jews to become true humans, which included the promise of having the same rights on German mental culture, the promise of being considered like true citizens.

But it was not the destiny of Jews to develop like Wagner desired. It was not our destiny to disappear, to meld and assimilate with Germans or any other people. And fortunately it depended not on desire, propositions and suggestions from any well-meaning stranger, but only on Divine Providence. We had to remain Jews and, as always when Jewry was endangered by assimilation, Providence for once constrained us by her powerful hand to fulfil our duties as God's elected people and made the new-starting racial anti-Semitism her instrument.

What always happens with ideas when camp-followers develop them also happened in the case of Wagner: if Wagner were relatively mild, so his followers were harsh; if Wagner gave the Jews the possibility of living like citizens, his followers insisted on nationalism; if Wagner considered only the mental and moral accomplishments of Jews, his followers stated the racial differences. Followers always carry on to excess, and so we had soon to learn from men like Houston Chamberlain that there is a racial difference between Jews and Germans—that not only is the Aryan race a very superior race destined to rule the world, that not only is the Jewish race an inferior race and one to be detested, but, we had also to realize, the Jewish race possessed no creative capacity. It was of no value to argue against the very superficial philosophy of this poor man, nor against his theories, which are based on unproved statements, nor against the evident untruthfulness he brought about.

You have to understand the effect of such statements on young artists. An artist cannot create without being convinced of his creative capacity—at least an artist of higher art needs confidence in the necessity and originality of his doings. But though our situation was a very regrettable one, I do not want to speak more about it. Rather, I would like to speak about the effect of this racial condemnation on our contemporaries.

A surprising matter of fact—the influence of these theories on pure Aryan people was not very great. There were only small groups, among students mostly, which were subdued by them. And all the great Jewish thinkers, scientists, artists, writers and innovators, like Einstein, Freud, Karl Kraus, Max Liebermann, Jakob Wassermann, Franz Werfel, Fritz Kreisler, and all the others on a very long list, had as many admirers, followers and pupils, corresponding to their work, without any regard for their Jewish origin. And from my own experience I can tell you that the number of my Aryan pupils and followers was very much larger than I could have expected. It exceeded far over the rate which corresponds to the Jewish and non-Jewish population. Indeed, I personally found myself far more appreciated by Aryans than by Jews.

And now here is the point where you can recognize the terrible influence of racial theories—not on Aryans, but on Jews. The latter, deprived of their racial self-confidence, doubted a Jew's creative capacity more than the Aryans did. They were at best cautious and believed only when supported by Aryans, as, for instance, in the cases of Einstein and Kreisler. But generally they preferred to believe in Aryans and even in mediocre ones, so that, unfortunately, this lack of self-confidence led often to disdain of Jewish doings. 'He is only a Jew' (only!!), 'he cannot be of any importance.' And they turned toward non-Jewish celebrities.

Here are these deplorable facts, which make me appreciate so much your movement of Mailam. Helping the Hebrew University to build up and to maintain a music department is a very great contribution to the high aim of this institute.

I certainly neither neglect to appreciate highly the absolute scientific value of this institute, nor do I make light of the impression which Jewish scientific and artistic accomplishments cannot fail to produce on non-Jewish people. But I personally believe the most in the moral effect of such aims on *Jews*. To restore the Jewish self-confidence, to restore faith in ourselves, the belief in our creative capacity, the belief in our high morality, in our destiny. We should never forget that we are God's elected people.

He is only a Jew. No, he is a Jew and therefore he is probably of great importance!

I consider the activity of Mailam as a very important part of those activities which support our national and religious feelings and which will guarantee the eternal life of Jewry.

Let me thank you for the great honour I have enjoyed and for the occasion you have given me to express these ideas.

Mailam Reception. March 29, 1935

6

MY ATTITUDE TOWARD POLITICS
1950

I am at least as conservative as Edison and Ford have been. But I am, unfortunately, not quite as progressive as they were in their own fields.

In my early twenties, I had friends who introduced me to Marxian theories. When I thereafter had jobs as *Chormeister*—director of men's choruses[1]—they called me 'Genosse'—comrade, and at this time, when the Social Democrats fought for an extension of the right of suffrage, I was strongly in sympathy with some of their aims.

But before I was twenty-five, I had already discovered the difference between me and a labourer; I then found out that I was a *bourgeois* and turned away from all political contacts.

I was much too busy with my own development as a composer, and, I am sure, I could never have acquired the technical and aesthetic power I developed had I spent any space of time to politics. I never made speeches, nor propaganda, nor did I try to convert people.

When the First World War began, I was proud to be called to arms and as a soldier I did my whole duty enthusiastically as a true believer in the house of Habsburg, in its wisdom of 800 years in the art of government and in the consistency of a monarch's lifetime, as compared with the short lifetime of every republic. In other words, I became a monarchist. Also at this time and after the

505

unfortunate ending of the war and for many years thereafter, I considered my-self as a monarchist, but also then did not participate in any action. I was then and thereafter only a quiet believer in this form of government, though the chance for a restoration were at zero.

Evidently when I came to America such considerations were superfluous. My viewpoint since then has been one of gratitude for having found a refuge. And I decided that I, as only a naturalized citizen, had no right to participate in the politics of the natives. In other words, I had to stand by and to be still. This, I have always considered to be the rule of my life. But I was never a communist.[2]

February 16, 1950

7

HUMAN RIGHTS
1947

I

It is sad to have to admit that most men consider it their human right to dispute, even to overpower, the human rights of their fellows. Even sadder is the aspect of the world today, which offers no hope of improvement in the foreseeable future.

But this should not stifle our longing for a state of affairs in which the sanctity of each man's human rights is intangibly self-evident. Humanity has been benefited by all such blessings only because an ever-increasing number of people have yearned passionately for redemption until it was granted. All progress in social thinking and feeling which eliminated friction in community life has come about only through the force of such longing.

We must never give up our longing.

Let heathens continue to dispute the immortality of the soul, the faithful must never cease to feel its self-evidence. For even if the heathens were right at present, the force of the longing of the faithful would eventually generate an immortal soul.

And the same thing will happen with human rights, if only we do not stop believing in them—although they are as yet far from being universally recognized or defined.

II

Should the rights of the general law, i.e. the civil law, differ from the human rights, such differences should be designated as follows:

(a) Human rights should strive to improve the balance between claims and resistance, even in cases where the civil law has not as yet discovered a solution.

(b) A certain minimum of rights unchangeably valid for all peoples and races should be searched for.

The authority to make a declaration of human rights belongs to an organization which views itself as the avant-garde for the development of civil rights.

III

Law is only in the slightest degree an attempt to secure balance. In reality, it is nearly always an expression of power. True, the right of the feeble has enforced recognition up to a point, but it has enforced it in the manner a power enforces its ends. Disagreement arises, if unforeseen consequences had to be accepted because one had been overwhelmed by pity; reaction then is provoked.

IV

The difficulty of establishing right lies in the mutual opposition of those interests which are entitled to protection. Galileo, who cast doubt upon the credibility of the story of Creation, and the Church, which could not permit attacks upon the inviolability of the Scriptures, were equally in need of protection—and equally entitled to it.

In our much-vaunted civilization burning at the stake is out of custom. To a certain degree, at least, one can say what one likes (though let us not forget the 'third degree'). After all, Pasteur and Zola had not to suffer physically—but mentally only. And hardly anything (except some annoyance) happened to the doctor who propounded a new theory about diabetes, ten years too early.

War, the father of all things, has again furnished to the world new models, recommended for imitation. Troublesome expressions of all-too-free thinking are eradicated together with their originators. Their books are burned, their authors hanged, full-dressed generals without trial; they have no special rights, and feelings of shame are ignored because right is what benefits the German, and only remotely related to human right.

V

Fifty-one per cent could hardly be sure of winning a battle against forty-nine per cent. But by an election, they gain the ascendancy over a minority, subjugate them, and turn them into slaves.

The claim of protection is acknowledged even if the relation is two per cent to ninety-eight per cent. But the forty-nine per cent minority has lost all its rights—oftentimes even some of its civil rights.

But let us also not forget that microscopic one-man minority, not more than five to ten of whom are to be found, even in Western civilisation, in each century.

VI

A progressive development of civilization and culture, based upon scientific knowledge alone, would eventually have to accomplish equilibrium of conflicting interests. This might not take place for several centuries, for powerful opponents are struggling, and all such interests are recognized. But the more refined the methods of testing rights might become, the more numerous will become the demands. The Archbishop could dare to cuff Mozart without so much as suspecting that thereby he had won his place in the history of music. Who could know, in these days, to what an extent the artist's sense of his own dignity would develop? Who could foresee in these days that a creator might lose lust for life if he faced suddenly a thought contradictory to his dignity?

But, on the other hand, who could foresee that the contumely which was heaped upon the heads of Wagner, Ibsen, Strindberg, Mahler and others by the critics would finally be looked upon as a code of honour? No one could be a really great man without such enemies.

When will human rights—well, not prevent a man from having to undergo such experiences, but at least cause the others to be informed that it is shameful to have occasioned such suffering?

508

VII

Every scientist, technician, discoverer, poet, painter, or musician who has profited from the acquisitions of one of his predecessors contributes something to the development of his profession—whether this one or that one be an original thinker, or merely one who imitates or utilizes. One must not underestimate the honest craftsman who reworks familiar materials, and one should also not overestimate the original thinker. No one owes everything to himself alone.

Whether or not it must be tolerated that infringement is more highly rewarded than the alien property from which it was borrowed (though never repaid) is after all of subordinate importance. But, often enough, the real originator is taken for the imitator, when the real imitator is a clever propagandist. That is a falsification of the history of the intellectuals—but who cares, except the victim?

VIII

A gold mine, an oil well, a store, a bank, a factory, or even an oil painting cannot be taken away from the remotest descendants of their possessor by anyone. But the protection of owner-rights on intellectual works is restricted by a time limit during which it is a punishable crime to steal from the author or creator, not because such a theft is immoral and dishonourable, but because it would impinge upon the interests of belligerent powers. Because, after this period has lapsed, competition will force the publisher to sell more cheaply, but will still leave him sufficient profit, because he need not pay the author any more. Supposedly the work of art then belongs to the commonwealth, but in reality it belongs to the exploiters. After this period has lapsed, the taking of what is not one's own property ceases to be a punishable crime, though it has not ceased to be a theft. The commonwealth has only that title of possession granted to it by its power. This is senseless not only morally, but also economically; for the interest of the public in the work of art is far too slight to justify its taking upon itself the responsibility of exposing the descendants of the genius to the same misery as the genius himself.

IX

It is tragic that a code of human rights lacks the capacity of defending itself against attacks and annihilation to the same extent as does democracy. Everything which one might undertake in their name would violate the human rights of the attackers—just as everything is undemocratic which might protect democracy.

Their last resort is only persuasion.

X

It looks as if the code of human rights will have to limit itself to a smaller number of claims than its high-sounding title would imply.

XI

Most forms of faith are exclusive, and antagonistic—even militant, challenging, quarrelsome. It would be self-destruction were they tolerant. Think, for example, of Communistic or Fascistic states, in which faith functions as an instrument of government.

XII

Is it the duty of man to believe in truth? Is the right to believe what is false worthy of protection?

XIII

Surely, the Ten Commandments represent one of the first *déclarations des droits humaines* set forth in word and script. They assure the right to live and to have possessions; they protect marriage, vows, and work, but deny from the very beginning freedom of faith, because there is only ONE God.

XIV

'How can I truly love the good without hating the bad?' asks Strindberg. Consequently, he wants to combat evil—in fact, he *must*. This is why one man has to fight against 'bourgeois art', while another must fight against the Palestinian style of architecture because it is qualified foreign to the race, though, however, it stems from the great Adolf Loos.

He who fights will and must conquer, will and must oppress the conquered.

But what are the human rights of those who still believe in defeated art, in defeated ideas?

XV

Music speaks in its own language of purely musical matters—or, perhaps, as most aestheticians believe, of matters of feeling and fantasy. One can pass over Richard Strauss' good joke: 'I can express in music the moving of a pencil from one place to another.' That is not the language in which a musician unconsciously gives himself away, as he does when he formulates ideas which might even frighten him if he did not know that no one can find out what he hides while he says it.

But one day the children's children of our psychologists and psychoanalysts will have deciphered the language of music. Woe, then, to the incautious who thought his innermost secrets carefully hidden and who must now allow tactless men to besmirch his most personal possessions with their own impurities. Woe, then, to Beethoven, Brahms, Schumann and all other 'Unknown'[1] composers, when they fall into such hands—these men who used their human right to free speech only in order to conceal their true thoughts!

Is the right to keep silent not worthy of protection?

XVI

One must also recognize the rights of cannibals. Their claims are based on the instinctive recognition that blood becomes blood, flesh becomes flesh. In view of the primitive devices used to establish this as a scientific fact, one must grant a high rank to such an instinct. It functions more reliably than 'tests' on the basis of which suffering humanity is dosed with medicines the deleterious effects of which are already after one year observable.

XVII

Is it human right to be born or is birth control a human right? Is birth control permissible, or is it tolerable to let children decay as if they were surplus? What attitude do religions take?

XVIII

Let us think of the Hindus. They die, millions of them, in a famine, yet it would never occur to them to slaughter a cow, a sacred cow. How can we explain to people of such faith what is the right of men and, in spite of that, expect that they believe in human rights—these men who would die in silence rather than act in a manner contrary to the sanctity of their faith? Compare this attitude to that of the old lady who, when one of her favourite hens was designated for the supper table, first stroked and fondled it tenderly. When she then turned it over to her cook for the necessary preparations, she said, 'Poor hen! But you'll taste so good in wine sauce.'

XIX

These are real problems, and one could easily become pessimistic about them.

Nevertheless, one must never give up the longing for the universal sanctity of human rights.

In our soul there lies the power of longing with creative intensity.

Los Angeles. July 21, 1947

SOURCES AND NOTES

(References to: *Style and Idea* (1st edition, Dika Newlin, editor), Philosophical Library, Inc., New York, 1950; *Arnold Schoenberg Letters* (Erwin Stein, editor), English edition, Faber and Faber Ltd., London, 1964. Translations of German articles by Leo Black, unless otherwise noted.)

ON MY FIFTIETH BIRTHDAY   PAGE 23

Zu meinem fünfzigsten Geburtstag, in a special issue of *Musikblätter des Anbruch*, Vienna, August–September, 1924, honouring Schoenberg's fiftieth birthday.

1   Begun in 1917, *Die Jakobsleiter* remained unfinished. The first large section of it was performed in Vienna on June 16, 1961.

2   Neither the music nor the text of this choral work can be identified. The *Four Pieces for Mixed Chorus*, Op. 27, were not composed until the fall of 1925, although two of the texts may have been written at an earlier date.

3   The first twelve-tone pieces include the *Sonnet* from the *Serenade*, Op. 24; the *Waltz*, No. 5 of the *Five Piano Pieces*, Op. 23; the *Suite for Piano*, Op. 25; and the *Wind Quintet*, Op. 26.

4   *Satzkunst* and *Setzkunst*.

5   *Die Lehre vom musikalischen Zusammenhang, Die Gesetze der musikalischen Komposition, Theorie der mehrstimmigen (kontrapuntischen) Komposition, Gesetze der Komposition mit zwölf Tönen* (see p. 207).

6   *Eine wirkliche Zwölfton-Notenschrift* (see p. 354), *Eine neue Erklärung der Verzierung, Manieren, Vorschläge, etc.* (see p. 298), *Erläuterung, Darstellung und richtige Beschreibung aller Tempo- und Vortragsbezeichnungen*.

CIRCULAR TO MY FRIENDS ON MY SIXTIETH BIRTHDAY   PAGE 25

Rundschreiben an Freunde, three mimeographed pages, dated November, 1934. (See also Letter 163.)

1   A publication honouring Schoenberg on his sixtieth birthday, September 13, 1934. Published by Universal Edition, Vienna.

2   The clarinettist, Victor Pollatschek, had often performed *Pierrot Lunaire* with Schoenberg in Europe.

3   Chautauqua, in western New York State, was famous for many years as a summer centre of artistic and educational activities.

4   Otto Klemperer was musical director of the Los Angeles Philharmonic Orchestra from 1933 to 1939.

5   Suburbs of Vienna. At one time Schoenberg made his home in Mödling.

6   Schoenberg finally moved with his family in 1936 to Brentwood Park, West Los Angeles.

7   *Moses und Aron.*

8   The *Suite for String Orchestra* was composed in 1934 and first performed by Otto Klemperer and the Los Angeles Philharmonic Orchestra on May 18, 1935. Prof. Martin Bernstein of New York University also conducted the Chautauqua Symphony Orchestra.

HONORARY CITIZENSHIP OF VIENNA   PAGE 29

Speech of acceptance, delivered in English by Schoenberg, at a concert of the Los Angeles Chamber Symphony on October 23, 1949, a month after his 75th birthday. (See Letter 247 to the Burgomaster of Vienna, October 5, 1949.)

HOW ONE BECOMES LONELY   PAGE 30

Presented in English as a Cooke-Daniels Memorial Lecture under the auspices of the Denver (Colorado) Art Museum, at the Colorado Consistory Auditorium on October 11, 1937, during a festival of Schoenberg's music in which the Kolisch Quartet participated. The musical examples were recorded.

1   *Verklärte Nacht* was composed in 1899; its first performance actually took place in 1903.

2   The *First String Quartet*, Op. 7, was completed in 1905 and first performed in 1907.

3 Actually the *Kammersymphonie*, Op. 9, was composed in 1906, two years before the *Second String Quartet*, Op. 10. It was also performed a year before the latter, in 1907.

4 The *Chamber Symphony No. 2*, Op. 38, was begun in 1906, put aside shortly thereafter, and not taken up again until 1939, at which time it was completed in quite a different form than originally conceived.

5 The 'atonal revolution' must actually be dated from 1908 or 1909, when the *George-Lieder*, Op. 15, and the *Three Piano Pieces* were written.

6 *Pierrot Lunaire* is written for a chamber ensemble consisting of flute (and piccolo), clarinet (and bass clarinet), violin (and viola), 'cello and piano.

7 See *The Young And I*, p. 92.

8 Paraphrasing the end of the *Gurrelieder*:

Seht die Sonne!	See the sun rise!
Farbenfroh am Himmelssaum	Golden-hued in heav'n he gleams
Oestlich grüsst ihr Morgentraum!	Lights the East with morning dreams.

HEART AND BRAIN IN MUSIC   PAGE 53

First draft in English, January 18, 1946; rewritten April 22, 1946, for a lecture at the University of Chicago in May. Published in *The Works of the Mind* (1947, University of Chicago Press) and in *Style and Idea*, 1950.

A SELF-ANALYSIS   PAGE 76

Originally entitled *Maturity* (March 3, 1948), this essay was subsequently translated into German as *Selbstanalyse*. It was first published in English in the *Program Book of the New Friends of Music*, New York (November 13, 1949), and ultimately appeared in *Musical America* (February, 1953).

MY EVOLUTION   PAGE 79

The original manuscript, in English, dated August 2, 1949, was intended for publication in *Nuestra Música*, Mexico City, October, 1949. Corrections in the English manuscript and a German translation were made on August 16; the latter, under the title *Rückblick*, appeared in the September issues of *Stimmen* (Berlin) and *Oesterreichische Musikzeitschrift* (Vienna), in honour of Schoenberg's 75th birthday (September 13). As a lecture, in the original English form, it was presented at the University of California at Los Angeles on November 29. Publication of the article took place in the October, 1952, issue of *The Musical Quarterly*.

THE YOUNG AND I PAGE 92

Die Jugend und Ich, three typewritten pages and handwritten postscript, 1923.

1   *links liegend lassen*, literally 'leave lying on the left'—a reference, perhaps, to Schoenberg's more radical position. (Trans.)

2   In the meantime this has become true, as became known to me later through an utterance of Scherchen which is treated in one of my letters to him. Since this essay was written between the 19th and 21st of August, 1923, I had a premonition of this at that time. (AS). (The reference is not clear. (Ed.))

3   Handwritten postscript: 'This essay needs a reconciliatory ending from which can be elucidated that I am addressing the loud-mouths and not the young talents like Hindemith, Krenek, Korngold, etc. I mean: they should bear their cross as I bear my own! But not to court success.' September 25, 1923.

MY BLIND ALLEY PAGE 95

Meine Sackgasse, one handwritten page, 1926.

1   *die Katze in der Sackgasse.*
2   *Hinter mir beginnt heute die Sackgasse.*

MY PUBLIC PAGE 96

Mein Publikum, in *Der Querschnitt*, Berlin, April 1930. Schoenberg also attempted an English translation in 1933 or 1934.

NEW MUSIC: MY MUSIC PAGE 99

Neue Musik: Meine Musik, an unfinished project in a notebook, including, in handwriting, four pages of outline, twelve pages of sketches, and the first draft of five topics (24 pages in all): *Gedanken, Melodie, Wiederholung, Oper, Splitter* (see p. 337). No date is given, although Schoenberg himself noted later that it must have been before 1930.

1   Some of the passages (marked − + − + − +) are indecipherable.

1. IDEAS   PAGE 99

1   See bar 29 of the Prelude in c-sharp minor, No. 4 of *Das Wohltemperierte Klavier*, Book I.

4. OPERA   PAGE 105

1   Schoenberg notes, 'das ist also vor 1930 geschrieben', since his fourth opera, *Moses und Aron*, which was begun in 1930, is not mentioned.

2   The librettist, of course, was his wife, Gertrud, who wrote the text under the pseudonym, Max Blonda.

CONSTRUCTED MUSIC   PAGE 106

Konstruierte Musik: four handwritten pages, undated, but found with other short essays dated 1931 to 1934.

ON REVIENT TOUJOURS   PAGE 108

Original English manuscript dated October 1948. First published in *New York Times*, December 19, 1948; later in *Style and Idea*, 1950. German translation in *Stimmen*, Berlin, September 1949.

1   See Letter 224 to Josef Rufer, May 25, 1948.

MY TECHNIQUE AND STYLE   PAGE 110

Consists of two short handwritten pages in English, presumably written in answer to a questionnaire. It was never published, has no date, but undoubtedly belongs to the very last years of Schoenberg's life—thus around 1950.

1   Schoenberg probably means here the *Two Songs*, Op. 14, rather than the still very tonal *Two Ballads*, Op. 12.

Original manuscript in German, *Neue und Veraltete Musik, oder Stil und Gedanke* (completed February 10, 1933), described by the author as 'about New Music (from a lecture spoken at Prague)'. Among Schoenberg's first lectures in English in the United States, given in Boston in 1933 (or 1934), under the title, 'New and Antiquated Music or Style and Idea'; later revised, to the present form, for a lecture at the University of Chicago on May 16, 1946. Published in *Style and Idea*, 1950.

Draft of a lecture, *Kriterien musikalischen Werte*, in 1927; further attempts in both German and English during the ensuing years. English manuscript completed on April 24, 1946, for a lecture at the University of Chicago, May 23. Published in *Style and Idea*, 1950.

1   The winning opera was Humperdinck's *Hänsel und Gretel*.

Neue Musik, three handwritten pages, 1923.

Although both a German title, *Zeitwende*, and an alternative English title, *Change of Direction*, were considered, the manuscript, dated 1948, exists only in an English form with the above title. It was published posthumously in *Nuestra Música* (Mexico City, 1952) as *Momento de Transición*. Corrections in the English text by Dika Newlin, 1950.

Das Verhältnis zum Text, in *Der Blaue Reiter*, Wassily Kandinsky and Franz Marc, editors (München, R. Piper and Co., Verlag, 1912). Translation by Dika Newlin in *Style and Idea*, 1950.

Original English manuscript dates from 1949. Published in *Style and Idea*, 1950.

THE RADIO: REPLY TO A QUESTIONNAIRE   PAGE 147

> *Antwort auf eine Rundfrage*, two handwritten pages, 1930. The question-
> naire itself was not available.

1   The sender cannot be identified.

2   It is not clear to whom or what this refers.

3   Postscript added later by Schoenberg: 'Ibach did not acknowledge this
       letter. He neither said "thank you", nor do I know whether he printed it.'

'SPACE-SOUND', VIBRATO, RADIO, ETC.   PAGE 148

> '*Raumton*', *Vibrato, Radio, etc.*, five handwritten pages, 1931.

1   On 'open' strings a *true* vibrato is impossible. (AS)

MODERN MUSIC ON THE RADIO   PAGE 151

> *Moderne Musik im Rundfunk*, in *Radiowelt*, Vienna, April 8, 1933.

ART AND THE MOVING PICTURES   PAGE 153

> In *California Arts and Architecture*, April, 1940.

FOLKLORISTIC SYMPHONIES   PAGE 161

> Original English article appeared in *Musical America*, February, 1947;
> later in *Style and Idea*, 1950. Also translated by Schoenberg into German
> under the title, *Symphonien aus Volksliedern* (published in *Stimmen*,
> Berlin, November, 1947).

1   See measures 196ff and measures 409–15 in the same movement. (AS)

FOLK-MUSIC AND ART-MUSIC   PAGE 167

> *Volksmusik und Kunstmusik*, two handwritten pages with no date given,
> although there is reason to believe that it was written around the time of
> the Foreword to *Three Satires*, Op. 28—that is, 1926.

NATIONAL MUSIC (1)   PAGE 169

> *Nationale Musik*, seven handwritten pages, 1931.

NATIONAL MUSIC (2)   PAGE 172

Zu Nationale Musik, continuation of preceding article, four handwritten pages, 1931.

ITALIAN NATIONAL MUSIC   PAGE 175

Italienische Nationalmusik, two handwritten pages, 1927.

WHY NO GREAT AMERICAN MUSIC?   PAGE 176

The title of an article by W. J. Henderson, which appeared in the *American Mercury*, July, 1934. Schoenberg's reply to it is in German, 10 typewritten pages.

A LEGAL QUESTION   PAGE 185

Eine Rechtsfrage, five handwritten pages, 1909.

1   *Extrablatt*. The Viennese newspaper is not identified.
2   *Ein Notschrei vom Alsergrund*.
3   *The Second String Quartet*, Op. 10, which was first performed in December, 1908.
4   Literally: 'Mr. Liebstöckl has once again not picked out an eye of Mr. Karpath; on the contrary, he has closed one of his own.'
5   Schoenberg appended the following note: 'I wrote this article after the scandal at the first performance of the *Kammersymphonie* (1906 or 7), and sent it to Karl Kraus, who, instead of helping me to improve it, refused it with some rather objectionable explanation. How much I could have learned from Kraus in those days.' July, 1940.

AN ARTISTIC IMPRESSION   PAGE 189

Ein Kunsteindruck (no title given by Schoenberg), three handwritten pages. No date, although probably written at about the same time as the preceding article (1909).

1   Schoenberg wrote on the first page of this article, 'My scandal seems to have taught me to write, for although this essay (after the first performance of the Second Quartet) is still somewhat overblown and discursive, I was already writing better.' July, 1940.

As the date is given for the first performance of the Quartet—December 21, 1908—we may assume that this and the preceding article (which is dated January 16, 1909) were written shortly after that event and as a strong reaction to its criticisms.

ABOUT MUSIC CRITICISM   PAGE 191

Über Musikkritik, in *Der Merker*, Vienna, October, 1909.

1   'der nichts weiss von der Tabulatur.'—Hans Sachs.

2   'Der Stimmungskritiker', the critic concerned only with moods, feelings and intuition.

3   *Können*: ability, knowledge, power.

4   A reference to Brahms' Cello Sonata in F major, Op. 99.

5   Editor's note at the end: 'These remarks by the well-known radical leader of Vienna's musical avant-garde offer so much matter for disputation that we gladly throw them open to public discussion.'

SLEEPWALKER   PAGE 197

Schlafwandler, in *Pan*, Berlin, February 22, 1912.

1   The Maeterlinck song was *Herzgewaechse*, Op. 20, composed in 1911. The piano pieces played by Mr. Closson were the *Sechs kleine Klavierstücke*, Op. 19, also written in 1911. (Programme of February 4, 1912.)

2   Editor's remark: 'An artist of the seriousness of Arnold Schoenberg cannot be forbidden the opportunity to speak out. After he had stated his accusation against Leopold Schmidt we asked him to verify it thoroughly. His attitude remained unchanged.'

THE MUSIC CRITIC   PAGE 198

Der Musikkritiker (Schoenberg claims that the title was not his) in *Pan*, Berlin, February 29, 1912. A reply to Leopold Schmidt's reply to *Schlafwandler* (see 'Sleepwalker'), which appeared in *Pan*, February 22.

1   *Pelleas und Melisande*, Op. 5.

MUSICAL HISTORIANS PAGE 201

Musikhistoriker, one page typed, 1915.

1   Julius Korngold, the influential music critic of the *Neue Freie Presse* in
Vienna, and father of the composer, Eric.

THOSE WHO COMPLAIN ABOUT THE DECLINE PAGE 203

Untergangs-Raunzer, one typewritten page, 1923. The title suggests
Oswald Spengler's *Der Untergang des Abendlandes* (*The Decline of the
West*), which was published in 1918.

TWELVE-TONE COMPOSITION PAGE 207

In der Komposition mit 12 Tönen, no title given by Schoenberg: two typewritten pages, 1923.

HAUER'S THEORIES PAGE 209

These three articles were written during 1923 in response to various books
and articles by Josef Matthias Hauer expounding his own twelve-tone
theories. None of them was ever published. The first, without title, is
one typewritten page long; the second, entitled *Kosmische Gesetze* (*Cosmic
Laws*), occupies only one-half typed page; the third, consisting of three
large typewritten pages, is called *Hauers Theorien* (*Hauer's Theories*). (See
also Letters 78 and 79.)

1   *kosmische Aufschneiderei*, which means also 'cosmic boasting' or 'exaggeration'.
2   Entitled *Atonale Musik*.
3   'unartistic', 'not touched by the muse'.
4   Beggars, paupers (*gueux*).
5   Handwritten note at the end: 'Should be continued.'

'SCHOENBERG'S TONE-ROWS' PAGE 213

Commentary, in English, on Richard S. Hill's article in the January, 1936
issue of *The Musical Quarterly*, entitled 'Schoenberg's Tone-Rows and

the Tonal Systems of the Future.' Marginal notes establish date of writing as following shortly on the appearance of the article.

1   Schoenberg most likely means *Vom Wesen des Musikalischen*, which was published in 1923, rather than *Vom Melos zur Pauke*, which appeared in 1925—and was dedicated to Schoenberg.

2   Cf. *Composition With Twelve Tones*, p. 224.

COMPOSITION WITH TWELVE TONES (1)   PAGE 214

Published in *Style and Idea*, 1950. Notes for lecture (translated from German) at Princeton University, on March 6, 1934. Also presented at University of Southern California, Summer, 1935. Research lecture, in present form, at University of California at Los Angeles, March 26, 1941. Repeated at University of Chicago, May 2, 1946, with Addendum.

1   Curiously and wrongly, most people speak of the 'system' of the chromatic scale. Mine is no system but only a method, which means a *modus* of applying regularly a preconceived formula. *A method can, but need not,* be one of the consequences of a system. I am also not the inventor of the chromatic scale; somebody else must have occupied himself with this task long ago. (AS)

2   Still sometimes occurring in my first compositions in this style. (AS)

3   There are scores of mathematical geniuses who can square and cube in their minds. There are scores of chess players who play blindfolded, and every chess player has to work out in his mind the possibilities of the next five moves. There must not be many who can exceed ten moves, but only to them should one compare the imaginative capacity of a real musical mind. (AS)

4   As, for instance, in the fourth of the Diabelli Variations, Beethoven omits, in an inexplicable manner, one measure. (AS)

COMPOSITION WITH TWELVE TONES (2)   PAGE 245

Three and one half typewritten pages. Undated, but some references to retirement from the university, renewed interest in composing *Die Jakobsleiter*, and work on *Structural Functions of Harmony*, suggest that this article was written after 1946 and perhaps as late as 1948.

IS IT FAIR?   PAGE 249

Original English manuscript, dated December 2, 1947. Published in *Music and Dance in California and the West*, Hollywood, 1948.

THEORY OF FORM   PAGE 253

Formenlehre, six short typewritten pages, 1924.

TONALITY AND FORM   PAGE 255

Original manuscript in German, *Tonalität und Gliederung*, dated July 29, 1925. First published, however, in English, on December 19, 1925 in *The Christian Science Monitor*, Boston (translator unknown), and subsequently in *The Pacific Coast Musician* (May 4, 1935), in *Schoenberg* (edited by Merle Armitage, New York, 1937), and in *Music and Dance in California* (Hollywood, 1940).

OPINION OR INSIGHT?   PAGE 258

Gesinnung oder Erkenntnis?, in *Jahrbuch 1926 der Universal-Edition, 25 Jahre Neue Musik*, Vienna; later in *Le Monde Musical*, Paris, December 31, 1927, under the title *Tonal ou Atonal*.

1   *Der musikalische Gedanke und seine Darstellung* constitutes one of Schoenberg's most ambitious projects. It was first formulated in 1925, worked on intermittently until, at least, 1934, but never finished. It appears that many of its main topics were dealt with in later books and articles. For a discussion of its contents see Josef Rufer, *The Works of Arnold Schoenberg* (English edition, Faber and Faber, London, 1962, pp. 137–8).

FOR A TREATISE ON COMPOSITION   PAGE 264

Zur Kompositionslehre, in *Die Musik*, Berlin, May 1931.

PROBLEMS OF HARMONY   PAGE 268

Original article, *Probleme der Harmonie* (January 20, 1927), presented as a lecture at the Berlin *Akademie der Künste*. Revised for publication in

Modern Music (New York, May–June, 1934) with translation by Adolph Weiss.

CONNECTION OF MUSICAL IDEAS PAGE 287

Four handwritten pages in English; no date (*c.* 1948).

OLD AND NEW COUNTERPOINT PAGE 288

Alter und Neuer Kontrapunkt, two handwritten pages, 1928.

LINEAR COUNTERPOINT PAGE 289

Der Lineare Kontrapunkt, eight handwritten pages, 1931; commentary on the book by Ernst Kurth, *Grundlagen des linearen Kontrapunkts*, Bern, 1917.

1   Here Schoenberg makes a play on words: *vorgesehen, vorausgesehen, Vorsehung, Vorsicht, Voraussicht*, whose English equivalents are, respectively, 'foreseen', 'predicted', 'foresight', 'precaution', 'prediction'. (Trans.) Both the author (E. Curth!) and title are misspelled here and elsewhere.

3   In *Volksliederbuch für die Jugend* (C. F. Peters, 1930).

4   *Das Unaufhörliche*, published in 1931.

LINEAR COUNTERPOINT: LINEAR POLYPHONY PAGE 295

Linearer Kontrapunkt—Lineare Polyphonie, five handwritten pages; no date given, but obviously a companion piece to the preceding article, 'Linear Counterpoint'.

1   Ernst Kurth, whose book *Grundlagen des linearen Kontrapunkts* was also referred to in the preceding article, 'Linear Counterpoint'.

2   See 'Linear Counterpoint', p. 289.

FUGUE PAGE 297

zu Marc-André Souchaux 'Das Thema in der Fuge Bachs', one page handwritten commentary on 'The Theme in Bach's Fugue' by Marc-André Souchaux, 1936.

Ueber Verzierungen, Primitive Rhythmen, Etc., und Vogelgesang (also, on the first page, another version of the title: *Vorschlaege, Negerrhythmen, Zigeuner- und Naturvölker-Rhythmen und der Vogelgesang*); seventeen typewritten pages, including one page of outline and notes, dated 1922.

1   Long ago I tried to describe this fairly consistently in a study I carried out. (AS)

The reference may be to *Zur Vortragslehre* ('For a Treatise on Performance', see p. 319), 1923 or 1924. (Ed.)

2   Perhaps this also disposes of the view that 'fear of dissonance' led to this kind of notation. One could add the further counter-argument that, logically speaking, it should not have been the rhythm which one was allowed to write wrongly, but the note. And the note does not become any more consonant just because one writes the rhythm wrongly! (AS)

3   May I refer here to what I say on a related subject in my *Harmonielehre* (3rd edition, p. 24)? '... and the true relationship of these (exotic) cultures to that in Europe (and vice versa) may be compared to the relationship between a courier on horseback to optical telegraphy, or between the latter and wireless telegraphy: the most primitive form of the second surpasses in speed the highest form of the first, and the most primitive form of the third is just as superior to the highest form of the second.' (AS)

ORNAMENTS AND CONSTRUCTION   PAGE 312

Verzierungen und Konstruktion, one typewritten page, 1923.

1   Schoenberg's son Georg by his first marriage.

GLOSSES ON THE THEORIES OF OTHERS   PAGE 313

Glossen zu den Theorien anderer, 1929; seven and one half handwritten pages. Reference is made to Hindemith, Krenek, Gutmann, Westphal, Wiesengrund (-Adorno) and Redlich, whose articles or theories appeared in two leading modern-music publications, *Anbruch* (Vienna) and *Melos* (Mainz).

1   Collaboration with Bertolt Brecht for the Baden-Baden music festival in the summer of 1929.

2   Smoked bacon with pineapple, a favourite Viennese dish.

3   See 'Opinion or Insight?', p. 258.

4   Pun on the periodical *Anbruch*: *Anbrecher* means 'those who break in'.

5   See 'Criteria for the Evaluation of Music', p. 124.

FOR A TREATISE ON PERFORMANCE   PAGE 319

> *Zur Vortragslehre*, each article one typewritten page. No date for the first article, the second identified—later by hand—as 'about 1923 or 24'. It is presumed that both articles were written at about the same time and were intended for a text on performance.

TODAY'S MANNER OF PERFORMING CLASSICAL MUSIC   PAGE 320

> Three typewritten pages, in English, dated 1948. Corrections by Dika Newlin, 1950.

THE FUTURE OF ORCHESTRAL INSTRUMENTS   PAGE 322

> *Die Zukunft der Orchesterinstrumente* in *Pult und Taktstock*, Vienna, December 1924. Article signed by pseudonym, JENS.QU. ('Jenerseits Querkopf'), but authorship later acknowledged by Schoenberg (July 30, 1932).

1   *Setzkunst* and *Satzkunst* respectively.

2   *As-Klarinette*, may be a misprint for *A-Klarinette*, although a very high A-flat Clarinet was used in German military bands (see Adam Carse, *Musical Wind Instruments*, Macmillan and Co., 1939).

MECHANICAL MUSICAL INSTRUMENTS   PAGE 326

> *Mechanische Musikinstrumente* in *Pult und Taktstock*, Vienna, March–April, 1926.

INSTRUMENTATION   PAGE 330

> *Instrumentation* (German), seven handwritten pages, 1931.

THE FUTURE OF THE OPERA
PAGE 336

Two-page handwritten reply to an article on *Die Zukunft der Oper* in *Neues Wiener Tagblatt*, 1927.

I   This was obviously written before the advent of motion pictures with sound.

OPERA: APHORISMS
PAGE 337

Splitter, shortened form of *Gedankensplitter*, 'aphorisms' or 'aperçus'. Five handwritten pages, undated; continuation of article 'Opera' (see 'New Music: My Music', p. 99).

I   The distinction here is between *Schauspieler*—literally a player who is on show, i.e. an actor—and *Hörspieler*—a player who is heard. (Trans.)

PERFORMANCE INDICATIONS (DYNAMICS)
PAGE 340

Vortragszeichen, one typewritten page, 1923.

MUSICAL DYNAMICS
PAGE 341

Musikalische Dynamik, one handwritten page, 1929.

1   Postscript: I have written down this idea immediately, just as it came to me. So it is still very imperfect and unclear! (AS)

ABOUT METRONOME MARKINGS
PAGE 342

Zur Metronomisierung, two typewritten pages, 1926.

I   Cf. Heinrich Heine's 'Die Beiden Grenadiere': 'Was schert mich Weib, was schert mich Kind . . . lass sie betteln gehn, wenn sie hungrig sind.'

TRANSPOSITION
PAGE 343

Transposition (German), two typewritten pages, 1923.

I   Walter Seligmann was a pupil of Schoenberg. About the article Schoenberg comments: 'He wrote it at my instigation; the criticism, of course, came from me.'

2   'Enforces' means that they apply in all circumstances, and are quite impossible to avoid. (AS)

3   As noted by Schoenberg in the manuscript of his Wind Quintet, Op. 26.

VIBRATO   PAGE 345

In German, no title given. Undated, but references to recordings heard on the radio place this article some time around 1940.

PHRASING   PAGE 347

Phrasierung, two handwritten pages, 1931.

1   No mention is made of any specific book by Heinrich Schenker, although Schoenberg wrote considerable marginalia in his copy of Schenker's 'Der Tonwille', vol. 1, 1921.

THE MODERN PIANO REDUCTION   PAGE 348

Der Moderne Klavierauszug, part of a symposium in *Die Musik*, Berlin, November 1923; response to an article with the same title by Max Broesike-Schoen in *Die Musikwelt*, Hamburg, September 15, 1922.

ON NOTATION   PAGE 350

Zur Notenschrift, two typewritten pages, 1923.

1   See 'A New Twelve-Tone Notation', p. 354.

2   The reference is to musical works by these composers (not specified) and not to any of their writings about notation.

PICTORIAL NOTATION   PAGE 351

Noten-Bilder-Schrift, one typewritten page, 1923.

1   These signs, as far as is known, did not appear in subsequent compositions.

REVOLUTION—EVOLUTION, NOTATION (ACCIDENTALS)   PAGE 353

Revolution-Evolution: Notierung (Vorzeichen), one handwritten page, 1931.

A NEW TWELVE-TONE NOTATION   PAGE 354

> *Eine Neue Zwölfton-Schrift*, manuscript dated November, 1924; published in *Anbruch*, Vienna, January, 1925.

1   Busoni gives his proposal the title, 'Attempt at an Organic Piano Notation' (*Versuch einer organischen Klaviernotenschrift*, Leipzig, 1910) and says very aptly, '. . . and it has finally become clear to me that our present-day octave consists no longer of seven intervals but of twelve; and that each of these intervals must have its own place on the staff.' (AS)

2   But I do not really believe this will be necessary. (AS)

3   Universal Edition has had music-paper prepared according to my instructions. (AS)

PROBLEMS IN TEACHING ART   PAGE 365

> *Probleme des Kunstunterrichts* in *Musikalisches Taschenbuch*, Vienna, 1911.

MUSIC (FROM 'GUIDE-LINES FOR A MINISTRY OF ART')   PAGE 369

> *Musik, aus 'Richtlinien für ein Kunstamt'*, originally appeared in the weekly publication, *Der Friede*, Vienna, March 28, 1919. The other articles in 'Guide-Lines', on the visual arts, the theatre and literature, as well as the foreword, were written by the architect, Adolf Loos. The whole symposium was then published as a pamphlet (Verlag Richard Lanyi, Vienna, 1919). Finally Schoenberg's article by itself appeared in the collection, *Von Neuer Musik* (F. J. Marcan-Verlag, Cologne, 1924), with the 'Preliminary Remark' added.

1   According to Adolf Loos's proposal the Viennese state theatres are to serve to perform dramatic works as perfectly as possible. Each work is to be presented with such care and such expensive production and casting that thirty performances a season justify the work and expense involved. In this way each of the state theatres would perform some ten works annually. The system of distributing tickets provides for one attendance by each theatre-goer at each of the various productions that year. At the end of the season the works included in one years' repertoire will disappear for a long time, to make way for new productions. For the state theatres all literary experiments (first performances) will be ruled out; they will be left to the private theatres. For the provinces touring theatres will be organized. (Editorial note at time of reprint).

ON THE QUESTION OF MODERN COMPOSITION TEACHING PAGE 373

Zur Frage des modernen Kompositionsunterrichtes in *Deutsche Tonkünstler-Zeitung*, Berlin, November 5, 1929.

TEACHING AND MODERN TRENDS IN MUSIC PAGE 376

Two typewritten pages, in English, 1938.

EARTRAINING THROUGH COMPOSING PAGE 377

Speech presented at the Music Teachers National Association convention in Kansas City, Missouri, on December 30, 1939; subsequently published in the *Volume of Proceedings* for 1939 of that organization. Also in *Modern Music*, Fall 1946, under the title, 'On the Appreciation of Music'.

THE BLESSING OF THE DRESSING PAGE 382

The manuscript, in English, dates from 1948. Published in *Style and Idea*, 1950.

1   The reference is obviously to Nadia Boulanger.
2   In Thomas Mann's *Doktor Faustus*.

AGAINST THE SPECIALIST PAGE 387

Two typewritten pages, in English. No date given, but one of the anecdotes related occurred while Schoenberg was teaching at the University of California, around 1940.

THE TASK OF THE TEACHER PAGE 388

The manuscript is dated February 14, 1950; it was published posthumously in *Music and Dance in New York State*, 1952.

Eight typewritten pages, in English, dated March 10, 1950. Corrections by Dika Newlin.

1   'Hair-pulling, head-slapping, ear-pulling.'

2   I am not sure whether all this has not already been described by competent theorists. However, as I already said in my *Harmonielehre*, I have not learned this by reading but by thinking; therefore it is my own. But it seems to me that today's musical education is not always benefited by the tradition of the great line of Viennese teachers and theorists—the line of Porpora, Fux, Albrechtsberger, Sechter, Bruckner and Schenker. It seems that only musicians five or six years older or younger than I have had part of it. Many of them are dead; curiously, none of them was an advanced composer. (AS)

3   I have made use of such possibilities in the first movement of my Suite (in ancient style) for String Orchestra, which I had planned as a *Lehrstück* for students of composition, omitting, of course, those combinations which are not interesting enough. (AS)

In *Style and Idea*, 1950. 'This essay was originally a lecture delivered in February, 1933, on the occasion of Brahms's 100th birthday. This year, 1933, was also the 50th anniversary of Wagner's death. This is a fully reformulated version of my original lecture. Many things and some of my opinions have changed during that time, and now 1947 is again an anniversary of Brahms; he died fifty years ago.' (AS)

1   As misrepresented by Robert Haven Schauffler in his book of the same name. (AS)

2   I use in my music for similar purposes the symbols ′ and ˘, borrowed from prosody. Thus changes of accentuation and rhythmic shifts are indicated. See Ex. 51c. (AS)

Franz Liszts Werk und Wesen in the Liszt-issue (100th anniversary of the composer's birth) of *Allgemeine Musik-Zeitung*, Berlin, October 20, 1911.

GUSTAV MAHLER: IN MEMORIAM   PAGE 447

Gustav Mahler in the Mahler commemorative issue of *Der Merker*, March 1, 1912. Mahler had died on May 18, 1911.

1   Matthew 26:36.

GUSTAV MAHLER   PAGE 449

Manuscript for lecture in German dated October 13, 1912. Revised and partly translated by Schoenberg in 1948. Final translation by Dika Newlin for inclusion in *Style and Idea*, 1950.

'ROBERT SCHUMANN AS CRITIC'   PAGE 472

Der Kritiker Robert Schumann, Hundert Jahre Davidsbündler by Otto Reiner. Comments written by hand on two pages, dated November 11, 1931. Only passages pertaining to commentary have been reproduced.

1   *Neue Zeitschrift für Musik*, founded by Schumann and others in 1834 and edited by him from 1835–44.

ALBAN BERG (1)   PAGE 474

One typewritten page, in English, 1949.

ALBAN BERG (2)   PAGE 475

Alban Berg in *Die Theaterwelt*, Düsseldorf, April 10, 1930, on the occasion of a performance of *Wozzeck*.

GEORGE GERSHWIN   PAGE 476

In *George Gershwin*, edited by Merle Armitage (Longmans, Green and Company, 1938).

KRENEK'S *Sprung über den Schatten*   PAGE 477

Two typewritten pages, in German, 1923.

IGOR STRAVINSKY: *Der Restaurateur* PAGE 481

Der Restaurateur, one handwritten page, 1926. The title has the double meaning of 'the restaurant-owner' or, as Schoenberg probably intended it, 'the restorer (of art)'.

STRAVINSKY'S *Oedipus* PAGE 482

Oedipus von Strawinsky, one handwritten page, 1928.

ANTON WEBERN: FOREWORD TO HIS *Six Bagatelles for String Quartet, Op. 9* PAGE 483

Published by Universal Edition, Vienna, 1924.

ANTON WEBERN: *Klangfarbenmelodie* PAGE 484

One and one-half typewritten pages in German, 1951; no title given.

1   Frederick Dorian, musicologist and conductor, was born in Vienna and participated in the Schoenberg Seminars there after the First World War.
2   Literally 'tone-colour-melodies'.

ZEMLINSKY PAGE 486

Published in the Zemlinsky-issue of *Der Auftakt*, Prague, 1921, under the title, *Gedanken über Zemlinsky*—which Schoenberg disclaimed. Alexander von Zemlinsky composed at least six operas and was a well-known conductor of opera, particularly in Prague.

PARSIFAL AND COPYRIGHT PAGE 491

Parsifal und Urheberrecht in *Konzert-Taschenbuch*, Berlin, February, 1912.

COPYRIGHT PAGE 497

Two typewritten pages in English. Undated, but probably written around February or March, 1949, when Schoenberg was interested in a copyright case involving Stravinsky.

SUCCESS—THE END OF BOHEMIANISM   PAGE 499

Erfolg—das Ende der Boheme, part of a symposium on 'The Dying Bohemian' in *Berliner Tageblatt*, May 13, 1928.

DOES THE WORLD LACK A PEACE-HYMN?   PAGE 500

Fehlt der Welt ein Friedenshymne?, a symposium in *8-Uhr Abendblatt der Berliner National-Zeitung*, May 26, 1928. Schoenberg is introduced here as 'one of the leaders of the modernists in German music'.

1   A follow-up to the publication of the article is this letter from Schoenberg to the Editor of the *8-Uhr Abendblatt*:

I am most upset at having sent an article (for your questionnaire in the Whitsun edition) without saying I wanted to see a proof. I can understand it if the person who does this proof-reading job for you is so pressed for time that he fails to notice when two lines are missing. I am convinced that it is not any sort of cut, when part of the sentence about 'God save the King', beginning with 'and' is missing. After all, it would be carrying incompetence too far to try and improve my article and yet fail to see that the sentence does not end there. But apart from that, it would also be too much of an insult to an artist of my standing to make cuts in my work without asking. Nowadays, perhaps, that happens only to beginners, even in the Wild West (or East).

I shall have to learn a lesson from this: no more contributions about Peace-Hymns! At any rate, not until people in Germany have taken note of the difference between being the man fairly generally regarded abroad as having founded the modern music of our time, and being 'one of the leaders of the modernists in German music'.

Do not take it amiss that I am so petty; or rather, forgive my not being pettier in matters of artistic honour.

Yours most respectfully

(dated May 30, 1928)

TWO SPEECHES ON THE JEWISH SITUATION   PAGE 501

Among Schoenberg's first speeches in the United States, written and delivered by him in English, 1934 and 1935.

MY ATTITUDE TOWARD POLITICS   PAGE 505

Two typewritten pages in English, 1950.

1   In 1895, when he was twenty-one, Schoenberg conducted the metal workers' choral society in Stockerau near Vienna.

2   This statement, and the whole article in fact, shows Schoenberg's sensitivity to the 'Loyalty Oath' controversy at the University of California, although, having been retired from that institution for more than six years, he was in no way involved.

HUMAN RIGHTS   PAGE 506

The original German manuscript, *Menschenrechte*, dated July 21, 1947, was translated by Dika Newlin for inclusion in *Style and Idea*, 1950.

1   Cf. *The Unknown Brahms* (by Robert Haven Schauffler). Under this title an author undertakes to pollute the image of the composer. (AS)

APPENDIX I

CHRONOLOGICAL ORDER OF THE SELECTED WRITINGS
Date of manuscript given wherever possible

UNDATED WRITINGS

APPENDIX II

ORIGINAL GERMAN AND ENGLISH ARTICLES AND ENGLISH
TRANSLATIONS, LISTED ALPHABETICALLY

543

INDEX

553

DATE DUE
